Fodor's

PHILADELPHIA & THE PENNSYLVANIA DUTCH COUNTRY

14TH EDITION

Where to Stay and Eat for All Budgets

Must-See Sights and Local Secrets

Ratings You Can Trust

Fodor's Travel Publications New York, Toronto, London, Sydney, Auckland

www.fodors.com

FODOR'S PHILADELPHIA & THE PENNSYLVANIA DUTCH COUNTRY
Editors: Mary Beth Bohman and Mark Sullivan

Editorial Production: David Downing
Editorial Contributors: Laura Knowles Callanan, Rob DiGiacomo, Joyce Eisenberg, Andrea Lehman, Piers Marchant, Barbara Ann Rosenberg, Bernard Vaughan
Maps: David Lindroth, *cartographer;* Bob Blake and Rebecca Baer, *map editors*
Design: Fabrizio La Rocca, *creative director;* Guido Caroti, *art director;* Melanie Marin, *senior picture editor*
Production/Manufacturing: Colleen Ziemba
Cover Photo (Elfreth's Alley): Bob Krist

COPYRIGHT

Fourteenth Edition

ISBN 1-4000-1567-7

ISSN 1098-9358

SPECIAL SALES

This book is available for special discounts for bulk purchases for sales promotions or premiums. Special editions, including personalized covers, excerpts of existing books, and corporate imprints, can be created in large quantities for special needs. For more information, write to Special Markets/Premium Sales, 1745 Broadway, MD 6-2, New York, New York 10019, or e-mail specialmarkets@randomhouse.com.

AN IMPORTANT TIP & AN INVITATION

Although all prices, opening times, and other details in this book are based on information supplied to us at press time, changes occur all the time in the travel world, and Fodor's cannot accept responsibility for facts that become outdated or for inadvertent errors or omissions. So **always confirm information when it matters,** especially if you're making a detour to visit a specific place. Your experiences—positive and negative—matter to us. If we have missed or misstated something, **please write to us.** We follow up on all suggestions. Contact the Philadelphia editor at editors@fodors.com or c/o Fodor's at 1745 Broadway, New York, New York 10019.

PRINTED IN THE UNITED STATES OF AMERICA

10 9 8 7 6 5 4 3 2 1

Be a Fodor's Correspondent

Your opinion matters. It matters to us. It matters to your fellow Fodor's travelers, too. And we'd like to hear it. In fact, we *need* to hear it.

When you share your experiences and opinions, you become an active member of the Fodor's community. That means we'll not only use your feedback to make our books better, but we'll publish your names and comments whenever possible. Throughout our guides, look for "Word of Mouth," excerpts of your unvarnished feedback.

Here's how you can help improve Fodor's for all of us.

Tell us when we're right. We rely on local writers to give you an insider's perspective. But our writers and staff editors—who are the best in the business—depend on you. Your positive feedback is a vote to renew our recommendations for the next edition.

Tell us when we're wrong. We're proud that we update most of our guides every year. But we're not perfect. Things change. Hotels cut services. Museums change hours. Charming cafés lose charm. If our writer didn't quite capture the essence of a place, tell us how you'd do it differently. If any of our descriptions are inaccurate or inadequate, we'll incorporate your changes in the next edition and will correct factual errors at fodors.com *immediately.*

Tell us what to include. You probably have had fantastic travel experiences that aren't yet in Fodor's. Why not share them with a community of like-minded travelers? Maybe you chanced upon a bistro or B&B that you don't want to keep to yourself. Tell us why we should include it. And share your discoveries and experiences with everyone directly at fodors.com. Your input may lead us to add a new listing or highlight a place we cover with a "Highly Recommended" star or with our highest rating, "Fodor's Choice."

Give us your opinion instantly at our feedback center at www.fodors.com/feedback. You may also e-mail editors@fodors.com with the subject line "Philadelphia Editor." Or send your nominations, comments, and complaints by mail to Philadelphia Editor, Fodor's, 1745 Broadway, New York, NY 10019.

You and travelers like you are the heart of the Fodor's community. Make our community richer by sharing your experiences. Be a Fodor's correspondent.

Happy traveling!

Tim Jarrell, Publisher

CONTENTS

ABOUT OUR WRITERS

New Jersey native Laura Knowles Callanan has lived in the Lititz area for more than 25 years, yet she can still remember when she first saw Lancaster County and experienced her initial fascination with the Amish and their unique way of life.

Robert DiGiacomo is a freelance writer and regular Fodor's contributor. A Philadelphia resident, he has written for many national and regional publications, including *Travel Holiday, Woman's Day,* and *Elegant Wedding.*

Joyce Eisenberg has spent most of her career writing about her native Philadelphia, much of it for Fodor's; she penned the first Fodor's guide to the city in 1985. The self-described travel maven and author of the JPS Dictionary of Jewish Words has taken family trips this year to Trinidad, China and Botswana.

Editor, writer, and Trenton resident Andrea Lehman is the author of *Around Philadelphia with Kids* and has contributed to guides to Pennsylvania and New Jersey. She loves to explore natural and historical treasures on both sides of the Delaware and counts among her pastimes hiking, biking, and crossing the Scudder Falls Bridge.

Piers Marchant is a fiction writer who has also published numerous articles and reviews in the *Tucson Weekly,* the *Philadelphia Weekly,* and the *Philadelphia City Paper.* He is happily ensconced in the Queen Village section of Philly.

Barbara Ann Rosenberg is a Center City–based food and travel writer. She is the Dateline correspondent for the James Beard House, a columnist for *Cuizine* magazine, and a frequent contributor to the *Robb Report,* as well as an advisory-board member for the Culinary Institute, and the mid-Atlantic bureau chief for the East-West News Bureau.

Philadelphia native Bernard Vaughan was born and raised in Chestnut Hill. He has written news stories for various local papers and has a master's degree in journalism from Temple University. His fiction and poetry has been published in literary journals in Philadelphia, New Orleans, and Seattle.

ABOUT THIS BOOK

Our Ratings

Sometimes you find terrific travel experiences and sometimes they just find you. But usually the burden is on you to select the right combination of experiences. That's where our ratings come in.

As travelers we've all discovered a place so wonderful that its worthiness is obvious. And sometimes that place is so experiential that superlatives don't do it justice: you just have to be there to know. These sights, properties, and experiences get our highest rating, **Fodor's Choice**, indicated by orange stars throughout this book.

Black stars highlight sights and properties we deem **Highly Recommended**, places that our writers, editors, and readers praise again and again for consistency and excellence.

By default, there's another category: any place we include in this book is by definition worth your time, unless we say otherwise. And we will.

Disagree with any of our choices? Care to nominate a place or suggest that we rate one more highly? Visit our feedback center at www.fodors.com/feedback.

Budget Well

Hotel and restaurant price categories from **¢ to $$$$** are defined in the opening pages of each chapter. For attractions, we always give standard adult admission fees; reductions are usually available for children, students, and senior citizens. Want to pay with plastic? **AE, D, DC, MC, V** following restaurant and hotel listings indicate if American Express, Discover, Diner's Club, MasterCard, and Visa are accepted.

Restaurants

Unless we state otherwise, restaurants are open for lunch and dinner daily. We mention dress only when there's a specific requirement and reservations only when they're essential or not accepted—it's always best to book ahead.

Hotels

Hotels have private bath, phone, TV, and air-conditioning and operate on the European Plan (a.k.a. EP, meaning without meals), unless we specify that they use the Continental Plan (CP, with a Continental breakfast), Breakfast Plan (BP, with a full breakfast), or Modified American Plan (MAP, with breakfast and dinner) or are all-inclusive (including all meals and most activities). We always list facilities but not whether you'll be charged an extra fee to use them, so when pricing accommodations, find out what's included.

Many Listings

- ★ Fodor's Choice
- ★ Highly recommended
- ✉ Physical address
- ✥ Directions
- Mailing address
- ☎ Telephone
- Fax
- On the Web
- E-mail
- Admission fee
- Open/closed times
- Start of walk/itinerary
- Credit cards

Hotels & Restaurants

- Hotel
- Number of rooms
- Facilities
- Meal plans
- ✕ Restaurant
- Reservations
- Dress code
- Smoking
- BYOB
- Hotel with restaurant that warrants a visit

Other

- Family-friendly
- Contact information
- ⇨ See also
- Branch address
- ☞ Take note

WHAT'S WHERE

Back in the 18th century William Penn laid out his new city of Philadelphia as though it were a huge chessboard. Charles Dickens lamented in 1842 that "it is a handsome city but distractingly regular: After walking about it for an hour or two, I felt that I would have given the world for a crooked street." Two main thoroughfares intersect the center of the city: Broad Street (the city's spinal column, which runs north to south), and Market Street (which runs east to west). Where Broad and Market meet, neatly dividing the city center into four segments, you'll find City Hall, Philadelphia's center of gravity.

The Historic Area & the Old City

No matter how you first approach Philadelphia, all things start at Independence National Historical Park. As the birthplace of the country, "America's most historic square mile" was the arena across which the nation strode to its national identity and independence. It's impossible to list the historical highlights because *everything* is a highlight. Independence Hall—where the Declaration of Independence was approved and the U.S. Constitution adopted—Congress Hall, Old City Hall, Carpenters' Hall, Franklin Court, Declaration House, and, of course, the Liberty Bell are just some of the attractions. If seeing these sights doesn't bring out your gee-whiz patriotism, nothing will.

Long considered one of Society Hill's poorer neighbors and known as a melting pot for immigrants, Old City, north of the Historic Area, is associated with three historic monuments: Christ Church, Elfreth's Alley, and the Betsy Ross House. Today the area is also known for its chic art galleries, cafés, and restaurants, and its rehabbed houses and residential lofts. The presence of theater and dance companies, art workshops, and design firms adds to the neighborhood's renewed vitality as a cultural, shopping, and dining district.

Society Hill & Penn's Landing

Society Hill, south of the Historic Area, is Philadelphia as it has been for more than 200 years. Old chimney pots, hidden courtyards, ornate door knockers, and cobblestone streets: untouched by neon lights, Society Hill basks in its own patina. Although many houses are "trinity" abodes (one room to a floor), others are numbered among America's Federal-style showplaces, including the Physick House and the Powel House. Sit outside them for a while and watch the people go by, and not just those of the 21st century: guides in colonial dress sometimes lead candlelight strolls through the district. Funky South Street, a destination in itself, provides a dividing line between Society Hill and its more down-to-earth neighbor, Southwark.

Ever since William Penn sailed up the Delaware into Dock Creek, Philadelphia's waterfront has been a vibrant part of the city's life. Once home to sailing ships and counting houses and still one of the world's largest freshwater ports, Penn's Landing today has become a 37-acre-long riverside park, the site of concerts and festivals all summer long. It's also home to the Independence Seaport Museum and a flotilla of ship museums: the USS *Becuna,* the USS *Olympia,* and the *Gazela of Philadelphia.* A ferry link to the Adventure Aquarium and Camden Children's Garden in New Jersey has helped revitalize part of Camden's waterfront as well.

Center City

Philadelphia has many pasts, but if you're interested in its present and future, head for Center City. This is Philly's business district, anchored by Oz-like skyscrapers and solidly Victorian City Hall, which is crowned by the enormous statue of William Penn. From Chinatown to Rittenhouse Square, Center City is crammed with sights. A sample? How about the Academy of Music; that leviathan horn of plenty, the Reading Terminal Market; the bustling Pennsylvania Convention Center; Thomas Jefferson University (home to Philly's greatest painting, Thomas Eakins's *Gross Clinic*); and for those with itchy credit cards, the Shops at Liberty Place. In broad local usage, Center City refers to the entire area between the Delaware and Schuylkill rivers (east and west boundaries) and Vine and South streets (north and south)—an area that would be synonymous with downtown in another city—but here it refers specifically to the business district around City Hall and Market Street.

Rittenhouse Square

The prettiest of Philadelphia's public squares, Rittenhouse Square beckons frazzled city dwellers to slow down. Today the park is the heart of upper-crust Philly. Swank hotels and modern office buildings now intrude, but the trappings of onetime grandeur remain on view in its Victorian town houses. Many treasures are tucked away here, including the Curtis Institute of Music and the Rosenbach Museum and Library, home to 130,000 manuscripts, including James Joyce's *Ulysses.*

Benjamin Franklin Parkway

From City Hall the Benjamin Franklin Parkway stretches northwest to a Greco-Roman temple on a hill—the Philadelphia Museum of Art. The parkway is the city's Champs-Elysées, a grand boulevard designed by French architects and alive with flowers, trees, and fountains. Along the way are many of the city's finest cultural institutions: the Academy of Natural Sciences, the Franklin Institute, and the Rodin Museum.

Fairmount Park

When in need of elbow room, Philadelphians head for Fairmount Park, whose 8,500 acres make it the largest landscaped city park in the world. Deemed by many Philly dwellers to be their own backyard, Fairmount beckons with a wide range of pleasures. Joggers, walkers, and bicyclists consider it prime territory. Along Kelly Drive stand the Victorian houses of Boathouse Row, headquarters of the rowing clubs that make up what's called the "Schuylkill Navy." The Mann Center for the Performing Arts hosts open-air concerts in summer. Children flock to the Philadelphia Zoo. Many people are also drawn to the centuries-old houses that dot the park, including Mt. Pleasant, Strawberry Mansion, and Lemon Hill. Here you can also find the noted Greek Revival Fairmount Waterworks. The Wissahickon, in the northern section of the park, beckons the adventurous with miles of paths through the gorge carved by Wissahickon Creek.

Southwark & South Philadelphia

Chiseled in stone on the facade of an old Southwark building are the words ON THIS SITE IN 1879, NOTHING HAPPENED! Today a great deal is happening in this district, which stretches from Front to 6th streets and from South Street to Washington Avenue. The renovation generation has helped make the Queen Village area of the neighborhood a winner in the revival-of-the-fittest contest. As a result, rents here are catching up to nearby Society Hill. Although Southwark has never been as renowned as its ritzy neighbor, it contains some of the most charming streets in the city, such as Hancock and Queen. For real Philly flash, check out the Mummers Museum, on Washington Avenue.

South Philadelphia is the neighborhood that gave the world Rocky Balboa, as well as Bobby Rydell, Frankie Avalon, and Fabian. The city's "Little Italy" can sometimes seem more Naples than Philly—just take in the five-block outdoor Italian Market, with its piles of peppers and mountains of mozzarella. You can satisfy your cravings in any number of eateries here, many of them simple neighborhood spots.

University City

Once known as the "Athens of America," Philadelphia claims an astonishing concentration of colleges and universities, nearly unrivaled in the country. Two of the larger institutions, the University of Pennsylvania and Drexel University, are in an area dubbed University City in West Philadelphia. Here, too, is the University Museum, containing one of the world's finest archaeology and anthropology collections. City buses travel along Walnut Street from Society Hill to University City; 34th and Walnut streets is the stop for Penn. One block north is the Institute of Contemporary Art, with its innovative exhibitions. Take Locust Walk to explore this Ivy League campus; ivy really does cling to the buildings.

Manayunk

This old mill town, wedged between the Schuylkill River and some very steep hills 7 mi northwest of Center City, was once crucial to Philadelphia's industrial fortune; it became part of the city in 1854. Today it's bringing in dollars with its restaurants and boutiques—it has become one of the city's hottest neighborhoods. More than a half mile of stores stretch along Main Street, and behind it are remnants of the Schuylkill Navigational Canal that originally brought life to this area.

Germantown & Chestnut Hill

When Germantown, an area north of Center City, was settled by Germans fleeing economic and religious turmoil, it was way out in the country, linked to the city 6 mi away by a dirt road. Before long, the Germans' modest homes and farms were interspersed with the grand homes of affluent Philadelphians who hoped to escape the city's summer heat. They escaped the heat but not the British, who occupied the town and deployed troops from here during the Battle of Germantown. Today Germantown is an integrated neighborhood prized for its large old homes; several of the historic houses that line Germantown Avenue are open for tours. Over the years, development continued along the avenue, farther from the city, culminating in Chestnut Hill, today one of Philadelphia's prettiest neighborhoods.

Brandywine Valley & Valley Forge

Think of the Brandywine Valley, and the paintings of Andrew Wyeth come to mind: stone or clapboard farmhouses, forests that could tell a story or two, and meadows with getaway space and privacy. The valley's palette is quintessentially Wyeth, too—russet, fieldstone gray, shades of amber. Chadds Ford, the heart of Wyeth Country, is near the splendid homes and estates of the du Ponts: Winterthur, Nemours, and Longwood Gardens. Nearby, the Valley Forge area offers a radical juxtaposition of the hardships of the past with the abundance of today—within a few miles of each other are the site of George Washington's heroic 1777–78 encampment and the massive King of Prussia Mall.

Bucks County

Long a vacation spot for New Yorkers and Philadelphians, Bucks County is a day-tripper's delight, filled with historic sites, artists' colonies, nature preserves, old fieldstone inns, and country-chic restaurants. Once hailed as the "Genius Belt" and home to such luminaries as Dorothy Parker, James Michener, and Oscar Hammerstein II, the region is packed with attractions: New Hope and Lahaska offer delightful shopping and antiquing; Doylestown has Fonthill, a millionaire's do-it-yourself castle right out of the Brothers Grimm; and the Delaware Canal towpath runs through countryside that conjures up England's Cotswolds.

Lancaster County, Hershey & Gettysburg

An hour's drive from Philadelphia are Lancaster County and the Pennsylvania Dutch Country, known for delicious foods and tranquil farmlands. Around the hub of Lancaster you can tour farmers' markets (shoofly pie should be at the top of your take-home goody list) or replicas of Amish villages, or you can stop in at the oldest pretzel bakery in the country and twist your own pretzel. Shoppers will find antiques, crafts, and abundant outlet stores in the area, too. For dessert head west to Hershey, the only town in the world that has streetlights shaped like foil-wrapped Hershey Kisses. About 55 mi from Lancaster is Gettysburg, where the greatest artillery battle on this continent was fought in July 1863—and later immortalized through the words of Lincoln's Gettysburg Address.

Philadelphia in 6 Days

In a city with as many richly stocked museums and matchless marvels as Philadelphia, you risk seeing half of everything or all of nothing. So use the efficient itineraries below to keep you on track as you explore both the famous sights and those off the beaten path.

Day 1: Begin your first day with an exploration of the city's historic district. Sign up at the Independence National Historical Park Visitor Center for a walking tour hosted by a National Park Service guide; try a go-at-your-own-pace tour offered by Audio Walk and Tour; or take a walk on your own. For lunch, proceed to the Reading Terminal Market, where you can sample the real Philadelphia "cuisine"—cheese steaks, soft pretzels, and Bassett's ice cream—or something else from the dozens of food stalls. (The market is closed Sunday.) After lunch, walk nine blocks east on Arch Street (or take a bus on Market Street) to Old City; Christ Church, the Betsy Ross House, and Elfreth's Alley are all in close proximity. The galleries and cafés in the area may tempt you to take a short break from your pursuit of history. In the late afternoon, head back to Independence Hall for a horse-drawn carriage ride. Have dinner in Old City; then catch the Lights of Liberty walking sound-and-light show (March–December, weather permitting).

Day 2: Spend the morning of Day 2 exploring the Philadelphia Museum of Art on Benjamin Franklin Parkway, followed by lunch in the museum's lovely dining room. Afterward, depending on your interests and the day of the week, you could head to Merion by bus or car to see the world-renowned collection of impressionist paintings at the Barnes Foundation (open Friday–Sunday). Or you could walk to Eastern State Penitentiary Historic Site for a tour of a former prison or to the Franklin Institute Science Museum.

Day 3: Start Day 3 in Center City with a ride to the top of City Hall for a pigeon's-eye view of the city. Next, head across the street to the Masonic Temple for a surreal tour through time—and architectural history—led by a Mason. Art lovers may prefer a visit to the Pennsylvania Academy of the Fine Arts, two blocks north of City Hall at Broad and Cherry streets. Eat lunch at the Reading Terminal Market.

If you want to stay inside, head to Rittenhouse Square's Rosenbach Museum and Library, which has a diverse collection ranging from the original manuscript of James Joyce's *Ulysses* to the works of beloved children's author Maurice Sendak. If you prefer being outdoors, visit Penn's Landing, where you can check out the Independence Seaport Museum and/or take the ferry across the river to the Adventure Aquarium and Camden Children's Garden. At sunset, have a drink on the deck of the *Moshulu,* which is docked on the Camden side of the Delaware River.

Day 4: Begin Day 4 by exploring either Society Hill or the Rittenhouse Square area. Then take a bus west on Walnut Street to the University Museum of Archaeology and Anthropology, in University City. You can have lunch at the museum or on campus. In the afternoon, return to Center City to the corner of 16th Street and John F. Kennedy Boulevard, to pick up the Philadelphia Trolley Works' narrated tour of Fairmount Park; or if you have children along, visit the Philadelphia Zoo. Afterward, drive or catch the SEPTA R6 train to Manayunk, where you can have dinner in one of the restaurants lining Main Street; many stores here are open late, too.

Day 5: On Day 5, head out of the city by car to Valley Forge National Historical Park, where you can hike or picnic after you've taken the self-guided auto tour of General Washington's winter encampment. If you like to shop, spend the afternoon at the nearby King of Prussia Mall. Or drive back toward the city to take in the Barnes Foundation, the Eastern State Penitentiary, or the Franklin Institute—whichever ones you didn't see on Day 2.

Another option for Day 5 is to stay in the city and explore Queen Village in Southwark and South Philadelphia. Follow up a visit to the Mummers Museum with a strut along 9th Street, site of the outdoor Italian Market. You can pick up the makings for a great picnic, or duck into one of the restaurants here for lunch. In the afternoon, visit the museums you missed on Day 2. Check the local papers for an evening activity—perhaps a sporting event at the South Philadelphia stadiums, a show in Center City, or live music at a jazz club.

Day 6: Get out of the city again with a day trip by car to the Brandywine Valley. Your first stop will be the Brandywine River Museum in Chadds Ford, which showcases the art of Andrew Wyeth and his family, as well as works by other area painters and illustrators. Next, head south to Winterthur and feast your eyes on Henry Francis du Pont's extraordinary collection of American decorative art in an equally extraordinary mansion. Spend the balance of your day strolling through Longwood Gardens in Kennett Square, which is in bloom even in winter. If it's a Tuesday, Thursday, or Saturday in summer, stay for dinner and the fountain light show.

If You Have More Time

More time means you'll be able to delve even deeper into Philly's other—and outer—neighborhoods. Check out Chinatown in Center City, take a drive through Germantown and Chestnut Hill (stopping at Cliveden), or devote a full day to shopping in trendy Manayunk. If the weather's nice, you can drive to the northwestern tip of Fairmount Park and check out the Wissahickon—a local favorite for all sorts of activities, from strolling to cycling.

You can also break up your city exploring with longer side trips to Bucks County or Lancaster County. Both have an abundance of charming bed-and-breakfasts that make for perfect overnight or weekend stays.

If You Have 2 Days

You could easily spend two weeks exploring Philadelphia, but if you have only a few days, you can still get a good taste of what the city has to offer. You'll want to get the tour of the historic sights out of the way on Day 1. Either follow the itinerary above, or forgo the Lights of Liberty show and check out Old City's bars and clubs instead. Then spend a leisurely day exploring either the Philadelphia Museum of Art or the Barnes Foundation. Wrap up Day 2 with a stroll around Rittenhouse Square or through Fairmount Park.

A Kid's-Eye View of Philadelphia

Philadelphia has fantastic activities and sights for tots. Best of all, these stops appeal to adults as well.

Day 1: There's plenty of interest for the whole family in the Historic Area. Start at Independence Hall and be sure to hit the Liberty Bell and Franklin Court. Kids love the evening Lights of Liberty show. The City Tavern is fun for dinner and has a good kids' menu.

Day 2: Head over to Penn's Landing to check out the Independence Seaport Museum before taking the ferry across the river to the Camden Waterfront to explore the Adventure Aquarium and the Camden Children's Garden. Back in Philadelphia, head to Chinatown for dinner. Make sure to look into discount passes—the RiverPass, for example, includes round-trip ferry travel and admission to the aquarium and children's garden. CityPass covers the seaport and ships, the aquarium and children's garden, as well as several other sights around Philadelphia, such as the Philadelphia Zoo and the Philadelphia Museum of Art.

Day 3: Take a trip to Fairmount Park to watch crew teams row on the Schuylkill River. Don't miss the giant indoor slide at the Smith Memorial Playground and Playhouse—by the reservoir in the East Park. While you're here, you might as well check out the Philadelphia Zoo. If the weather's bad, make Day 3 a museum day. The Philadelphia Museum of Art, the grand dame, is always an option, but the Pennsylvania Academy of Fine Arts is equally interesting to kids and has a wonderful Family Resource Center. Nearby Reading Terminal Market makes a good lunch stop.

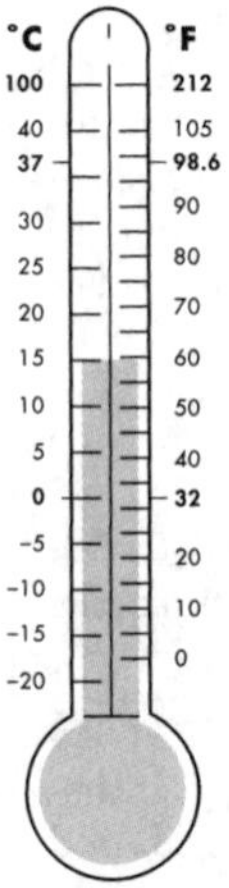

Any time is right to enjoy the area's attractions, and a variety of popular annual events takes place throughout the year. The period around July 4th is particularly festive; there are special activities in the historic area throughout the summer. Concert and theater seasons run from October through the beginning of June. You may find some better lodging deals in winter. In spring, the city's cherry blossoms bloom, and they rival those of Washington, D.C.

Climate

Like other northern American cities, Philadelphia can be hot and humid in summer and cold in winter (winter snowfall averages 21 inches).

Forecasts **Weather Channel** www.weather.com

PHILADELPHIA

Jan.	40F	4C	May	72F	22C	Sept.	76F	24C
	27	– 3		54	12		61	16
Feb.	41F	5C	June	81F	27C	Oct.	67F	19C
	27	– 3		63	17		50	10
Mar.	49F	9C	July	85F	29C	Nov.	54F	12C
	34	– 1		68	20		40	– 4
Apr.	61F	16C	Aug.	83F	28C	Dec.	43F	6C
	43	6		67	19		31	– 1

ON THE CALENDAR

The Mummers Parade on New Year's Day may be the most notorious of Philly's special events, but you'll find something special going on no matter when you visit, from seasonal walking tours to arts festivals to premier sporting events. For exact dates and other information about the following events, contact the Independence Visitor Center.

ONGOING

Memorial Day–September	At the **Head House Crafts Fair** (✉ 2nd and Pine Sts. ☎ 215/790–0782), more than 30 artisans exhibit jewelry, stained glass, leather, and quilts on summer weekends, noon–11 Saturday and noon–6 Sunday.
Mid-August–mid-October	In Lancaster County, the **Pennsylvania Renaissance Faire** (☎ 717/665–7021) is a re-creation of Elizabethan England, with jousting, craftspeople demonstrating ancient arts, a human chess game, and food of the period.

WINTER

December	During **Elfreth's Alley Christmas Open House,** (✉ Elfreth's Alley, surrounded by Front, 2nd, Arch, and Race Sts. ☎ 215/574–0560), held the second Friday in December, the community opens its early-18th-century homes to the public for evening tours.
	The Nutcracker (☎ 215/893–1999), the Pennsylvania Ballet's production of the Tchaikovsky classic, is a Philadelphia tradition.
	Washington Crossing the Delaware (☎ 215/493–4076) is reenacted on December 25th with four 40-ft reproductions of Durham boats. On Christmas Day 1776, George Washington and his troops took the Hessian camp at Trenton by surprise.
	Neighbors in the New Year (☎ 215/965–7676 or 800/537–7676), held between December 27 and January 1, is six days of entertaining events, including a Mummers Fest at the Pennsylvania Convention Center. The culmination is a New Year's Eve celebration with fireworks over the Delaware River.
January	The daylong **Mummers Parade** (☎ 215/965–7676 or 800/537–7676) kicks off the New Year as some 30,000 sequined and feathered paraders march west on Market Street to City Hall on January 1.
February	**Black History Month** is celebrated with exhibits, lectures, and music at the African American Museum in Philadelphia, plus related events around the city.

SPRING	
March	The **Philadelphia Flower Show** (☎ 215/988–8800), in early March, is the nation's largest and most prestigious indoor flower show, with acres of exhibits and themed displays. Other events for gardening enthusiasts are part of Flower Show Week.
	The **St. Patrick's Day Parade** (☎ 215/965–7676 or 800/537–7676) brings the wearing of the green to Benjamin Franklin Parkway.
	The Book & The Cook (☎ 215/545–4543) teams the city's best chefs and the world's top cookbook authors in a weeklong event held in more than 80 restaurants. Festivities include wine tastings, market tours, food sampling, and demonstrations at the Fort Washington Expo Center.
April	The **Philadelphia Antiques Show** (☎215/387–3500) showcases museum-quality antiques and decorative arts of 56 antiques dealers from throughout the country.
	The **Philadelphia Film Festival** (☎ 267/765–9700) presents more than 100 features, documentaries, and short films from more than 30 countries at venues throughout the city.
	Penn Relays (☎ 215/898–6145) is one of the world's oldest and largest amateur track meets for high school and college athletes, with more than 350 races and events.
	Valborgsmässoafton (☎ 215/389–1776), the traditional Swedish welcome to spring, has food, song, dance, and bonfires at the American-Swedish Historical Museum.
Late April–May	**Philadelphia Open House** (☎ 215/928–1188) is a three-week period when selected private homes, gardens, and historic buildings in neighborhoods around the city open their doors to the public on walking and bus tours.
	PrideFest Philadelphia (☎ 215/732–3378) is the nation's most comprehensive gay and lesbian symposium and festival, with a street fair and meetings and parties at locations around the city.
Mid-May	On Mother's' Day weekend the **Dad Vail Regatta** (🌐 www.dadvail.org), the largest collegiate rowing event in the country, takes place. Up to 500 shells from more than 100 colleges race on a 2,000-meter course on the Schuylkill River in Fairmount Park.
Mid-May–early June	The Pennsylvania Academy of the Fine Arts's annual **Student Art Exhibition** (☎ 215/972–7600 🌐 www.pafa.org) presents the work of this talented student body for viewing and purchase.
3rd week in May	For more than 80 years, the **Rittenhouse Square Flower Market** (☎ 215/271–7149) has held this two-day sale of plants, flowers, and food, including the traditional candy lemon stick.

Memorial Day Weekend	**Jam on the River** (✉ Penn's Landing ☎ 215/965–7676 or 800/537–7676) is Philadelphia's kickoff to summer, showcasing the best of the bayou with a weekend of music, food, and crafts from New Orleans, in a family-oriented event.
SUMMER	
Late May–early June	The **Devon Horse Show and Country Fair** (☎ 610/964–0550 🌐 www.thedevonhorseshow.org), first held in 1896, is a nine-day event in which top riders compete for more than $200,000 in prize money.
Late May–August	Longwood Gardens' **Summer Festival of Fountains** (☎ 610/388–1000 🌐 www.longwoodgardens.com) includes fountain displays during the day and fountain light shows set to music several nights a week.
Early June	The **Rittenhouse Square Fine Arts Annual** (☎ 877/689–4112), America's oldest (1931) and largest outdoor juried art show, exhibits works by more than 100 Philadelphia-area artists.
Early June	The **U.S. Pro Cycling Championship** (🌐 www.procyclingtour.com), the country's premier bicycle race, attracts the world's top cyclists to its 156-mi course, including the grueling Manayunk Wall.
2nd weekend in June	**Elfreth's Alley Fete Days** (☎ 215/574–0560 🌐 www.elfrethsalley.org) is the time for open houses on America's oldest continuously occupied street, along with food and fife-and-drum music.
Last weekend in June	The **Manayunk Annual Arts Fest** (✉ Main St. ☎ 215/482–9565) lines this neighborhood's main drag with more than 250 artists from all over the country displaying arts and crafts.
June–July	The **Philadelphia Orchestra's Summer Season** (✉ Mann Center for the Performing Arts, 52nd St. and Parkside Ave. ☎ 215/893–1999) showcases noted guest conductors and soloists in six weeks of outdoor concerts.
Late June–July 4	Philadelphia's premier event, the **Sunoco Welcome America Festival** (☎ 215/683–2211) celebrates America's birthday in America's birthplace. Highlights of the more than 80 free happenings are big-name outdoor concerts and fireworks and music in front of the Philadelphia Museum of Art.
Sun. before July 14	The Eastern State Penitentiary (☎ 215/236–3300) reenacts the storming of the Bastille at a **Bastille Day Celebration**, which includes an appearance by Marie Antoinette.
Labor Day Weekend	The big **Long's Park Art & Craft Festival** (☎ 717/295–7054) in Lancaster offers three days of contemporary fine art and crafts, a food fair, and children's activities.

FALL	
September	The **Philadelphia Distance Run** (☎ 215/564–6499 🌐 philadelphiadistancerun.org) is the country's premier half-marathon, with more than 7,000 runners completing a 13-mi course through downtown and along the Schuylkill River.
Early–mid-September	The **Philadelphia Fringe Festival** (☎ 215/413–1318 🌐 www.pafringe.org) presents 11 days of avant-garde dance, music, theater, poetry, puppetry, and performance art by performers from all over the world at various sites in Old City.
Late September	The **Von Steuben Day Parade** (☎ 215/965–7676 or 800/537–7676), along Benjamin Franklin Parkway, honors the Prussian general who trained the Continental soldiers at Valley Forge.
October	The **Pulaski Day Parade** (☎ 215/965–7676 or 800/537–7676) marches up Broad Street; the Polish-American Congress honors this Polish general, a hero of the Revolutionary War.
2nd Mon. in October	The **Columbus Day Parade** (☎ 215/965–7676 or 800/537–7676) includes both a parade on South Broad Street and a festival at Marconi Plaza.
October	**Candlelight Tours of the Edgar Allan Poe National Historic Site** (✉ 532 N. 7th St. ☎ 215/597–8780) celebrate Halloween and Poe with "ghostly" weekend walks through the house.
Last 2 weeks in October	The Eastern State Penitentiary (☎ 215/236–3300) presents **Terror Behind the Walls**, a Halloween-theme tour through its cells and corridors featuring costumed actors and ghoulish tales.
Early November	The **Philadelphia Museum of Art Craft Show** (☎ 215/235–7469) is four days of exhibits by 190 top national craftspeople.
Late November	The **Thanksgiving Day Parade** (✉ Benjamin Franklin Pkwy. ☎ 215/965–7676 or 800/537–7676) has thousands of marchers, floats, and local personalities.
November or December	The **Philadelphia Dog Show** (☎ 215/641–4500), sponsored by the Kennel Club of Philadelphia, includes 2,500 entries and 140 breeds.

PLEASURES & PASTIMES

The Spirit of 1776 Many Americans think they know something about the birthplace of the nation: Benjamin Franklin, the signing of the Constitution, etc. Still, grade-school facts and figures do little to prepare you for the actual Philadelphia experience. To walk through Independence National Historical Park is a tour that exercises not only the feet but the spirit. Who can fail to be moved by the words PROCLAIM LIBERTY THRO' ALL THE LAND, inscribed on America's best-loved relic, the Liberty Bell?

Oh, Dem Golden Slippers Buttoned-up Philadelphia explodes in a tidal wave of sequins, feathers, riotous sound, and pageantry every New Year's Day: the Mummers Parade. The city dons "dem Golden Slippers" and cakewalks up Market Street in a parade that outglitters Las Vegas. This little shindig, initially brought from England, had its American beginnings early in the 19th century, when costumed groups rang doorbells and recited—for a donation—rhymes that explained their strange garb. Nowadays, you get 12 nonstop hours of song, dance, and costumed splendor. The Mummers also stage a summer parade around July 4.

Philly Flavors For decades gourmet groupies wrote the city off as a lackluster dining center. How things have changed! In this city known for its revolutionary spirit, innovative chefs have been wielding kitchen utensils with the zeal of a patriot's quill. Today the city has stellar Italian and Chinese restaurants as well as notable seafood and steak houses, not to mention a wide variety of ethnic eateries from Mexican to Vietnamese. And, of course, there's always the cheese steak.

The Emerald City Envisioned by William Penn as a "greene countrie towne," Philadelphia is famous as a city with a green thumb. It counts its trees as avidly as a miser counts gold and now claims more than 2 million scattered among city squares, parks, streets, and innumerable backyards. The city's main "garden" is Fairmount Park, the largest municipal park in the world. For Philly at its flower-spangled best, check out some of the great Society Hill house gardens and the annual Philadelphia Flower Show—the largest indoor horticultural event in the world.

Museums & Masterpieces Artistically, Philadelphia has always been fertile aesthetic territory. From the probing realism of such 19th-century masters as Thomas Eakins and Robert Henri to famous collectors such as the McIlhennys and the Arensbergs, Philadelphia has always played off the contrast between its traditionally staid origins and a lively interest in the new. Nowhere is this more evident than at the Barnes Foundation, with its collection of 175 Renoirs. The Brandywine River Museum showcases the art of Andrew Wyeth and his famous family. Thanks to the Philadelphia Museum of Art, Philadelphia Art Alliance, the Painted Bride Art Center, and the Pennsylvania Academy of the Fine Arts, the city's art scene remains as spirited as ever.

FODOR'S CHOICE

Fodor'sChoice ★

The sights, restaurants, hotels, and other travel experiences on these pages are our editors' top picks—our Fodor's Choices. They're the best of their type in the area covered by the book—not to be missed and always worth your time. In the destination chapters that follow, you will find all the details.

LODGING

$$$$ **Four Seasons, Philadelphia.** Philly's poshest hotel has the best restaurants, service, and—if you get a room overlooking the fountains in Logan Circle—the most romantic views.

$$$$ **Hotel Hershey, Hershey.** This may well be Pennsylvania's only Mediterranean-style villa. The spa pays homage to the candy man with chocolate-themed treatments.

$$$$ **Westin Philadelphia.** Colonial touches coexist with modern convenience at this accommodating luxury hotel.

$$$–$$$$ **Barley Sheaf Farm, Bucks County.** From in-room spa treatments to carefully restored architectural details in buildings dating from 1740, the former estate of playwright George S. Kaufman is equal parts treat and retreat.

$$$–$$$$ **Park Hyatt Philadelphia at the Bellevue.** You can't get more luxurious—and you can't get more downtown—than this hotel, a Philadelphia institution for almost a century.

$$–$$$ **Rittenhouse Square Bed & Breakfast, Philadelphia.** This refined, European-style mansion offers the luxury of a large hotel in an intimate setting.

$–$$$ **The Inn at Whitewing Farm, Brandywine Valley.** This elegant gentleman's farm overlooks a rolling landscape that would have inspired Andrew Wyeth.

$$ **Penn's View Inn, Philadelphia.** Urban charm and a fine Italian restaurant distinguish this Old City inn.

$–$$ **Smithton Inn, Lancaster County.** Tough decisions abound here: a cozy room with a fireplace or a suite with cathedral ceilings?

RESTAURANTS

$$$$ **Dilworthtown Inn, Brandywine Valley.** This Colonial-era country inn is a West Chester favorite for romantic candlelit dining.

$$$$ **Fountain, Philadelphia.** Its classy setting in the Four Seasons and outstanding contemporary fare consistently draw locals and visitors alike.

$$$$ **Le Bec-Fin, Philadelphia.** *Formidable!* The most prestigious restaurant in town, the Bec is internationally renowned for its impeccable service, elegance, and the soufflés of owner Georges Perrier.

$$$–$$$$	**Gibraltar, Lancaster County.** A Mediterranean flair is an unexpected twist in the heart of Pennsylvania's Dutch Country.
$$$–$$$$	**Jake's, Manayunk.** Fine contemporary crafts decorate a stellar eatery in Manayunk; the scallops are a taste of perfection.
$$$–$$$$	**The Log Cabin, Lancaster County.** Yes, this is a real log cabin, but the dining rooms and food are as elegant as they come.
$$–$$$$	**Hamilton's Grill Room, Bucks County.** An open grill in the main dining room is the source for simply prepared, yet highly regarded, fare.
$$–$$$$	**Overtures, Philadelphia.** A bit of Paris exists just off funky South Street at this stylish, creative restaurant.
$$–$$$	**Lily's (on James and on Main), Lancaster County.** American cuisine gets a dusting-off at both Lily's locations, and the results will make you see old standbys in a new light.
¢–$	**Continental Restaurant & Martini Bar, Philadelphia.** A hip and kitschy restaurant in Old City serves up inexpensive yet inventive eats.

AFTER HOURS

Brasserie Perrier, Center City. This sophisticated bar and bistro will let you see-and-be-seen and sample some of the famed Perrier cuisine without breaking the bank.

Delaware River waterfront. You can club-hop by river taxi to more than a dozen nightspots near the Ben Franklin Bridge.

Kimmel Center for the Performing Arts. This massive center hosts everything from the Philadelphia Orchestra to modern dance groups.

Lights of Liberty. When the sun goes down, the streets around Independence Hall become a stage set for a dazzling sound-and-light show (April through October) that brings to life early U.S. history.

South Street. From art galleries to tattoo parlors, South Street—the stretch between Front and 7th streets—is, as the song says, "the hippest place in town."

Standard Tap, Northern Liberties. This cozy neighborhood staple offers a fine array of dining options, lots of beer choices, and a friendly ambiance.

Swann Lounge, Center City. With live jazz, dancing, and a Viennese-style dessert buffet, this lounge in the Four Seasons covers a lot of bases.

EXCURSIONS

Farmers' markets. For the best "sweets and sours" and chowchow, head for the Central Market in downtown Lancaster or the Green Dragon Farmers Market and Auction in Ephrata.

Longwood Gardens, Brandywine Valley. The valley's No. 1 attraction has more than 1,000 acres of flowers, trees, color, and beauty, 365 days a year.

Pennsylvania Dutch Country. Backcountry roads will take you past Amish farms, roadside stands, and the occasional horse-drawn buggy; all-you-can-eat restaurants will give you a crash course on the region's hearty food.

MUSEUMS

Barnes Foundation. This Merion mansion holds one of the world's finest collections of impressionist and postimpressionist art, including 65 works by Matisse, 66 Cézannes, and 175 Renoirs.

Brandywine River Museum. A converted 19th-century gristmill on the banks of the Brandywine showcases the art of three generations of the Wyeth family.

Landis Valley Museum, Lancaster. Not a typical museum, Landis Valley lets you witness 1800s Pennsylvania German rural life with a tour around 15 historic buildings.

Philadelphia Museum of Art. Rocky fans may have the urge to run up the steps. Go ahead, indulge! Then go inside and discover one of the world's great art collections.

Winterthur Museum & Gardens, Brandywine Valley. An unrivaled collection of American decorative arts from 1640 to 1860 fills Henry Francis du Pont's nine-story mansion. The gardens are particularly lovely in spring.

SHOPPING

King of Prussia Mall. Massive is the best way to describe this two-malls-in-one complex, where it's impossible to go away empty-handed.

Kitchen Kettle Village, Lancaster. Over 30 shops provide a good sampling of Amish crafts, not to mention the samples of jams and relishes.

Reading Terminal Market. This Center City market has everything from Amish baked goods to clothes and crafts.

Rittenhouse Row. You'll find some of the swankiest stores and galleries here, and the location by Rittenhouse Square makes it a pleasant place to stroll and window-shop.

QUINTESSENTIAL PHILADELPHIA

Boathouse Row at night. Hundreds of tiny white lights outline the dozen or so houses along the Schuylkill River just beyond the Philadelphia Museum of Art.

Forbidden Drive in Fairmount Park. Walking, jogging, or biking along Forbidden Drive is a meditative must for those wishing to forget about the city for a few hours.

Fourth of July celebration. This spectacular 10-day birthday party includes several nights of fireworks, an illuminated boat parade, outdoor concerts, and the awarding of the Philadelphia Liberty Medal to world leaders.

Independence National Historical Park. Start at the visitor center and follow the redbrick road past a dozen stirring sites, including Independence Hall and the Liberty Bell.

Lunch in Rittenhouse Square. Grab a bench at the city's toniest downtown park. With majestic elms, Victorian statues, and playing children, it seems to have sprung from the brush of Mary Cassatt.

The 76ers. Philadelphia's basketball games are always fast-paced and action-packed, and at the First Union Center there's always a good seat.

SMART TRAVEL TIPS

Finding out about your destination before you leave home means you won't spend time organizing everyday minutiae once you've arrived. You'll be more streetwise when you hit the ground as well, better prepared to explore the aspects of Philadelphia that drew you here in the first place. The organizations in this section can provide information to supplement this guide; contact them for up-to-the-minute details, and consult the A to Z sections that end each chapter for facts on the various topics as they relate to the areas around Philadelphia. Happy landings!

ADDRESSES

Philadelphia is a city of distinct neighborhoods, and some named streets (as opposed to numbered streets) repeat in more than one neighborhood. You will find several streets coming to an end at the Schuylkill River or Fairmount Park only to resume at the other side. It is important therefore to phone ahead for driving directions if you are traveling to destinations in neighborhoods beyond Center City.

AIR TRAVEL TO & FROM PHILADELPHIA

BOOKING

When you book, look for nonstop flights and remember that "direct" flights stop at least once. Try to avoid connecting flights, which require a change of plane. Two airlines may operate a connecting flight jointly, so ask whether your airline operates every segment of the trip; you may find that the carrier you prefer flies you only part of the way. To find more booking tips and to check prices and make online flight reservations, log on to www.fodors.com.

CARRIERS

All major airlines offer service to and from Philadelphia. It's a hub for US Airways, which offers the most nonstop domestic flights. You can find discounted airfares on Southwest Airlines and smaller carriers like Air Tran. Both US Airways and British Airways offer daily nonstop service from London, and Air France frequently offers discounted fares from London with a stop in Paris. American, United, and Virgin Atlantic are also popular

Airlines **Air Canada** ☎ 888/247-2262 🌐 www.aircanada.com. **Air France** ☎ 800/237-2747 in the U.S., 0825/864-864 in France 🌐 www.airfrance.com. **Air Tran** ☎ 800/247-8726 🌐 www.airtran.com. **American** ☎ 800/433-7300 in the U.S. 🌐 www.aa.com. **America West** ☎ 800/235-9292 🌐 www.americawest.com. **British Airways** ☎ 800/247-9297 in the U.S., 0870/8509-850 in the U.K. 🌐 www.britishairways.com. **Continental** ☎ 800/523-3273 🌐 www.continental.com. **Delta** ☎ 800/221-1212 🌐 www.delta.com. **Northwest** ☎ 800/225-2525 🌐 www.nwa.com. **Southwest** ☎ 800/435-9792 🌐 www.southwest.com. **United** ☎ 800/864-8331 🌐 www.united.com. **US Airways** ☎ 800/943-5436 🌐 www.usairways.com. **Virgin Atlantic** ☎ 800/862-8621 in the U.S., 08705/747-747 in the U.K. 🌐 www.virginatlantic.com.

CHECK-IN & BOARDING

Always **find out your carrier's check-in policy.** Plan to arrive at the airport about 2 hours before your scheduled departure time for domestic flights and 2½ to 3 hours before international flights. You may need to arrive earlier if you're flying from one of the busier airports or during peak air-traffic times. To avoid delays at airport-security checkpoints, try not to wear any metal. Jewelry, belt and other buckles, steel-toe shoes, barrettes, and underwire bras are among the items that can set off detectors.

Assuming that not everyone with a ticket will show up, airlines routinely overbook planes. When everyone does, airlines ask for volunteers to give up their seats. In return, these volunteers usually get a several-hundred-dollar flight voucher, which can be used toward the purchase of another ticket, and are rebooked on the next available flight out. If there are not enough volunteers, the airline must choose who will be denied boarding. The first to get bumped are passengers who checked in late and those flying on discounted tickets, so get to the gate and check in as early as possible, especially during peak periods.

Always **bring a government-issued photo I.D.** to the airport; even when it's not required, a passport is best.

CUTTING COSTS

The least expensive airfares to Philadelphia are often priced for round-trip travel and must usually be purchased in advance. Airlines generally allow you to change your return date for a fee; most low-fare tickets, however, are nonrefundable. It's smart to call a number of airlines and check the Internet; when you are quoted a good price, book it on the spot—the same fare may not be available the next day, or even the next hour. Always check different routings and look into using alternate airports. Also, price off-peak flights and red-eye, which may be significantly less expensive than others. Travel agents, especially low-fare specialists (⇨ Discounts & Deals), are helpful.

Consolidators are another good source. They buy tickets for scheduled flights at reduced rates from the airlines, then sell them at prices that beat the best fare available directly from the airlines. (Many also offer reduced car-rental and hotel rates.) Sometimes you can even get your money back if you need to return the ticket. Carefully read the fine print detailing penalties for changes and cancellations, purchase the ticket with a credit card, and confirm your consolidator reservation with the airline.

When you fly as a courier, you trade your checked-luggage space for a ticket deeply subsidized by a courier service. There are restrictions on when you can book and how long you can stay. Some courier companies list with membership organizations, such as the Air Courier Association and the International Association of Air Travel Couriers; these require you to become a member before you can book a flight.

Many airlines, singly or in collaboration, offer discount air passes that allow foreigners to travel economically in a particular country or region. These visitor passes usually must be reserved and purchased before you leave home. Information about passes often can be found on airlines' international Web pages, which tend to be aimed at travelers from outside the carrier's home country. Also, try typing the name of the pass into a search engine, or search for "pass" within the carrier's Web site.

Consolidators **AirlineConsolidator.com** 888/468-5385 www.airlineconsolidator.com; for international tickets. **Best Fares** 800/880-1234 www.bestfares.com; $59.90 annual membership. **Cheap Tickets** 800/377-1000 or 800/652-4327 www.cheaptickets.com. **Expedia** 800/397-3342 or 404/728-8787 www.expedia.com. **Hotwire** 866/468-9473 or 920/330-9418 www.hotwire.com. **Now Voyager Travel** 1717 Avenue M, Brooklyn, NY 11230 212/459-1616 718/504-4762 www.nowvoyagertravel.com. **Onetravel.com** www.onetravel.com. **Orbitz** 888/656-4546 www.orbitz.com. **Priceline.com** www.priceline.com. **Travelocity** 888/709-5983, 877/282-2925 in Canada, 0870/111-7061 in the U.K. www.travelocity.com.

Courier Resources **Air Courier Association/Cheaptrips.com** 800/211-5119 www.aircourier.org or www.cheaptrips.com; $20 annual membership. **Courier Travel** 303/570-7586 313/625-6106 www.couriertravel.org; $50 annual membership. **International Association of Air Travel Couriers** 308/632-3273 308/632-8267 www.courier.org; $45 annual membership. **Now Voyager Travel** 1717 Avenue M, Brooklyn, NY 11230 212/459-1616 718/504-4762 www.nowvoyagertravel.com.

ENJOYING THE FLIGHT

State your seat preference when purchasing your ticket, and then repeat it when you confirm and when you check in. For more legroom, you can request one of the few emergency-aisle seats at check-in, if you're capable of moving obstacles comparable in weight to an airplane exit door (usually between 35 pounds and 60 pounds)—a Federal Aviation Administration requirement of passengers in these seats. Seats behind a bulkhead also offer more legroom, but they don't have underseat storage. Don't sit in the row in front of the emergency aisle or in front of a bulkhead, where seats may not recline. SeatGuru.com has more information about specific seat configurations, which vary by aircraft.

Ask the airline whether a snack or meal is served on the flight. If you have dietary concerns, request special meals when booking. These can be vegetarian, low-cholesterol, or kosher, for example. It's a good idea to pack some healthful snacks and a small (plastic) bottle of water in your carry-on bag. On long flights, try to maintain a normal routine, to help fight jet lag. At night, get some sleep. By day, eat light meals, drink water (not alcohol), and **move around the cabin** to stretch your legs. For additional jet-lag tips consult *Fodor's FYI: Travel Fit & Healthy* (available at bookstores everywhere).

Smoking policies vary from carrier to carrier. Most airlines prohibit smoking on all of their flights; others allow smoking only on certain routes or certain departures. Ask your carrier about its policy.

FLYING TIMES

Flying time from Boston is 1 hour; from Chicago, 2¼ hours; from Miami, 2½ hours; from Los Angeles, 6 hours; from London, 7 hours.

HOW TO COMPLAIN

If your baggage goes astray or your flight goes awry, complain right away. Most carriers require that you **file a claim immediately.** The Aviation Consumer Protection Division of the Department of Transportation publishes *Fly-Rights,* which discusses airlines and consumer issues and is available online. You can also find articles and information on mytravelrights.com, the Web site of the nonprofit Consumer Travel Rights Center.

Airline Complaints **Aviation Consumer Protection Division** U.S. Department of Transportation, Office of Aviation Enforcement and Proceedings, C-75, Room 4107, 400 7th St. SW, Washington, DC 20590 202/366-2220 airconsumer.ost.dot.gov. **Federal Aviation Administration Consumer Hotline** for inquiries: FAA, 800 Independence Ave. SW, Washington, DC 20591 800/322-7873 www.faa.gov.

RECONFIRMING

Check the status of your flight before you leave for the airport. You can do this on your carrier's Web site, by linking to a flight-status checker (many Web booking services offer these), or by calling your carrier or travel agent.

AIRPORTS & TRANSFERS

The major gateway to Philadelphia is Philadelphia International Airport (PHL), 8 mi from downtown in the southwest part of the city. Renovations in the past few years have made the terminals more appealing; shops and more eating options are welcome additions.

Airport Information Philadelphia International Airport ✉ 8900 Essington Ave., off I-95 ☎ 215/937-6937 and 800/745-4283 🌐 www.phl.org.

AIRPORT TRANSFERS

Allow at least a half hour, more during rush hour, for the 8-mi trip between the airport and Center City. By car the airport is accessible via I–95 south or I–76 east.

Taxis at the airport are plentiful but expensive—a flat fee of $20 plus tip. Follow the signs in the airport and wait in line for a taxi. Limousine service and shuttle buses are also available. Shuttle buses cost $10 and up per person and will make most requested stops downtown as well as to the suburbs. You can make shuttle arrangements at the centralized ground transportation counter in the baggage claim areas.

The Southeastern Pennsylvania Transportation Authority (SEPTA) runs the Airport Rail Line R1, which leaves the airport every 30 minutes from 6:10 AM to 12:10 AM. The trip to Center City takes about 20 minutes and costs $5.50. Trains serve the 30th Street, Suburban (Center City), Market East, and University City stations.

Limousines Carey Limousine Philadelphia ☎ 215/492-8402. London Limousine & Town Car Service ☎ 800/834-0708.

Train Airport Information Desk ☎ 800/745-4283. SEPTA ☎ 215/580-7800 🌐 www.septa.com.

BUSINESS HOURS

Banks are open weekdays 9–3; a few are open Saturdays and Sundays, with limited hours. The main post office is open 24 hours daily; some branches are open 9 to 5 weekdays, and Saturday 9 to noon. All banks and post offices are closed on national holidays.

MUSEUMS & SIGHTS

Many museums and sights are open 10–5; a few stay open late one or two evenings a week, and a number are closed on Monday. Historic area sights are open daily, with longer hours in summer, but it's wise to check ahead.

PHARMACIES

Most downtown pharmacies are open 9–6. Hours vary in the outlying neighborhoods and suburbs.

SHOPS

Downtown shopping hours are generally 9:30 or 10 to 5 or 6. Many stores are open until 9 PM on Wednesday. Most downtown stores are closed on Sunday, but the Gallery, the Shops at Liberty Place, and some stores in the Bellevue are open noon–5 or 6. The Bourse is open Sundays 11–5 from spring to fall. Antiques stores and art galleries may be closed some mornings or weekdays; it's wise to call ahead for hours.

BUS TRAVEL TO & FROM PHILADELPHIA

Greyhound operates long-haul service to Baltimore, Washington, D.C., New York, Wilmington, and points beyond out of the terminal at 10th and Filbert streets, just north of the Market East commuter rail station. For lower fares, Apex and New Century are two companies that connect Philadelphia with New York, Boston, and Washington, D.C. The Chinatown-based companies depart from different points on 11th Street between Arch and Vine streets. New Jersey Transit stops at the Greyhound terminal and offers service between Philadelphia and Atlantic City and other New Jersey destinations.

PAYING

You may purchase long-haul bus tickets with cash, traveler's checks, or major credit cards.

Bus Information Greyhound ☎ 215/931-4075 or 800/231-2222 🌐 www.greyhound.com. Apex ☎ 215/351-9167 🌐 www.apexbus.com. New Century Travel ☎ 215/627-2666 🌐 www.2000coach.com. New Jersey Transit ☎ 800/722-2222 🌐 www.njtransit.com.

BUS TRAVEL AROUND PHILADELPHIA

Buses make up the bulk of the SEPTA system, with 110 routes extending throughout the city and into the suburbs. Although the buses are comfortable and reliable, they should be used only when you are not in a hurry, as traffic on the city's major thoroughfares can add some time to your trip.

The distinctive purple minibuses you'll see around Center City are SEPTA's convenience line for visitors, the PHLASH. The 33 stops in the loop run from the Philadelphia Museum of Art on the Benjamin Franklin Parkway through Center City to Penn's Landing. Since a ride on the PHLASH costs $1 for a one-way ticket, **consider the handy all-day, unlimited-ride pass available for $4 per passenger or $10 for up to five passengers.** These buses run daily from 10 AM to midnight from mid-May to mid-September, 10 to 6 the rest of the year. There's service every 10 minutes.

FARES & SCHEDULES

The base fare for subways, trolleys, and buses is $2, paid with exact change or a token. Transfers cost 60¢. Senior citizens (with valid I.D.) ride free during off-peak hours and holidays. Up to two children (less than 42 inches tall) ride free with each paying adult. Tokens sell for $1.30 and can be purchased in packages of 2, 5, or 10 from cashiers along the Broad Street subway and Market-Frankford lines and in many downtown stores (including some Rite Aid pharmacies). You can also purchase them online at www.buyphilly.com.

If you plan to travel extensively within Center City, it's a good idea to **get a SEPTA pass.** The Day Pass costs $5.50 and is good for 24 hours of unlimited use on all SEPTA vehicles within the city, plus one trip on any regional rail line, including the Airport Express train. A weekly transit pass costs $18.75. Tokens and transit passes are good on buses and subways but not on commuter rail lines.

You can purchase tokens and transit passes in the SEPTA sales offices in the concourse below the northwest corner of 15th and Market streets; in the Market East station (8th and Market Sts.); and in 30th Street Station (30th and Market Sts.) Though SEPTA's automated answering system has cut down on your phone wait, be prepared for a busy signal and a long time on hold.

Bus Information **PHLASH** ☎ 215/474-5274 🌐 www.gophila.com/phlash. **SEPTA** ☎ 215/580-7800 🌐 www.septa.org.

CAMERAS & PHOTOGRAPHY

Contemporary and classic architecture, beautiful parks, and interesting historic sites provide you with plenty of great photo ops in and around Philadelphia. You'll want to remember your camera when you travel to the communities in Lancaster County. When you are visiting among the Amish, remember that they do not like their photos taken.

The *Kodak Guide to Shooting Great Travel Pictures* (available at bookstores everywhere) is loaded with tips.

Photo Help **Kodak Information Center** ☎ 800/242-2424 🌐 www.kodak.com.

EQUIPMENT PRECAUTIONS

Don't pack film or equipment in checked luggage, where it is much more susceptible to damage. X-ray machines used to view checked luggage are extremely powerful and therefore are likely to ruin your film. Try to ask for hand inspection of film, which becomes clouded after repeated exposure to airport X-ray machines, and keep videotapes and computer disks away from metal detectors. Always keep film, tape, and computer disks out of the sun. Carry an extra supply of batteries, and be prepared to turn on your camera, camcorder, or laptop to prove to airport security personnel that the device is real.

CAR RENTAL

Rates in Philadelphia begin around $20 a day and $120 a week for an economy car with air-conditioning, an automatic transmission, and unlimited mileage. This does not include airport surcharges and the tax on car rentals, which is 9%.

Major Agencies **Alamo** ☎ 800/327-9633 🌐 www.alamo.com. **Avis** ☎ 800/331-1212, 800/879-2847 or 800/272-5871 in Canada, 0870/606-0100 in the U.K., 02/9353-9000 in Australia, 09/526-2847 in New Zealand 🌐 www.avis.com. **Budget** ☎ 800/527-0700 🌐 www.budget.com. **Dollar** ☎ 800/800-4000,

0800/085-4578 in the U.K. www.dollar.com. **Hertz** 800/654-3131, 800/263-0600 in Canada, 0870/844-8844 in the U.K., 02/9669-2444 in Australia, 09/256-8690 in New Zealand www.hertz.com. **National Car Rental** 800/227-7368 www.nationalcar.com.

CUTTING COSTS

For a good deal, book through a travel agent who will shop around. Also, price local car-rental companies—whose prices may be lower still, although their service and maintenance may not be as good as those of major rental agencies—and research rates on the Internet. Consolidators that specialize in air travel can offer good rates on cars as well (⇨ Air Travel). Remember to ask about required deposits, cancellation penalties, and drop-off charges if you're planning to pick up the car in one city and leave it in another. If you're traveling during a holiday period, also make sure that a confirmed reservation guarantees you a car.

INSURANCE

When driving a rented car you are generally responsible for any damage to or loss of the vehicle. You also may be liable for any property damage or personal injury that you may cause while driving. Before you rent, see what coverage you already have under the terms of your personal auto-insurance policy and credit cards.

For about $9 to $25 a day, rental companies sell protection, known as a collision- or loss-damage waiver (CDW or LDW), that eliminates your liability for damage to the car; it's always optional and should never be automatically added to your bill. In most states you don't need a CDW if you have personal auto insurance or other liability insurance. However, **make sure you have enough coverage to pay for the car.** If you do not have auto insurance or an umbrella policy that covers damage to third parties, purchasing liability insurance and a CDW or LDW is highly recommended.

REQUIREMENTS & RESTRICTIONS

In Philadelphia and the surrounding areas you must be 21 to rent a car, and rates may be higher if you're under 25. Child seats are compulsory for children under eight. Non-U.S. residents need a reservation voucher (for prepaid reservations that were made in the traveler's home country), a passport, a driver's license, and a travel policy that covers each driver, when picking up a car.

SURCHARGES

Before you pick up a car in one city and leave it in another, ask about drop-off charges or one-way service fees, which can be substantial. Also inquire about early-return policies; some rental agencies charge extra if you return the car before the time specified in your contract while others give you a refund for the days not used. Most agencies note the tank's fuel level on your contract; to avoid a hefty refueling fee, return the car with the same tank level. If the tank was full, refill it just before you turn in the car, but be aware that gas stations near the rental outlet may overcharge. It's almost never a deal to buy a tank of gas with the car when you rent it; the understanding is that you'll return it empty, but some fuel usually remains. Surcharges may apply if you're under 25 or if you take the car outside the area approved by the rental agency. You'll pay extra for child seats (about $8 a day), which are compulsory for children under five, and usually for additional drivers (up to $25 a day, depending on location).

CAR TRAVEL

Getting to and around Philadelphia by car can be difficult—at rush hour it can be a nightmare. The main east–west freeway through the city, the Schuylkill Expressway (I–76), is often tied up for miles.

The main north–south highway through Philadelphia is the Delaware Expressway (I–95). To reach Center City heading southbound on I–95, take the Vine Street exit.

From the west the Pennsylvania Turnpike begins at the Ohio border and intersects the Schuylkill Expressway (I–76) at Valley Forge. The Schuylkill Expressway has several exits in Center City. The Northeast Extension of the turnpike, renamed I–476, runs from Scranton to Plymouth Meeting, north of Philadelphia. From the east the

New Jersey Turnpike and I–295 access U.S. 30, which enters the city via the Benjamin Franklin Bridge, or New Jersey Route 42 and the Walt Whitman Bridge into South Philadelphia.

With the exception of a few wide streets (notably the Benjamin Franklin Parkway, Broad Street, Vine Street, and part of Market Street), streets in Center City are narrow and one-way. Philadelphia's compact 2-square-mi downtown is laid out in a grid. The traditional heart of the city is Broad and Market streets, where City Hall stands. Market Street divides the city north and south; 130 South 15th Street, for example, is in the second block south of Market Street. North–south streets are numbered, starting with Front (1st) Street, at the Delaware River, and increasing to the west. Broad Street, recently renamed the Avenue of the Arts, is the equivalent of 14th Street. The diagonal Benjamin Franklin Parkway breaks the grid pattern by leading from City Hall out of Center City into Fairmount Park.

EMERGENCY SERVICES

If you have a AAA membership card, you can dial the group's toll-free number for emergency road service.

AAA Mid-Atlantic ✉ 2040 Market St. ☎ 215/864–5000, 800/222–4357.

PARKING

Parking in Center City can be tough. A spot at a parking meter, if you're lucky enough to find one, costs between 50¢ and $1 per hour. Parking garages are plentiful, especially around Independence Hall, City Hall, and the Pennsylvania Convention Center, but can charge up to $1.50 per 15 minutes and up to $20 or so for the day. Police officers are vigilant about ticketing illegally parked cars and fines begin at $25. Fortunately the city is compact, and you can easily get around downtown on foot or by bus after you park your car.

ROAD CONDITIONS

Use extra caution when maneuvering the narrow one-way streets of Center City. Drivers on the Philadelphia stretch of the Schuylkill Expressway (I–76) routinely drive well over the speed limit (and the many accidents on this highway attest to this). If you can, choose gentler routes to your destination, such as Kelly Drive or West River Drive.

RULES OF THE ROAD

Pennsylvania law requires all children under age four to be strapped into approved child-safety seats and children ages five to eight to ride in toddler booster seats. All passengers must wear seat belts. In Pennsylvania, unless otherwise indicated, you may turn right at a red light after stopping if there is no oncoming traffic. When in doubt, wait for the green. Speed limits in Philadelphia are generally 35–40 mph on side streets, 55 mph on the surrounding highways.

CHILDREN IN PHILADELPHIA

Philadelphia has many attractions and activities for youngsters. The Please Touch Museum is designed for ages one to seven. Several museums, including the Franklin Institute, Academy of Natural Sciences, and the Independence Seaport Museum, are entertaining for children of all ages. Others, such as the Philadelphia Museum of Art, offer weekly children's activities and entertainment. Playgrounds abound in Center City and in the outlying neighborhoods. Many restaurants offer children's menus.

Pick up copies of the free monthly publications *Parents Express* and *Metrokids,* which include up-to-date listings of museum exhibitions, festivals, films, and bookstore readings for children. These are available in bookstores, cafés, and libraries.

Fodor's Around Philadelphia with Kids can help you plan your days together. For general advice about traveling with children, consult *Fodor's FYI: Travel with Your Baby.* They are available in bookstores everywhere.

Local Information **Metrokids** ☎ 215/291–5560 🌐 www.metrokids.com. **Parents Express** ☎ 215/648–3580 🌐 www.parents-express.net.

FLYING

Experts agree that it's a good idea to use safety seats aloft for children weighing less than 40 pounds. Airlines set their own policies: if you use a safety seat, U.S. carriers usually require that the child be ticketed, even if he or she is young enough to ride free, because the seats must be strapped into regular seats. And even if you pay the full adult fare for the seat, it may be worth it, especially on longer trips. Do **check your airline's policy about using safety seats during takeoff and landing.** Safety seats are not allowed everywhere in the plane, so get your seat assignments as early as possible.

When reserving, request children's meals or a freestanding bassinet (not available at all airlines) if you need them. But note that bulkhead seats, where you must sit to use the bassinet, may lack an overhead bin or storage space on the floor.

LODGING

Most hotels in Philadelphia allow children under a certain age to stay in their parents' room at no extra charge, but others charge for them as extra adults; be sure to find out the cutoff age for children's discounts.

SIGHTS & ATTRACTIONS

Places that are especially appealing to children are indicated by a rubber-duckie icon (🐤) in the margin.

TRANSPORTATION

Up to two children under four years of age ride free with each paying adult on SEPTA buses, subways, and trolleys. On weekends, an additional two children under 11 can ride for a reduced fare.

CONCIERGES

Concierges, found in many hotels, can help you with theater tickets and dinner reservations: a good one with connections may be able to get you seats for a hot show or prime-time dinner reservations at the restaurant of the moment. You can also turn to your hotel's concierge for help with travel arrangements, sightseeing plans, services ranging from aromatherapy to zipper repair, and emergencies. **Always tip** a concierge who has been of assistance (⇨ Tipping).

CONSUMER PROTECTION

Whether you're shopping for gifts or purchasing travel services, **pay with a major credit card** whenever possible, so you can cancel payment or get reimbursed if there's a problem (and you can provide documentation). If you're doing business with a particular company for the first time, contact your local Better Business Bureau and the attorney general's offices in your state and (for U.S. businesses) the company's home state as well. Have any complaints been filed? Finally, if you're buying a package or tour, always consider travel insurance that includes default coverage (⇨ Insurance).

BBBs **Council of Better Business Bureaus** ✉ 4200 Wilson Blvd., Suite 800, Arlington, VA 22203 ☎ 703/276-0100 📠 703/525-8277 🌐 www.bbb.org.

CUSTOMS & DUTIES

When shopping, **keep receipts** for all purchases. Travelers from outside the United States may be required to show their purchases to customs officials.

IN AUSTRALIA

Australian residents who are 18 or older may bring home A$900 worth of souvenirs and gifts (including jewelry), 250 cigarettes or 250 grams of cigars or other tobacco products, and 2.25 liters of alcohol (including wine, beer, and spirits). Residents under 18 may bring back A$450 worth of goods. If any of these individual allowances are exceeded, you must pay duty for the entire amount (of the group of products in which the allowance was exceeded). Members of the same family traveling together may pool their allowances. Prohibited items include meat products. Seeds, plants, and fruits need to be declared upon arrival.

Australian Customs Service Customs House, 10 Cooks River Dr., Sydney International Airport, Sydney, NSW 2020 ☎ 02/6275-6666 or 1300/363263, 02/8334-7444 or 1800/020-504 quarantine-inquiry line 📠 02/8339-6714 🌐 www.customs.gov.au.

IN CANADA

Canadian residents who have been out of Canada for at least seven days may bring in C$750 worth of goods duty-free. If you've been away fewer than seven days but more than 48 hours, the duty-free allowance drops to C$200. If your trip lasts

24 to 48 hours, the allowance is C$50; if the goods are worth more than C$50, you must pay full duty on all of the goods. You may not pool allowances with family members. Goods claimed under the C$750 exemption may follow you by mail; those claimed under the lesser exemptions must accompany you. Alcohol and tobacco products may be included in the seven-day and 48-hour exemptions but not in the 24-hour exemption. If you meet the age requirements of the province or territory through which you reenter Canada, you may bring in, duty-free, 1.5 liters of wine *or* 1.14 liters (40 imperial ounces) of liquor *or* 24 12-ounce cans or bottles of beer or ale. Also, if you meet the local age requirement for tobacco products, you may bring in, duty-free, 200 cigarettes, 50 cigars or cigarillos, and 200 grams of tobacco. You may have to pay a minimum duty on tobacco products, regardless of whether or not you exceed your personal exemption. Check ahead of time with the Canada Border Services Agency or the Department of Agriculture for policies regarding meat products, seeds, plants, and fruits.

You may send an unlimited number of gifts (only one gift per recipient, however) worth up to C$60 each duty-free to Canada. Label the package UNSOLICITED GIFT—VALUE UNDER $60. Alcohol and tobacco are excluded.

Canada Border Services Agency ✉ Customs Information Services, 191 Laurier Ave. W, 15th fl., Ottawa, Ontario K1A 0L5 ☎ 800/461-9999 in Canada, 204/983-3500, 506/636-5064 🌐 www.cbsa.gc.ca.

IN NEW ZEALAND

All homeward-bound residents may bring back NZ$700 worth of souvenirs and gifts; passengers may not pool their allowances, and children can claim only the concession on goods intended for their own use. For those 17 or older, the duty-free allowance also includes 4.5 liters of wine or beer; one 1,125-ml bottle of spirits; and either 200 cigarettes, 250 grams of tobacco, 50 cigars, *or* a combination of the three up to 250 grams. Meat products, seeds, plants, and fruits must be declared upon arrival to the Agricultural Services Department.

New Zealand Customs ✉ Head office: The Customhouse, 17-21 Whitmore St., Box 2218, Wellington ☎ 09/300-5399 or 0800/428-786 🌐 www.customs.govt.nz.

IN THE U.K.

From countries outside the European Union, including United States, you may bring home, duty-free, 200 cigarettes, 50 cigars, 100 cigarillos, or 250 grams of tobacco; 1 liter of spirits or 2 liters of fortified or sparkling wine or liqueurs; 2 liters of still table wine; 60 ml of perfume; 250 ml of toilet water; plus £145 worth of other goods, including gifts and souvenirs. Prohibited items include meat and dairy products, seeds, plants, and fruits.

HM Customs and Excise ✉ Portcullis House, 21 Cowbridge Rd. E, Cardiff CF11 9SS ☎ 0845/010-9000 or 0208/929-0152 advice service, 0208/929-6731 or 0208/910-3602 complaints 🌐 www.hmce.gov.uk.

DISABILITIES & ACCESSIBILITY

People with disabilities will find that most attractions and the larger hotels in Philadelphia will accommodate their needs. Theaters and stadiums contain ramps and/or elevators. Some of Philadelphia's older, bumpier sidewalks and walkways may be difficult to navigate with wheelchairs, but all of the major streets in Center City have curb cuts. Handicapped parking is available on streets in front of major attractions and in parking lots.

An 80-page booklet from ARTREACH, Inc., *Access the Arts: A Guide for People with Disabilities,* contains information on more than 75 of the region's theaters, performing-arts centers, and museums for people with physical disabilities. Listings include wheelchair accessibility of entrances and rest rooms; phone and TTY numbers; and large-print or Braille materials or assistive listening devices. The book is available on audiocassette for individuals who are blind.

Artreach, Inc. ☎ 215/951-0316 🌐 www.artreach.org.

LODGING

Despite the Americans with Disabilities Act, the definition of accessibility seems to differ from hotel to hotel. Some properties may be accessible by ADA standards for people with mobility problems but not for people with hearing or vision impairments, for example.

If you have mobility problems, ask for the lowest floor on which accessible services are offered. If you have a hearing impairment, check whether the hotel has devices to alert you visually to the ring of the telephone, a knock at the door, and a fire/emergency alarm. Some hotels provide these devices without charge. Discuss your needs with hotel personnel if this equipment isn't available, so that a staff member can personally alert you in the event of an emergency.

If you're bringing a guide dog, get authorization ahead of time and write down the name of the person with whom you spoke.

RESERVATIONS

When discussing accessibility with an operator or reservations agent, ask hard questions. Are there any stairs, inside *or* out? Are there grab bars next to the toilet *and* in the shower/tub? How wide is the doorway to the room? To the bathroom? For the most extensive facilities meeting the latest legal specifications, opt for newer accommodations. If you reserve through a toll-free number, consider also calling the hotel's local number to confirm the information from the central reservations office. Get confirmation in writing when you can.

SIGHTS & ATTRACTIONS

Museums and theaters have brought their facilities in line with federal regulations and all include wheelchair access, barrier-free entrances, and accessible rest rooms and elevators. Some, such as the Philadelphia Museum of Art and the Pennsylvania Academy of the Fine Arts, offer wheelchair rentals. Some of the attractions in Independence National Historical Park may pose obstacles to people with disabilities, as their historic designation occasionally precludes structural improvements. The Independence Visitor Center and Liberty Bell Pavilion are entirely accessible. A captioned version of a film shown at the visitor center and a printed script of an audio program may be obtained on request.

TRANSPORTATION

More than half of SEPTA's buses are wheelchair accessible and one-third have wheelchair lifts and computerized, recorded announcements of stops. Fares for travelers with disabilities are reduced for off-peak travel. Specialized pick-up and drop-off service is available by calling SEPTA Paratransit. A complete list of accessible bus routes and times is available on SEPTA's Web site. The PHLASH buses are accessible.

For general complaints, call the Disability Rights Section. The Aviation Consumer Protection Division handles airline-related problems, and the Civil Rights Office deals with problems with surface transportation.

The U.S. Department of Transportation Aviation Consumer Protection Division's online publication *New Horizons: Information for the Air Traveler with a Disability* offers advice for travelers with a disability, and outlines basic rights. Visit DisabilityInfo.gov for general information.

SEPTA Paratransit ☎ 215/580-7853 TTY 🌐 www.septa.org/service/accessible_septa.html.

Information and Complaints **Aviation Consumer Protection Division** (⇨ Air Travel) for airline-related problems; 🌐 airconsumer.ost.dot.gov/publications/horizons.htm for airline travel advice and rights. **Departmental Office of Civil Rights** ✉ for general inquiries, U.S. Department of Transportation, S-30, 400 7th St. SW, Room 10215, Washington, DC 20590 ☎ 202/366-4648, 202/366-8538 TTY 📠 202/366-9371 🌐 www.dotcr.ost.dot.gov. **Disability Rights Section** ✉ NYAV, U.S. Department of Justice, Civil Rights Division, 950 Pennsylvania Ave. NW, Washington, DC 20530 ☎ ADA information line 202/514-0301, 800/514-0301, 202/514-0383 TTY, 800/514-0383 TTY 🌐 www.ada.gov. **U.S. Department of Transportation Hotline** ☎ for disability-related air-travel problems, 800/778-4838 or 800/455-9880 TTY.

TRAVEL AGENCIES

In the United States, the Americans with Disabilities Act requires that travel firms serve the needs of all travelers. Some agencies specialize in working with people with disabilities.

Access Adventures is run by a former physical-rehabilitation counselor. CareVacations handles group tours and cruises.

Travelers with Mobility Problems **Access Adventures/B. Roberts Travel** ✉ 1876 East Ave., Rochester, NY 14610 ☎ 800/444-6540 🌐 www.brobertstravel.com. **Accessible Vans of America** ✉ 37 Daniel Rd. W, Fairfield, NJ 07004 ☎ 877/282-8267, 888/282-8267, 973/808-9709 reservations 📠 973/808-9713 🌐 www.accessiblevans.com. **CareVacations** ✉ No. 5, 5110-50 Ave., Leduc, Alberta, Canada, T9E 6V4 ☎ 780/986-6404 or 877/478-7827 📠 780/986-8332 🌐 www.carevacations.com, for group tours and cruise vacations. **Flying Wheels Travel** ✉ 143 W. Bridge St., Box 382, Owatonna, MN 55060 ☎ 507/451-5005 📠 507/451-1685 🌐 www.flyingwheelstravel.com.

Travelers with Developmental Disabilities **New Directions** ✉ 5276 Hollister Ave., Suite 207, Santa Barbara, CA 93111 ☎ 805/967-2841 or 888/967-2841 📠 805/964-7344 🌐 www.newdirectionstravel.com. **Sprout** ✉ 893 Amsterdam Ave., New York, NY 10025 ☎ 212/222-9575 or 888/222-9575 📠 212/222-9768 🌐 www.gosprout.org.

DISCOUNTS & DEALS

Be a smart shopper and compare all your options before making decisions. A plane ticket bought with a promotional coupon from travel clubs, coupon books, and direct-mail offers or purchased on the Internet may not be cheaper than the least expensive fare from a discount ticket agency. And always keep in mind that what you get is just as important as what you save.

If you're planning to visit some of the city's top museums, **look into CityPass,** which offers 50% savings on admission to six attractions and is valid for nine days. The pass costs $36 and covers the Academy of Natural Sciences, the Franklin Institute Science Museum, the Independence Seaport Museum, the National Constitution Center, the Philadelphia Zoo, and the Philadelphia Trolley Tour. You can buy the pass at any of the attractions; because the passes are tickets, you also avoid any ticket lines.

CityPass ☎ 707/256-0490 🌐 www.citypass.com.

DISCOUNT RESERVATIONS

To save money, look into discount reservations services with Web sites and toll-free numbers, which use their buying power to get a better price on hotels, airline tickets (⇨ Air Travel), even car rentals. When booking a room, always **call the hotel's local toll-free number** (if one is available) rather than the central reservations number—you'll often get a better price. Always ask about special packages or corporate rates.

Hotel Rooms **Accommodations Express** ☎ 800/444-7666 or 800/277-1064. **Hotels.com** ☎ 800/246-8357 🌐 www.hotels.com. **Quikbook** ☎ 800/789-9887 🌐 www.quikbook.com. **Turbotrip.com** ☎ 800/473-7829 🌐 w3.turbotrip.com.

PACKAGE DEALS

Don't confuse packages and guided tours. When you buy a package, you travel on your own, just as though you had planned the trip yourself. Fly/drive packages, which combine airfare and car rental, are often a good deal. In cities, ask the local visitor's bureau about hotel and local transportation packages that include tickets to major museum exhibits or other special events.

EMERGENCIES

Pennsylvania Hospital is near the historic district. Hahnemann University Hospital is near City Hall, Jefferson Hospital is near Chinatown and the Convention Center, and Graduate Hospital is near Rittenhouse Square.

Emergency Services **Ambulance, fire, police** ☎ 911.

Hospitals **Graduate Hospital** ✉ 1800 Lombard St. ☎ 215/893-2000 information, 215/893-2350 emergency room. **Hahnemann University Hospital** ✉ Broad and Vine Sts. ☎ 215/762-7000 information, 215/762-7963 emergency room. **Jefferson Hospital** ✉ 11th and Sansom Sts. ☎ 215/955-6000 **Pennsylvania Hospital** ✉ 8th and Spruce Sts. ☎ 215/829-3000 information, 215/829-3358 emergency room.

Hot Lines **Poisoning Control Center** ☎ 800/222-1222. **Suicide and Crisis Intervention Center** ☎ 215/686-4420. **Women Against Abuse** ☎ 215/386-7777.

24-Hour Pharmacies **CVS Pharmacy** ✉ 1826-30 Chestnut St. ☎ 215/972-1401. **Rite Aid** ✉ 2017-2023 S. Broad St. ☎ 215/467-0850.

FERRY TRAVEL

The RiverLink Ferry, a seasonal (April–mid-November) passenger ferry, offers service between Philadelphia and Camden, site of the Advennture Aquarium, the Tweeter Center, Battleship New Jersey, and Campbell's Field. Ferries depart every 40 minutes from Penn's Landing and from Camden's waterfront daily between 9:40 and 5:20, with extended hours and continuous service for Penn's Landing and Tweeter Center concerts, and Camden Riversharks baseball games. The cost is $6 round-trip, the ride takes 12 minutes, and the ferry is wheelchair-accessible.

FARES & SCHEDULES

RiverLink Ferry tickets must be purchased at the terminal at Penn's Landing (Walnut Street and Columbus Avenue), outside the Independence Seaport Museum or at the Camden terminal. Payment can be made by cash only.

RiverLink Ferry ✉ Penn's Landing near Walnut St. ☎ 215/925-5465 ⊕ www.riverlinkferry.org.

GAY & LESBIAN TRAVEL

Philadelphia is the first major city in the country to woo gay visitors through television ads. The campaign, launched in 2004, features a man in a tricorner hat urging his beloved to visit him in Philadelphia. The ad runs on cable stations such as Bravo, Comedy Central, and VH1.

In Center City, the gay scene revolves around an area between Lombard and Walnut streets and 11th and 13th streets, where there are a good number of gay bars, cafés, and shops. One hub of the Philadelphia gay experience is Giovanni's Room, a bookstore founded in 1973. It has plenty of maps, guides, and free advice for visitors. You can also check out the local weekly newspaper, the *Philadelphia Gay News*.

For details about the gay and lesbian scene, consult *Fodor's Gay Guide to the USA* (available in bookstores everywhere).

Gay- & Lesbian-Friendly Businesses **Giovanni's Room** ✉ 345 S. 12th St. ☎ 215/923-2960 ⊕ www.giovannisroom.com. **Philadelphia Gay News** ✉ 505 S. Fourth St. ☎ 215/625-8501 ⊕ www.pgn.com.

Gay- & Lesbian-Friendly Travel Agencies **Different Roads Travel** ✉ 1017 N. LaCienega Blvd., Suite 308, West Hollywood, CA 90069 ☎ 310/289-6000 or 800/429-8747 (Ext. 14 for both) 📠 310/855-0323 ✉ lgernert@tzell.com. **Kennedy Travel** ✉ 130 W. 42nd St., Suite 401, New York, NY 10036 ☎ 800/237-7433 or 212/840-8659 📠 212/730-2269 ⊕ www.kennedytravel.com. **Now, Voyager** ✉ 4406 18th St., San Francisco, CA 94114 ☎ 415/626-1169 or 800/255-6951 📠 415/626-8626 ⊕ www.nowvoyager.com. **Skylink Travel and Tour/Flying Dutchmen Travel** ✉ 1455 N. Dutton Ave., Suite A, Santa Rosa, CA 95401 ☎ 707/546-9888 or 800/225-5759 📠 707/636-0951; serving lesbian travelers.

HOLIDAYS

Major national holidays are New Year's Day (Jan. 1); Martin Luther King Day (3rd Mon. in Jan.); Presidents' Day (3rd Mon. in Feb.); Memorial Day (last Mon. in May); Independence Day (July 4); Labor Day (1st Mon. in Sept.); Columbus Day (2nd Mon. in Oct.); Thanksgiving Day (4th Thurs. in Nov.); Christmas Eve and Christmas Day (Dec. 24 and 25); and New Year's Eve (Dec. 31).

INSURANCE

The most useful travel-insurance plan is a comprehensive policy that includes coverage for trip cancellation and interruption, default, trip delay, and medical expenses (with a waiver for preexisting conditions).

Without insurance you'll lose all or most of your money if you cancel your trip, regardless of the reason. Default insurance covers you if your tour operator, airline, or cruise line goes out of business—the chances of which have been increasing. Trip-delay covers expenses that arise because of bad weather or mechanical delays. Study the fine print when comparing policies.

U.K. residents can buy a travel-insurance policy valid for most vacations taken during the year in which it's purchased (but check preexisting-condition coverage).

Always **buy travel policies directly from the insurance company**; if you buy them from a cruise line, airline, or tour operator that goes out of business you probably won't be covered for the agency or operator's default, a major risk. Before making any purchase, review your existing health and home-owner's policies to find what they cover away from home.

Travel Insurers In the U.S.: **Access America** ✉ 2805 N. Parham Rd., Richmond, VA 23294 ☎ 800/284-8300 🖷 804/673-1469 or 800/346-9265 🌐 www.accessamerica.com. **Travel Guard International** ✉ 1145 Clark St., Stevens Point, WI 54481 ☎ 800/826-1300 or 715/345-1041 🖷 800/955-8785 or 715/345-1990 🌐 www.travelguard.com.

FOR INTERNATIONAL TRAVELERS

For information on customs restrictions, *see* Customs & Duties.

CAR RENTAL

When picking up a rental car, non-U.S. residents need a reservation voucher for any prepaid reservations that were made in the traveler's home country, a passport, a driver's license, and a travel policy that covers each driver.

CAR TRAVEL

Gasoline costs about $1.90 to $2.50 per gallon in Philadelphia. Most downtown gas stations can be found on Broad Street or Delaware Avenue. Most gas stations in the area stay open late (24 hours in some locations), except in rural areas, where Sunday hours are limited and where you may drive long stretches without a refueling opportunity. Highways are well paved. Interstate highways—limited-access, multilane highways whose numbers are prefixed by "I–"—are the fastest routes. Interstates with three-digit numbers encircle urban areas, which may have other limited-access expressways, freeways, and parkways as well. Tolls may be levied on limited-access highways. So-called U.S. highways and state highways are not necessarily limited-access but may have several lanes.

Along larger highways, roadside stops with rest rooms, fast-food restaurants, and sundries stores are well spaced. State police and tow trucks patrol major highways and lend assistance. If your car breaks down on an interstate, pull onto the shoulder and wait for help, or have your passengers wait while you walk to an emergency phone (available in most states). If you carry a cell phone, dial 911, noting your location on the small green roadside mileage markers.

Driving in the United States is on the right. Do obey speed limits posted along roads and highways. Watch for lower limits in small towns and on back roads. **Pennsylvania requires all passengers to wear seat belts.** On weekdays between 6 and 10 AM and again between 4 and 7 PM expect heavy traffic. To encourage carpooling, some freeways have special lanes for so-called high-occupancy vehicles (HOV)—cars carrying more than one passenger.

Bookstores, gas stations, convenience stores, and rest stops sell maps (about $3) and multiregion road atlases (about $10).

CONSULATES

Philadelphia has its own British consulate, but the nearest consulates for Australia, Canada, and New Zealand are in New York City.

British Consulate ✉ 1818 Market St., 33rd fl., Philadelphia 19103 ☎ 215/557-7665.

CURRENCY

The dollar is the basic unit of U.S. currency. It has 100 cents. Coins are the copper penny (1¢); the silvery nickel (5¢), dime (10¢), quarter (25¢), and half-dollar (50¢); and the golden $1 coin, replacing a now-rare silver dollar. Bills are denominated $1, $5, $10, $20, $50, and $100, all mostly green and identical in size; designs and background tints vary. In addition, you may come across a $2 bill, but the chances are slim. The exchange rate at this writing is US$1.91 per British pound, 80¢ per Canadian dollar, 78¢ per Australian dollar, and 73¢ per New Zealand dollar.

ELECTRICITY

The U.S. standard is AC, 110 volts/60 cycles. Plugs have two flat pins set parallel to each other.

EMERGENCIES

For police, fire, or ambulance, **dial 911** (0 in rural areas).

INSURANCE

Britons and Australians need extra medical coverage when traveling overseas.

Insurance Information In the U.K.: **Association of British Insurers** ✉ 51 Gresham St., London EC2V

7HQ ☎ 020/7600-3333 🖷 020/7696-8999 🌐 www.abi.org.uk. In Australia: **Insurance Council of Australia** ✉ Level 3, 56 Pitt St. Sydney, NSW 2000 ☎ 02/9253-5100 🖷 02/9253-5111 🌐 www.ica.com.au. In Canada: **RBC Insurance** ✉ 6880 Financial Dr., Mississauga, Ontario L5N 7Y5 ☎ 800/387-4357 or 905/816-2559 🖷 888/298-6458 🌐 www.rbcinsurance.com. In New Zealand: **Insurance Council of New Zealand** ✉ Level 7, 111-115 Customhouse Quay, Box 474, Wellington ☎ 04/472-5230 🖷 04/473-3011 🌐 www.icnz.org.nz.

MAIL & SHIPPING

You can buy stamps and aerograms and send letters and parcels in post offices. Stamp-dispensing machines can occasionally be found in airports, bus and train stations, office buildings, drugstores, and the like. You can also deposit mail in the stout, dark blue, steel bins at strategic locations everywhere and in the mail chutes of large buildings; pickup schedules are posted. You can deposit packages at public collection boxes as long as the parcels are affixed with proper postage and weigh less than one pound. Packages weighing one or more pounds must be taken to a post office or handed to a postal carrier.

For mail sent within the United States, you need a 37¢ stamp for first-class letters weighing up to 1 ounce (23¢ for each additional ounce) and 23¢ for postcards. You pay 80¢ for 1-ounce airmail letters and 70¢ for airmail postcards to most other countries; to Canada and Mexico, you need a 60¢ stamp for a 1-ounce letter and 50¢ for a postcard. An aerogram—a single sheet of lightweight blue paper that folds into its own envelope, stamped for overseas airmail—costs 70¢.

To receive mail on the road, have it sent c/o General Delivery at your destination's main post office (use the correct five-digit ZIP code). You must pick up mail in person within 30 days and show a driver's license or passport.

PASSPORTS & VISAS

When traveling internationally, carry your passport even if you don't need one (it's always the best form of I.D.) and **make two photocopies of the data page** (one for someone at home and another for you, carried separately from your passport). If you lose your passport, promptly call the nearest embassy or consulate and the local police.

Visitor visas aren't necessary for Canadian or European Union citizens, or for citizens of Australia who are staying fewer than 90 days.

i Australian Citizens **Passports Australia** ☎ 131-232 🌐 www.passports.gov.au. **United States Consulate General** ✉ MLC Centre, Level 59, 19-29 Martin Pl., Sydney, NSW 2000 ☎ 02/9373-9200, 1902/941-641 fee-based visa-inquiry line 🌐 usembassy-australia.state.gov/sydney.

i Canadian Citizens **Passport Office** ✉ to mail in applications: 70 Cremazie St., Gatineau, Québec J8Y 3P2 ☎ 800/567-6868, 866/255-7655 TTY 🌐 www.ppt.gc.ca.

i New Zealand Citizens **New Zealand Passports Office** ✉ For applications and information, Level 3, Boulcott House, 47 Boulcott St., Wellington ☎ 0800/22-5050 or 04/474-8100 🌐 www.passports.govt.nz. **Embassy of the United States** ✉ 29 Fitzherbert Terr., Thorndon, Wellington ☎ 04/462-6000 🌐 usembassy.org.nz. **U.S. Consulate General** ✉ Citibank Bldg., 3rd fl., 23 Customs St. E, Auckland ☎ 09/303-2724 🌐 usembassy.org.nz.

i U.K. Citizens **U.K. Passport Service** ☎ 0870/521-0410 🌐 www.passport.gov.uk. **American Consulate General** ✉ Danesfort House, 223 Stranmillis Rd., Belfast, Northern Ireland BT9 5GR ☎ 028/9038-6100 🖷 028/9068-1301 🌐 www.usembassy.org.uk. **American Embassy** ✉ for visa and immigration information or to submit a visa application via mail (enclose an SASE), Consular Information Unit, 24 Grosvenor Sq., London W1A 2LQ ☎ 090/5544-4546 or 090/6820-0290 for visa information (per-minute charges), 0207/499-9000 main switchboard 🌐 www.usembassy.org.uk.

TELEPHONES

All U.S. telephone numbers consist of a three-digit area code and a seven-digit local number. Within many local calling areas, you dial only the seven-digit number. Within some area codes, you must dial "1" first for calls outside the local area. To call between area-code regions, dial "1" then all 10 digits; the same goes for calls to numbers prefixed by "800," "888," "866," and "877"—all toll free. For calls to numbers preceded by "900" you must pay—usually dearly.

For international calls, dial "011" followed by the country code and the local number. For help, dial "0" and ask for an overseas operator. The country code is 61 for Australia, 64 for New Zealand, 44 for the United Kingdom. Calling Canada is the same as calling within the United States. Most local phone books list country codes and U.S. area codes. The country code for the United States is 1.

For operator assistance, dial "0." To obtain someone's phone number, call directory assistance at 555–1212 or occasionally 411 (free at many public phones). To have the person you're calling foot the bill, phone collect; dial "0" instead of "1" before the 10-digit number.

At pay phones, instructions often are posted. Usually you insert coins in a slot (usually 25¢–50¢ for local calls) and wait for a steady tone before dialing. When you call long-distance, the operator tells you how much to insert; prepaid phone cards, widely available in various denominations, are easier. Call the number on the back, punch in the card's personal identification number when prompted, then dial your number.

MAIL & SHIPPING

Post Offices **Main Post Office** ✉ 2970 Market St. ☎ 215/895-8980. **Middle City Branch** ✉ 2037 Chestnut St. ☎ 215/568-6329. **University City Branch** ✉ 228 S. 40th St. ☎ 215/568-6391.

Major Services **DHL** ✉ 510 Walnut St. ☎ 800/225-5345 🌐 www.dhl.com **Fed Express** ✉ 1201 Market St. ☎ 800/463-3339 🌐 www.fedex.com **UPS** ✉ 211 South St. ☎ 215/733-9200 🌐 www.ups.com.

MEDIA

NEWSPAPERS & MAGAZINES

The *Philadelphia Inquirer* and the *Philadelphia Daily News* are the city's main daily newspapers. They share a Web site (🌐 www.philly.com). The two alternative weeklies are the *City Paper* (🌐 www.citypaper.net) and the *Philadelphia Weekly* (🌐 www.philadelphiaweekly.com). The monthly *Philadelphia* magazine (🌐 www.phillymag.com) contains listings and advertisements of interest to visitors as well as residents.

RADIO & TELEVISION

AM radio: KYW 1060 plays news and weather, and WIP 610 dispenses all the vitriol of the average Philly sports fan. FM radio: Run by the University of Pennsylvania, WXPN 88.5 is the place for jazz and other types of music, WHYY 90.1 is the local National Public Radio affiliate, WMMR 93.3 focuses on album rock, WXTU 92 plays country, and WUSC 98.9 is known for urban contemporary.

The local affiliates of the major networks are channel 3, CBS; channel 6, ABC; channel 10, NBC; channel 12, PBS; and channel 29, FOX.

MONEY MATTERS

Philadelphia can be expensive, although it's less so than New York. A cup of coffee will cost $1 at a diner but $2–$3 at an upscale restaurant; a sandwich will set you back $4–$8. Taxi rides begin at $2.10 and can quickly add up to $6 or more for a ride across Center City. Most sites in Independence National Historical Park are free; museums in the city cost $3–$14.

Prices throughout this guide are given for adults. Substantially reduced fees are almost always available for children, students, and senior citizens. For information on taxes, *see* Taxes.

ATMS

Automatic teller machines are available in the lobbies or on the outside walls of most banks. They can also be found at branches of the local convenience store chain Wawa, and in larger grocery stores.

ATM Locations **Cirrus** ☎ 800/424-7787. **Plus** ☎ 800/843-7587.

CREDIT CARDS

Throughout this guide, the following abbreviations are used: **AE,** American Express; **D,** Discover; **DC,** Diners Club; **MC,** MasterCard; and **V,** Visa.

Reporting Lost Cards **American Express** ☎ 800/992-3404. **Diners Club** ☎ 800/234-6377. **Discover** ☎ 800/347-2683. **MasterCard** ☎ 800/622-7747. **Visa** ☎ 800/ 847-2911.

PACKING

Portage and luggage trolleys are hard to find, so **pack light.** Philadelphia is a fairly casual city, although men will need a jacket and tie in some of the better restaurants. Jeans and sneakers or other casual clothing is fine for sightseeing. You'll need a heavy coat and boots for winter, which can be cold and snowy. Summers are hot and humid, but you'll need a shawl or jacket for air-conditioned restaurants. Many areas are best explored on foot, so **bring good walking shoes.**

In your carry-on luggage, pack an extra pair of eyeglasses or contact lenses and enough of any medication you take to last a few days longer than the entire trip. You may also ask your doctor to write a spare prescription using the drug's generic name, as brand names may vary from country to country. In luggage to be checked, **never pack prescription drugs, valuables, or undeveloped film.** And don't forget to carry with you the addresses of offices that handle refunds of lost traveler's checks. Check *Fodor's How to Pack* (available at online retailers and bookstores everywhere) for more tips.

To avoid customs and security delays, carry medications in their original packaging. Don't pack any sharp objects in your carry-on luggage, including knives of any size or material, scissors, nail clippers, and corkscrews, or anything else that might arouse suspicion.

To avoid having your checked luggage chosen for hand inspection, don't cram bags full. The U.S. Transportation Security Administration suggests packing shoes on top and placing personal items you don't want touched in clear plastic bags.

CHECKING LUGGAGE

You're allowed to carry aboard one bag and one personal article, such as a purse or a laptop computer. Make sure what you carry on fits under your seat or in the overhead bin. Get to the gate early, so you can board as soon as possible, before the overhead bins fill up.

Baggage allowances vary by carrier, destination, and ticket class. On international flights, you're usually allowed to check two bags weighing up to 70 pounds (32 kilograms) each, although a few airlines allow checked bags of up to 88 pounds (40 kilograms) in first class. Some international carriers don't allow more than 66 pounds (30 kilograms) per bag in business class and 44 pounds (20 kilograms) in economy. If you're flying to or through the United Kingdom, your luggage cannot exceed 70 pounds (32 kilograms) per bag. On domestic flights, the limit is usually 50 to 70 pounds (23 to 32 kilograms) per bag. In general, carry-on bags shouldn't exceed 40 pounds (18 kilograms). Most airlines won't accept bags that weigh more than 100 pounds (45 kilograms) on domestic or international flights. Expect to pay a fee for baggage that exceeds weight limits. Check baggage restrictions with your carrier before you pack.

Airline liability for baggage is limited to $2,500 per person on flights within the United States. On international flights it amounts to $9.07 per pound or $20 per kilogram for checked baggage (roughly $640 per 70-pound bag), with a maximum of $634.90 per piece, and $400 per passenger for unchecked baggage. You can buy additional coverage at check-in for about $10 per $1,000 of coverage, but it often excludes a rather extensive list of items, shown on your airline ticket.

Before departure, itemize your bags' contents and their worth, and label the bags with your name, address, and phone number. (If you use your home address, cover it so potential thieves can't see it readily.) Include a label inside each bag and **pack a copy of your itinerary.** At check-in, make sure each bag is correctly tagged with the destination airport's three-letter code. Because some checked bags will be opened for hand inspection, the U.S. Transportation Security Administration recommends that you leave luggage unlocked or use the plastic locks offered at check-in. TSA screeners place an inspection notice inside searched bags, which are re-sealed with a special lock.

If your bag has been searched and contents are missing or damaged, file a claim with the TSA Consumer Response Center as soon as possible. If your bags arrive damaged or fail to arrive at all, file a written report with the airline before leaving the airport.

Complaints **U.S. Transportation Security Administration Contact Center** ☎ 866/289-9673 🌐 www.tsa.gov.

RESTROOMS

Public restrooms are located near Independence Mall on the west side of 5th Street and in the Independence Visitor Center on 6th Street between Market and Arch streets.

SAFETY

Center City and the major tourist destinations are generally safe during the day but it is wise to take certain precautions. Avoid wearing flashy jewelry and leave all valuables in your hotel's safe. Wear a money belt; if you bring a handbag, keep it on your lap—not on the floor or dangling on the back of your chair—in restaurants and theaters. Exercise caution, particularly after dark, in the areas north of Center City and west of University City; avoid deserted streets. You can ask hotel personnel or guides at the Independence Visitor Center about the safety of places you're interested in visiting. As you would in any city, keep your car locked and watch your possessions carefully. Remember to remove items from your car.

Subway crime has diminished in recent years. During the day cars are crowded and safe. However, platforms and cars can be relatively empty in the late evening hours. Instead of waiting for a subway or train in off-hours, **take a cab late at night.**

SENIOR-CITIZEN TRAVEL

Most museums and attractions in and around Philadelphia, including the Philadelphia Museum of Art, the Franklin Institute, and the Pennsylvania Academy of the Fine Arts, offer reduced rates for seniors. Many hotels and restaurants offer discounts as well. Seniors can ride free on the SEPTA system during off-peak hours.

To qualify for age-related discounts, mention your senior-citizen status up front when booking hotel reservations (not when checking out) and before you're seated in restaurants (not when paying the bill). Be sure to have identification on hand. When renting a car, ask about promotional car-rental discounts, which can be cheaper than senior-citizen rates.

Educational Programs **Elderhostel** ✉ 11 Ave. de Lafayette, Boston, MA 02111 ☎ 877/426-8056, 978/323-4141 international callers, 877/426-2167 TTY 📠 877/426-2166 🌐 www.elderhostel.org.

SIGHTSEEING TOURS

BOAT TOURS

Liberty Belle Cruises, aboard a 600-passenger Mississippi paddle-wheel riverboat, offers lunch, dinner, and Sunday brunch cruises with a banjo player, sing-alongs, and a buffet. Board at Penn's Landing (Columbus Blvd. at Lombard Circle).

The *Spirit of Philadelphia* runs lunch and dinner cruises along the Delaware River. This three-deck ship leaves Penn's Landing at Lombard Circle and Columbus Boulevard for lunch, dinner, and starlight cruises. Dinner cruises include a live musical revue and dance music.

Fees & Schedules ***Liberty Belle* Cruises** ☎ 215/757-0800 🌐 www.libertybelle.com. ***Spirit of Philadelphia*** ☎ 215/923-4354 🌐 www.spiritcruises.com.

BUS TOURS

Philadelphia Trolley Works offers narrated tours in buses designed to resemble Victorian-style trolleys. The fare is an all-day pass, allowing unlimited stops. Board at any stop, including the Pennsylvania Convention Center and the Liberty Bell.

The tour takes about 90 minutes and costs $20. It makes 20 stops on a route covering the Historic Area, the Benjamin Franklin Parkway, the Avenue of the Arts (South Broad Street), Fairmount Park, the Philadelphia Zoo, Eastern State Penitentiary, and Penn's Landing.

Fees & Schedules **Philadelphia Trolley Works** ☎ 215/925-8687 🌐 www.phillytour.com.

CARRIAGE RIDES

Numerous horse-drawn carriages wind their way through the narrow streets of the Historic Area. Tours last anywhere from 15 minutes to an hour and cost from $25 to $70 for up to four people. Carriages line up on Chestnut and 6th streets near Independence Hall between 10 AM and 6 PM and at South Street and 2nd Street between 7 PM and midnight. You can reserve a carriage and be picked up anywhere downtown. Carriages operate year-round, except when the temperature is below 20°F or above 92°F.

'76 Carriage Company ☎ 215/925-8687 🌐 www.phillytour.com.

DUCK TOURS

Ride the Ducks offers 80-minute surf-and-turf tours of Philadelphia's historic district, Penn's Landing, and the Delaware River using military-designed land-sea vehicles. The "ducks" are circa-1945 Army DUKW trucks with watertight hulls converted into 38-passenger open-air vehicles. Tours run from mid-March through November and start at $23.

Ride the Ducks ☎ 215/227-3825 🌐 www.phillyducks.com.

SPECIAL-INTEREST TOURS

The Constitutional Walking Tour is a free, self-guided exploration around some of the city's most popular historic areas. It covers many of the most important sights, including Independence Hall, the Liberty Bell, and the National Constitution Center. The brochure can be found at the Independence Visitors Center and other locations. Remember that each site may charge a separate entrance fee.

Italian Market Tours gives an afternoon's introduction to this vibrant area's cultural and historic sites with visits to cheese, meat, and pastry shops for food-making demonstrations and tastings. Celeste Morello, author of the *Italian Market Cookbook,* leads the walking tour, with a six-person minimum.

Harry Boonin, historian and author of *The Jewish Quarter of Philadelphia,* heads up Jewish Walking Tours of Philadelphia. Two mornings a week he guides visitors through Society Hill and Queen Village, where Eastern European Jews settled at the turn of the last century.

Constitutional Walking Tour ☎ 215/525-1776 🌐 www.theconstitutional.com. **Italian Market Tours** ☎ 215/334-6008 🌐 www.fantes.com/italianmarket.htm. **Jewish Walking Tours of Philadelphia** ☎ 215/918-0326 🌐 www.boonin.com.

WALKING TOURS

Centipede Tours offers tours of Independence Park led by guides in Colonial dress. Tours of the city's ethnic heritage and of its circles and squares are also available, as are multilingual guides. Walk Philadelphia's 50 different tours of the city and the region focus on architecture and history.

Fees & Schedules **Centipede Tours** ☎ 215/735-3123 🌐 www.centipedeinc.com. **Walk Philadelphia** ☎ 215/625-9255 🌐 www.centercityphila.org/goingout/tours.aspx.

STUDENTS IN PHILADELPHIA

The majority of museums and attractions in and around Philadelphia offer reduced rates to students presenting a valid student I.D.

I.D.s & Services **STA Travel** ✉ 10 Downing St., New York, NY 10014 ☎ 212/627-3111, 800/777-0112 24-hr service center 📠 212/627-3387 🌐 www.sta.com. **Travel Cuts** ✉ 187 College St., Toronto, Ontario M5T 1P7 Canada ☎ 800/592-2887 in the U.S., 416/979-2406 or 866/246-9762 in Canada 📠 416/979-8167 🌐 www.travelcuts.com.

SUBWAY TRAVEL

The Broad Street Subway runs from Fern Rock station in the northern part of the city to Pattison Avenue and the sports complex (First Union Center and Veterans Stadium) in South Philadelphia. The Market-Frankford line runs across the city from the western suburb of Upper Darby to Frankford in Northeast Philadelphia. Both lines shut down from midnight to 5 AM, during which time "Night Owl" buses operate along the same routes. Tickets may be purchased at all subway stations. The one-way fare within the city is $2, with transfers costing 60¢.

While the subway does have its limitations, it can still be a good way to maneuver around the city and avoid having to park a car, which, during business hours, can be a frustrating experience.

Fares & Schedules **SEPTA** ☎ 215/580-7800 🌐 www.septa.org.

TAXES

SALES TAX

The main sales tax in Philadelphia and the surrounding areas is 7%. This tax also applies to restaurant meals. Various other taxes—including a liquor tax—may apply. There is no sales tax on clothing. Hotel taxes are 14% in Philadelphia, 8% in Bucks County, and 6% in Lancaster County.

TAXIS

Cabs cost $2.10, plus $1.80–$2.30 per mile. They are plentiful during the day downtown—especially along Broad Street and near major hotels and train stations. At night and outside Center City, taxis are scarce. Your best bet is to go to a hotel and have the doorman hail a taxi for you. Or, you can call for a cab, but they frequently show up late and occasionally never arrive. Be persistent: calling back if the cab is late will often yield results. The standard tip for cabdrivers is about 15% of the total fare.

Taxi Companies **Olde City Taxi** ☎ 215/338-0838. **Quaker City Cab** ☎ 215/728-8000. **Yellow Cab** ☎ 215/333-3333.

TELEPHONES

Philadelphia has two area codes: 215 and 267, which is being assigned to new numbers. Because of this, you must dial "1" followed by all 10 digits—even for local calls.

TIME

Philadelphia and the surrounding areas are in the eastern time zone. Daylight saving time is in effect from early April through late October; Eastern standard time, the rest of the year. Clocks are set ahead one hour when daylight saving time begins, back one hour when it ends. Philadelphia is 3 hours ahead of Los Angeles, 1 hour ahead of Chicago, 6 hours behind London, and 15 hours behind Sydney.

TIPPING

At restaurants, a 15% tip is standard for servers; up to 20% may be expected at more expensive establishments. The same goes for taxi drivers, bartenders, and hairdressers. Coat checkers usually expect $1–$2; bellhops and hotel and airport porters should get $1 per bag. Hotel maids in upscale hotels should get about $1 per day of your stay. For local sightseeing tours, you may individually tip the driver-guide $1–$5, depending on the length of the tour and the number of people in your party, if he or she has been helpful or informative. Ushers in theaters do not expect tips.

A concierge typically receives a tip of $5–$10, with an additional gratuity for special services or favors.

TOURS & PACKAGES

Because everything is prearranged on a prepackaged tour or independent vacation, you spend less time planning—and often get it all at a good price.

BOOKING WITH AN AGENT

Travel agents are excellent resources. But it's a good idea to collect brochures from several agencies, as some agents' suggestions may be influenced by relationships with tour and package firms that reward them for volume sales. If you have a special interest, find an agent with expertise in that area. The American Society of Travel Agents (ASTA) has a database of specialists worldwide; you can log on to the group's Web site to find one near you.

Make sure your travel agent knows the accommodations and other services of the place being recommended. Ask about the hotel's location, room size, beds, and whether it has a pool, room service, or programs for children, if you care about these. Has your agent been there in person or sent others whom you can contact?

Do some homework on your own, too: local tourism boards can provide information about lesser-known and small-niche operators, some of which may sell only direct.

BUYER BEWARE

Each year consumers are stranded or lose their money when tour operators—even large ones with excellent reputations—go out of business. So check out the operator. Ask several travel agents about its reputation, and try to **book with a company that has a consumer-protection program.** (Look for information in the company's brochure.) In the United States, members of the United States Tour Operators Association are required to set aside funds (up to $1 million) to help eligible customers cover payments and travel arrangements in the event that the company defaults. It's also a good idea to choose a company that participates in the American Society of Travel Agents' Tour Operator Program; ASTA will act as mediator in any disputes between you and your tour operator.

Remember that the more your package or tour includes, the better you can predict the ultimate cost of your vacation. Make sure you know exactly what is covered, and beware of hidden costs. Are taxes, tips, and transfers included? Entertainment and excursions? These can add up.

Tour-Operator Recommendations **American Society of Travel Agents** (⇨ Travel Agencies). **CrossSphere-The Global Association for Packaged Travel** ✉ 546 E. Main St., Lexington, KY 40508 ☎ 859/226-4444 or 800/682-8886 📠 859/226-4414 🌐 www.CrossSphere.com. **United States Tour Operators Association** (USTOA) ✉ 275 Madison Ave., Suite 2014, New York, NY 10016 ☎ 212/599-6599 📠 212/599-6744 🌐 www.ustoa.com.

TRAIN TRAVEL

Philadelphia's beautifully restored 30th Street Station, at 30th and Market streets, is a major stop on Amtrak's Northeast Corridor line. The 90-minute Philadelphia to New York trip is about $50 each way. Amtrak's high-speed *Acela* trains run frequently between Washington and Boston, always stopping in Philadelphia. You can shave 20 minutes off the Philadelphia–New York trip, but it'll cost you about $95 each way. The trains cater to business travelers and are equipped with conference tables and electrical outlets at every seat.

You can **travel by train between Philadelphia and New York City on the cheap** by taking the SEPTA commuter line R7 to Trenton, New Jersey, and transferring to a NJ Transit commuter line to Manhattan. Ask for the excursion rate. The trip takes an extra 30 minutes, but costs about $17 one-way.

Amtrak also serves Philadelphia from points west, including Harrisburg, Pittsburgh, and Chicago.

Philadelphia's fine network of commuter trains, operated by SEPTA, serves both the city and the suburbs. The famous Main Line, a cluster of affluent suburbs, got its start—and its name—from the Pennsylvania Railroad route that ran westward from Center City. All SEPTA commuter trains stop at 30th Street Station and connect to Suburban Station (16th Street and John F. Kennedy Boulevard, near major hotels), and Market East Station (10th and Market streets), near the historic section and beneath the Gallery at Market East shopping complex. Fares, which vary according to route and time of travel, range from $3 to $7 each way. These trains are your best bet for reaching Germantown, Chestnut Hill, Merion (site of the Barnes Foundation), and other suburbs.

PATCO (Port Authority Transit Corporation) High Speed Line trains run underground from 16th and Locust streets to Lindenwold, New Jersey. Trains stop at 13th and Locust, 9th and Locust, and 8th and Market streets, then continue across the Benjamin Franklin Bridge to Camden. It's one way to get to the Adventure Aquarium or the Tweeter Center; NJ Transit has a shuttle bus from the Broadway stop to the aquarium on weekends and to the center during concerts. Fares run from $1.15 to $2.45. **Sit in the very front seat for a great view going across the bridge.**

FARES & SCHEDULES

You can get train schedules and purchase tickets at the 30th Street, Market East, and Suburban stations or online from the SEPTA Web site. Several smaller stations are open for ticket sales in the morning. You may also purchase tickets on the train but will pay a surcharge if you are departing from a station that sells tickets. PATCO schedules can be obtained from their station at 16th and Locust streets. Tickets for both SEPTA and PATCO train travel may be purchased with cash or a major credit card.

Train Information **Amtrak** ☎ 215/349-2135 or 800/872-7245 🌐 www.amtrak.com. **New Jersey Transit** ☎ 800/772-2222 🌐 www.njtransit.com. **PATCO** ☎ 215/922-4600 🌐 www.drpa.org/patco/index.asp. **SEPTA** ☎ 215/580-7800 🌐 www.septa.org.

RESERVATIONS
Although reservations are not always necessary, it's a good idea to purchase Amtrak tickets in advance, particularly for travel during peak holiday times. SEPTA and PATCO reservations are not necessary.

TRANSPORTATION AROUND PHILADELPHIA
If you're staying in Center City, the best way to get around is on foot or by taking the PHLASH bus, which stops at all of the major museums and attractions. The subway system does not service the western section of Center City between City Hall and 30th Street Station.

Taxis are also plentiful around tourist destinations. SEPTA's commuter trains service most attractions in the Philadelphia suburbs; PATCO will get you to the Camden attractions. You'll want a car to get to the Brandywine Valley, Lancaster, and Bucks County attractions.

TRAVEL AGENCIES
A good travel agent puts your needs first. Look for an agency that has been in business at least five years, emphasizes customer service, and has someone on staff who specializes in your destination. In addition, **make sure the agency belongs to a professional trade organization.** The American Society of Travel Agents (ASTA) has more than 10,000 members in some 140 countries, enforces a strict code of ethics, and will step in to mediate agent-client disputes involving ASTA members. ASTA also maintains a directory of agents on its Web site; ASTA's TravelSense.org, a trip planning and travel advice site, can also help to locate a travel agent who caters to your needs. (If a travel agency is also acting as your tour operator, *see* Buyer Beware *in* Tours & Packages.)

Local Agent Referrals **American Society of Travel Agents** (ASTA) ✉ 1101 King St., Suite 200, Alexandria, VA 22314 ☎ 703/739-2782 or 800/965-2782 24-hr hotline 🖷 703/684-8319 🌐 www.astanet.com and www.travelsense.org. **Association of British Travel Agents** ✉ 68-71 Newman St., London W1T 3AH ☎ 020/7637-2444 🖷 020/7637-0713 🌐 www.abta.com. **Association of Canadian Travel Agencies** ✉ 130 Albert St., Suite 1705, Ottawa, Ontario K1P 5G4 ☎ 613/237-3657 🖷 613/237-7052 🌐 www.acta.ca.**Australian Federation of Travel Agents** ✉ Level 3, 309 Pitt St., Sydney, NSW 2000 ☎ 02/9264-3299 or 1300/363-416 🖷 02/9264-1085 🌐 www.afta.com.au. **Travel Agents' Association of New Zealand** ✉ Level 5, Tourism and Travel House, 79 Boulcott St., Box 1888, Wellington 6001 ☎ 04/499-0104 🖷 04/499-0786 🌐 www.taanz.org.nz.

TROLLEYS
Philadelphia once had an extensive trolley network, and a few trolley lines are still in service and run by SEPTA. Routes 10 and 13 begin west and north of Center City and end on Market Street. Due to the frequent construction along these routes, they are not reliable. For privately run trolleys, *see* Bus Tours *in* Sightseeing Tours.

VISITOR INFORMATION
For general information before you go, call or check the Web sites of the Greater Philadelphia Tourism Marketing Corporation and the Pennsylvania Office of Travel and Tourism. When you arrive, stop by the Independence Visitor Center on 6th Street between Market and Arch streets.

If you are planning to make side trips from Philadelphia or are traveling on to Bucks County or Lancaster County, you should also *see* Visitor Information *in* the A to Z sections of Chapters 7, 8, and 9.

Tourist Information **Greater Philadelphia Tourism Marketing Corporation** ☎ 215/599-0776 and 888/467-4452 🌐 www.gophila.com. **Independence Visitor Center** ✉ 6th St. between Market and Arch Sts. ☎ 215/965-7676 or 800/537-7676 🌐 www.independencevisitorcenter.com. **Pennsylvania Office of Travel and Tourism** ☎ 800/847-4872 🌐 www.experiencepa.com. **Philadelphia Convention and Visitors Bureau** ✉ 1700 Market St., Suite 3000, 19102 ☎ 215/636-3300 🖷 215/636-3327 🌐 www.pcvb.org. In the U.K.: **Pennsylvania Tourism Office** ✉ Suite 302, 11-15 Betterton St. Covent Garden, London WC2H 9BP ☎ 020/7470-8801 🖷 020/7470-8810.

Government Advisories **Consular Affairs Bureau of Canada** ☎ 800/267-6788 or 613/944-6788 🌐 www.voyage.gc.ca. **U.K. Foreign and Commonwealth Office** ✉ Travel Advice Unit, Consular Directorate, Old Admiralty Building, London SW1A 2PA ☎ 0870/606-0290 or 020/7008-1500 🌐 www.fco.gov.uk/travel. **Australian Department of Foreign**

Affairs and Trade ☎ 300/139–281 travel advisories, 02/6261–1299 Consular Travel Advice 🌐 www.smartraveller.gov.au or www.dfat.gov.au. **New Zealand Ministry of Foreign Affairs and Trade** ☎ 04/439–8000 🌐 www.mft.govt.nz.

WEB SITES

Check out the World Wide Web when planning your trip. You'll find everything from weather forecasts to virtual tours. Be sure to visit Fodors.com (🌐 www.fodors.com), a complete travel-planning site. You can research prices and book plane tickets, hotel rooms, rental cars, vacation packages, and more. In addition, you can post your pressing questions in the Travel Talk section. Other planning tools include a currency converter and weather reports, and there are loads of links to travel resources.

DigitalCity Philadelphia (🌐 www.digitalcity.com/philadelphia) and CitySearch Philadelphia (🌐 www.philadelphia.citysearch.com) have reviews and events listings. The home page for the *Philadelphia Inquirer* (🌐 Philly.com) has hundreds of articles on the region. The Web site for *Philadelphia* magazine (🌐 www.phillymag.com) has information on arts, nightlife, shopping, and dining.

Exploring Philadelphia

1

WORD OF MOUTH

"All of downtown [Philadelphia] is walkable, so if the weather is nice, just grab a map and wander."

—lesliec1

"But the 'must-sees' for one day could be so many things: I'd say that the Liberty Bell/Independence Hall area would certainly be among them . . . The new Constitution Center is super and in that area as well."

—Amy

"[Philadelphia] is a great kid city—the Please Touch Museum is just right for five- and six-year-olds . . . also the zoo, Reading Terminal Market, duck tours . . ."

—elmom

www.fodors.com/forums

By Robert DiGiacomo

"ON THE WHOLE, I'D RATHER BE IN PHILADELPHIA." W. C. Fields may have been joking when he wrote his epitaph, but if he were here today, he would eat his words. They no longer roll up the sidewalks at night in Philadelphia. A construction boom, a restaurant renaissance, and cultural revival have helped transform the city. For more than a decade, there has been an optimistic mood, aggressive civic leadership, and national recognition of what the locals have long known: Philadelphia can be a very pleasant place to live—a city with an impressive past and a fascinating future.

Philadelphia is a place of contrasts: Grace Kelly and Rocky Balboa; Le Bec-Fin—one of the nation's finest French haute cuisine restaurants—and the fast-food heaven of Jim's Steaks; Independence Hall and the Mario Lanza Museum; 18th-century national icons with 21st-century–style skyscrapers soaring above them. The world-renowned Philadelphia Orchestra performs in a stunning concert hall—the focal point of efforts to transform Broad Street into a multicultural Avenue of the Arts. Along the same street, 25,000 Mummers dressed in outrageous sequins and feathers historically have plucked their banjos and strutted their stuff to the strains of "Oh, Dem Golden Slippers" on New Year's Day. City residents include descendants of the staid Quaker founding fathers, the self-possessed socialites of the Main Line (remember Katharine Hepburn and Cary Grant in *The Philadelphia Story*?), and the unrestrained sports fans, who are as vocal as they are loyal.

Historically speaking, Philadelphia is a city of superlatives: the world's largest municipal park; the best collection of public art in the United States; the widest variety of urban architecture in America; and according to some experts, the greatest concentration of institutions of higher learning in the country.

A City of Neighborhoods

Philadelphia is known as a city of neighborhoods (109 by one count). Shoppers haggle over the price of tomatoes in South Philly's Italian Market; families picnic in the parks of Germantown; street vendors hawk soft pretzels in Logan Circle; and all over town kids play street games such as stickball, stoopball, wireball, and chink. It's a city of neighborhood loyalty: ask a native where he's from and he'll tell you: Fairmount, Fishtown, or Frankford, rather than Philadelphia. The city's population is less transient than that of other large cities; people who are born here generally remain, and many who leave home to study or work eventually return. Although the population is nearly 1.5 million, its residents are intricately connected; on any given day, a Philadelphian is likely to encounter someone with whom he grew up. The "it's-a-small-world" syndrome makes people feel like they belong.

The Philadelphia Story

William Penn founded the city in 1682 and chose to name it Philadelphia—Greek for "brotherly love"—after an ancient Syrian city, site of one of the earliest and most venerated Christian churches. Penn's Quakers settled on a tract of land he described as his "greene countrie towne." After the Quakers, the next waves of immigrants to arrive were Anglicans and Presbyterians (who had a running conflict with the "stiff Quakers" and their distaste for music and dancing). The new residents forged traditions that remain strong in parts of Philadelphia today: united families, comfortable houses, handsome furniture, and good education. From these early years came the attitude Mark Twain summed up as: "In Boston, they ask: 'What does he know?' In New York, 'How much does he make?' In Philadelphia, 'Who were his parents?' "

The city became the queen of the English-speaking New World from the late 1600s to the early 1800s. In the latter half of the 1700s Philadelphia was the largest city in the colonies, a great and glorious place. So, when the delegates from the colonies wanted to meet in a centrally located, thriving city, they chose Philadelphia. They convened the First Continental Congress in 1774 at Carpenters' Hall. The rest, as they say, is history. It is here that the Declaration of Independence was written and adopted, the Constitution was framed, the capital of the United States was established, the Liberty Bell was rung, the nation's flag was sewn by Betsy Ross (though scholars debate this), and George Washington served most of his presidency.

Getting Your Bearings

Today you will find Philadelphia's compact 2-square-mi downtown (William Penn's original city) between the Delaware and the Schuylkill (pronounced *skoo*-kull) rivers. Thanks to Penn's grid system of streets—laid out in 1681—the downtown area is a breeze to navigate. The traditional heart of the city is Broad and Market streets (Penn's Center Square), where City Hall now stands. Market Street divides the city north and south; 130 South 15th Street, for example, is in the second block south of Market Street. North–south streets are numbered, starting with Front (1st) Street, at the Delaware River, and increasing to the west. Broad Street is the equivalent of 14th Street. The diagonal Benjamin Franklin Parkway breaks the rigid grid pattern by leading from City Hall out of Center City into Fairmount Park, which straddles the Schuylkill River and the Wissahickon Creek for 10 mi.

Although Philadelphia is the sixth-largest city in the nation (nearly 1.5 million people live in the city, 6.2 million in the metropolitan area), it maintains a small-town feel. It's a cosmopolitan, exciting, but not overwhelming city, a town that's easy to explore on foot yet big enough to keep surprising even those most familiar with it.

AROUND INDEPENDENCE HALL

THE MOST HISTORIC SQUARE MILE IN AMERICA

Fodor's Choice ★

Any visit to Philadelphia, whether you have one day or several, should begin in the city area that comprises **Independence National Historical Park.** Philadelphia was the birthplace of the United States, the home of the country's first government, and nowhere is the spirit of those miraculous early days—the boldness of conceiving a brand-new nation—more palpable than along the cobbled streets of the city's most historic district.

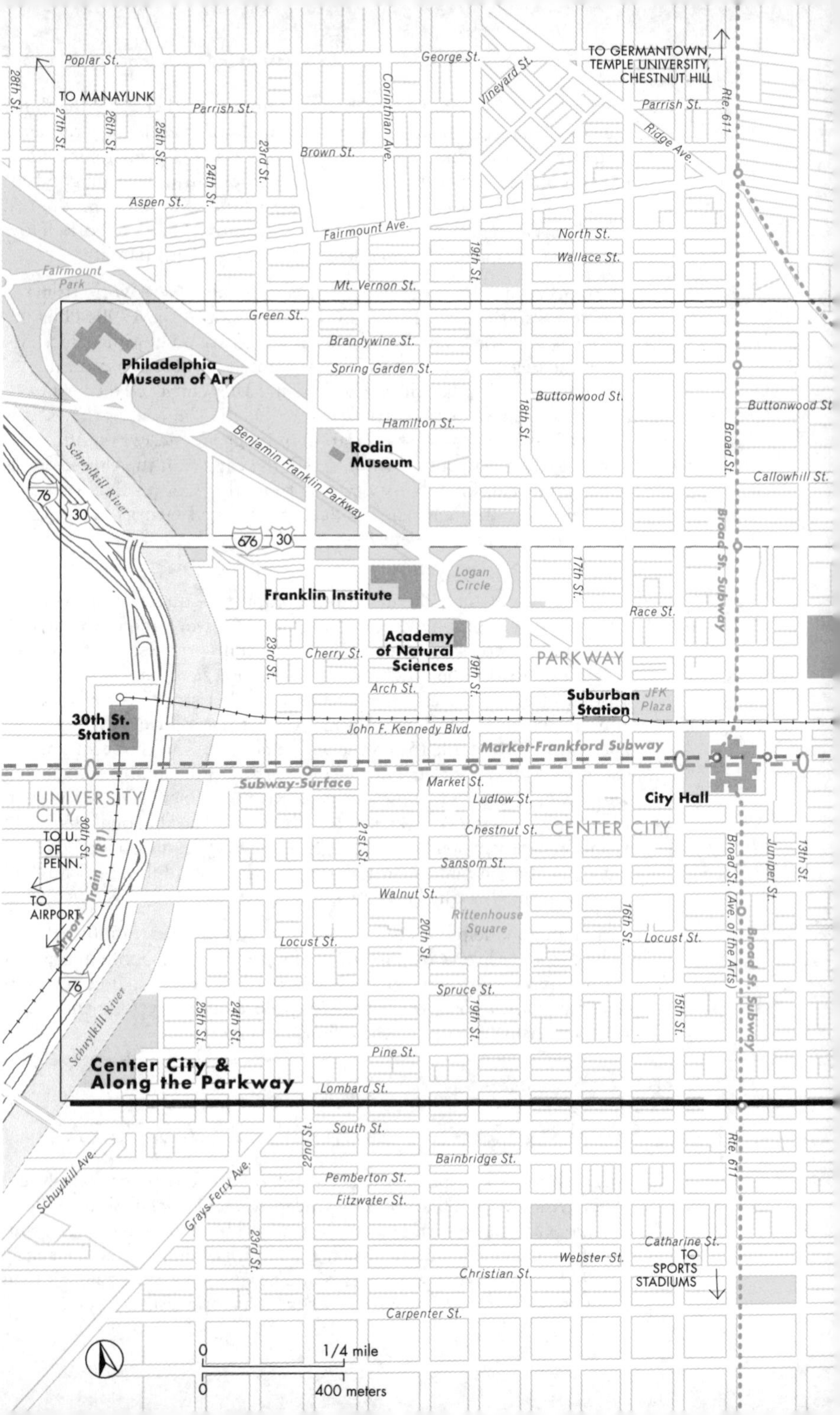
Center City &
Along the Parkway
TO MANAYUNK
TO GERMANTOWN,
TEMPLE UNIVERSITY,
CHESTNUT HILL
Poplar St.
George St.
Vineyard St.
28th St.
27th St.
26th St.
25th St.
24th St.
23rd St.
Parrish St.
Corinthian Ave.
Brown St.
Ridge Ave.
Rte. 611
Aspen St.
Fairmount Ave.
North St.
Wallace St.
19th St.
Fairmount
Park
Mt. Vernon St.
Green St.
Brandywine St.
Philadelphia
Museum of Art
Spring Garden St.
Buttonwood St.
18th St.
Hamilton St.
Broad St.
Benjamin Franklin Parkway
Schuylkill River
Rodin
Museum
Callowhill St.
76
30
676
Broad St. Subway
Logan
Circle
17th St.
Franklin Institute
Race St.
Academy
of Natural
Sciences
Cherry St.
PARKWAY
Arch St.
Suburban
Station
JFK
Plaza
30th St.
Station
John F. Kennedy Blvd.
Market-Frankford Subway
Subway-Surface
Market St.
UNIVERSITY
CITY
Ludlow St.
City Hall
TO U.
OF
PENN.
30th St.
Airport Train (R1)
Chestnut St.
CENTER CITY
21st St.
Sansom St.
Broad St. (Ave. of the Arts)
Juniper St.
13th St.
TO
AIRPORT
Walnut St.
Rittenhouse
Square
20th St.
16th St.
Locust St.
Spruce St.
15th St.
Pine St.
Lombard St.
South St.
22nd St.
Rte. 611
Schuylkill Ave.
Grays Ferry Ave.
Bainbridge St.
Pemberton St.
Fitzwater St.
Catharine St.
TO
SPORTS
STADIUMS
Webster St.
Christian St.
Carpenter St.
0
1/4 mile
0
400 meters

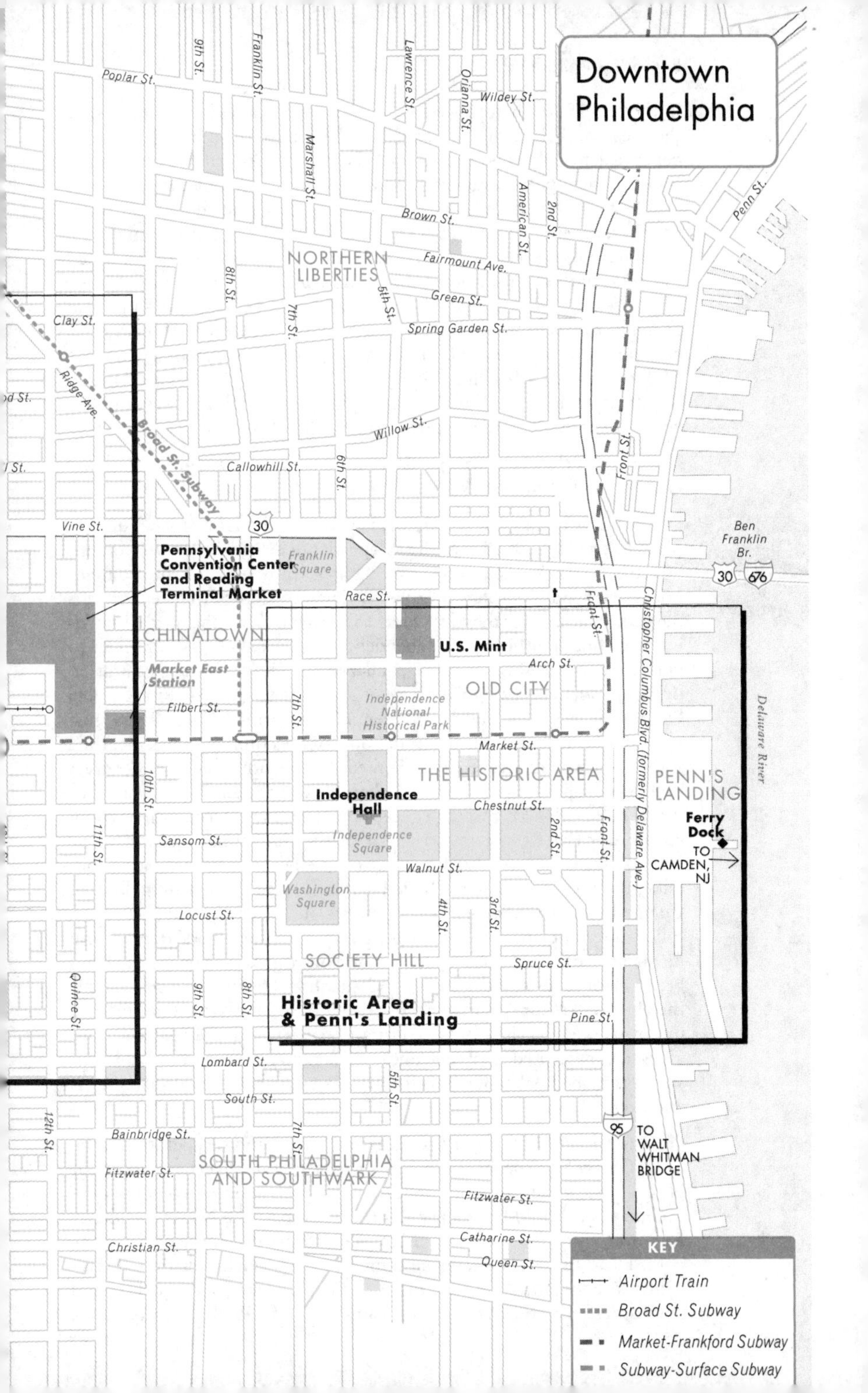

Downtown Philadelphia
Poplar St.
9th St.
Franklin St.
Lawrence St.
Orianna St.
Wildey St.
Marshall St.
American St.
2nd St.
Brown St.
Penn St.
NORTHERN LIBERTIES
Fairmount Ave.
8th St.
5th St.
Green St.
7th St.
Spring Garden St.
Clay St.
Ridge Ave.
Broad St. Subway
Willow St.
Front St.
Callowhill St.
6th St.
Vine St.
30
Ben Franklin Br.
676
Pennsylvania Convention Center and Reading Terminal Market
Franklin Square
Race St.
Christopher Columbus Blvd. (formerly Delaware Ave.)
CHINATOWN
U.S. Mint
Market East Station
Arch St.
OLD CITY
Filbert St.
Independence National Historical Park
Delaware River
Market St.
10th St.
THE HISTORIC AREA
PENN'S LANDING
Independence Hall
Chestnut St.
11th St.
Independence Square
Ferry Dock
Sansom St.
TO CAMDEN, NJ
Walnut St.
Washington Square
4th St.
3rd St.
Locust St.
SOCIETY HILL
Spruce St.
Quince St.
Historic Area & Penn's Landing
Pine St.
Lombard St.
South St.
12th St.
95
TO WALT WHITMAN BRIDGE
Bainbridge St.
SOUTH PHILADELPHIA AND SOUTHWARK
Fitzwater St.
Christian St.
Catharine St.
Queen St.
KEY
Airport Train
Broad St. Subway
Market-Frankford Subway
Subway-Surface Subway

In the late 1940s, before civic-minded citizens banded together to save the area and before the National Park Service stepped in, the Independence Hall neighborhood was crowded with factories and run-down warehouses. Then the city, state, and federal government took interest. Some buildings were restored, and others were reconstructed on their original sites; several attractions were built for the 1976 Bicentennial celebration. In recent years, a flurry of construction has again transformed the area, with several notable buildings—including an expanded visitor center, a more attractive home for the Liberty Bell, and a national museum to celebrate the U.S. Constitution. Today the park covers 42 acres and holds close to 40 buildings. Urban renewal in Independence Mall plaza and in Washington Square East (Society Hill) have ensured that Independence Hall will never again keep unsightly company. The city's most historic area is now also one of its loveliest.

Numbers in the text correspond to numbers in the margin and on the Historic Area and Penn's Landing map.

a good walk

This walk back in time will immerse you in Colonial history. The best place to orient yourself is at the **Independence Visitor Center** 1 on 6th Street between Market and Arch. A block to the north is the contemporary **National Constitution Center** 2. Directly across Market Street is the gathering area for the new **Liberty Bell Pavilion** 3, an angled glass building with fine sightlines of Independence Hall. Cross Chestnut Street to **Independence Square,** site of **Independence Hall** 4, where the Declaration of Independence was signed; tours begin in the courtyard alongside **Old City Hall** 5, home of the U.S. Supreme Court from 1791 to 1800. Just in front of it is Philosophical Hall, home of the country's oldest learned society. Independence Hall is flanked on the other side by **Congress Hall** 6, which holds the restored chambers of the first U.S. Congress. Next, cross 5th Street to the cobblestoned Library Street, where you'll see **Library Hall** 7, a reconstruction of the first public library in the United States. Just before 4th Street on the left is the Parthenon look-alike, the **Second Bank of the United States** 8, with its portrait gallery of Colonial Americans; its entrance is on Chestnut Street. Crossing 4th Street, follow a redbrick path to the Carpenters' Court; **Carpenters' Hall** 9, with its displays of 18th-century tools, is on your right. On your left is Pemberton House, now a bookstore and gift shop. Behind the bookstore is the **New Hall Military Museum** 10; it contains a variety of weapons and uniforms. Leave Carpenters' Court and continue on the redbrick path alongside manicured lawns and ancient oaks and maples east to 3rd Street, site of the **First Bank of the United States** 11, a handsome example of Federal architecture.

Walk north on 3rd Street, cross Chestnut Street, and turn left to the **National Liberty Museum** 12; the exhibits here celebrate diversity and honor Nobel peace prize winners. Your next stop, particularly if you have children in tow, should be **Franklin Court** 13. Just past the National Liberty Museum, turn right through the gates and walk down the cobblestone path. Head into the underground museum that celebrates the achievements of Benjamin Franklin, and visit the Colonial-era print shop and post office. Exit on Market Street and turn left. Walk several blocks, passing the Liberty Bell and the visitor center, and turn left on 7th Street. On your right, you'll see the reconstructed **Declaration House** 14, where Thomas Jefferson wrote his rough draft of the Declaration of Independence, and a branch of the Free Library of Philadelphia. Across 7th Street is the **Atwater Kent Museum** 15, which chronicles the city's history. Next to the museum is a walkway under the Rohm and Haas Building. You'll pass the sculpture-fountain *Milkweed Pod*. Installed in 1959, it was one of the first examples of Philadelphia's law requiring public buildings to spend 1% of construction costs for art. At 6th Street turn right and walk south almost to Walnut Street to the **Curtis Center** 16; peek into the lobby to see the spectacular glass mosaic mural by Maxfield Parrish and Louis Comfort Tiffany.

If you have more time and energy, continue east on Walnut Street. On the corner of 4th and Walnut streets is the **Todd House** 17, the simply furnished home of Dolley Madison, which has a lovingly maintained 18th-century garden; it stands in contrast with the lavishly furnished **Bishop White House** 18, at 3rd and Walnut streets. Follow Walnut a half block east to see the Philadelphia Merchant's Exchange, the city's commercial center for part of the 19th century. Around the corner at 2nd, between Walnut and Sansom, is **Welcome Park** 19, marking the spot where William Penn once lived.

TIMING If you've put on your walking shoes and are good at negotiating the cobblestones, you can wander through this compact area in about two hours. But the city's atmospheric historic district warrants a slower pace. For more information about planning your time in the historic district, *see* Visiting Independence Park CloseUp *later in this chapter.*

What to See

15 **Atwater Kent Museum.** Philadelphia's official history museum tells the city's story, from its founding more than 300 years ago until today. Started in 1938 by Atwater Kent, a wealthy inventor, radio magnate, and manufacturer, the museum houses more than 100,000 objects—everything from textiles to toys—that illustrate what everyday life was like for generations of Philadelphians. It occupies an elegant 1826 Greek Revival building designed by John Haviland, who was also the architect of the Eastern State Penitentiary. The museum owns a sizable collection of works by Norman Rockwell, the most well-known American illustrator of the 20th century, including the artist's 332 covers for the *Saturday Evening Post* (about 50 are on display at any given time). ✉ *15 S. 7th St., Historic Area* ☎ *215/685–4830* 🌐 *www.philadelphiahistory.org* 🎫 *$5* ⏲ *Wed.–Mon. 10–5.*

18 **Bishop White House.** Built in 1786, this restored upper-class house embodies Colonial and Federal elegance. It was the home of Bishop William White (1748–1836), rector of Christ Church, first Episcopal bishop of Pennsylvania, and spiritual leader of Philadelphia for 60 years. White, a founder of the Episcopal church after the break with England, was chaplain to the Continental Congress and entertained many of the country's first families, including Washington and Franklin. The 2nd-floor study contains much of the bishop's own library. Unlike most

TO NORTHERN LIBERTIES
TO EDGAR ALLEN POE NATIONAL HISTORIC SITE
TO BENJAMIN FRANKLIN BRIDGE
25
United States Mint
Cherry St.
Bread St.
2
National Constitution Center
Betsy Ross House
23
28
Arch St.
24
OLD CITY
Christ Church Burial Ground
26
27
P
Filbert St.
American St.
Independence Visitor Center
1
Commerce St.
3rd St.
Church St.
Market-Frankford Subway
Market St.
14
13
Franklin Court
Strawberry St.
7th St.
15
Independence National Historic Park
Ludlow St.
The Bourse
Ranstead St.
Ranstead St.
3
Liberty Bell
6th St.
5th St.
4th St.
Bank St.
12
Chestnut St.
6
4
5
8
10
7
Pemberton House
9
11
Independence Hall
Philosophical Hall
Sansom St.
16
Independence Square
17
18
Philadelphia Merchant's Exchange
Walnut St.
Chancellor St.
46
43
45
Washington Square
Willings Alley
St. James Pl.
Locust St.
St. Joseph's Way
42
SOCIETY HILL
Locust St.
Marshalls Ct.
44
Spruce St.
Cypress St.
Cypress St.
7th St.
6th St.
5th St.
Lawrence Ct.
37
3rd St.
American St.
Phillip St.
Panama St.
4th St.
41
TO SOUTH STREET
Pine St.
39
40
38
Addison St.
Stamper

The Historic Area & Penn's Landing

houses of the period, the bishop's house had an early form of flush toilet. The house tour is not recommended for small children, who may be bored. You may obtain free tickets at the visitor center for one-hour tours that include the Todd House. ✉ *309 Walnut St., Historic Area* ☎ *215/965–2305* 🌐 *www.nps.gov/inde* 🎫 *Free* 🕐 *Hrs vary; check Web site or visitor center.*

❾ **Carpenters' Hall.** This handsome, patterned red-and-black brick building dating from 1770 was the headquarters of the Carpenters' Company, a guild founded to support carpenters, who were both builders and architects in this era, and to aid their families. In September 1774 the First Continental Congress convened here and addressed a declaration of rights and grievances to King George III. Today re-creations of Colonial settings include original Windsor chairs and candle sconces and displays of 18th-century carpentry tools. The Carpenters' Company still owns and operates the building. ✉ *320 Chestnut St., Historic Area* ☎ *215/965–2305* 🌐 *www.nps.gov/inde* 🎫 *Free* 🕐 *Jan. and Feb., Wed.–Sun. 10–4; Mar.–Dec., Tues.–Sun. 10–4.*

❻ **Congress Hall.** Formerly the Philadelphia County Courthouse, Congress Hall was the meeting place of the U.S. Congress from 1790 to 1800—one of the most important decades in our nation's history. Here the Bill of Rights was added to the Constitution; Alexander Hamilton's proposals for a mint and a national bank were enacted; and Vermont, Kentucky, and Tennessee became the first new states after the original colonies. On the 1st floor is the House of Representatives, where President John Adams was inaugurated in 1797. On the 2nd floor is the Senate chamber, where in 1793 George Washington was inaugurated for his second term. Both chambers have been authentically restored. ✉ *6th and Chestnut Sts., Historic Area* ☎ *215/965–2305* 🌐 *www.nps.gov/inde* 🎫 *Free* 🕐 *Daily 9–5.*

⓰ **Curtis Center.** The lobby of the Curtis Publishing Company building has a great treasure: a 15- by 50-foot glass mosaic mural, *The Dream Garden,* based on a Maxfield Parrish painting. It was executed by the Louis C. Tiffany Studios in 1916. The work's 260 colors and 100,000 pieces of opalescent hand-fired glass laced with gold leaf make it perhaps the finest Tiffany mural in the world. The mural has also been designated a "historic object" by the Philadelphia Historical Commission after its owner, the estate of a local art patron, put it up for sale for $9 million in 1998; the designation, the first in the city's history, stopped the sale and the mural remains in public view. ✉ *6th and Walnut Sts., Historic Area* ☎ *215/238–6450* 🎫 *Free* 🕐 *Weekdays 8–6, Sat. 8–1.*

⓮ **Declaration House.** In a 2nd-floor room that he had rented from bricklayer Jacob Graff, Thomas Jefferson (1743–1826) drafted the Declaration of Independence in June 1776. The home was reconstructed for the Bicentennial celebration; the bedroom and parlor in which Jefferson lived that summer were re-created with period furnishings. The 1st floor has a Jefferson exhibition and a seven-minute film, *The Extraordinary Creation.* The display on the Declaration of Independence shows some of the changes Jefferson made while writing it. You can see Jefferson's original version—which would have abolished slavery had the passage not been stricken by the committee that included Benjamin Franklin and John Adams. ✉ *7th and Market Sts., Historic Area* ☎ *215/965–2305* 🌐 *www.nps.gov/inde/declaration-house.html* 🎟 *Free* ⏲ *Hrs vary; check Web site or visitor center.*

⓫ **First Bank of the United States.** A fine example of Federal architecture, the oldest bank building in the country was headquarters of the government's bank from 1797 to 1811. Designed by Samuel Blodget Jr. and erected in 1795–97, the bank was an imposing structure in its day, exemplifying strength, dignity, and security. Head first to the right, to the north side of the structure, to find a wrought-iron gateway topped by an eagle. Pass through it into the courtyard, and you magically step out of modern-day Philadelphia and into Colonial America. Before you do so, check out the bank's pediment. Executed in 1797 by Clodius F. Legrand and Sons, its cornucopia, oak branch, and American eagle are carved from mahogany—a late-18th-century masterpiece that has withstood acid rain better than the bank's marble pillars. ✉ *120 S. 3rd St., Historic Area* ⏲ *Interior closed to the public.*

⓭ **Franklin Court.** In 1763, at the age of 57, Benjamin Franklin (1706–90) built his first permanent home in Philadelphia, in a courtyard off Market Street. This underground museum on the site of the house is an imaginative tribute to a Renaissance man: scientist and inventor (of bifocals and the lightning rod), philosopher and writer, savvy politician and successful businessman. Franklin, publisher of *Poor Richard's Almanac,* helped draft the Declaration of Independence and negotiate the peace with Great Britain. He also helped found Pennsylvania Hospital, the University of Pennsylvania, the Philadelphia Contributionship, and the American Philosophical Society.

In the courtyard adjacent to the museum, architect Robert Venturi erected a steel skeleton of Franklin's former home. You can peek through "windows" into cutaways to see wall foundations, outdoor privy wells, and other parts of his home that were uncovered during excavations. Within the museum the accomplishments of the statesman, diplomat, scientist, inventor, printer, and author are brought to life. Dial-a-quote to hear his thoughts or pick up a telephone and listen to what his contemporaries really thought of him. There's also an informative 20-minute film on Franklin's life. At the Market Street side are several houses, now exhibition halls, that Franklin had rented in addition to his main home. In one, you can see how Franklin fireproofed the building: his interest in fireproofing led him to experiment with kite flying and lightning (remember the delightful rendition of those experiments in Disney's animated cartoon *Ben and Me?*). Here, too, you'll find a restoration of a Colonial-era print shop and a post office. Don't forget to get a letter hand-stamped with a "B. FREE FRANKLIN" cancellation. Organizations throughout the region planned to mark Franklin's 300th birthday, in 2006, with all manner of exhibits, lectures, debates, readings, theater events, and concerts, under the auspices of the federal Benjamin Franklin Tercentenary Commission (www.benfranklin300.com). ✉ *314–322 Market St., or enter from Chestnut St. walkway, Historic Area* ☎ *215/*

965–2305 🌐 *www.nps.gov/inde/franklin_court* 🎫 *Free* 🕑 *Hrs vary; check Web site or visitor center.*

★ 4 **Independence Hall.** The birthplace of the United States, this redbrick building with its clock tower and steeple is one of the nation's greatest icons. America's most historic building was constructed in 1732–56 as the Pennsylvania State House. What happened here between 1775 and 1787 changed the course of American history—and the name of the building to Independence Hall. The delegates to the Second Continental Congress met in the hall's Assembly Room in May 1776, united in anger over the blood that had been shed when British troops fired on citizens in Concord, Massachusetts. In this same room George Washington was appointed commander in chief of the Continental Army, Thomas Jefferson's eloquent Declaration of Independence was signed, and later the Constitution of the United States was adopted. Here the first foreign minister to visit the United States was welcomed; the news of Cornwallis's defeat was announced, signaling the end of the Revolutionary War; and, later, John Adams and Abraham Lincoln lay in state. The memories this building holds linger in the collection of polished muskets, the silver inkstand used by delegates to sign the Declaration of Independence, and the "Rising Sun" chair in which George Washington sat. (After the Constitution was adopted, Benjamin Franklin said about the sun carving on the chair, "I have the happiness to know that it is a rising and not a setting sun.")

In the **East Wing**—attached to Independence Hall by a short colonnade—you can embark on free tours that start every 15 to 20 minutes and last 35 minutes. Admission is first-come, first-served; you may have to wait. The **West Wing** of Independence Hall contains an exhibit of the national historical park's collection of our nation's founding documents: the final draft of the Constitution, a working copy of the Articles of Confederation, and the first printing of the Declaration of Independence.

In front of Independence Hall, next to the statue of George Washington, note the plaques marking the spots where Abraham Lincoln stood on February 22, 1861, and where John F. Kennedy delivered an address on July 4, 1962. Each year on July 4, the Philadelphia Liberty Medal is presented here to a world leader. With Independence Hall in front of you and the Liberty Bell behind you, this is a place to stand for a moment and soak up a sense of history. From March through December and on major holidays, free, timed tickets from the visitor center are required for entry. Tickets also can be reserved by calling 800/967–2283 or by logging on to www.reservations.nps.gov. ✉ *Chestnut St. between 5th and 6th Sts., Historic Area* ☎ *215/965–2305* 🌐 *www.nps.gov/inde/indep-hall.html* 🎫 *Free* 🕑 *Daily 9–5.*

⚑ 1 **Independence Visitor Center.** The 47,500-square-foot facility, besides being a gateway to Independence National Historical Park, also houses the city's official visitor center. On hand are park rangers to answer questions and distribute maps and brochures on park sites and other historic locations. There's also a fully staffed concierge and trip planning desk, which will provide information on other attractions, from the

VISITING INDEPENDENCE PARK

YOU CAN EASILY EXPLORE *the park on your own; in each building a park ranger can answer all your questions. In summer, under the title, "Once Upon a Nation," more than a dozen storytellers wander through the park, perching on benches to tell tales of the times. At Harmony Lane, 4th and Walnut Streets, there is a Colonial street scene, with games such as hoops and scotch hoppers (known today as hopscotch) and activities such as butter churning. A rotating schedule of feature-length stories, including tales of Edgar Allen Poe and stories about George Washington and Thomas Jefferson will be performed at the Free Quaker Meeting House. Special paid guided tours are also available through the Independence Visitor Center.*

Hours & Fees: *The Independence Visitor Center, Independence Hall, and the Liberty Bell Pavilion are open daily year-round from 9 to 5, later in summer. Other park buildings are also open daily, although their hours may vary from season to season. Call 800/537–7676, the 24-hour hotline, for current hours plus a schedule of park programs; or visit www.nps.gov/inde. Except as noted, all attractions run by the park are free.*

When to Go: *The best time to visit America's birthplace is on America's birthday; just expect big crowds. The city throws the weeklong* ***Sunoco Welcome America!*** *party. From June 27 to July 4, there are more than 50 free events, including parades (the Mummers and an illuminated boat procession), outdoor concerts, historical reenactments, elaborate fireworks, and the awarding of the prestigious Philadelphia Liberty Medal to a world leader. The rest of the summer is also busy, with plays, musicals, and parades. For information on the entertainment schedule, call* ***Historic Philadelphia, Inc.*** *(800/764–4786 www.historicphiladelphia.org).*

Lights of Liberty: *A nighttime multimedia extravaganza, billed as the "world's first walkable sound-and-light show," takes place in five acts throughout the park. The one-hour show, which dramatizes the events that led up to the American Revolution, culminates at Independence Hall on July 8, 1776, with the first public reading of the Declaration of Independence. You wear 3-D, sound, wireless headsets and view high-definition five-story projections on the area's historic buildings. The walking distance is a half mile, and wheelchairs are available. There are six shows per hour.* PECO Energy Liberty Center, 6th and Chestnut Sts., Historic Area 215/542–3789 or 877/462–1776 www.lightsofliberty.org $20, $50 family package with 2 adult and 2 children's tickets Apr.–Oct., daily, from just after dark, weather permitting.

How Long to Stay: *Budget a full day here. An early start lets you reserve timed tickets for a tour of the Todd and Bishop White houses and adjust your schedule to catch some of the special events on the visitor center's daily schedule. Allow about 40 minutes for the Independence Hall tour and another hour each at Franklin Court and the Todd and Bishop White houses. Allow 30 minutes each at Declaration House and the visitor center, where it's a good idea to see the film* Independence *before you set out. You might want to dine in the area and then catch the Lights of Liberty show.*

Philadelphia Museum of Art to the Philadelphia Zoo, as well as a reservation and ticketing service. Before you set off on a walking tour, acquaint yourself with Colonial American history by watching the founding fathers come to life in the 30-minute movie *Independence,* one of the films being shown in the center's three theaters. There are also a coffee bar and an excellent bookstore, where you can stock up on books, videos, brochures, prints, wall hangings, and souvenirs about historic figures and events. The most popular items are the tiny Liberty Bell reproductions. An atrium connects the visitor center to a renovated underground parking facility.

To see two of the city's famous historic homes—the Bishop White and Todd houses—you'll need to stop at the information desk to obtain a free, timed ticket, and reserve a spot on one of the hour-long tours. ✉ *6th and Market Sts., Historic Area* ☎ *215/965–7676 or 800/537–7676* 🌐 *www.independencevisitorcenter.com* ⏲ *Sept.–June, daily 8:30–5; July and Aug., daily 8:30–6.*

Independence Square. On July 8, 1776, the Declaration of Independence was first read in public here. Although the square is not as imposing today, it still has great dignity. You can imagine the impact the reading had on the colonists. ✉ *Bounded by Walnut and Chestnut Sts. and 5th and 6th Sts., Historic Area.*

★ ❸ **Liberty Bell.** The bell fulfilled the biblical words of its inscription when it rang to "proclaim liberty throughout all the land unto all the inhabitants thereof," beckoning Philadelphians to the State House yard to hear the first reading of the Declaration of Independence. Ordered in 1751 and originally cast in England, the bell cracked during testing and was recast in Philadelphia by Pass and Stow two years later. To keep it from falling into British hands during the Revolution—they would have melted it down for ammunition—the bell was spirited away by horse and wagon to Allentown, 60 mi to the north. The bell is the subject of much legend; one story says it cracked when tolled at the funeral of Chief Justice John Marshall in 1835. Actually, the bell cracked slowly over a period of years. It was repaired but cracked again in 1846 and was then forever silenced. It was called the State House Bell until the 1830s, when a group of abolitionists adopted it as a symbol of freedom and renamed it the Liberty Bell.

After being housed in Independence Hall for more than 200 years, the bell was moved to a glass-enclosed pavilion for the 1976 Bicentennial, that for many seemed an incongruous setting for such a historic object. In mid-2003, the bell once again moved to another glass-enclosed pavilion with redbrick accents. This time, great care was taken to improve access to the bell and the view of its former home at Independence Hall, which is seen against the backdrop of the sky—rather than 20th-century buildings. The Liberty Bell complex houses a bell chamber, an interpretive exhibit area with historic displays and memorabilia, and a covered area for waiting in line. Construction was delayed in part by the discovery that the bell—a symbol of the abolition movement—would be located near the remains of the former slave quarters of President George Washington. (The presidential mansion, once located on the site, was torn down in the 1830s.) The original design for the current pavilion did not make note of the slave quarters, but the National Park Service, following an outcry from the public and historians, revised the exhibits to present a more complete history of the site. ✉ *6th and Chestnut Sts., Historic Area* ☎ *215/965–2305* 🌐 *www.nps.gov/inde/liberty-bell.html* 🎫 *Free* 🕒 *Daily 9–5.*

need a break?

Enter the **Bourse** (✉ 5th St. across from the Liberty Bell Pavilion, Historic Area ☎ 215/625–0300) and you're in another century. The skylighted Great Hall, with its Corinthian columns, marble, wrought-iron stairways, and Victorian gingerbread details, has been magnificently restored. Built in 1895 as a stock exchange, it now houses shops and a food court, where you can grab a cup of cappuccino or a Philly cheese steak.

1

7 **Library Hall.** This 20th-century building is a reconstruction of Franklin's Library Company of Philadelphia, the first public library in the colonies. The American Philosophical Society, one of the country's leading institutions for the study of science, has its library at this scholarly research facility. The vaults contain such treasures as a copy of the Declaration of Independence handwritten by Thomas Jefferson, William Penn's 1701 Charter of Privileges, and journals from the Lewis and Clark expedition of 1803–06. The library's collection also includes first editions of Newton's *Principia Mathematica,* Franklin's *Experiments and Observations,* and Darwin's *On the Origin of Species.* The lobby has fascinating changing exhibitions that showcase the society's collection. ✉ *105 S. 5th St., Historic Area* ☎ *215/440–3400* 🌐 *www.amphilsoc.org/about/libhall.htm* 🎫 *Free* 🕒 *Weekdays 9–4:45.*

Living History Center. The park's former visitor center now houses the ongoing archaeological work on the more than one million artifacts unearthed during the construction of the National Consitution Center. You watch archaelogists at work and ask them questions. The center also offers screenings of the movie musical, "1776," with audience participation. ✉ *3rd and Chestnut Sts. Historic Area* ☎ *800/537–7676* 🌐 *www.independencevisitorcenter.com* 🎫 *Free for archaeological displays; $1 for "1776"* 🕒 *daily 9–5; check visitor center for movie times.*

2 **National Constitution Center.** This 160,000-square-foot museum brings the U.S. Constitution alive through a series of highly interactive exhibits tracing the development and adoption of the nation's landmark guiding document. The heart of the sprawling museum, "The Story of We the People," takes you from the American Revolution through the Constitution's ratification to major events in the nation's constitutional history. Later, you can play the role of a Supreme Court justice deciding an important case, and walk among the framers in Signers Hall, where you can decide whether to add your signature to the list of founding fathers. The $132-million facility has 100-plus exhibits and plays host to many events—from the regular taping of National Public Radio's "Justice Talking" program to speeches by current and former world leaders. ✉ *525 Arch St., His-*

toric Area ☎ *215/923–0004* 🌐 *www.constitutioncenter.org* 🎫 *$7* ⏲ *Sun.–Fri. 9:30–5, Sat. 9:30–6.*

⓬ **National Liberty Museum.** Using interactive exhibits, video, and works of art, the museum aims to combat bigotry in the United States by putting a spotlight on the nation's rich traditions of freedom and diversity. Galleries celebrate outstanding Americans, including 19 Nobel peace prize winners and heroes of September 11, 2001, as well as heroes from around the world. The museum's collection of glass art is symbolic of the fragility of peace; its highlight is Dale Chihuly's 20-foot-tall red glass sculpture, *Flame of Liberty.* Sandy Skoglund's colorful Jelly Bean People is a reminder that we're all the same inside regardless of the color of our skin. ✉ *321 Chestnut St., Historic Area* ☎ *215/925–2800* 🌐 *www.libertymuseum.org* 🎫 *$5* ⏲ *Sept.–May, Tues.–Sun. 10–5; June–Aug., daily 10–5.*

❿ **New Hall Military Museum.** The original of this reconstructed 1790 building briefly served as headquarters for the U.S. Department of War. On display are Revolutionary War uniforms, medals, and authentic weapons, including powder horns, swords, and a 1763 flintlock musket. Dioramas depict highlights of the Revolutionary War. The building also houses a Marine Corps memorial. ✉ *Chestnut St. east of 4th St., Historic Area* ☎ *215/965–2305* 🌐 *www.nps.gov/inde/new-hall.html* 🎫 *Free* ⏲ *Hrs vary; check Web site or visitor center.*

❺ **Old City Hall.** Independence Hall is flanked by Congress Hall to the west and Old City Hall to the east: three distinctive Federal-style buildings erected to house the city's growing government. But when Philadelphia became the nation's capital in 1790, the just-completed city hall was lent to the federal government. It housed the U.S. Supreme Court from 1791 to 1800; John Jay was the Chief Justice. Later, the boxlike building with a peaked roof and cupola was used as the city hall. Today an exhibit presents information about the early days of the federal judiciary. ✉ *5th and Chestnut Sts., Historic Area* ☎ *215/965–2305* 🌐 *www.nps.gov/inde/old-city-hall.html* 🎫 *Free* ⏲ *Hrs vary; check Web site or visitor center.*

Philadelphia Merchant's Exchange. Designed by the well-known Philadelphia architect William Strickland and built in 1832, this impressive Greek Revival structure served as the city's commercial center for 50 years. It was both the stock exchange and a place where merchants met to trade goods. In the tower a watchman scanned the Delaware River and notified merchants of arriving ships. The exchange stands behind Dock Street, a cobblestone thoroughfare closed to traffic. The building houses a small exhibit on its history and park offices. ✉ *3rd and Walnut Sts., Historic Area* ☎ *215/965–2305* 🎫 *Free* ⏲ *Weekdays 8:30–4:30.*

Philosophical Hall. This is the headquarters of the American Philosophical Society, founded by Benjamin Franklin in 1743 to promote "useful knowledge." The members of the oldest learned society in America have included Washington, Jefferson, Lafayette, Emerson, Darwin, Edison, Churchill, and Einstein. Erected between 1785 and 1789 in what has been called a "restrained Federal style" (designed, probably, to complement, not outshine, adjacent Independence Hall), Philosophical Hall is brick with marble trim and has a handsome arched entrance. The society's library is across the street in Library Hall. ✉ *104 S. 5th St., Historic Area* ☎ *215/440–3400* 🌐 *www.amphilsoc.org* 🎫 *Free* 🕐 *Oct.–Mar., Thurs.–Sun. noon–5; Apr.–Sept., Wed.–Sun. noon–5.*

8 **Second Bank of the United States.** When Second Bank President Nicholas Biddle held a design competition for a new building, he required all architects to use the Greek style; William Strickland, one of the foremost architects of the 19th century, won. Built in 1824, the bank, with its Doric columns, was based on the design of the Parthenon and helped establish the popularity of Greek Revival architecture in the United States. The interior banking hall, though, was Roman, with a dramatic, barrel-vault ceiling. Housed here are portraits of prominent Colonial Americans by noted artists such as Charles Willson Peale, William Rush, and Gilbert Stuart. Don't miss Peale's portraits of Jefferson and Lewis and Clark: The former is the only one that shows the third president with red hair, and the latter is the only known portrait of the famous explorers. The permanent exhibition, "The People of Independence," has a life-size wooden statue of George Washington by William Rush; a mural of Philadelphia in the 1830s by John A. Woodside Jr.; and the only known likeness of William Floyd, a lesser-known signer of the Declaration of Independence. ✉ *420 Chestnut St., Historic Area* ☎ *215/965–2305* 🌐 *www.nps.gov/inde/second-bank.html* 🎫 *Free* 🕐 *Hrs vary; check Web site or visitor center.*

17 **Todd House.** Built in 1775 by John Dilworth, Todd House has been restored to its 1790s appearance, when its best-known resident, Dolley Payne Todd (1768–1849), lived here. She lost her husband, the Quaker lawyer John Todd, to the yellow fever epidemic of 1793. Dolley later married James Madison, who became the fourth president. Her time as a hostess in the White House was quite a contrast to her years in this simple home. There's an 18th-century garden next to Todd House. Obtain free tickets at the visitor center for one-hour tours that include the Bishop White House. ✉ *4th and Walnut Sts., Historic Area* ☎ *215/965–2305* 🌐 *www.nps.gov/inde/todd-house.html* 🎫 *Free* 🕐 *Hrs vary; check Web site or visitor center.*

19 **Welcome Park.** A scale model of the Penn statue that tops City Hall sits on a 60-foot-long map of Penn's Philadelphia, carved in the pavement of Welcome Park. (The *Welcome* was the ship that transported Penn to America.) The wall surrounding the park displays a time line of William Penn's life, with information about his philosophy and quotations from his writings. The park was the site of the slate-roof house where Penn lived briefly and where he granted the Charter of Privileges in 1701. Written by Penn, the Charter of Privileges served as Pennsylvania's constitutional framework until 1776; the Liberty Bell was commissioned to commemorate the charter's 50th anniversary. The City Tavern, across the street, marks the site where George Washington once dined. It's still open for historically correct lunches and dinners. ✉ *2nd St. just north of Walnut St., Historic Area.*

OLD CITY

LIVING "NORTH OF MARKET"

In Colonial days, the rich folks in residential Society Hill whispered of those who lived "north of Market," for this area, between Front and 5th streets and Chestnut and Vine streets, was the city's commercial district for industry and wholesale distributors, filled with wharves and warehouses and taverns. It also held the modest homes of craftsmen and artisans. Old City (as it became known some 40 years ago, to distinguish it from the national park area) is aptly named: it is one of the city's oldest and most historic neighborhoods, home to Elfreth's Alley; the Betsy Ross House; and Christ Church, where George Washington and John Adams came (across the tracks!) to worship at services. There's evidence of the Quaker presence here, too, in the Arch Street Meeting House.

Today Old City is Philadelphia's trendiest neighborhood, a local version of New York's SoHo. Many cast-iron building facades remain, though the old warehouses, with telltale names such as the Sugar Refinery and the Hoopskirt Factory, now house well-lighted loft apartments popular with artists and architects. There are small theaters—the Painted Bride, the Arden Theatre Company—and numerous art galleries and boutiques. In the past few years, more restaurants and bars have opened here than in any other part of the city. The Old City Arts Association hosts a festive, popular event the first Friday of each month—known, appropriately enough, as First Friday—when the galleries throw open their doors during evening hours.

Numbers in the text correspond to numbers in the margin and on the Historic Area and Penn's Landing map.

a good walk

A walk through Old City begins at 2nd and Market streets, location of the impressive **Christ Church** ⑳, attended by George and Martha Washington, among other notables. Continuing north on 2nd Street for a block and passing Arch Street, you'll come to a tiny Colonial street on the right, **Elfreth's Alley** ㉑; two houses are open to the public. Head back to 2nd Street, turn right (north), and a few footsteps will take you to the **Fireman's Hall Museum** ㉒, with exhibits on the history of fire fighting. If you then follow 2nd Street back to Arch and turn right (west), you'll find the most popular residence in Philadelphia, the **Betsy Ross House** ㉓.

A bit farther along, between 321 and 323 Arch Street, you can peer into the gated Loxley Court and its 18th-century houses and then cross the street to the Society of Friends' **Arch Street Meeting House** ㉔. Just ahead one block is the Christ Church Burial Ground, final resting place for Ben Franklin and other signers of the Declaration of Independence. Across 5th Street is the Free Quaker Meeting House, built for Friends who had been disowned by their pacifist meetings for participating in the Revolutionary War. Diagonally across Arch Street stands the **United States Mint** ㉕, where, by special arrangement with your congressional representative, you can watch coins being made. If you're up for an adventure—and a hearty 1¾-mi walk (each way)—you could cross the Benjamin

WILLIAM PENN & HIS LEGACY

WILLIAM PENN WAS A REBEL *with a cause. Born in London in 1644 into a nobleman's family, he attended Oxford University, studied law, and tried a military career (in emulation of his father, an admiral in the British Navy). It was at Oxford that Penn first heard Quaker preachers professing that each life is part of the Divine spirit, and that all people should be treated equally, even royalty. At age 23, Penn joined the Religious Society of Friends (Quakers), who at the time were considered religious zealots.*

Penn was imprisoned in the Tower of London a few times for his heretical pamphlets, but he was spared worse persecution because of his father's support of King Charles II. He petitioned the king to grant him land in the New World for a Quaker colony; he was given a 45,000-square-mi tract along the Delaware River in payment of a debt Charles owed to his late father. Indeed, the king named the land Pennsylvania in honor of the admiral.

On Penn's first visit to his colony, from 1662 to 1664, he began his "Holy Experiment," establishing his haven for Quakers. His early laws guaranteed religious freedom and an elected government. He bought land from the Native Americans and established a peace treaty with them that lasted for 70 years.

Penn was called back to England in 1684 and remained there until 1699, caring for his ill wife, Gulielma Maria Springett, who would die without ever seeing his beloved Pennsylvania. Penn was suspected of plotting with the former Catholic king, James II, to overthrow the current Protestant monarchy of William and Mary, who revoked his charter in 1692 for 18 months. Penn made his second trip to America with his second wife, Hannah Callowhill Penn, in 1699. The couple moved into ***Pennsbury Manor*** *along the upper Delaware River, where, while preaching about a life of simplicity, he lived in luxury. Penn issued a new frame of government, the Charter of Privileges, which became a model for the U.S. Constitution. He had to return to England yet again in 1701; there he was consumed by the political and legal problems of his colony, a term in prison for debt, and then illness. Penn died before he could return to Pennsylvania. After his death, his wife honored him by assuming the governorship for nine years.*

Although Penn spent only four of his 74 years in Pennsylvania, his legacy is profound. As a city planner, he mapped out a "greene countrie towne" with broad, straight streets. He positioned each house in the middle of its plot, so that every child would have green grass and play space; he named its streets—Walnut, Spruce, Chestnut—for trees, not for men. His original city plan has survived—and his statue looks out over it from atop City Hall. As a reformer, Penn replaced dungeons with workhouses, established the right of a jury to decide a verdict without harassment by a judge; provided schools where boys—and girls—could get a practical education; and limited the death penalty to two offenses—murder and treason—rather than the 200 mandated by English criminal law.

The ***Arch Street Meeting House*** *(✉ 4th and Arch Sts., Old City), on land Penn set aside as a Quaker burial ground, still holds weekly meetings for worship; they are open to the public, as is a museum honoring Penn.* ***Welcome Park*** *(✉ 2nd St. just north of Walnut, Old City), has a time line of Penn's life and a map of Penn's Philadelphia carved in the pavement.*

Franklin Bridge. The walkway entrance is about two blocks north of the Mint, on 5th Street. Otherwise, turn left (south) on 5th Street, cross Arch Street, and walk until you find a redbrick courtyard, entrance to the modern building that houses both the **National Museum of American Jewish History** 26 and **Mikveh Israel** 27, the oldest Jewish congregation in Philadelphia. Walking two blocks west on Arch Street to 7th Street brings you to the **African American Museum** 28, with displays that illuminate the black experience through the centuries. At this point you might want to follow 7th Street (on foot or by bus) five blocks north to the residence and exhibits at the Edgar Allan Poe National Historic Site.

TIMING If possible, set aside four or five hours on a Sunday for your visit to Old City. You could attend the 9 AM service at Christ Church, as George and Martha Washington did, and then join the 10:30 Quaker meeting at the Arch Street Friends Meeting House, where William Penn worshipped. Try to avoid scheduling a Monday visit from November through February, when two of the top sights—the Betsy Ross House and Elfreth's Alley—are closed. If you detour to the Poe House, allow another two hours. You can take this walk in any kind of weather and at any time of year since the neighborhood is a small one.

What to See

28 **African American Museum in Philadelphia.** Permanent and changing exhibits are dedicated to the history, fine art, artifacts, crafts, and culture of African-Americans in the United States—with a focus on Philadelphia and Pennsylvania. Past exhibitions have showcased African-American female sculptors, slavery artifacts, and sports in Philadelphia. The museum's gift shop stocks the area's widest selection of books on black culture, history, fiction, poetry, and drama, along with African textiles and sculpture and African-American jewelry, prints, and tiles. Opened in the Bicentennial year of 1976, this is the first museum of its kind funded and built by a city. ✉ *701 Arch St., Old City* ☎ *215/574–0380* 🌐 *www.aampmuseum.org* 🎫 *$8* ⏲ *Tues.–Sat. 10–5, Sun. noon–5.*

24 **Arch Street Meeting House.** Constructed in 1804 for the Philadelphia Yearly Meeting of the Society of Friends, this building of simple lines is still used for that purpose, as well as for biweekly services. Among the most influential members in the 19th century was Lucretia Mott (1793–1880), a leader in the women's suffrage, antiwar, and antislavery movements. A small museum in the meeting house presents a series of dioramas and a 14-minute slide show depicting the life and accomplishments of William Penn (1644–1718), who gave the land on which the meeting house sits to the Society of Friends. Quaker guides give tours year-round. ✉ *4th and Arch Sts., Old City* ☎ *215/627–2667* 🌐 *www.archstreetfriends.org* 🎫 *$2 minimum donation requested* ⏲ *Mon.–Sat. 10–4; worship Wed. at 7 PM and Sun. at 10:30 AM.*

off the beaten path

BENJAMIN FRANKLIN BRIDGE – When the bridge opened in 1926, its 1,750-foot main span made it the longest suspension bridge in the world. Paul Cret, architect of the Rodin Museum, was the designer. The bridge has been having some rust problems of late, but there's a massive project underway through 2006 to restore its glorious blue paint job. The bridge is most impressive at night, when it's lighted. Start the 1¾-mi walk (one-way) from either the Philadelphia side, two blocks north of the U.S. Mint, or the Camden, New Jersey, side. ✉ *5th and Vine Sts., Old City* ☎ *215/218–3750* 🌐 *www.drpa.org* 🎫 *Free* ⏲ *Daily 6 AM–around 6 PM weather permitting.*

★ ☝ 23 **Betsy Ross House.** It's easy to find this little brick house with the gabled roof: just look for the 13-star flag displayed from its 2nd-floor window. Whether Betsy Ross, also known as Elizabeth Griscom Ross Ashbourn Claypoole (1752–1836)—who worked in her family's flag-making and upholstery business—actually lived here and whether she really made the first Stars and Stripes is debatable. Nonetheless, the house, built about 1760, is a splendid example of a Colonial Philadelphia home and is fun to visit. Owned and maintained by the city, the eight-room house overflows with artifacts such as a family Bible and Betsy Ross's chest of drawers and reading glasses. The small rooms hold period pieces that reflect the life of this hardworking Quaker (who died at the age of 84, outliving three husbands). You may have to wait in line here, as this is one of the city's most popular attractions. The house, with its winding narrow stairs, is not accessible to people with disabilities. Alongside the house is brick-paved Atwater Kent Park, with a fountain, benches, and the graves of Betsy Ross and her third husband, John Claypoole. ✉ *239 Arch St., Old City* ☎ *215/686–1252* 🌐 *www.betsyrosshouse.org* 🎫 *$3* ⏲ *Apr.–Sept., daily 10–5; Oct.–Mar., Tues.–Sun 10–5.*

⚑ 20 **Christ Church.** The Anglicans of the Church of England built a wooden church on this site in 1697. When they outgrew it, they erected a new church, the most sumptuous in the colonies, designed by Dr. John Kearsley and modeled on the work of famed English architect Sir Christopher Wren. The symmetrical, classical facade with arched windows, completed in 1754, is a fine example of Georgian architecture; the church is one of the city's treasures. The congregation included 15 signers of the Declaration of Independence. The bells and the soaring 196-foot steeple, the tallest in the colonies, were financed by lotteries run by Benjamin Franklin. Brass plaques mark the pews of George and Martha Washington, John and Abigail Adams, Betsy Ross, and others. Two blocks west of the church is Christ Church Burial Ground. ✉ *2nd St. north of Market St., Old City* ☎ *215/922–1695* 🌐 *www.oldchristchurch.org* ⏲ *Mon.–Sat. 9–5, Sun. 1–5; services Sun. 9 and 11, Wed. at noon.*

need a break?

Metropolitan Bakery (✉ 126 Market St., Old City ☎ 215/928–9528) offers up a tantalizing array of artisan breads, brownies, and jumbo cookies, as well as coffee drinks and juices. You can also sit down inside or out—weather permitting—and enjoy a changing menu of sandwiches on fresh-sliced bread.

Christ Church Burial Ground. Weathered gravestones fill the resting place of five signers of the Declaration of Independence and other Colonial patriots. The best-known is Benjamin Franklin; he lies alongside his wife, Deborah, and their son, Francis, who died at age four. According to local legend, throwing a penny onto Franklin's grave will bring you good luck. The burial ground is open to the public for regular visits for the first time in 150 years. ✉ *5th and Arch Sts., Old City* ☎ *215/922–1695* 🌐 *www.oldchristchurch.org* 🎫 *$2* ⏲ *Mon.–Sat. 10–4, Sun. noon–4.*

off the beaten path

EDGAR ALLAN POE NATIONAL HISTORIC SITE – One of America's most original writers, Edgar Allan Poe (1809–49), lived here from 1843 to 1844; it's the only one of his Philadelphia residences still standing. During that time some of his best-known short stories were published: "The Telltale Heart," "The Black Cat," and "The Gold Bug." You can tour the three-story brick house; to evoke the spirit of Poe, the National Park Service deliberately keeps it empty. An adjoining house has exhibits on Poe and his family, his work habits, and his literary contemporaries; there's also an eight-minute film and a small Poe library and reading room. A statue of a raven helps set the mood. Special programs include Poetry Month tours (usually March or April) and popular "ghostly" tours in October (reservations required). The site, easily reached from the African-American Museum, is five blocks north of Market Street. SEPTA Bus 47 travels on 7th Street to Spring Garden Street, where you should disembark. ✉ *532 N. 7th St., Northern Liberties* ☎ *215/597–8780* 🌐 *www.nps.gov/edal* 🎫 *Free* ⏲ *Wed.–Sun. 9–5.*

★ 21 **Elfreth's Alley.** The alley, the oldest continuously occupied residential street in America, dates to 1702. Much of Colonial Philadelphia resembled this area, with its cobblestone streets and narrow two- or three-story brick houses. These were modest row homes, most built for rent, and lived in by craftsmen, such as cabinetmakers, silversmiths, and pewterers, and their families. They also housed captains and others who made their living in the city's busy shipping industry. The earliest houses (two stories) have pent eaves; taller houses, built after the Revolution, show the influence of the Federal style. The Elfreth's Alley Museum includes two homes that have been restored by the Elfreth's Alley Association: No. 124, home of a Windsor chair maker, and No. 126, a Colonial dressmaker's home, with authentic furnishings and a Colonial kitchen. In early June residents celebrate Fete Day, when some of the 30 homes are open to the public for tours hosted by guides in Colonial garb. On the second Friday evening in December, home owners again welcome visitors for a candlelight holiday tour. Both of these special events require advance tickets. ✉ *Front and 2nd Sts. between Arch and Race Sts., Old City* ☎ *215/574–0560* 🌐 *www.elfrethsalley.org* 🎫 *Alley free; museum $2, free on July 4* ⏲ *Mar.–Oct., Mon.–Sat 10–5, Sun. noon–5; Nov.–Feb., Thurs.–Sat. 10–5, Sun. noon–5.*

22 **Fireman's Hall Museum.** Housed in an authentic 1876 firehouse, this museum traces the history of fire fighting, from the volunteer company founded in Philadelphia by Benjamin Franklin in 1736 to the professional departments of the 20th century. The collection includes early hand- and horse-drawn fire engines, such as an 1815 hand pumper and a 1907 three-horse Metropolitan steamer; fire marks (18th-century building signs marking them as insured for fire); uniforms; and other memorabilia.

⊠ *147 N. 2nd St., Old City* ☎ *215/923–1438* ⊕ *www.gophila.com/culturefiles/museums/firemanshall* *Free, donations welcome* ⊙ *Tues.–Sat. 10–4:30 and 1st Fri. of each month 10–9.*

Free Quaker Meeting House. This was the house of worship for the Free "Fighting" Quakers, a group that broke away from the Society of Friends to take up arms against the British during the Revolutionary War. The building was designed in 1783 by Samuel Wetherill, one of the original leaders of the group, after they were disowned by their pacifist brothers. Among the 100 members were Betsy Ross (then Elizabeth Griscom) and Thomas Mifflin, a signer of the Constitution. After the Free Quaker group dissolved (many left to become Episcopalian), the building was used as a school, library, and warehouse. The meeting house, built in the Quaker plain style with a brick front and gable roof, has been carefully restored. ⊠ *500 Arch St., Old City* ☎ *215/965–2305* ⊕ *www.nps.gov/inde/fqmh.html* *Free* ⊙ *Hrs vary; check Web site or visitor center.*

Loxley Court. One of the restored 18th-century houses in this lovely court was once home to Benjamin Loxley, a carpenter who worked on Independence Hall. The court's claim to fame, according to its residents, is as the spot where Benjamin Franklin flew his kite in his experiment with lightning; the key tied to it was the key to Loxley's front door. ⊠ *321–323 Arch St., Old City* ⊙ *Closed to the public.*

27 **Mikveh Israel.** Nathan Levy, a Colonial merchant whose ship, the *Myrtilla,* brought the Liberty Bell to America, helped found this Jewish congregation in 1740, making it the oldest in Philadelphia and the second oldest in the United States. The original synagogue was at 3rd and Cherry streets; the congregation's current space (1976) is in the Sephardic style (following Spanish and Portuguese Jewish ritual) and occupies the same building as the **National Museum of American Jewish History.** The synagogue's Spruce Street Cemetery (about eight blocks away, beyond Old City) dates from 1740 and is the oldest surviving Jewish site in Philadelphia. It was the burial ground for the Spanish-Portuguese Jewish community. To arrange a tour, call the National Museum of American Jewish History. ⊠ *Synagogue: 44 N. 4th St., Old City* ☎ *215/922–5446* ⊙ *Mon.–Thurs. 10–5, Fri. 10–3, Sun. noon–5. Services Mon. and Fri. 7:15 AM, Fri. evening, Sat. 9 AM and evening, Sun. 8:15 AM* ⊠ *Cemetery: Spruce St. between 8th and 9th Sts., Old City* ☎ *215/922–5446* ⊕ *www.mikvehisrael.org* ⊙ *Guide present July and Aug., Mon.–Thurs. 10–4; Sept.–June, visiting arrangements can be made through synagogue office.*

need a break?

Located next door to its popular namesake restaurant, **Fork: etc.** (⊠ 308 Market St., Old City ☎ 215/625–9425) offers an ever-changing array of gourmet salads, soups, sandwiches, and pastries. You can dine in or take food out for a picnic in nearby Independence National Historical Park.

26 **National Museum of American Jewish History.** Established in 1976, this small museum is the only one in the nation dedicated exclusively to collecting, preserving, and interpreting artifacts pertaining to the Ameri-

can Jewish experience. It presents exhibits and programs exploring not only Jewish life but also issues of American ethnic identity, history, art, and culture. The museum shares a building with **Mikveh Israel** synagogue but planned to close in late 2006 to construct a new $100-million, 100,000-square-foot facility that's slated to open in 2009. ✉ *55 N. 5th St., Old City* ☎ *215/923–3811* 🌐 *www.nmajh.org* 🎫 *Free* ⏲ *Mon.–Thurs. 10–5, Fri. 10–3, Sun. noon–5.*

25 **United States Mint.** The first U.S. mint was built in Philadelphia at 16th and Spring Garden streets in 1792, when the Bank of North America adopted dollars and cents instead of shillings and pence as standard currency; the current mint was built in 1971. Every 45 minutes, self-guided tours open to groups of six or fewer are available by arrangement through your congressional representative. You can see blank disks being melted, cast, and pressed into coins, which are then inspected, counted, and bagged. The visitors' gallery has an exhibition of medals from the nation's wars, including the Medal of Honor, the Purple Heart, and the Bronze Star. Seven Tiffany glass tile mosaics depict coin making in ancient Rome. A shop in the lobby sells special coins and medals—in mint condition. ✉ *5th and Arch Sts., Old City* ☎ *215/408–0114* 🌐 *www.usmint.gov* 🎫 *Free* ⏲ *Make arrangements through your congressional representative.*

PENN'S LANDING & CAMDEN WATERFRONT

THE WATERFRONT CITY

The spot where William Penn stepped ashore in 1682 is the hub of a 37-acre riverfront park that stretches from Market Street south to Lombard Street. Walk along the waterfront and you'll see scores of pleasure boats moored at the marina and cargo ships chugging up and down the Delaware River. Philadelphia's harbor, which includes docking facilities in New Jersey and Delaware, is one of the world's largest freshwater ports. Attractions at Penn's Landing (215/922–2386, www.pennslandingcorp.com) include a maritime museum and historic marine vessels. The waterfront is also the scene of the annual Memorial Day Jam on the River and July 4th fireworks as well as jazz and big band concerts, ethnic festivals, and children's events.

The development of Penn's Landing—an ambitious effort to reclaim the Delaware River waterfront—began in 1967 and has continued in fits and starts. The Hyatt Regency Hotel and the Dockside Apartments have opened in the last five years, but a plan to create a family entertainment center with a movie theater, shops, and restaurants, and the aerial tram has been put on hold.

Meanwhile, the city of Camden has been sprucing up its waterfront and building attractions to lure visitors across the Delaware River. The lineup at Camden Waterfront (856/757–9400, www.camdenwaterfront.com) includes the Adventure Aquarium, the Camden Children's Garden, the Battleship *New Jersey,* and Campbell's Field, a minor-league park where the Camden Riversharks play. The indoor-outdoor Tweeter

Center amphitheater hosts concerts (big names like Paul Simon and Dave Matthews Band), Broadway theatrical productions, and family entertainment. The world's largest four-masted tall ship, the *Moshulu,* doubles as a restaurant.

To reach Penn's Landing, cross the Walnut Street Bridge at Front Street, which deposits you at the Independence Seaport Museum. The RiverLink Ferry connects Penn's Landing to Camden, New Jersey.

Numbers in the text correspond to numbers in the margin and on the Historic Area and Penn's Landing map.

TIMING You could easily spend a whole day here. If your kids are in tow, allow an hour and a half for the Independence Seaport Museum and its historic boats and another two or three hours for the ferry ride and visit to the aquarium, followed by a tour of the Battleship *New Jersey.*

What to See

★ 31 **Adventure Aquarium.** A $40-million renovation in 2005 transformed the former New Jersey State Aquarium into a high-tech, hands-on science education center, exhibiting nearly 6,000 species. You can observe the *Shark Realm,* a 550,000-gallon tank stretching two-stories high and thick with sharks, stingrays, and sawfish, or immerse yourself in it—the daring can "swim with the sharks" by snorkeling along the tank's perimeter under the careful supervision of aquarium staff. In the *West African River Experience,* hippopotamuses cohabit with birds, crocodiles, porcupines, and some 1,000 fish. There are also daily seal shows, penguin feedings, live animal talks, and "4-D" theater presentations, in which the 3-D on-screen action is choreographed to motion in the theater's seats. To get here, drive or take the ferry from Penn's Landing. ✉ *1 Riverside Dr., Camden Waterfront, Camden, NJ* ☎ *856/365–3300* 🌐 *www.adventureaquarium.com* 🎟 *$17* ⏲ *Daily 9:30–5.*

33 **Battleship *New Jersey.*** The World War II–era USS *New Jersey,* one of the most decorated battleships in the history of the U.S. Navy, is now a floating museum. It is docked in Camden, New Jersey, south of the Tweeter Center. The ship's current berth is across the Delaware River from the Philadelphia Naval Shipyard, which built and launched it in 1942. A 2½-hour guided tour takes visitors around the upper and lower decks of the ship, which was involved in a long list of Pacific operations, including the Marshalls, Iwo Jima, and Okinawa. ✉ *Beckett St., at the Delaware River, Camden Waterfront, Camden, NJ* ☎ *856/966–1652* 🌐 *www.battleshipnewjersey.org* 🎟 *$14* ⏲ *Jan.–Feb., Fri.–Mon. 9–3; Mar. and Oct.–Dec., daily 9–3; Apr.–Sept., daily 9–5.*

32 **Camden Children's Garden.** Located adjacent to the Adventure Aquarium on the Camden waterfront, this delightful 4-acre garden is an interactive horticultural playground with theme exhibits. You can smell, hear, touch, and even taste some of the elements in the Dinosaur, Butterfly, Picnic, and World's Kitchen gardens. The Storybook Gardens include a Three Little Pigs Garden, the Giant's Garden from "Jack in the Beanstalk," and a Frog Prince Grotto; there's also a maze, carousel, train ride, and tree house. To get here, drive or take the ferry from Penn's

Landing. ✉ *3 Riverside Dr., Camden Waterfront, Camden, NJ* ☎ *856/365–8733* 🌐 *www.camdenchildrensgarden.org* 🎫 *$5* 🕓 *Apr.–Sept., weekdays 9–5, weekends 10–5; Oct.–Mar., weekdays, 9:30–4:30, weekends 10–5.*

29 ***Gazela of Philadelphia.*** Built in 1883 and formerly named *Gazela Primeiro,* this 177-foot square-rigger is the last of a Portuguese fleet of cod-fishing ships. Still in use as late as 1969, it's the oldest and largest wooden square-rigger still sailing. As the Port of Philadelphia's ambassador of goodwill, the *Gazela* sails up and down the Atlantic coast from May to October to participate in harbor festivals and celebrations. It's also a ship school and a museum. An all-volunteer crew of 35 works on ship maintenance from November to April, while it's in port. ✉ *Penn's Landing at Market St., Penn's Landing* ☎ *215/238–0280* 🌐 *www.gazela.org* 🕓 *Call ahead; tours can be arranged when the ship is in port.*

★ 30 **Independence Seaport Museum.** Philadelphia's maritime museum houses many nautical artifacts, figureheads, and ship models as well as interactive exhibits that convey just what the Delaware and Schuylkill rivers have meant to the city's fortunes over the years. You can climb in the gray, cold wooden bunks used in steerage, unload cargo from giant container ships with a miniature crane, weld and rivet a ship's hull, or even hop in a scull and row along the Schuylkill. Enter the museum by passing under the three-story replica of the Benjamin Franklin Bridge. ✉ *211 S. Columbus Blvd., at Walnut St., Penn's Landing* ☎ *215/925–5439* 🌐 *www.phillyseaport.org* 🎫 *$9 includes museum and USS Olympia and USS Becuna; $29.95 RiverPass includes admission, round-trip ticket on RiverLink Ferry, and admission to Adventure Aquarium; free Sun. 10 AM–noon* 🕓 *Daily 10–5.*

RiverLink Ferry. This passenger ferry makes a 12-minute trip across the Delaware River; it travels back and forth between the Independence Seaport Museum at Penn's Landing and Camden's waterfront attractions, including the New Jersey State Aquarium, the Camden Children's Museum, and the Battleship New Jersey. You'll get a picturesque view of Philadelphia's skyline and the Ben Franklin Bridge. Besides its daytime schedule, the ferry runs express service two hours before and one hour after Tweeter Center concerts and Camden Riversharks baseball games. ✉ *Penn's Landing near Walnut St., Penn's Landing* ☎ *215/925–5465* 🌐 *www.riverlinkferry.org* 🎫 *$6 round-trip* 🕓 *Apr.–Oct., daily. Departs from Camden every 40 min 9–5:40, from Philadelphia every 40 min 9:20–5:20.*

34 **USS *Becuna.*** You can tour this 318-foot-long "guppy class" submarine, which was commissioned in 1944 and conducted search-and-destroy missions in the South Pacific. The guides—all World War II submarine vets—tell amazing stories of what life was like for a crew of 88 men, at sea for months at a time, in these claustrophobic quarters. Then you can step through the narrow walkways, climb the ladders, and glimpse the torpedoes in their firing chambers. Children will love it, but it's fascinating for adults, too. Note that the ticket booth by the boats is closed seasonally;

FREE DAYS

MANY OF PHILADELPHIA'S *most historic and best-known attractions are free every day. This lengthy list includes Independence Hall, the Liberty Bell, Carpenter's Hall, Franklin Court, and the other buildings and sites of Independence National Historic Park. You can check out free contemporary art at any time by taking a free tour of the city's many vibrant murals (see www.muralarts.org for details).*

Monday: *Curtis Institute of Music concert.*

Wednesday: *African American Museum (free from 5–7). Curtis Institute of Music concert.*

Friday: *First Fridays (first Friday of every month) in the Old City are celebrated with free admission to galleries and free music and food.*

Sunday: *Independence Seaport Museum (free 10–noon), Institute of Contemporary Art (free 11–1 PM), Philadelphia Art Museum (pay what you wish all day), University Museum of Archaeology and Anthropology (free all day, Sept.–May).*

For those attractions that always come with a hefty price tag, the city offers several discount passes that can save you a lot of money, especially if you're traveling with a large family. For example, Philadelphia City Pass offers savings on six attractions—Academy of Natural Sciences, Independence Seaport Museum, Franklin Institute Science Museum, National Constitution Center, Philadelphia Trolley Tour, and the Philadelphia Zoo. The pass costs $39 for adults (versus $78.70 if you purchase tickets at each site) and is valid for nine days from first use.

---

tickets must be purchased at the Independence Seaport Museum on weekdays mid-November–mid-April. ✉ *Penn's Landing at Spruce St., Penn's Landing* ☎ *215/922–1898* *www.geocities.com/Athens/Acropolis/7612/becuna.html* *$9 includes admission to USS Becuna, USS Olympia, and the Independence Seaport Museum.* *Daily 10–5.*

35 **USS *Olympia*.** Commodore George Dewey's flagship at the Battle of Manila in the Spanish-American War is the only remaining ship from that war. Dewey entered Manila Harbor after midnight on May 1, 1898. At 5:40 AM, he told his captain, "You may fire when ready, Gridley," and the battle began. By 12:30 the Americans had destroyed the entire Spanish fleet. The *Olympia* was the last ship of the "New Navy" of the 1880s and 1890s, the beginning of the era of steel ships. You can tour the entire restored ship, including the officers' staterooms, engine room, galley, gun batteries, pilothouse, and conning tower. Note that the ticket booth by the boats is closed seasonally; tickets must be purchased at the Independence Seaport Museum on weekdays mid-November–mid-April. ✉ *Penn's Landing at Spruce St., Penn's Landing* ☎ *215/922–1898* *www.spanamwar.com/olympia.htm* *$9 includes admission to USS Olympia, USS Becuna, and the Independence Seaport Museum* *Daily 10–5.*

SOCIETY HILL

ENDURING GRACE

During the 18th century Society Hill was Philadelphia's showplace. A carefully preserved district, it is easily the city's most photogenic neighborhood today, filled with hidden courtyards, delightful decorative touches such as chimney pots and brass door knockers, wrought-iron foot scrapers, and other remnants from the days of horse-drawn carriages and muddy, unpaved streets. Here time has not quite stopped but meanders down the cobblestone streets, whiling away the hours.

A trove of Colonial- and Federal-style brick row houses, churches, and narrow streets, Society Hill stretches from the Delaware River to 6th Street, south of Independence National Historical Park. Those homes built before 1750 in the Colonial style generally have 2½ stories and a dormer window jutting out of a steep roof. The less heavy, more graceful houses built after the Revolution were often in the Federal style, popularized in England during the 1790s.

Here lived the "World's People," wealthier Anglicans who arrived after William Penn and loved music and dancing—pursuits the Quakers shunned when they set up their enclave in Old City, north of Market Street, in a less desirable commercial area. The "Society" in the neighborhood's moniker refers, however, to the Free Society of Traders, a group of business investors who settled here on William Penn's advice.

Today many Colonial homes in this area have been lovingly restored by modern pioneers who moved into the area 40 years ago and rescued Society Hill from becoming a slum. Inspired urban renewal efforts have transformed vast empty factory spaces into airy lofts; new town houses were carefully designed to blend in with the old. As a result, Society Hill is not just a showcase for historic churches and mansions but a living, breathing neighborhood.

Numbers in the text correspond to numbers in the margin and on the Historic Area and Penn's Landing map.

a good walk

Begin your walk at the intersection of Columbus Boulevard and cobblestone Dock Street with your back to the Delaware River. Just ahead are the Society Hill Towers, three high-rise apartment buildings designed in the early '60s by I. M. Pei. These, along with the Society Hill town houses at 3rd and Locust streets, were the winning entries in a design competition for housing that would symbolize the renewal of Society Hill. Today the tall buildings seem out of scale with the rest of the neighborhood. At the dead end turn left. You'll be walking along 38th Parallel Place; in the park to your left is Philadelphia's Vietnam Veterans Memorial. Turn right (west) on Spruce Street and left (south) on 2nd Street to Delancey Street. On summer weekends you may want to continue a few blocks farther on 2nd Street to **Head House Square** 36, a Colonial marketplace that hosts a crafts and fine arts fair. One block ahead is South Street, with its funky shops, bookstores, restaurants, and bars.

Otherwise, walk west along Delancey Street, lined with some of the city's prized Colonial homes.

On your right at 4th Street is the freestanding **Physick House** 37, with its superb Federal and Empire furnishings. In the next few blocks, you'll see three of the city's historic churches. Follow 4th Street half a block south to Pine Street and turn right (west) toward 6th Street. Between Pine and Lombard streets, on what has been renamed Richard Allen Avenue, is **Mother Bethel African Methodist Episcopal Church** 38. Head east on Pine Street; on your right, just before 4th Street, is **Old Pine Street Presbyterian Church** 39. This, and **St. Peter's Episcopal Church** 40, which dominates most of the next block, were designed by Robert Smith. St. Peter's slim belfry tower is six stories high, topped by a wooden steeple. On the northwest corner of 3rd and Pine streets is the **Thaddeus Kosciuszko National Memorial** 41, honoring the Polish general who fought in the Revolution.

Turn left (north) on 3rd Street. Within a few blocks, you'll come across the brownstones of Bouvier's Row (Nos. 258–262), once owned by Jacqueline Kennedy Onassis's ancestors. A few doors up is the brick Georgian **Powel House** 42, filled with fine 18th-century furniture. Continue north on 3rd Street to Willings Alley (opposite the former Old St. Paul's Church). Turn left and then right into the courtyard of **Old St. Joseph's Church** 43, the city's first Catholic church. Walk up the alley to 4th Street and then a half block south to **Old St. Mary's Church** 44, another early Catholic church. Following 4th Street back north brings you to the nation's oldest fire-insurance company, the **Philadelphia Contributionship for the Insurance of Houses from Loss by Fire** 45. Turn left on Walnut Street to 6th Street, and you'll come upon tree-shaded Washington Square, one of the five in Penn's original city plan. On the east side of the square is the **Athenaeum** 46 research library and gallery. If you have an interest in medicine, walk two blocks south and two more west to Pennsylvania Hospital, the nation's oldest.

TIMING You'll need about one hour to walk through Society Hill, more if you tour the Powel and Physick houses. If walking is your main interest, save this excursion for a warm day, because it can be quite windy along the waterfront. The prime time for this walk? A summer Sunday, when Penn's Landing bustles with festivals and Head House Square turns into an open-air fine arts and crafts market.

What to See

46 **Athenaeum.** Housed in a national landmark Italianate brownstone dating from the mid-1800s and designed by John Notman, the Athenaeum is a research library specializing in architectural history and design. Its American Architecture Collection has close to a million items. The library, founded in 1814, contains significant materials on the French in America and on early American travel, exploration, and transportation. Besides books, the Athenaeum has notable paintings and period furniture; changing exhibits are presented in the gallery. ✉ *219 S. 6th St., Society Hill* ☎ *215/925–2688* 🌐 *www.philaathenaeum.org* 🎟 *Free* 🕒 *Gallery, weekdays 9–5; tours and research by appointment only.*

36 **Head House Square.** This open-air Colonial marketplace, extending from Pine Street to Lombard Street, is a reminder of the days when people went to central outdoor markets to buy food directly from farmers. It was first established as New Market in 1745. George Washington was among those who came here to buy butter, eggs, meat, fish, herbs, and vegetables. The Head House, a boxy building with a cupola and weather vane, was built in 1803 as the office and home of the market master, who tested the quality of the goods. Today, on summer weekends, the square is home to a crafts and fine arts fair featuring the work of more than 30 Delaware Valley artists. There are free children's workshops on Sundays from 1 to 3. ✉ *2nd and Pine Sts., Society Hill* ☎ *215/790–0782* ⏲ *Memorial Day–Sept., Sat. noon–11* PM*, Sun. noon–6.*

38 **Mother Bethel African Methodist Episcopal Church.** Society Hill holds a notable landmark in the history of African-Americans in the city. In 1787 Richard Allen led fellow blacks who left St. George's Methodist Church as a protest against the segregated worship. Allen, a lay minister and former slave who had bought his freedom from the Chew family of Germantown, purchased this site in 1791. It's believed to be the country's oldest parcel of land continuously owned by African-Americans. When the African Methodist Episcopal Church was formed in 1816, Allen was its first bishop. The current church, the fourth on the site, is an example of the 19th-century Romanesque Revival style, with broad arches and a square corner tower, opalescent stained-glass windows, and stunning woodwork. The earlier church buildings were the site of a school where Allen taught slaves to read and also a stop on the Underground Railroad. Allen's tomb and a small museum are on the lower level. ✉ *419 Richard Allen Ave., S. 6th St. between Pine and Lombard Sts., Society Hill* ☎ *215/925–0616* 🌐 *www.motherbethel.org* 🎫 *Free, donation requested* ⏲ *Museum and guided tours, Tues.–Sat. 10–3.*

39 **Old Pine Street Presbyterian Church.** Designed by Robert Smith in 1768 as a simple brick Georgian-style building, Old Pine is the only remaining Colonial Presbyterian church and churchyard in Philadelphia. Badly damaged by British troops during the Revolution, it served as a hospital and then a stable. In the mid-19th century, its exterior had a Greek Revival face-lift that included Corinthian columns. In the 1980s, the interior walls and ceiling were stenciled with thistle and wave motifs, a reminder of Old Pine's true name—Third, Scots, and Mariners Presbyterian Church, which documented the congregation's mergers. The beautifully restored church is painted in soft shades of periwinkle and yellow. In the churchyard are the graves of 100 Hessian soldiers from the Revolution—and of Eugene Ormandy, former conductor of the Philadelphia Orchestra. Jazz vespers are held here the third Sunday of each month at 5 PM. ✉ *412 Pine St., Society Hill* ☎ *215/925–8051* 🌐 *www.oldpine.org* 🎫 *Free* ⏲ *Weekdays 8–12:30 and 1:30–5.*

43 **Old St. Joseph's Church.** In 1733 a tiny chapel was established by Jesuits for Philadelphia's 11 Catholic families. It was one of the first places in the English-speaking colonies where Catholic mass could be legally celebrated, a right granted under William's Penn 1701 Charter of Privileges, which guaranteed religious freedom. But freedom didn't come easy;

on one occasion Quakers had to patrol St. Joseph's to prevent a Protestant mob from disrupting the service. The present church, built in 1839, is the third on this site. The late-19th-century stained-glass windows are notable. ✉ *321 Willings Alley, Society Hill* ☎ *215/923–1733* 🌐 *www.oldstjoseph.org* 🎫 *Free* 🕐 *Daily 9:30–4; mass Mon.–Sat. 12:05 PM, Sat. 5:30 PM, Sun. 7:30, 9:30, 11:30.*

44 **Old St. Mary's Church.** The city's second-oldest Catholic church, circa 1763, became its first cathedral when the archdiocese was formed in 1808. A Gothic-style facade was added in 1880; the interior was redone in 1979. The stained-glass windows, a ceiling mural of St. Mary, and brass chandeliers that hung in the Founders Room of Independence Hall until 1967 are highlights. Commodore John Barry, a Revolutionary War naval hero, and other famous Philadelphians are buried in the small churchyard. ✉ *252 S. 4th St., Society Hill* ☎ *215/923–7930* 🌐 *www.ushistory.org/tour/tour_stmary.htm* 🎫 *Free* 🕐 *Mon.–Sat. 10–4; mass Sat. 5 PM, Sun. 9 and 10:30 AM.*

off the beaten path

PENNSYLVANIA HOSPITAL – Inside the fine 18th-century original buildings of the oldest hospital in the United States are the nation's first medical library and first surgical amphitheater (an 1804 innovation, with a skylight). The hospital also has a portrait gallery, early medical instruments, art objects, and a rare-book library with items dating from 1762. The artwork includes the Benjamin West painting *Christ Healing the Sick in the Temple.* Dr. Thomas Bond thought of the idea of a community hospital to improve care for the poor and enrolled Benjamin Franklin in his vision. The Pennsylvania Assembly agreed to put up £2,000 if those interested in a hospital could do the same: it took Franklin only a month and a half to raise the money. Today Pennsylvania Hospital is a full-service modern medical center four blocks southwest of the Athenaeum. Pick up a copy of "Pennsylvania Hospital: A Walking Tour" at the Welcome Desk just off the 8th Street entrance. ✉ *8th and Spruce Sts., Society Hill* ☎ *215/829–3000, 215/829–3270 guided tours* 🌐 *www.pahosp.com* 🎫 *Free* 🕐 *Weekdays 8:30–4:30.*

45 **Philadelphia Contributionship for the Insurance of Houses from Loss by Fire.** The Contributionship, the nation's oldest fire insurance company, was founded by Benjamin Franklin in 1752; the present Greek Revival building with fluted marble Corinthian columns dates from 1836 and has some magnificently elegant salons (particularly the boardroom, where a seating plan on the wall lists Benjamin Franklin as the first incumbent of seat Number One). The architect, Thomas U. Walter, was also responsible for the dome and House and Senate wings of the U.S. Capitol in Washington, D.C. This is still an active business, but a small museum is open to the public. ✉ *212 S. 4th St., Society Hill* ☎ *215/627–1752* 🌐 *www.contributionship.com* 🎫 *Free* 🕐 *Weekdays 9–4.*

★ 37 **Physick House.** Built in 1786, this is one of two remaining freestanding houses from this era in Society Hill (you will see plenty of the famous Philadelphia row houses here). It's also one of the most beautiful homes

CloseUp

PARKING STRATEGIES

NARROW, 18TH-CENTURY STREETS *have resulted in a 21st-century challenge: parking.*

Your best option for the Historic District and Center City—especially if you plan to park once and walk or take public transit—is to use a garage.

The Philadelphia Parking Authority *(☎ 215/683–9600 ⊕ www.philapark.org) operates several garages in key locations, including 5th and Market streets (near Independence Mall), and offers some of the city's most competitive rates.*

Additional operators include ***Central Parking System*** *(☎ 215/564–4242) and* ***Parkway Corporation*** *(☎ 215/569–8400 ⊕ www.parkwaycorp.com). Also, hotel packages offered through* ***Greater Philadelphia Tourism Marketing Corp.*** *(⊕ www.gophila.com) often include parking.*

If you plan to move your car over the course of a day, or if you enjoy the thrill of the hunt, try for on-street parking. Meters and restrictions in many–but not all–parts of Center City are Monday through Saturday only.

Meters typically cost $1/hour, payable in change, or by using a ***Smart Card.*** *Available in $20 denominations, Smart Cards are sold through the Parking Authority Web site, or by calling 215/222–9100.*

While most meters restrict parking to two hours, there are longer-term (at least four hours) metered spaces in the Historic District on Front Street, between Market and Dock Streets, and on the Benjamin Franklin Parkway between 20th and 26th streets.

Let the street parker beware: meter attendants track spaces regularly during posted hours. Never leave your car unattended in a no-parking or tow away zone.

in America, with elegantly restored interiors and some of the finest Federal and Empire furniture in Philadelphia. Touches of Napoléon's France are everywhere: the golden bee motif woven into upholstery; the magenta-hue Aubusson rug (the emperor's favorite color); and stools in the style of Pompeii, the Roman city rediscovered at the time of the house's construction. Upstairs in the parlor, note the inkstand that still retains Benjamin Franklin's fingerprints. The house's most famous owner was Philip Syng Physick, the "Father of American Surgery" and a leading physician in the days before anesthesia. His most celebrated patient was Chief Justice John Marshall. The garden planted on three sides of the house is filled with plants common during the 19th century: complete with an Etruscan sarcophagus, a natural grotto, and antique cannon, it is considered by some to be the city's loveliest. ✉ *321 S. 4th St., Society Hill* ☎ *215/925–7866* ⊕ *www.philalandmarks.org* 🎫 *$5* ⏲ *Thurs.–Sat., noon–5, Sun. 1–5; guided tours on the hr, last tour at 4.*

★ 42 **Powel House.** The 1765 brick Georgian house purchased by Samuel Powel in 1769 remains one of the most elegant homes in Philadelphia. Powel—the "Patriot Mayor"—was the last mayor of Philadelphia under the Crown and the first in the new republic. The lavish home, a former wreck saved from demolition in 1930, is furnished with important pieces of 18th-century Philadelphia furniture. A mahogany staircase from Santo Domingo embellishes the front hall, and there is a signed Gilbert Stuart portrait in the parlor. In the 2nd-floor ballroom, Mrs. Powel—the city's hostess-with-the-mostest—served floating islands and whipped syllabubs to distinguished guests (including Adams, Franklin, and Lafayette) on Nanking china that was a gift from George and Martha Washington. Today the ballroom can be rented for parties and special events. ✉ *244 S. 3rd St., Society Hill* ☎ *215/627–0364* 🌐 *www.philalandmarks.org* 🎫 *$5* 🕒 *Thurs.–Sat. noon–5, Sun. 1–5.*

★ 40 **St. Peter's Episcopal Church.** Founded by members of Christ Church in Old City who were living in newly settled Society Hill, St. Peter's has been in continuous use since its first service on September 4, 1761. William White, rector of Christ Church, also served in that role at St. Peter's until his death in 1836. The brick Palladian-style building was designed by Scottish architect Robert Smith, who was responsible for Carpenters' Hall and the steeple on Christ Church. William Strickland's simple steeple, a Philadelphia landmark, was added in 1842. Notable features include the grand Palladian window on the chancel wall, high-back box pews that were raised off the floor to eliminate drafts, and the unusual arrangement of altar and pulpit at either end of the main aisle. The design has been called "restrained," but what is palpable on a visit is the silence and grace of the stark white interior. In the churchyard lie Commodore John Hazelwood, a Revolutionary War hero, painter Charles Willson Peale, and seven Native American chiefs who died of smallpox on a visit to Philadelphia in 1793. A guide is on hand weekends to answer questions. ✉ *313 Pine St., Society Hill* ☎ *215/925–5968* 🌐 *www.stpetersphila.org* 🕒 *Weekdays 9–4, Sat. 11–3, Sun. 1–3; tours can be arranged by calling ahead on weekdays; Sun. services 9, 10, and 11.*

South Street. Philadelphia's most bohemian neighborhood is crammed with craft shops and condom stores, coffee bars and tattoo parlors, ethnic restaurants, and New Age bookshops. At night it's crammed with people—those who hang out, and those who come to watch them, giving South Street the offbeat feel of Greenwich Village mixed with Bourbon Street. To some, it's still "the hippest street in town," as the Orlons called it in their 1963 song, although flower children have been replaced by teens with pierced eyebrows, and the crowds can get rowdy, especially late on weekend nights. ✉ *South St. from Front St. to about 10th St., Lombard St. to Bainbridge St., Society Hill/Queen Village* 🌐 *www.south-street.com.*

need a break?

Philadelphia Java Co. (✉ 518 S. 4th St. Society Hill ☎ 215/928–1811), offers respite from the bustle of nearby South Street. Inside is a cozy space with exposed brick walls and magazines and newspapers to peruse while you sip a favorite caffeinated beverage with a bagel or scone. Or you can dine al fresco on a panini or the cafe's signature labneh, an open faced sandwich with creamy Lebanese yogurt topped with green olives and olive oil.

41 **Thaddeus Kosciuszko National Memorial.** A Polish general who later became a national hero in his homeland, Kosciuszko came to the United States in 1776 to help fight in the Revolution; he distinguished himself as one of the first foreign volunteers in the war. The plain three-story brick house, built around 1776, has a portrait gallery; you can also view a six-minute film (in English and Polish) that portrays the general's activities during the Revolution. ✉ *301 Pine St., Society Hill* ☎ *215/597–9618* 🌐 *www.nps.gov/thko* 🎟 *Free* 🕒 *Hrs vary; check Web site or visitor center.*

Washington Square. This leafy area resembling a London square has been through numerous incarnations since it was set aside by William Penn. From 1705 until after the Revolution, the square was lined on three sides by houses and on the fourth by the Walnut Street Prison. The latter was home to Robert Morris, who went to debtors' prison after he helped finance the Revolution. The square served as a burial ground for victims of the 1793 yellow fever epidemic and for 2,600 British and American soldiers who perished during the Revolution. The square holds a Tomb of the Unknown Soldier, erected to the memory of unknown Revolutionary War soldiers. By the 1840s the square had gained prestige as the center of the city's most fashionable neighborhood. It later became the city's publishing center. ✉ *Bounded by 6th and 7th Sts. and Walnut and Locust Sts., Society Hill.*

CENTER CITY

CITY HALL & ENVIRONS

For a grand introduction to the heart of the downtown area, climb the few steps to the plaza in front of the Municipal Services Building at 15th Street and John F. Kennedy Boulevard. You'll be standing alongside a 10-foot-tall bronze statue of the late Frank L. Rizzo waving to the people. Rizzo, nicknamed the "Big Bambino," was the city's police commissioner, two-term mayor (in the 1970s), and a five-time mayoral candidate. He shaped the political scene just as the structures that surround you—City Hall, the PSFS Building, the Art Museum, the skyscrapers at Liberty Place, Oldenburg's *Clothespin,* and more—shape its architectural landscape.

The story behind this skyline begins with Philadelphia's historic City Hall, which reaches to 40 stories and was the tallest structure in the metropolis until 1987. No law prohibited taller buildings, but the tradition sprang from a gentleman's agreement not to build higher. In May 1984, when a developer proposed building two office towers that would break the 491-foot barrier, it became evident how entrenched this tradition was: the proposal provoked a public outcry. The traditionalists contended the height limitation had made Philadelphia a city of human scale, given character to its streets and public places, and showed respect for tradition. The opposing camp thought that a dramatic new skyline would shatter the city's conservative image and encourage economic growth. After painstaking debate the go-ahead was granted. In short order, the midtown area became the hub of the city's commercial center, Market Street west of City Hall became a district of high-rise office buildings, and the area became a symbol of the city's ongoing transformation from a dying industrial town to a center for service industries. Here, too, are a number of museums, the excellent Reading Terminal Market and the convention center, and Chinatown.

Numbers in the text correspond to numbers in the margin and on the Center City and Along the Parkway map.

a good walk

Ask most locals where "downtown" or "Center City" is, and you'll find they agree that Victorian **City Hall** 1 is at its heart. Take the elevator up to the tower for an incomparable bird's-eye view of the city. Leave City Hall by the north exit and cross John F. Kennedy Boulevard to the **Masonic Temple** 2, with its ornate interiors and collection of Masonic items. Two blocks north on Broad Street, at Cherry Street in a striking Victorian Gothic building, is the **Pennsylvania Academy of the Fine Arts** 3, filled with paintings by such artists as Winslow Homer and Andrew Wyeth. Head west on Cherry Street one block to 15th Street, turn left, and walk south three blocks to Market Street. This walk will take you from the classics to the avant-garde: Claes Oldenburg's 45-foot-high, 10-ton steel *Clothespin.*

Two blocks west of the sculpture are **Liberty Place One and Two** 4; the food court between them makes a convenient stop for lunch. Three blocks east at 13th Street is **Lord & Taylor** 5, formerly the John Wanamaker store, famous for its eagle statue and its nine-story grand court. Walk over to Market Street, turn right, and go one block to 12th Street. Here is the Philadelphia Saving Fund Society (PSFS) Building, an early (1930) skyscraper, now an upscale Loews Hotel. On the same block, SEPTA's headquarters holds the Transit Museum. Two blocks north on 12th Street is the **Reading Terminal Market** 6, filled with vendors of all kinds of food. Across Arch Street is the **Pennsylvania Convention Center** 7, which houses a terrific collection of contemporary art. Walking two blocks east on Arch Street brings you to the 40-foot-tall Chinese Friendship Gate, the unofficial entrance to the restaurants and stores of **Chinatown** 8.

TIMING To get a feel for the city at work, save this walk for a weekday, when the streets are bustling (on Sundays, especially, the area can be quite deserted). Besides, the City Hall Observation Tower is open weekdays only, and both the Reading Terminal Market and the Masonic Temple, two don't-miss spots, are closed Sunday. You could complete this walk in 45 minutes, but if you want to sightsee, reserve about half a day, with an hour each at the Masonic Temple, City Hall Tower, and the Pennsylvania Academy of the Fine Arts. If you get an early start, you can finish with lunch at the Reading Terminal Market.

What to See

8 **Chinatown.** Centered on 10th and Race streets two blocks north of Market Street, Chinatown serves as the residential and commercial hub of the city's Chinese community. Chinatown has grocery stores, souvenir and gift shops, martial arts studios, a fortune cookie store, bilingual street signs, red-and-green pagoda-style telephone booths, and more than 50

Center City & Benjamin Franklin Parkway

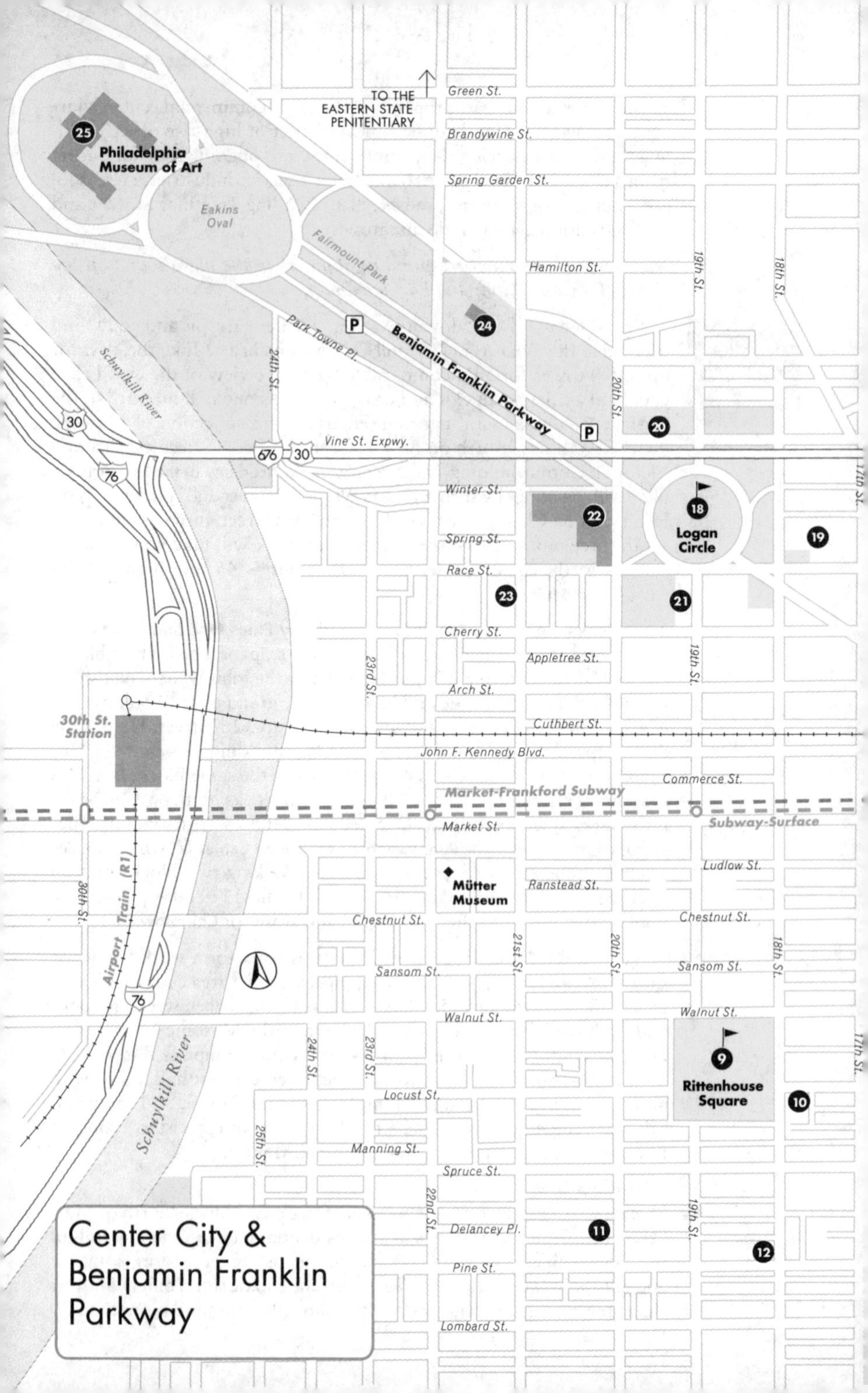

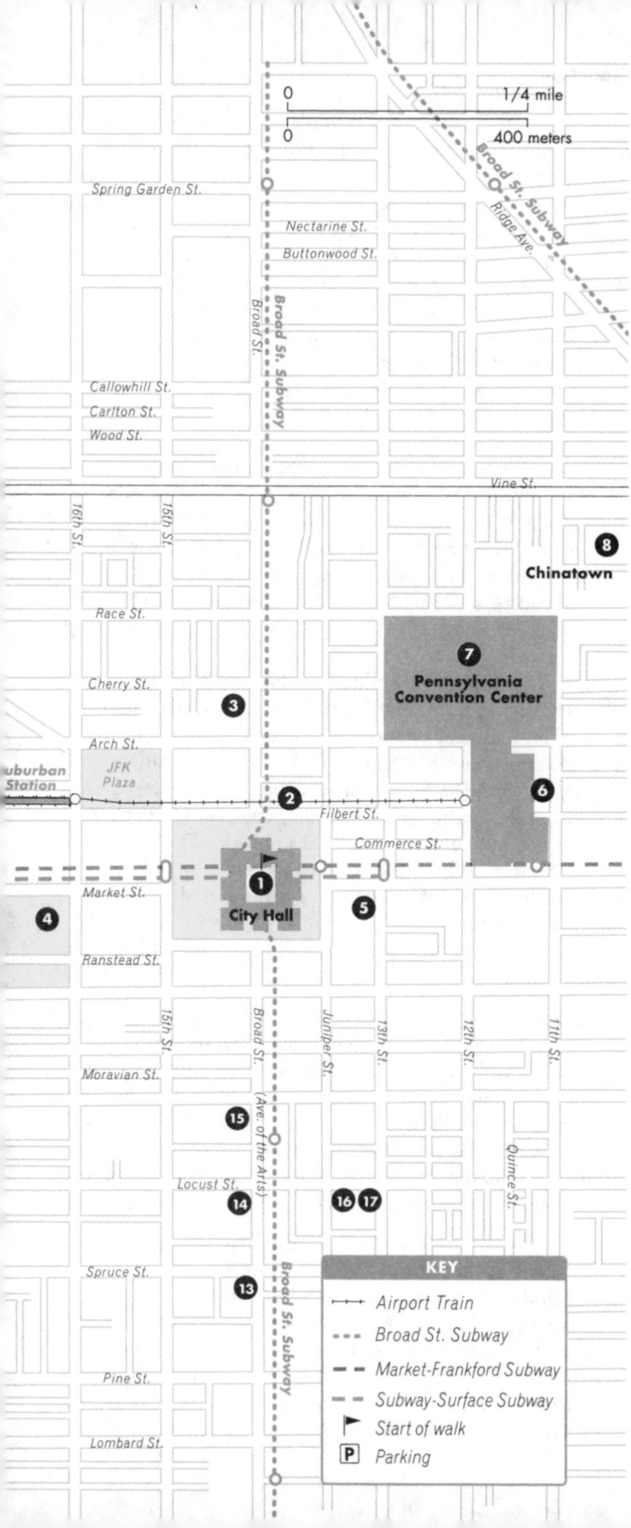

Academy of Music **14**
Academy of Natural Sciences **21**
Cathedral of Saints Peter and Paul **19**
Chinatown **8**
City Hall **1**
Civil War & Underground RR Museum **12**
Curtis Institute of Music **10**
Franklin Institute Science Museum **22**
Free Library of Philadelphia **20**
Historical Society of Pennsylvania **17**
Kimmel Center for the Performing Arts **13**
Liberty Place **4**
Library Company of Philadelphia **16**
Logan Circle **18**
Lord & Taylor **5**
Masonic Temple **2**
Park Hyatt Philadelphia at the Bellevue **15**
Pennsylvania Academy of the Fine Arts **3**
Pennsylvania Convention Center **7**
Philadelphia Museum of Art **25**
Please Touch Museum **23**
Reading Terminal Market **6**
Rittenhouse Square **9**
Rodin Museum **24**
Rosenbach Museum and Library **11**

restaurants. Over the past 20 years, Chinatown's population has become more diverse, reflecting the increase in immigration from other parts of Southeast Asia. As a result, the dining options are more varied; there now are restaurants serving authentic Vietnamese, Thai, Cambodian, and Burmese cuisine. One striking Chinatown site is the **Chinese Friendship Gate,** straddling 10th Street at Arch Street. This intricate and colorful 40-foot-tall arch—the largest authentic Chinese gate outside China—was created by Chinese artisans, who brought their own tools and construction materials. The citizens of Tianjin, Philadelphia's sister city in China, donated the building materials, including the ornamental tile. ✉ *9th to 11th Sts., Arch to Vine Sts., Chinatown* 🌐 *www.phillychinatown.com.*

need a break?

For a savory or sweet Chinese snack, stop at the **Hong Kong Bakery** (✉ 917 Race St., Chinatown ☎ 215/925–1288). Sample the "Hong Kong Hotdog," a smallish wiener encased in puff pastry (try it with mustard), or a sweet egg custard tart. Some of the items in the case defy description, but if you're feeling adventurous, try one or more. They're cheap (usually under $1) and you might just find a new taste thrill.

★ ⚑ ❶ **City Hall.** Topped by a 37-foot bronze statue of William Penn, City Hall was Philadelphia's tallest building until 1987; you can study the trappings of government and also get a panoramic view of the city here. With 642 rooms, it's the largest city hall in the country and the tallest masonry-bearing building in the world: no steel structure supports it. Designed by architect John McArthur Jr., the building took 30 years to build (1871–1900) and cost taxpayers more than $23 million. The result has been called a "Victorian wedding cake of Renaissance styles." Placed about the facade are hundreds of statues by Alexander Milne Calder, who also designed the statue of William Penn at the top. Calder's 27-ton cast-iron statue of Penn is the largest single piece of sculpture on any building in the world.

Not only the geographic center of Penn's original city plan, City Hall is also the center of municipal and state government. Many of the magnificent interiors—splendidly decorated with mahogany paneling, gold-leaf ceilings, and marble pillars—are patterned after the Second Empire salons of part of the Louvre in Paris. On a tour each weekday at 12:30, you'll see the Conversation Hall, the Supreme Court of Pennsylvania, the City Council chambers, and the mayor's reception room. You can attend often heated City Council meetings, held each Thursday morning at 10.

To top off your visit, take the elevator from the 7th floor up the tower to the observation deck at the foot of William Penn's statue for a 30-mi view of the city and surroundings. The elevator holds only six people per trip and runs every 15 minutes; the least crowded time is early morning. ✉ *Broad and Market Sts., tour office: E. Portal, Room 121, Center City* ☎ *215/686–1776, 215/686–2840 tour information* 🌐 *www.philadelphiacityhall.org* 🎫 *Donations suggested* 🕒 *Tower: weekdays 9:30–4:15; 90-min building tour including tower, weekdays at 12:30.*

Clothespin. Claes Oldenburg's 45-foot-high, 10-ton steel sculpture stands in front of the Center Square Building. Lauded by some and scorned by others, this pop art piece contrasts with the traditional statuary so common in Philadelphia. ✉ *15th and Market Sts., Center City.*

4 **Liberty Place One and Two. One Liberty Place** is the 945-foot, 63-story office building designed by Helmut Jahn that propelled Philadelphia into the "ultra-high" skyscraper era. Built in 1987, it became the tallest structure in Philadelphia. However, it will lose that distinction in the fall of 2007 when the 975-foot, 57-story Comcast Center office building is scheduled to open at 17th Street and John F. Kennedy Boulevard. The art deco–style structure, vaguely reminiscent of New York's Chrysler Building, is visible from almost everywhere in the city. In 1990 the adjacent 58-story tower, **Two Liberty Place,** opened. Zeidler Roberts designed this second building, which now holds the Westin Philadelphia. ✉ *One Liberty Pl., 1650 Market St., Market W* ✉ *Two Liberty Pl., 1601 Chestnut St., Market W.*

need a break?

The Shops at Liberty Place (✉ 1625 Chestnut St., between Liberty One and Liberty Two, Market W ☎ 215/851–9055) houses a large international food court on the second level, above the upscale boutiques. You'll find anything from salad to sushi to those familiar Philly cheese steaks.

5 **Lord & Taylor.** The former John Wanamaker department store, this building is almost as prominent a Philadelphia landmark as the Liberty Bell. Wanamaker began with a clothing store in 1861 and became one of America's most innovative and prominent retailers. The massive building, which occupies a city block with grace, was designed by the noted Chicago firm of D. H. Burnham and Company. Its focal point is the nine-story grand court with its 30,000-pipe organ—the largest ever built—and a 2,500-pound statue of an eagle, both remnants of the 1904 Louisiana Purchase Exposition in St. Louis. "Meet me at the Eagle" remains a popular way for Philadelphians to arrange a rendezvous. Happily, the current owners have kept the eagle and continue the famous Christmas sound-and-light show and the organ performances. ✉ *13th and Market Sts., Center City* ☎ *215/241–9000* 🌐 *www.lordandtaylor.com* ⏲ *Mon., Tues., Thurs., and Fri. 10–7; Wed. 10–8; Sat. 10–7; Sun. noon–6; free organ concerts Mon., Tues., and Thurs.–Sat., noon and 5; Wed., noon and 7.*

★ 2 **Masonic Temple.** The temple is one of the city's architectural jewels, but it remains a hidden treasure even to many Philadelphians. Historically, Freemasons were skilled stoneworkers of the Middle Ages who possessed secret signs and passwords. Their worldwide fraternal order—the Free and Accepted Masons—included men in the building trades, plus many honorary members; the secret society prospered in Philadelphia during Colonial times. Brother James Windrim designed this elaborate temple as a home for the Grand Lodge of Free and Accepted Masons of Pennsylvania. The trowel used here at the laying of the cornerstone in 1868, while 10,000 brothers looked on, was the same one that Brother George Washington used to set the cornerstone of the U.S. Capitol. The temple's ornate interior consists of seven lavishly decorated lodge halls built to exemplify specific styles of architecture: Corinthian, Ionic, Italian Renaissance, Norman, Gothic, Oriental, and Egyptian. The Egyptian room, with its accurate hieroglyphics, is the most famous. The temple also houses an interesting museum of Masonic items, including Benjamin Franklin's printing of the first book on Freemasonry published in America and Brother George Washington's Masonic Apron, which was embroidered by Madame Lafayette, wife of the famous marquis. ✉ *1 N. Broad St., Avenue of the Arts* ☎ *215/988–1917* 🌐 *www.pagrandlodge.org/tour/mtemple.html* 🎫 *$3 donation requested* 🕒 *45-min tours Sept.–June, Tues.–Fri. 11, 2, and 3, Sat. 10 and 11; July and Aug., weekdays 11, 2, and 3.*

★ ❸ **Pennsylvania Academy of the Fine Arts.** This High Victorian Gothic structure is a work of art in itself. Designed in 1876 by the noted, and sometimes eccentric, Philadelphia architects Frank Furness and George Hewitt, the multicolor stone-and-brick exterior is an extravagant blend of columns, friezes, and Richardsonian Romanesque and Moorish flourishes. The interior is just as lush, with rich hues of red, yellow, and blue and an impressive staircase. The nation's oldest art school and museum (founded in 1805) displays a fine collection that ranges from the Peale family, Gilbert Stuart, Benjamin West, and Winslow Homer to Andrew Wyeth and Red Grooms. *Fox Hunt* by Winslow Homer, *The Artist in His Museum* by Charles Willson Peale, and *Interior with Doorway* by Richard Diebenkorn are just a few notable works. The academy faculty has included Thomas Sully, Thomas Eakins, and Charles Willson Peale; the latter is one of the school's founders. Supplementing the permanent collection are constantly changing exhibitions of sculptures, paintings, and mixed-media artwork in the adjacent Samuel M.V. Hamilton Building; the 11-story facility, which opened for the academy's 200th anniversary, is also the home to the Sculpture Study Center, which offers changing displays from the permanent collection, classrooms, group and private studios for nearly 300 students, and Portfolio, the museum's gift shop. ✉ *118 N. Broad St., at Cherry St., Avenue of the Arts* ☎ *215/972–7600* 🌐 *www.pafa.org* 🎫 *$7* 🕒 *Tues.–Sat. 10–5, Sun. 11–5.*

❼ **Pennsylvania Convention Center.** Opened in June 1993 with galas, parties, and Vice President Al Gore cutting the ribbon, the convention center has helped rejuvenate Philadelphia's economy and fuel a hotel boom. It's big: with 313,000 square feet, the area of the main exhibition hall equals seven football fields. And it's beautiful: the 1.9 million square feet of space are punctuated by the largest permanent collection of contemporary art in a building of its kind. Many city and state artists are represented in the niches, nooks, and galleries built to house their multimedia works. To see the architectural highlight of the building—the Reading Terminal's magnificently restored four-story-high Victorian train shed, which has been transformed into the Convention Center's Grand Hall—enter the building through the century-old Italian Renaissance Headhouse structure on Market Street between 11th and 12th streets and ride up the escalator. The Headhouse is also home to Philadelphia's Hard Rock Cafe. ✉ *1101 Arch St., Market East* ☎ *215/418–4757* 🌐 *www.*

FLORAL FANTASY

IT TAKES ONE WEEK; *7,000 Belgian blocks; 3,500 volunteers; thousands of plumbers, carpenters, and electricians; more than a million plants; and 50 tractor-trailer loads of mulch to transform the Pennsylvania Convention Center into the annual* ***Philadelphia Flower Show*** *(☎ 215/988–8899 🌐 www.theflowershow.com), the world's largest indoor horticultural event. But the exhibitors—nursery owners, landscapers, and florists from the region and from Africa, Japan, and Europe—spend the better part of a year planning their displays. The astonishing, fragrant results of their efforts arrive in the city as a touch of spring in early March.*

It's a fitting tribute to William Penn that Philadelphia hosts this extravaganza, for this was Penn's "greene countrie town," which he laid out on a grid punctuated with tree-lined streets, pocket parks, small squares, and large public parks. It's also appropriate that this city gave root to the Pennsylvania Horticultural Society (PHS), the nation's first such organization. In 1829, two years after its founding, the society hosted its first show at the Masonic Hall in an 82-by-69-foot exhibition space; 25 society members showed off their green thumbs.

Today the show fills 10 acres of exhibition space at the convention center and spills throughout the area as local restaurants, hotels, and attractions offer special deals. (The show's Web site may have discounts and coupons.) Along with the more than 60 major exhibits, amateur gardeners contribute more than 2,000 entries in 330 competitive categories—from pressed plants and miniature settings to spectacular jewelry designs that use flowers. There are free cooking and gardening demonstrations, lectures, and an area where you can try out the latest gardening gadgets. Hundreds of vendors sell plants, birdhouses, topiaries, watering systems, botanical prints, and more.

Each year, the show has a theme, and the show's designers think big—very big. The entrance of the 2005 show, "America the Beautiful," took visitors through the original iron gates that once graced the White House of the 19th century, and continued through a virtual map of the nation's gardening styles, including "Country Casual" (prairie flowers, meadow grasses, evergreens, and cedars), "Suburban Soiree" (a bucolic backyard complete with a pool, teak deck, an outdoor kitchen, and brass planters), and "Tree House USA" (a woodland scene with a tree house, deck, and pavilion).

If you've made reservations, you can rest your weary feet during ***Garden Tea at the Flower Show*** *(☎ 215/988–8879), a proper English tea served at 12:30 and 3:45; it's $26 in addition to the show admission ($20–$26). For a more substantial lunch break, you can head across the street to the* ***Reading Terminal Market*** *(✉ 12th and Arch Sts., Market East), which has more than 80 stalls, shops, and lunch counters. Or walk two blocks east to the many restaurants of* ***Chinatown.***

Many people plan trips to Philadelphia around the show, so be sure to make reservations early. Wear good walking shoes, check your coat, and bring spending money for the many horticultural temptations. To avoid crowds, which can be daunting, arrive after 4 on weekdays and stay until the 9:30 closing, or show up when the doors open on weekend mornings, at 8.

paconvention.com 🎫 *Free* ⏲ *45-min tours by appointment only, subject to convention schedules.*

❻ **Reading Terminal Market.** The market is nothing short of a historical treasure and a food heaven to Philadelphians and visitors alike. One floor beneath the former Reading Railroad's 1891 train shed, the sprawling market has more than 80 food stalls and other shops, selling items from hooked rugs and handmade jewelry to South American and African crafts. Here, amid the local color, you can sample Bassett's ice cream, Philadelphia's best; down a cheese steak, a hoagie, a bowl of snapper soup, or a soft pretzel; or nibble Greek, Mexican, Thai, and Indian specialties. From Wednesday through Saturday the Amish from Lancaster County cart in their goodies, including Lebanon bologna, shoofly pie, and scrapple. Many stalls have their own counters with seating; there's also a central eating area. If you want to cook, you can buy a large variety of fresh food from fruit and vegetable stands, butchers, fish stores, and Pennsylvania Dutch markets. An open kitchen offers regular demonstrations by some of the region's top chefs. The entire building is a National Historic Landmark, and the train shed is a National Engineering Landmark. ✉ *12th and Arch Sts., Market East* ☎ *215/922–2317* 🌐 *www.readingterminalmarket.org* ⏲ *Mon.–Sat. 8–6.*

Fodor's Choice ★

Transit Museum. Located, appropriately enough, in the headquarters of the Southeastern Pennsylvania Transportation Authority (SEPTA), this small museum showcases the history and development of public transportation in the region and its impact on social, political, and economic life. ✉ *Concourse level, 1234 Market St., Market East* ☎ *215/580–7168* 🌐 *www.septa.org/store/museum.html* 🎫 *Free* ⏲ *Weekdays 10–5, Sat. 10–3.*

RITTENHOUSE SQUARE

LIVING THE GOOD LIFE

Rittenhouse Square, at 18th and Walnut streets, has long been one of the city's swankiest addresses. The square's entrances, plaza, pool, and fountains were designed in 1913 by Paul Cret, one of the people responsible for the Benjamin Franklin Parkway. The square was named in honor of one of the city's 18th-century stars: David Rittenhouse, president of the American Philosophical Society and a professor of astronomy at the University of Pennsylvania. The first house facing the square was erected in 1840, soon to be followed by other grand mansions. Almost all the private homes are now gone, replaced by hotels, apartments, and cultural institutions, and elegant restaurants and stylish cafés dot the neighborhood. The former home of banker George Childs Drexel was transformed into the Curtis Institute, alma mater of Leonard Bernstein and Gian Carlo Menotti. The former Samuel Price Wetherill mansion is now the Philadelphia Art Alliance, sponsor of exhibitions, drama, dance, and literary events.

The area south and west of the square is still largely residential and lovely, with cupolas and balconies, hitching posts and stained-glass windows. You can also find some small shops and two fine museum/library collections tucked in: the Civil War and Underground Railroad Museum and the Rosenbach Museum and Library. In the heart of the city there are green places, too. Peek in the streets behind these homes or through their wrought-iron gates, and you'll see well-tended gardens. On Delancey Place, blocks alternate narrow and wide. The wide blocks had the homes of the wealthy, and the smaller ones held dwellings for servants or stables (today these carriage houses are prized real estate). When he saw 18th Street and Delancey Place, author R. F. Delderfield, author of *God Is an Englishman,* said, "I never thought I'd see anything like this in America. It is like Dickensian London." Today the good life continues in Rittenhouse Square. Annual events include the Rittenhouse Square Flower Show and the Fine Arts Annual, an outdoor juried art show.

Four blocks east of the square is the Avenue of the Arts, also known as Broad Street. "Let us entertain you" could be the theme of the ambitious cultural development project that has transformed North and South Broad Street from a commercial thoroughfare to a performing arts district. Dramatic performance spaces have been built, old landmarks have been refurbished, and South Broad Street has been spruced up with landscaping, cast-iron lighting fixtures, and decorative sidewalk paving.

Numbers in the text correspond to numbers in the margin and on the Center City and Benjamin Franklin Parkway map.

a good walk

The lovely residential area around **Rittenhouse Square** 9 is dotted with small museums. A walk through this neighborhood logically begins at the square itself, on Walnut Street between 18th and 19th streets. East of the square are the former Barclay Hotel, celebrated for decades as the city's most fashionable hotel; the Philadelphia Art Alliance (251 S. 18th St.), housed in an 1890s mansion, with galleries open to the public; and the **Curtis Institute of Music** 10, whose talented students give free public recitals. West of the square you'll find a branch of the Free Library of Philadelphia, the Rittenhouse Hotel, and the Church of the Holy Trinity, presided over in the mid-19th century by the Reverend Phillips Brooks, who achieved renown as the lyricist of "O Little Town of Bethlehem."

Leave the square on its south side and continue south on 19th Street to Delancey Place, then turn right and take a look at this urban residential showcase with its grand houses. The 2000 block of Delancey wins the prize: at Number 2010 is the **Rosenbach Museum and Library** 11, a local gem, with paintings, manuscripts, and rare books. Heading east a block south of Delancey, you'll find the **Civil War and Underground Railroad Museum** 12, at 18th and Pine streets. Back at Rittenhouse Square, an elegant lunch can be enjoyed at the tony Lacroix at the Rittenhouse Hotel.

From Rittenhouse Square head east on Spruce Street four blocks to the **Kimmel Center for the Performing Arts** 13, the dramatic home of the Philadelphia Orchestra and other arts groups. Turn left on Broad Street, which has been rechristened the **Avenue of the Arts,** and walk one block to the **Academy of Music** 14, the orchestra's former home. As you walk along the west side of Broad between Spruce and Walnut streets, notice the more than 30 plaques in the sidewalk honoring some of those who contributed to Philadelphia's cultural history. Where else could Frankie

Avalon and Dizzy Gillespie rub shoulders with Anna Moffo and Eugene Ormandy? A block north of the venerable Academy of Music is another grande dame of South Broad Street, the former Bellevue Stratford Hotel, now the **Park Hyatt Philadelphia at the Bellevue** 15. As you continue up Broad Street, you'll pass a French Renaissance–style building, the Union League of Philadelphia. Cross Broad Street, double back to Locust Street, and walk east. Within the first block you come across two renowned collections, the **Library Company of Philadelphia** 16 and the **Historical Society of Pennsylvania** 17. If you have any time or energy remaining, you could walk three blocks east to 10th and Locust streets to see Thomas Eakins's masterpiece, *The Gross Clinic,* in Thomas Jefferson University's Alumni Hall.

TIMING This is one of the city's loveliest neighborhoods for strolling. Two hours would allow you enough time to wander through the Rittenhouse Square area and visit the Rosenbach Museum and Library (get there before 2:45). Add at least another hour for a stroll along South Broad Street, including afternoon tea or a cold lemonade at the Ritz-Carlton.

What to See

14 **Academy of Music.** The only surviving European-style opera house in America is the current home of the Opera Company of Philadelphia and the Pennsylvania Ballet; for the past century, it was home to the Philadelphia Orchestra. Designed by Napoleon Le Brun and Gustav Runge and completed in 1857, the building has a modest exterior; the builders ran out of money and couldn't put marble facing on the brick, as they had intended. The brick hides a lavish, neobaroque interior modeled after Milan's La Scala opera house, with gilt, carvings, murals on the ceiling, and a huge Victorian crystal chandelier. ✉ *Broad and Locust Sts., Avenue of the Arts* ☎ *215/893–1999 box office* 🌐 *www.academyofmusic.org.*

Avenue of the Arts. Broad Street, the city's main north–south thoroughfare, has been reinvented as a performing arts district. Although most of the cultural institutions are situated along South Broad Street from City Hall to Spruce Street, the avenue's cultural, education, and arts organizations span as far south as Washington Avenue in South Philadelphia and as far north as Dauphin Street in North Philadelphia. Joining the Merriam Theater and the University of the Arts on South Broad Street are the Wilma Theater, a 300-seat theater for this innovative company; a cabaret-style theater for the Philadelphia Clef Club of Jazz and the Performing Arts; the intimate Philadelphia Arts Bank at the University of the Arts; and the Prince Music Theater, a venue for musical theater and film. The newest venue is the Kimmel Center for the Performing Arts, at Broad and Spruce streets, which includes a 2,500-seat concert hall, specifically designed for the Philadelphia Orchestra, and a recital hall. On North Broad Street, the Pennsylvania Academy of the Fine Arts has completed structural renovations; the Liacouras Center, Temple University's multipurpose sports and concert complex, has opened; and the Freedom Theatre, the state's oldest African-American theater, has revamped and expanded the auditorium in its majestic Italianate mansion. Scheduled for an early 2007 opening is Symphony House, a $92-million, 31-story condominium tower that will also be home to the

400-seat Philadelphia Theatre Company. ✉ *Broad St., Avenue of the Arts* ☎ *215/731–9668* 🌐 *www.avenueofthearts.org.*

12 **Civil War and Underground Railroad Museum of Philadelphia.** The museum is one of the country's premier collections of Civil War memorabilia pertaining to the Union. Artifacts include two life masks of Abraham Lincoln; dress uniforms and swords that belonged to generals Grant and Meade; plus many other weapons, uniforms, and personal effects of Civil War officers and enlisted men. The library has more than 12,000 volumes about the war. ✉ *1805 Pine St., Rittenhouse Square* ☎ *215/735–8196* 🌐 *www.civilwarmuseumphiladelphia.org* 🎫 *$5* ⏲ *Thurs.–Sat. 11–4:30.*

10 **Curtis Institute of Music.** Graduates of this tuition-free school for outstanding students include Leonard Bernstein, Samuel Barber, Ned Rorem, and Anna Moffo. The school occupies four former private homes; the main building is in the mansion that belonged to banker George W. Childs Drexel. Built in 1893 by the distinguished Boston firm of Peabody and Stearns, it is notable for Romanesque and Renaissance architectural details. Free student and faculty concerts are given from October through May at 8, usually on Monday, Wednesday, and Friday evenings; there's also an opera, alumni recital, and symphony orchestra series. ✉ *1726 Locust St., Rittenhouse Square* ☎ *215/893–5261 recital hot line, 215/893–7902 Curtis ticket office* 🌐 *www.curtis.edu.*

Delancey Place. This fine residential area southwest of Rittenhouse Square was once the **address of Pearl S. Buck** (✉ 2019 Delancey Pl., Rittenhouse Square) and Rudolf Serkin. At one corner there is an interesting old **sea captain's house** (✉ 320 S. 18th St., Rittenhouse Square). At No. 2010 is the **Rosenbach Museum and Library.** Cypress Street, north of Delancey Place, and Panama Street (especially the 1900 block, one block south of Delancey) are two of the many intimate streets lined with trees and town houses characteristic of the area.

off the beaten path

THE GROSS CLINIC – Most art historians would put Thomas Eakins's magnificent medical painting *The Gross Clinic* (1875) on the list of top 10 American paintings; you can view it in Eakins Gallery in the alumni hall of Thomas Jefferson University. Eakins depicts Dr. Samuel D. Gross, Jefferson's celebrated surgeon and teacher, presiding over an operation for osteomyelitis in an amphitheater under a skylighted roof. His assistants are removing the bone, while the patient's mother stands off to the side. It's a dramatic piece in size (96 by 78 inches), composition (the light streaming into the murky room), and subject matter. Eakins, who studied anatomy at Jefferson Medical College, also painted portraits of two prominent professors, which are also on display here. The alumni hall is three blocks east of the Historical Society of Pennsylvania; request entry at the alumni hall information desk. ✉ *Jefferson Alumni Hall, 1020 Locust St., Washington Square West* ☎ *215/503–7926* 🌐 *www.tju.edu/eakins/grossclinic.cfm* 🎫 *Free* ⏲ *Mon.–Sat. 10–4, Sun. noon–4.*

17 **Historical Society of Pennsylvania.** Following a merger with the Balch Institute for Ethnic Studies, this superlative special collections library now

houses more than 500,000 books, 300,000 graphic works, and 19 million manuscript items; the emphasis is on Colonial, early national, and Pennsylvania history, as well as immigration history and ethnicity. Founded in 1824, the society also owns one of the largest family history libraries in the nation. This is the place to go to trace your family roots. Notable items from the collection include the Penn family archives, President James Buchanan's papers, a printer's proof of the Declaration of Independence, and the first draft of the Constitution. The library is open to anyone over 13 years old. ✉ *1300 Locust St., Washington Square West* ☎ *215/732–6200* 🌐 *www.hsp.org* 🎟 *$6* ⏲ *Tues. and Thurs. 12:30–5:30, Wed. 12:30–8:30, Fri. 10–5:30.*

⓭ **Kimmel Center for the Performing Arts.** Intended to make a contemporary design statement in this Colonial city, the Kimmel Center for the Performing Arts evokes Philadelphia's traditional redbrick structures, while providing architectural oomph with its dramatic vaulted glass roof. The 450,000-square-foot facility by architect Raphael Viñoly includes the 2,500-seat, cello-shaped Verizon Hall; the more intimate 650-seat Perelman Theater; a café and restaurant; a gift shop; a rooftop terrace; and a public plaza. Together, with the venerable Academy of Music, it makes up the Regional Performing Arts Center. Making their home at the Kimmel are the Philadelphia Orchestra, Philadanco, Philadelphia Chamber Music Society, Concerto Soloists Chamber Orchestra, and American Theater Arts for Youth. Free performances are given on Wednesdays, Saturdays, and Sundays in the center's Commonwealth Plaza; check Web site or call for schedule. ✉ *Broad and Spruce Sts., Avenue of the Arts* ☎ *215/790–5800 or 215/893–1999* 🌐 *www.kimmelcenter.org* 🎟 *Free* ⏲ *Daily 10–6, and evenings when there are performances; tours Tues.–Sun. at 1.*

⓰ **Library Company of Philadelphia.** Founded in 1731, this is one of the oldest cultural institutions in the United States and the only major Colonial American library that has survived virtually intact, despite having moved from building to building. You can stop by and read the rare books, although nothing circulates. Ben Franklin and his Junto, a group of people who read and then discussed philosophical and political issues, started the Library Company; they also founded the American Philosophical Society. From 1774 to 1800 it functioned as the de facto Library of Congress, and until the late 19th century it was the city library. Ten signers of the Declaration of Independence were members, among them Robert Morris, Benjamin Rush, and Thomas McKean. The 500,000-volume collection includes 200,000 rare books. Among the first editions—many acquired when they were first published—are Herman Melville's *Moby Dick* and Walt Whitman's *Leaves of Grass*. The library is particularly rich in Americana up to 1880, black history to 1915, the history of science, and women's history. Changing exhibits showcase the library's holdings. ✉ *1314 Locust St., Washington Square West* ☎ *215/546–3181* 🌐 *www.librarycompany.org* 🎟 *Free* ⏲ *Weekdays 9–4:45.*

⓯ **Park Hyatt Philadelphia at the Bellevue.** Though its name has been changed many times, this building will always be "the Bellevue" to Philadelphians. The hotel has had an important role in city life, much like the heroine of a long-running soap opera. The epitome of the opulent hotels characteristic of the early 1900s, the Bellevue Stratford was the city's leading hotel for decades. It closed in 1976 after the first outbreak of Legionnaires' disease, which spread through the building's air-conditioning system during an American Legion convention. Reopened as the Fairmont several years later, the hotel failed to regain its luster and closed again in 1986. When renovations were completed in 1989, this magnificent building debuted as home to a number of upscale shops (the Shops at the Bellevue), restaurants, and a food court, as well as the luxurious Hotel Atop the Bellevue. Although the hotel has been renamed, its character seems to have remained the same. ✉ *Broad and Walnut Sts., Avenue of the Arts* ☎ *215/893–1776* 🌐 *www.hyatt.com.*

need a break?

For a most civilized break from touring, enter the luxurious world of the Ritz-Carlton's soaring **Rotunda** (✉ 10 S. Broad St., Avenue of the Arts ☎ 215/735–7700). Here, surrounded by white marble columns and soothed with live music from a piano or harp, you can relax on an overstuffed sofa and enjoy a cool drink, afternoon tea, or a cocktail.

9 Fodor's Choice ★ **Rittenhouse Square.** Once grazing ground for cows and sheep, Philadelphia's most elegant square is reminiscent of a Parisian park. One of William Penn's original five city squares, the park was named in 1825 to honor David Rittenhouse, 18th-century astronomer, clock maker, and the first director of the United States Mint. Many of Philadelphia's movers, shakers, and celebrities have lived here. Extra paths were made for Dr. William White, a leader in beautifying the square, so he could walk directly from his home to the exclusive Rittenhouse Club across the square and lunch with the likes of Henry James. Until 1950 town houses bordered the square, but they have now been replaced on three sides by swank apartment buildings and hotels. Some great houses remain, including the celebrated former residence of Henry P. McIlhenny (on the southwest corner), once home to one of the world's great art collections, now on view at the Philadelphia Museum of Art. If you want to join the office workers who have lunch-hour picnics in the park, you'll find scores of restaurants and sandwich shops along Walnut, Sansom, and Chestnut streets east of the square. Or you can dine alfresco at one of several upscale open-air cafés across from the square on 18th Street between Locust and Walnut. The term "Rittenhouse Row" describes the greater Rittenhouse Square area, bordered by Pine, Market, 21st, and Broad streets. ✉ *Walnut St. between 18th and 19th Sts., Rittenhouse Square* 🌐 *www.phila.gov/fairpark/squares/rittenhouse.html.*

need a break?

A block north of Rittenhouse Square is **Pronto** (✉ 103 S. 18th St., Rittenhouse Square ☎ 215/564–2772), which features a fantastic selection of prepared foods, salads, and sandwiches, perfect for a quick lunch or snack. You'll smell the mouthwatering aroma down the block. It's take-out only, but claim a bench in nearby Rittenhouse Square for the best alfresco seat in town.

★ 11 **Rosenbach Museum and Library.** This 1863 three-floor town house, and an adjoining building, both renovated in 2003, are filled with Persian rugs and 18th-century British, French, and American antiques (plus an entire living room that once belonged to poet Marianne Moore), but the real treasures are the artworks, books, and manuscripts here. Amassed by Philadelphia collectors Philip H. and A. S. W. Rosenbach, the collection includes paintings by Canaletto, Sully, and Lawrence; drawings by Daumier, Fragonard, and Blake; book illustrations ranging from medieval illuminations to the works of Maurice Sendak, author of *Where the Wild Things Are;* the only known copy of the first edition of Benjamin Franklin's *Poor Richard's Almanack;* and the library's most famous treasure—the original manuscript of James Joyce's *Ulysses*. The Rosenbach celebrates "Bloomsday" on June 16 with readings from *Ulysses* by notable Philadelphians. The library has more than 130,000 manuscripts and 30,000 rare books. ✉ *2010 Delancey Pl., Rittenhouse Square* ☎ *215/732–1600* 🌐 *www.rosenbach.org* 🎫 *$8* ⏲ *Tues., Thurs., and Fri. 10–5, Wed. 10–8, weekends 10–5; free Tues. in July–Aug.; guided tour on the hour 11–4; additional tour at 6:30 on Wed.*

THE BENJAMIN FRANKLIN PARKWAY

MUSEUMS & MARVELS

Alive with colorful flowers, flags, and fountains, the Benjamin Franklin Parkway stretches northwest from the John F. Kennedy Plaza to the Kelly (East) and West River drives. This 250-foot-wide boulevard is crowned by the Philadelphia Museum of Art. French architects Jacques Greber and Paul Cret designed the parkway in the 1920s. Today a distinguished assemblage of museums, institutions, hotels, and apartment buildings line the road, competing with each other in grandeur.

Here you'll find the Free Library of Philadelphia and the Family Court, housed in buildings whose designs are copied from the palaces on Paris's Place de la Concorde. A newer addition is the Four Seasons Hotel, though its dignified design has made it look like a local institution since the day it opened. A grand processional path, the parkway occasionally lets down its hair as the route for city parades and the site of many festivals and events, including the Thanksgiving and Columbus Day parades and the First Union U.S. Pro Cycling championship.

Numbers in the text correspond to numbers in the margin and on the Center City and Along the Parkway map.

a good walk

Begin at John F. Kennedy Plaza, on the west side of City Hall, site of the LOVE sculpture. If you'd prefer not to walk the length of the Benjamin Franklin Parkway, you could pick up one of Philadelphia Trolley Works's trolley buses here; the 90-minute narrated tour of the city includes stops at the parkway museums. From the plaza walk northwest on the parkway about four blocks to **Logan Circle** 18 ⚑ and its lovely fountain sculpture. Next visit the Italian Renaissance–style **Cathedral of Saints Peter and Paul** 19, at 18th Street.

Walking counterclockwise around Logan Circle, you'll see twin marble Greek Revival buildings off to your right. The nearer of the two is the city's Family Court; the other is the **Free Library of Philadelphia** ⑳. Cross Logan Circle to see the dinosaur exhibition and more at the **Academy of Natural Sciences** ㉑. From the academy walk west on Race Street to 20th Street and tour the hands-on exhibits at the **Franklin Institute Science Museum** ㉒. If it's a warm day, head outside to the **Wachovia Science Park,** a play-and-learn area just behind the museum on 21st Street. If you have children under the age of seven, don't miss the interactive displays at the **Please Touch Museum** ㉓, a half block south on 21st Street. If your kids are older and if you and they appreciate the macabre, it's worth walking a few blocks south to see the Mütter Museum's collection of skulls and specimens.

Head back to the north side of the parkway and walk northwest. On your right is the Youth Study Center (a detention center for juvenile offenders) with two striking tableaux depicting families. At the next corner, guarded by a bronze cast of the famous sculpture *The Thinker,* is the **Rodin Museum** ㉔. Just ahead, atop Faire Mount, the plateau at the end of Franklin Parkway, is the **Philadelphia Museum of Art** ㉕, with its world-class collections. Before you see the beauty at the art museum, you could choose to tour the "beast." Half a mile north at 22nd Street and Fairmount Avenue is Eastern State Penitentiary, a former prison that is now an offbeat attraction. From there, following Fairmount Avenue west toward the higher numbers is the quickest route back to the art museum.

TIMING The parkway is at its most colorful in spring, when the trees and flowers are in bloom. Leave early in the morning and plan to spend an entire day—and possibly the evening—in this area. On Wednesday you can cap off your day of culture with dinner and entertainment at the Philadelphia Museum of Art. If it's a Friday or Saturday, save the Franklin Institute for midafternoon, head out to dinner in the neighborhood, and return for a film on the giant screen of the Omniverse Theater, followed by a rock-and-roll laser light show in Fels Planetarium (the last show is at midnight). How much time you spend at each museum depends on your interests; be aware that the art museum and the Rodin Museum are closed on Monday.

What to See

㉑ **The Academy of Natural Sciences.** The dioramas of animals from around the world displayed in their natural habitats give this natural history museum an old-fashioned charm. The most popular attraction is Dinosaur Hall, with reconstructed skeletons of a Tyrannosaurus rex and the latest paleontological find—the giganotosaurus, the biggest meat-eating dinosaur ever discovered. Dinosaur Hall features fossils dating as far back as 160 million years ago. Other draws are Living Downstream, an interactive watershed model with multimedia kiosks for visitors to engage in a role-playing game called Tough Choices; The Big Dig, where you can dig for real fossils; and the live butterflies that flutter all around you in a tropical rain forest setting. Outside-In is an interactive children's nature museum where kids can crawl through a log, investigate a real bee hive, and touch a tarantula. If you're keeping track of Philadelphia firsts, note that the academy, the oldest science research institution in the Western Hemisphere and a world leader in the fields of natural science research, education, and exhibition, was founded in 1812; the present building dates from 1868. ✉ *19th St. and Benjamin Franklin Pkwy., Logan Circle* ☎ *215/299–1000* 🌐 *www.acnatsci.org* 🎫 *$9* ⏲ *Weekdays 10–4:30, weekends 10–5.*

19 **Cathedral of Saints Peter and Paul.** The basilica of the archdiocese of Philadelphia is the spiritual center for the Philadelphia area's 1.4 million Roman Catholics. Topped by a huge copper dome, it was built between 1846 and 1864 in the Italian Renaissance style. Many of the interior decorations were done by Constantino Brumidi, who painted the dome of the U.S. Capitol. Six Philadelphia bishops and archbishops are buried beneath the altar. ✉ *18th and Race Sts., Logan Circle* ☎ *215/561–1313* 🌐 *www.archdiocese-phl.org/parishes/7000.htm* 🎫 *Free* ⏲ *Daily 7–5. Masses weekdays 7:30, 12:05, 12:35; Sat. 5:15; Sun. 8:30, 10:30, 12:15, 5.*

off the beaten path

EASTERN STATE PENITENTIARY HISTORIC SITE – Designed by John Haviland and built in 1829, Eastern State was at the time the most expensive building in America; it influenced penal design around the world and was the model for some 300 prisons from China to South America. Before it closed in 1971, the prison was home to Al Capone, Willie Sutton, and Pep the Dog, who killed the cat that belonged to a governor's wife. The audio tour of this stabilized ruin (included with admission) leads to 25 stops, including Capone's former cell, and features narration by former guards and inmates—punctuated by cell doors slamming and other sounds of prison life. Guided tours on specific topics are also given; check the Web site or call ahead for a schedule. The penitentiary, just a half mile north of the Rodin Museum, hosts changing art exhibitions, haunted house tours around Halloween, and a Bastille Day celebration the Sunday before July 14, with a reenactment of the storming of the Bastille. ✉ *22nd St. and Fairmount Ave., Fairmount* ☎ *215/236–3300* 🌐 *www.easternstate.org* 🎫 *$9* ⏲ *Apr.–Nov., Wed.–Sun. 10–5.*

need a break?

Across the street from the brooding Eastern State Penitentiary is a more welcoming spot—**Mugshots Coffeehouse and JuiceBar** (✉ 21st St. and Fairmount Ave., Fairmount ☎ 267/514–7145), a neighborhood hangout offering organic, fair trade coffee, fresh juices and smoothies, as well as an all-day chalkboard menu of bagel-and-egg sandwiches, soups, mini-frittata, veggie wraps and even good old reliable peanut butter and jelly.

★ 22 **Franklin Institute Science Museum.** Founded more than 175 years ago to honor Benjamin Franklin, the institute is a science museum that is as clever as its namesake, thanks to an abundance of dazzling hands-on exhibits. To make the best use of your time, study the floor plan before you begin exploring. You can sit in the cockpit of a T-33 jet trainer, trace

BEN FRANKLIN'S SPARK

UNLIKE THE BRONZE STATUE *of William Penn perched atop City Hall, the marble likeness of Benjamin Franklin is within the* ***Franklin Institute Science Museum.*** *Perhaps that's as it should be: noble-born Penn above the people and common-born Franklin sitting more democratically among them.*

Franklin (1706–1790) was anything but a common man. In fact, biographer Walter Isaacson called him "the most accomplished American of his age." Franklin's insatiable curiosity, combined with his ability to solve problems in his own life, inspired his invention of bifocals, an odometer to measure postal routes, a "long arm" to reach books high on his shelves, and a flexible urinary catheter for his brother who was suffering with kidney stones. His great intellect inspired his launching of the American Philosophical Society, the oldest learned society in America. He was the only "Founding Father" who shaped and signed all of the nation's founding documents, including the Declaration of Independence, the Constitution, and treaties with France and England. He was a citizen of the world—a representative in the Pennsylvania General Assembly, a minister to France.

It's fortunate for Philadelphians that Franklin spent so many of his 84 years here. That might have been an act of fate or early recognition that "time is money," as he wrote in Advice to a Young Tradesman *in 1748. Born in Boston in 1706, Franklin ran away from home and the oppression of his job as a printer's apprentice at his brother's shop. When he couldn't find work in New York, he didn't waste time; he moved on to Philadelphia. Within 10 years Franklin had opened his own printing office. His* Pennsylvania Gazette *was the most successful newspaper in the Colonies; his humor propelled his* Poor Richard: An Almanack *to best-seller status in the Colonies. In Franklin's Print Shop in the* ***Franklin Court*** *complex, site of Ben's first permanent home in Philadelphia, you can get a letter hand-stamped with a B. Free Franklin cancellation.*

Franklin had time and passion for civic duties. As Postmaster, he set up the city's postal system. He founded the city's first volunteer fire company and ***Library Company of Philadelphia,*** *its first subscription library. After his famous kite experiment, he opened the first fire insurance company, the* ***Philadelphia Contributionship for the Insurance of Houses from Loss by Fire.*** *He proposed the idea for the* ***University of Pennsylvania*** *and personally raised money to finance* ***Pennsylvania Hospital,*** *the nation's first.*

Though Franklin spent the majority of his later years in Europe, he was laid to rest in the city that he called home—alongside his wife, Deborah, and one of his sons, Francis—in the ***Christ Church Burial Ground.***

January 17, 2006, marks the 300th birthday of Philadelphia's most beloved historical figure. The city that has honored him with a parkway, a bridge, a football stadium, a science museum, and a mall has planned a yearlong celebration that includes debates, theater performances, parades and other special events (🌐 www.benfranklin300.org). An international exhibit, "Benjamin Franklin: In Search of a Better World" will debut in Philadelphia at the ***National Constitution Center*** *on December 15, 2005 and run until April 30, 2006 before traveling through the United States and to Paris.*

the route of a corpuscle through the world's largest artificial heart (15,000 times life size), and ride to nowhere on a 350-ton Baldwin steam locomotive. The many exhibits cover energy, motion, sound, physics, astronomy, aviation, ships, mechanics, electricity, time, and other scientific subjects. You'll also find a working weather station, the world's largest pinball machine, and Franklin's famous lightning rod.

The **Franklin Air Show** celebrates powered flight with the Wright Model B Flyer, and the museum's beloved walk-through heart will be the centerpiece of **The Giant Heart: A Healthy Interactive Experience**, an exhibit about bioscience, health and wellness, and health-care technology. **The Sports Challenge** conveys the physics, physiology, and material science behind your favorite sport through such activities as simulating surfing, climbing a rock wall, and comparing your sneaker size to Shaquille O'Neal's size 22s. The **Fels Planetarium**—which has a state-of-the-art aluminum dome, lighting and sound systems, and a related astronomy exhibit, "Space Command"—has shows about the stars, space exploration, comets, and other phenomena. The **Mandell Center** includes the Cyberzone computer lab with 20 computers linked to the Web; Material Matters, a chemistry lesson; and the Tuttleman IMAX Theater, with a 79-foot domed screen and a 56-speaker high-tech sound system; recent movies include *Lewis & Clark: Great Journey West* and *Mystery of the Nile*. One don't-miss: the 30-foot-tall statue of Benjamin Franklin. ✉ *20th St. and Benjamin Franklin Pkwy., Logan Circle* ☎ *215/448–1200, 215/448–1388 laser show hot line* 🌐 *www.fi.edu* 🎫 *Ticket packages $13.75–$18.75* ⏲ *Daily 9:30–5. The Tuttleman Theater remains open until 9 Fri. and Sat.*

20 **Free Library of Philadelphia.** Philadelphia calls its vast public library system the "Fabulous Freebie." Founded in 1891, the central library has more than 1 million volumes. With its grand entrance hall, sweeping marble staircase, 30-foot ceilings, enormous reading rooms with long tables, and spiral staircases leading to balconies, this Greek Revival building looks the way libraries should. With more than 12,000 musical scores, the Edwin S. Fleisher collection is the largest of its kind in the world. Tormented by a tune whose name you can't recall? Hum it to one of the music room's librarians, and he or she will track it down. The department of social science and history has nearly 100,000 charts, maps, and guidebooks. The rare-book room is a beautiful suite housing first editions of Dickens, ancient Sumerian clay tablets, illuminated medieval manuscripts, and more modern manuscripts, including Poe's *Murders in the Rue Morgue* and "The Raven." With 100,000 books for children from preschool to eighth grade, the children's department houses the city's largest collection of children's books in a made-for-kids setting. ✉ *19th St. and Benjamin Franklin Pkwy., Logan Circle* ☎ *215/686–5322* 🌐 *www.library.phila.gov* 🎫 *Free* ⏲ *Mon.–Wed. 9–9, Thurs.–Sat. 9–5, Sun. 1–5 (closed Sun. late May–Sept.); tours of rare book room weekdays at 11.*

18 **Logan Circle.** One of William Penn's five squares, Logan Circle was originally a burying ground and the site of a public execution by hanging in 1823. It found a fate better than death, though. In 1825 the square was named for James Logan, Penn's secretary; it later became a circle and is

now one of the city's gems. The focal point of Logan Circle is the **Swann Fountain** of 1920, designed by Alexander Stirling Calder, son of Alexander Milne Calder, who created the William Penn statue atop City Hall. You'll find many works by a third generation of the family, noted modern sculptor Alexander Calder, the mobile- and stabile-maker, in the nearby **Philadelphia Museum of Art.** The main figures in the fountain symbolize Philadelphia's three leading waterways: the Delaware and Schuylkill rivers and Wissahickon Creek. Around Logan Circle are some examples of Philadelphia's magnificent collection of outdoor art, including *General Galusha Pennypacker,* the Shakespeare Memorial (*Hamlet and the Fool,* by Alexander Stirling Calder), and *Jesus Breaking Bread.*

off the beaten path

MÜTTER MUSEUM – Skulls, antique microscopes, and a cancerous tumor removed from President Grover Cleveland's mouth in 1893 form just part of the unusual medical collection in the Mütter Museum, in the College of Physicians of Philadelphia, a few blocks south of the Please Touch Museum. The museum has hundreds of anatomical and pathological specimens, medical instruments, and organs removed from patients, including a piece of John Wilkes Booth's neck tissue. The collection contains 139 skulls; items that belonged to Marie Curie, Louis Pasteur, and Joseph Lister; and a 7-foot, 6-inch skeleton, the tallest on public exhibition in the United States. ✉ *19 S. 22nd St., Rittenhouse Square* ☎ *215/563–3737* 🌐 *www.collphyphil.org* 🎟 *$10* ⏲ *Daily 10–5.*

25 **Philadelphia Museum of Art.** The city's premier cultural attraction is one of the country's leading museums. Actually, one of the greatest treasures of the museum is the building itself. Constructed in 1928 of Minnesota dolomite, it's modeled after ancient Greek temples but on a grander scale. The museum was designed by Julian Francis Abele, the first African-American to graduate from the University of Pennsylvania School of Architecture. You can enter the museum from the front or the rear; choose the front, and you can run up the 99 steps made famous in the movie *Rocky* (Rocky only ran up 72).

Fodor's Choice ★

Once inside, you'll see the grand staircase and Saint-Gaudens's statue of *Diana;* she formerly graced New York's old Madison Square Garden. The museum has several outstanding permanent collections: the John G. Johnson Collection covers Western art from the Renaissance to the 19th century; the Arensberg and A. E. Gallatin collections contain modern and contemporary works by artists such as Brancusi, Braque, Matisse, and Picasso. Famous paintings in these collections include Van Eyck's *St. Francis Receiving the Stigmata,* Rubens's *Prometheus Bound,* Benjamin West's *Benjamin Franklin Drawing Electricity from the Sky,* van Gogh's *Sunflowers,* Cézanne's *The Large Bathers,* and Picasso's *Three Musicians.* Two important recent (2002) acquisitions are an 18th century glazed stoneware Korean dragon jar from the Choson Dynasty and *Taboo,* a 1963 painting by American Jacob Lawrence.

The enigmatic Marcel Duchamp, whose varied creations influenced many 20th-century artists, is a specialty of the house; the museum has the world's most extensive collection of his works, including the world-famous *Nude Descending a Staircase* and *The Bride Stripped Bare by Her Bachelors, Even.* Among the American art worth seeking out is a fine selection of the works by 19th-century Philadelphia artist Thomas Eakins, including *The Concert Singer* and some notable portraits. The most spectacular "objects" in the museum are entire structures and great rooms moved lock, stock, and barrel from around the world: a 12th-century French cloister, a 16th-century Indian temple hall, a 16th-century Japanese Buddhist temple, a 17th-century Chinese palace hall, and a Japanese ceremonial teahouse. Among the other collections are costumes, Early American furniture, and Amish and Shaker crafts. An unusual touch—and one that children especially like—is the Kienbusch Collection of Arms and Armor. At this writing, a 100,000-square-foot annex, the Ruth and Raymond G. Perelman Building, is scheduled in 2007 to open across the street from the museum in the former Reliance Standard Life Insurance building. Designed by the same architect as the museum and built at the same time, the renovated facility will offer rotating works from the museum's permanent collection in photography, costume, and contemporary design, as well as classrooms and a library.

Friday evenings feature live jazz performances in the Great Hall. The museum has a fine restaurant and a surprisingly good cafeteria. ✉ *26th St. and Benjamin Franklin Pkwy., Fairmount* ☎ *215/763–8100, 215/684–7500 24-hr taped message* 🌐 *www.philamuseum.org* 🎟 *$10, Sun. pay what you wish* ⏲ *Tues. and Thurs.–Sun. 10–5, Wed. and Fri. 10–8:45.*

23 **Please Touch Museum.** Philadelphia's children's museum, one of the country's best, is designed for youngsters ages one to seven. Highlights include Alice's Adventures in Wonderland, a 2,300-square-foot re-creation of Wonderland that encourages children to develop problem-solving and literacy skills; Sendak, an interactive exhibit of oversize settings and creatures from books by celebrated author-illustrator Maurice Sendak; and SuperMarket Science, with large shopping and kitchen play settings and a lab where science and math-related demonstrations are held. The museum also has a child-size television studio, an exhibit on transportation, a farm-theme area for toddlers, and interactive theater shows. At this writing, the museum is scheduled to move to Fairmount Park in 2007. The new $72 million, 135,000-square-foot facility incorporates Memorial Hall, the only remaining building from the 1876 Centennial Exposition. ✉ *210 N. 21st St., Logan Circle* ☎ *215/963–0667* 🌐 *www.pleasetouchmuseum.org* 🎟 *$9.95* ⏲ *Daily, 9–4:30.*

★ 24 **Rodin Museum.** This jewel of a museum holds the best collection outside France of the work of sculptor Auguste Rodin (1840–1917). You'll pass through Rodin's *Gates of Hell*—a 21-foot-high sculpture with more than 100 human and animal figures—into an exhibition hall where the sculptor's masterworks are made even more striking by the use of light and shadow. Here are the French master's *The Kiss, The Burghers of Calais,* and *Eternal Springtime.* A small room is devoted to one of Rodin's most famous sitters, the French novelist Balzac. Photographs by Edward Steichen showing Rodin at work round out the collection. The museum occupies a 20th-century building designed by

French architects Jacques Greber and Paul Cret. ✉ *22nd St. and Benjamin Franklin Pkwy., Fairmount* ☎ *215/763–8100* 🌐 *www.rodinmuseum.org* *$3 donation requested* ⏲ *Tues.–Sun. 10–5.*

Wachovia Science Park. A cooperative venture between the Franklin Institute Science Museum and the Please Touch Museum, the park presents interactive displays in an outdoor setting—which means children get a chance to run around and play while they learn. Swings demonstrate the laws of gravity and energy, and golf illustrates physics in motion. ✉ *21st St. between Winter and Race Sts., Logan Circle* *Free with admission to the Franklin Institute or the Please Touch Museum* ⏲ *May–Sept., daily 10–3.*

FAIRMOUNT PARK

THE EMERALD CITY

Stretching from the edge of downtown to the city's northwest corner, Fairmount Park is the largest landscaped city park in the world. With more than 8,500 acres and 2 million trees (someone claims to have counted), the park winds along the banks of the Schuylkill River—which divides it into west and east sections—and through parts of the city. Quite a few city dwellers consider the park their backyard. On weekends the 4-mi stretch along Kelly Drive is crowded with joggers, bicycling moms and dads with children strapped into kiddie seats atop the back wheel, hand-holding senior citizens out for some fresh air, collegiate crew teams sculling along the river, and budding artists trying to capture the sylvan magic just as Thomas Eakins once did.

Fairmount Park encompasses natural areas—woodlands, meadows, rolling hills, two scenic waterways, and a forested 5½-mi gorge. It also contains tennis courts, ball fields, playgrounds, trails, exercise courses, several celebrated cultural institutions, and some historic Early American country houses that are operated by the Philadelphia Museum of Art and open to visitors. Philadelphia has more works of outdoor art than any other city in North America, and more than 200 of these works—including statues by Frederic Remington, Jacques Lipchitz, and Auguste Rodin—are scattered throughout Fairmount Park. Some sections of the park that border depressed urban neighborhoods are neglected, but it's better maintained along the Schuylkill.

The park was established in 1812 when the city purchased 5 acres behind Faire Mount, the hill upon which the Philadelphia Museum of Art now stands, for waterworks and public gardens. Through private bequests and public purchases (which continue today), it grew to its present size and stature.

The following tour highlights many of the park's treasures. You can tour by car (get a good city map), starting near the Philadelphia Museum of Art. Signs help point the way, and the historic houses have free parking. Before you set out, call **Park House Information** (☎ 215/684–7926 🌐 www.phila.gov/fairpark), to find out which historic houses are open

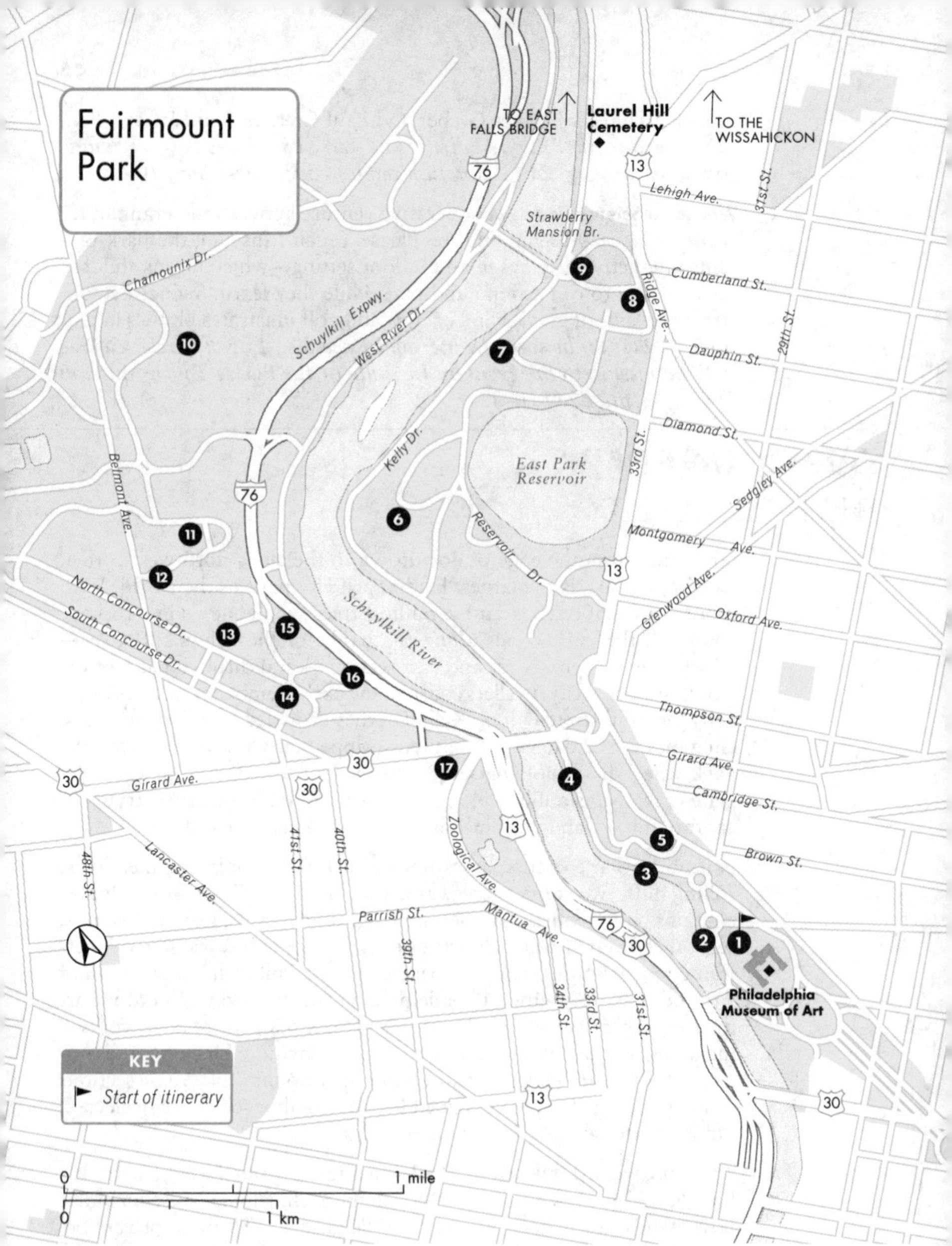

- Belmont Plateau **10**
- Boathouse Row **3**
- Cedar Grove **15**
- Ellen Phillips Samuel Memorial Sculpture Garden **4**
- Faire Mount **1**
- Fairmount Waterworks **2**
- Horticulture Center **11**
- Japanese House **12**
- Laurel Hill **7**
- Lemon Hill **5**
- Memorial Hall **13**
- Mt. Pleasant **6**
- Philadelphia Zoo **17**
- Smith Civil War Memorial **14**
- Strawberry Mansion **9**
- Sweetbriar **16**
- Woodford **8**

that day and what special events are planned. Another option is to take the narrated tour given by Philadelphia Trolley Works (board it at the Philadelphia Museum of Art or at John F. Kennedy Plaza, at 16th Street and John F. Kennedy Boulevard). The trolley bus visits many of these sites, and you can get on and off all day for $10.

Numbers in the text correspond to numbers in the margin and on the Fairmount Park map.

a good drive

Your visit can start where the park began, at **Faire Mount** 1 . If it's a nice day, you could begin this outing with a short walk before you set off by car. Park behind the art museum and walk down the stairs. To your right is the museum's Azalea Garden, designed in the English romantic style. Straight ahead, overlooking the Schuylkill River, is the **Fairmount Waterworks** 2, an elegant group of Greek Revival buildings. A few steps north of the Waterworks you'll see the Victorian structures of **Boathouse Row** 3; watch for rowers on the river here, too. Walking north along Kelly Drive, alongside the river, you soon reach the **Ellen Phillips Samuel Memorial Sculpture Garden** 4, with works by 16 artists.

Now's the time to walk back to your car for a driving tour of East Fairmount Park. Follow Kelly Drive to the end of Boathouse Row; turn right up the hill to a Federal-style country house, **Lemon Hill** 5. Head back to Kelly Drive, turn right, pass through the rock archway, and turn right again at the equestrian statue of Ulysses S. Grant. The first left takes you to **Mt. Pleasant** 6, a Georgian mansion. Continue along the road that runs to the right of the house (as you face it) past Rockland, a handsome Federal house that's currently closed. At the dead end turn left onto Reservoir Drive. You'll pass the redbrick Georgian-style Ormiston, also closed. Take the next left, Randolph Drive, to another Georgian house, **Laurel Hill** 7, on Edgely Drive, which becomes Dauphin Street. Just about 10 feet before reaching 33rd Street, turn left on Strawberry Mansion Drive, and you're at **Woodford** 8, which has an interesting collection of household goods. A quarter mile northwest of Woodford stands the house that gave its name to the nearby section of Philadelphia, **Strawberry Mansion** 9. It has furniture from three periods of its history.

If you're a fan of historic cemeteries, you can visit Laurel Hill Cemetery before you cross the river to West Fairmount Park. Drive back down the driveway of Strawberry Mansion, turn left at the stop sign, and follow the narrow road as it winds right to the light. Turn left onto Ridge Avenue and follow it to the entrance gate, which sits between eight Greek columns. To skip the cemetery and continue your tour, proceed down the Strawberry Mansion driveway to the stop sign, turn left, and follow the road as it loops down and around to the Strawberry Mansion Bridge. Cross the river and follow the road; when it splits, stay left. You'll come to Chamounix Drive, a long straightaway. Turn left and then left again on Belmont Mansion Drive for a fine view from **Belmont Plateau** 10. Follow Belmont Mansion Drive down the hill. Where it forks, stay to the left, cross Montgomery Drive, and bear left to reach the **Horticulture Center** 11 with its greenhouse and garden. Loop all the way around the Horticulture Center to visit the serene **Japanese House** 12 and its waterfall and gardens.

Drive back around the Horticulture Center and continue through the gates to Montgomery Drive. Turn left and then left again at the first light (Belmont Avenue). Turn left again on North Concourse Drive. On your left is **Memorial Hall** 13, a building from the 1876 Centennial Exposition that will become the new home of the Please Touch Museum in spring 2007. The two towers just ahead are part of the **Smith Civil War Memorial** 14. Turn left just past them to see furniture from over the centuries at **Cedar Grove** 15. Just south of Cedar Grove, atop a hill sloping down to the Schuylkill, is a Federal mansion, **Sweetbriar** 16. Continue past the house, make the first left, and turn left again at the stop sign onto Lansdowne Drive. Follow the signs straight ahead to the **Philadelphia Zoo** 17. If you enjoy hiking, you could continue on to the Wissahickon, in the northwest section of Fairmount Park.

TIMING Any time but winter is a fine time to explore the great outdoors in Fairmount Park. In spring the cherry blossoms are lovely; in fall the changing leaves blaze with color. In winter you can explore the indoors, on Christmas tours of the historic houses. Hikers, bikers, and joggers will enjoy a recreational trail that connects Bartram's Garden in Southwest Philadelphia with Valley Forge National Historical Park west of the city. If you leave the driving to the Philadelphia Trolley Works, your narrated tour will take just 40 minutes. If you drive, after you've explored Kelly Drive on foot, you'll need about two hours. Add another 20–30 minutes for each historic house you tour. Because each property keeps its own quirky schedule, it's hard to choose one day that's best for seeing the interiors, although a summer weekend is your best bet. Animal lovers can spend half a day at the Philadelphia Zoo.

What to See

10 **Belmont Plateau.** Literally the high point of your park tour, Belmont Plateau has a view from 243 feet above river level. In front of you lie the park, the Schuylkill River winding down to the Philadelphia Museum of Art, and—4 mi away—the Philadelphia skyline. ✉ *Belmont Mansion Dr., W. Fairmount Park, Fairmount Park.*

3 **Boathouse Row.** These architecturally varied 19th-century buildings—in Victorian Gothic, Gothic Revival, and Italianate styles—are home to the rowing clubs that make up the "Schuylkill Navy," an association of boating clubs organized in 1858. The view of the boathouses from the west side of the river is splendid—especially at night, when they're outlined with hundreds of small lights. The row's newest addition, Lloyd Hall, has a gymnasium, bicycle and skate rentals in season, and a two-story café. ✉ *Kelly Dr., E. Fairmount Park, Fairmount Park.*

Fodor's Choice ★

15 **Cedar Grove.** Five styles of furniture—Jacobean, William and Mary, Queen Anne, Chippendale, and Federal—reflect the accumulations of five generations of the Paschall-Morris family. The house stood in Frankford, in northeastern Philadelphia, for 180 years before being moved to this location in 1927. ✉ *Lansdowne Dr. off N. Concourse Dr., W. Fairmount Park, Fairmount Park* ☎ *215/235–7469* 🌐 *www.philamuseum.org/collections/parkhouse* 🎫 *$3* ⏲ *Tues.–Sun. 10–5.*

4 **Ellen Phillips Samuel Memorial Sculpture Garden.** Bronze and granite sculptures by 16 artists stand in a series of tableaux and groupings on riverside terraces. Portraying American themes and traits, they include *The Quaker,* by Harry Rosen; *Birth of a Nation,* by Henry Kreis; and *Spirit of Enterprise,* by Jacques Lipchitz. ✉ *Kelly Dr., E. Fairmount Park, Fairmount Park.*

1 **Faire Mount.** This is now the site of the Philadelphia Museum of Art. In 1812 a reservoir was built here to distribute water throughout the city.

★ 2 **Fairmount Waterworks.** Designed by Frederick Graff, this National Historic Engineering Landmark built in 1815 was the first steam-pumping station of its kind in the country. The notable assemblage of Greek Revival buildings—one of the city's most beautiful sights—has undergone a $29-million renovation. The revamped Fairmount Waterworks, located just behind the Philadelphia Museum of Art, has an interpretive center with original machinery and modern exhibits, an art gallery, and an information center. On weekends there's an outdoor marketplace with crafts, flowers, souvenirs, and pastries; musicians, jugglers, and mimes provide free entertainment on the deck of the New Mill House. A restaurant was scheduled to open in late 2005 ✉ *Waterworks Dr., off Kelly Dr., Fairmount Park* ☎ *215/334–3472* 🌐 *www.fairmountwaterworks.org* 🎫 *Free* ⏲ *Daily, sunrise–sunset for site; Tues.–Sat. 10–5, Sun. 1–5 interpretive center.*

11 **Horticulture Center.** On the Horticulture Center's 27 wooded acres are a butterfly garden, a greenhouse where plants and flowers used on city property are grown, and a pavilion in the trees for bird-watching from the woodland canopy. Don't miss the whimsical *Seaweed Girl* fountain in the display house. The center stands on the site of the 1876 Centennial Exposition's Horticultural Hall. ✉ *N. Horticultural Dr., W. Fairmount Park, Fairmount Park* ☎ *215/685–0096* 🎫 *Free* ⏲ *Visitor center and greenhouses, daily 9–3; grounds, July–Sept., 9–6, Oct.–June, 9–5.*

12 **Japanese House.** This reconstructed 16th-century samurai's dwelling, built in Japan, was exhibited temporarily at the Museum of Modern Art in New York, then reassembled here in 1958. The architectural setting and the waterfall, gardens, Japanese trees, and pond make a serene contrast to the busy city. The house is called Shofu-So, which means "pine breeze villa," and has a roof made of the bark of hinoki, a cypress that grows only in the mountains of Japan. Call ahead or check Web site to see if a traditional tea ceremony is scheduled. ✉ *Lansdowne Dr. east of Belmont Ave., W. Fairmount Park, Fairmount Park* ☎ *215/878–5097* 🌐 *www.shofuso.com* 🎫 *$4* ⏲ *May–Oct., Tues.–Fri. 10–4, weekends 11–5.*

7 **Laurel Hill.** Built around 1767, this Georgian house on a laurel-covered hill overlooking the Schuylkill River once belonged to Dr. Philip Syng Physick (also owner of Society Hill's Physick House). On some Sunday evenings during the summer, Women for Greater Philadelphia sponsors candlelight chamber music concerts here. ✉ *E. Edgely Dr., E. Fairmount Park, Fairmount Park* ☎ *215/235–1776* 🌐 *www.philamuseum.org/collections/parkhouse* 🎫 *$3* ⏲ *July–Dec., Tues.–Sat., 10–4, Sun. noon–4.*

off the beaten path

LAUREL HILL CEMETERY – John Notman, architect of the Athenaeum and many other noted local buildings, designed Laurel Hill in 1836. The cemetery is an important example of an early rural burial ground and the first cemetery in America designed by an architect. Its rolling hills overlooking the Schuylkill River, its rare trees, and its monuments and mausoleums sculpted by greats such as Notman, Alexander Milne Calder, Alexander Stirling Calder, William Strickland, and Thomas U. Walter made it a popular picnic spot in the 19th century; today it's a great place for a stroll. Those buried in this 99-acre necropolis include prominent Philadelphians and Declaration of Independence signers. Burials still take place here. ✉ *3822 Ridge Ave., Fairmount Park* ☎ *215/228–8200, 215/228–8817 tours through the Friends of Laurel Hill Cemetery* 🌐 *www.forever-care.com* ☞ *Walking tour brochure at office for $5* ⏲ *Weekdays 8–4, Sat. 9:30–1:30.*

5 **Lemon Hill.** An impressive example of a Federal-style country house, Lemon Hill was built in 1800 on a 350-acre farm. Its most distinctive features are oval parlors with concave doors and the entrance hall's checkerboard floor of Valley Forge marble. ✉ *Poplar Dr., E. Fairmount Park, Fairmount Park* ☎ *215/232–4337* 🌐 *www.philamuseum.org/collections/parkhouse* 🎫 *$3* ⏲ *Apr.–mid-Dec., Wed.–Sun. 10–4.*

13 **Memorial Hall.** Architect Hermann J. Schwarzmann's grand stone building with a glass dome and Palladian windows served as an art museum during the Philadelphia Centennial Exposition, a celebration of the nation's 100th birthday. Close to 10 million people attended the exposition to see the novel exhibits of machinery, produce, and art sent by foreign countries. The hall, a notable example of beaux arts architecture, influenced the design of many American and European museums and government buildings. It is the only major building remaining from the event. At this writing, the building was slated to begin extensive renovations to become the new home of the Please Touch Museum, which is scheduled to open in late spring 2007. ✉ *N. Concourse Dr., W. Fairmount Park, Fairmount Park* ☎ *215/685–0000* ⏲ *Closed to the public.*

6 **Mt. Pleasant.** Built in 1761 by John Macpherson, a Scottish sea captain, Mt. Pleasant is one of the finest examples of Georgian architecture in the country. The historically accurate furnishings are culled from the Philadelphia Museum of Art's collection of Philadelphia Chippendale furniture. According to legend, Revolutionary War traitor Benedict Arnold purchased this house as an engagement gift for Peggy Shippen, but he was banished before the deal was signed. ✉ *Mt. Pleasant Dr., E. Fairmount Park, Fairmount Park* ☎ *215/235–7469* 🌐 *www.philamuseum.org/collections/parkhouse* 🎫 *$3* ⏲ *Tues.–Sun. 10–5.*

17 **Philadelphia Zoo.** Chartered in 1859 and opened in 1874, America's first zoo is home to more than 2,000 animals representing six continents. It's small and well landscaped enough to feel pleasantly intimate, and the naturalistic habitats allow you to get close enough to hear the animals breathe. At each exhibit an old-fashioned Talking Storybook provides narration when activated by an elephant-shape key. The Amphibian and Rep-

tile House houses 87 species, from 15-foot-long snakes to frogs the size of a dime. The state-of-the-art 2½-acre Primate Reserve is home to 11 primate species from around the world. Notable attractions include the zoo's "Big Cat Falls," a $20-million naturalistic home to more than a dozen rare white lions, leopards, jaguars, mountain lions, and tigers, scheduled to open in spring 2006; a terrific Bird House; and the African Plains, stomping ground of giraffes and zebras. The TaskyKake Children's Zoo has a bunny "village," with a post office, hospital, and toy store, where kids find out how rabbits communicate and reproduce; two animal "exercise yards" with macaws, porcupines, hedgehogs, and owls; pony rides; and a barnyard animal petting and feeding area. You can get a bird's-eye view of the zoo and Fairmount Park on the Channel 6 Zooballoon, a 30-passenger helium balloon anchored by a high tensile steel cable that "travels" to a height of 400 feet. ✉ *34th St. and Girard Ave., W. Fairmount Park, Fairmount Park* ☎ *215/243–1100* 🌐 *www.phillyzoo.org* 🎫 *Mid-Mar.–Oct., $16.95; Nov.–mid-Mar., $10.95; Zooballoon, $12 additional; $26.95 for general admission and Zooballoon* ⏲ *Feb.–Nov., weekdays 9:30–5, weekends 9:30–6; Dec.–Feb., daily 10–4.*

⓮ **Smith Civil War Memorial.** Built from 1897 to 1912 with funds donated by wealthy foundry owner Richard Smith, the memorial honors Pennsylvania heroes of the Civil War. Among those immortalized in bronze are Generals Meade and Hancock—and Smith himself. At the base of each tower is a curved wall with a bench. If you sit at one end and listen to a person whispering at the other end, you'll understand why they're called the Whispering Benches. Unfortunately, the litter around the site reflects its location near an economically struggling neighborhood. ✉ *N. Concourse Dr., W. Fairmount Park, Fairmount Park.*

❾ **Strawberry Mansion.** The largest mansion in Fairmount Park has furniture from the three main phases of its history: Federal, Regency, and Empire. In the parlor is a collection of rare Tucker porcelain; the attic holds fine antique dolls. ✉ *Near 33rd and Dauphin Sts., E. Fairmount Park, Fairmount Park* ☎ *215/228–8364* 🌐 *www.philamuseum.org/collections/parkhouse* 🎫 *$3* ⏲ *Tues.–Sun. 10–4.*

⓰ **Sweetbriar.** This three-story Federal mansion dating from 1797 was the first year-round residence in what is now Fairmount Park. It was built by Samuel and Jean Breck to escape the yellow fever epidemic that ravaged the city. ✉ *Lansdowne Dr. off N. Concourse Dr., W. Fairmount Park, Fairmount Park* ☎ *215/222–1333* 🌐 *www.philamuseum.org/collections/parkhouse* 🎫 *$3* ⏲ *July–mid-Dec., Wed.–Sun. 10–4.*

off the beaten path

THE WISSAHICKON – Of the Philadelphia areas that William Penn encountered, the Wissahickon has changed the least. In the northwestern section of Fairmount Park, this gorge was carved out by the Wissahickon Creek—5½ mi of towering trees, cliffs, trails, and animals. You can easily visualize the Leni-Lenape who lived here and gave the creek its name. Many inns once stood along the banks of the Wissahickon; only two remain. One is now a police station; the other is the **Valley Green Inn** (✉ Springfield Ave. and Wissahickon Creek, Fairmount Park ☎ 215/247–1730 🌐 www.valleygreeninn.com), built in 1850. It is in one of the loveliest parts of the Wissahickon gorge. You can sit on a bench alongside the creek, look at the stone bridge reflected in the water, and savor the tranquility of this spot.

Forbidden Drive, a dirt-and-gravel pathway along the west side of the creek, is a haunt of joggers, bikers, horseback riders, anglers, and nature lovers. There are foot trails along both sides of the creek and interesting statues along the route. Walking less than ½ mi south of the Valley Green Inn brings you to Devil's Pool; Shakespeare Rock, with a quotation carved on its face; and Hermit's Cave, where German mystic Johannes Kelpius and his followers came in 1694 to await the millennium. A visit to Historic RittenhouseTown, America's first paper mill, requires a 3-mi hike south. To the north of the inn are Indian Rock and a covered bridge that was built around 1855, the last still standing within the boundaries of a major American city.

You'll need a car to get here: to reach Valley Green Inn from downtown, take the Schuylkill Expressway west to the Lincoln Drive–Wissahickon Park exit (Exit 32). Follow Lincoln Drive to Allen's Lane, then turn right. At Germantown Avenue turn left, go about a mile, turn left at Springfield Avenue, and follow it to the end. A map of the Wissahickon showing all the trails and sites can be purchased for $6 at the Valley Green Inn's snack-booth window, open daily in warmer months from 9 to 5, weekends only the rest of the year.

8 **Woodford.** The Naomi Wood collection of antique household goods, including Colonial furniture, unusual clocks, and English delftware, can be seen in this fine Georgian mansion built about 1756. ✉ *Near 33rd and Dauphin Sts., E. Fairmount Park, Fairmount Park* ☎ *215/229–6115* 🌐 *www.philamuseum.org/collections/parkhouse* 🎫 *$3* ⏲ *Tues.–Sun. 10–4.*

SOUTHWARK & SOUTH PHILADELPHIA

STRUTTING SOUTH OF SOUTH

Two of the city's most interesting neighborhoods lie south of South Street—Southwark and South Philadelphia. Southwark, stretching from Front to 6th Street and from South Street to Washington Avenue, was the center of the commercial and ship-building activity that made Philadelphia the biggest port in the Colonies and in the young United States. One of the oldest sections of the city, Southwark was already settled by the Swedes when the English arrived; the Swedish influence shows in street names such as Swanson, Christian, and Queen.

Directly south of Society Hill, Southwark is neither as glamorous nor as historically renowned as its neighbor. Chiseled in stone on one facade are these words: ON THIS SITE IN 1879, NOTHING HAPPENED! But like Society Hill, Southwark's Queen Village neighborhood has been gentrified by young professionals; the restoration attracted chic restaurants and interesting shops.

Through the years South Philadelphia has absorbed boatloads of immigrants—European Jews, Italians, and most recently, Asians and Mexicans. The city's Little Italy, it is a huge area of identical row houses, many with gleaming white marble steps, stretching south and west of Southwark. At the heart of the neighborhood's Bella Vista section, along 9th Street, is the outdoor Italian Market, packed with vendors hawking crabs and octopus, eggplants and tomatoes. From butcher-shop windows hang skinned animals; cheese shops are crammed with barrels of olives. Sylvester Stallone walked along 9th Street in the films *Rocky* and *Rocky II,* and almost every campaigning president has visited the market on his swing through Philadelphia. It's a great photo op for them—and for you.

Although there are chic eateries in South Philadelphia, the majority of the neighborhood's Italian restaurants are not fancy (decor such as red-check vinyl tablecloths and plastic grapes hanging from plastic vines is not uncommon), but the food can be terrific and—more important—authentic. You'll wonder if Mama is in the kitchen preparing a southern Italian specialty just for you. This is the neighborhood that gave the world Mario Lanza, Bobby Rydell, Frankie Avalon, and Fabian, and some area restaurants proudly display gold records earned by these neighborhood celebrities. Plenty of locals and visitors alike head for South Philly's competing culinary shrines, Pat's King of Steaks and Geno's, both at the corner of 9th Street and Passyunk Avenue. One of their cheese steaks makes a perfect prelude to an evening spent at the city's sports complexes, at the southern end of South Philadelphia.

Numbers in the text correspond to numbers in the margin and on the Southwark & South Philadelphia map.

a good walk

A leisurely stroll through Southwark and South Philadelphia is a fun day's outing. From Bainbridge Street, proceed south (right turn) on 2nd Street, which old-timers call Two Street. The homes along these streets are the oldest in the city, dating from the mid-1700s. Even when their construction dates are not chiseled on the facades, the settling bricks above the overhangs, the crooked windows, and the shutters that don't hang straight all attest to their vintage. Turn east (left) on Catharine Street and then south (right) on Hancock Street, one of the most charming streets in the city. The tiny clapboard houses at Nos. 813 and 815 were built by a shipwright and are the last of their type. Detour onto Queen Street to see the old firehouse with gas lamps at No. 117. It has been beautifully converted to a single-family home.

Continue down Hancock to Christian Street; go east (left) about one block (under the I–95 overpass) to Swanson Street. Here is **Gloria Dei** 1, the oldest church in Pennsylvania. Return to 2nd Street by way of Christian Street and walk south (left turn), past a neighborhood landmark, the Shot Tower, where lead shot was made during the War of 1812. At Washington Avenue is the **Mummers Museum** 2, where you can get a feeling for this local institution. From the museum walk west

Gloria Dei 1
Italian Market . . 3
Mario Lanza Museum 4
Mummers Museum 2
Samuel S. Fleischer Art Memorial . . 5

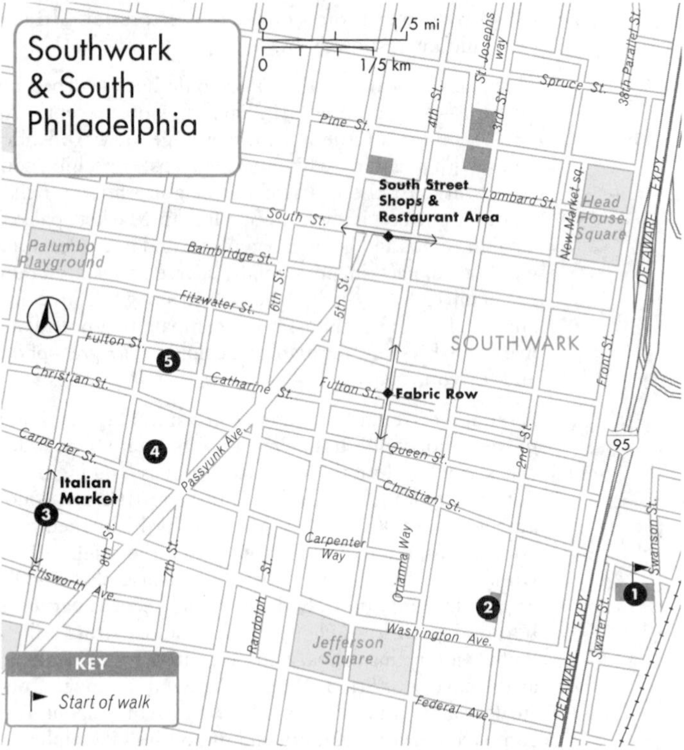

on Washington Avenue to 9th Street and then proceed north along the busiest stretch of the five-block open-air **Italian Market** ❸. At Christian Street walk east to 7th Street, half a block south to Montrose Street to the **Mario Lanza Museum** ❹, with memorabilia and photos of the singer. Returning to Christian, head one block north to Catharine to the **Samuel S. Fleisher Art Memorial** ❺, a tuition-free art school with exhibits of fine contemporary art. Finally, head east on Catharine to 4th Street and continue to South Street. Dry-goods merchants line 4th Street south of South Street in an area called Fabric Row; you'll find an amazing variety of designer and ethnic textiles, upholstery, and draperies.

TIMING It's best to visit this neighborhood Tuesday through Saturday, because the Italian Market is closed Sunday afternoon and Monday, and the Mummers Museum is closed Sundays in July and August and every Monday. Start early—the Italian Market winds down by late afternoon—and allow three to four hours.

What to See

❺ **The Samuel S. Fleisher Art Memorial.** Based on founder Samuel S. Fleisher's invitation to "the world to come and learn art," this school and gallery has offered tuition-free classes since 1898. Now administered by the Philadelphia Museum of Art, the Fleisher offers regular exhibits of contemporary art, which are selected through its competitive "Challenge" series, as well as works by faculty and students. The Memorial consists of four connected buildings on Catharine Street—including The Sanctuary, a Romanesque Revival Episcopal church designed by the architectural firm of Frank Furness and featuring European art from the 13th to the 15th centuries—as well as a satellite building at 705 Christian Street dedicated to works on paper. ✉ *709–721 Catharine St., Southwark* ☎ *215/922–3456* 🌐 *www.fleisher.org* 🎫 *Free* ⏲ *Weekdays 11–5; additional hrs when school is in session, Mon.–Thurs. 6:30–9:30* PM*, Sat. 10–3.*

❶ **Gloria Dei.** One of the few remnants of the Swedes who settled Pennsylvania before William Penn, Gloria Dei, also known as Old Swedes' Church, was organized in 1642. Built in 1698, the church has numerous intriguing religious artifacts, such as a 1608 Bible once owned by Sweden's Queen Christina. The carvings on the lectern and balcony were salvaged from the congregation's first church, which was destroyed by fire. Models of two of the ships that transported the first Swedish settlers hang from the ceiling—right in the center of the church. Grouped around the church are the parish hall, the caretaker's house, the rectory, and the guild house. The church sits in the center of its graveyard; it forms a picture that is pleasing in its simplicity and tranquillity. ✉ *916 Swanson St., near Christian St. and Columbus Blvd., Queen Village* ☎ *215/389–1513* 🌐 *www.nps.gov/glde* 🎫 *Free* ⏲ *Daily 9–5, but call first.*

❸ **Italian Market.** It's more Naples than Philadelphia: vendors crowd the sidewalks and spill out onto the streets; live crabs and caged chickens wait for the kill; picture-perfect produce is piled high. The market dates back to the turn of the century, when it was founded by Italian immigrants. You'll find imported and domestic products, kitchenware, fresh pastas, cheeses, spices, meats, fruits and vegetables, and dry goods. These days the market has lost some of its charm; food stalls share the already crowded street with vendors selling bootleg CDs, logo T-shirts, and dollar-store bargains, but it's still enjoyable to stroll and to duck into a cheese or spice shop. ✉ *9th St. between Washington Ave. and Christian St., Bella Vista/S. Philadelphia* 🌐 *www.phillyitalianmarket.com* ⏲ *Tues.–Sat., 9–late afternoon, Sun. 9–12:30.*

need a break?

When you're ready for an atmospheric break, stop by **Anthony's Italian Coffee House** (✉ 903 S. 9th St., Bella Vista/S. Philadelphia ☎ 215/627–2586) in the heart of the Italian Market. Here, to the strains of Frank Sinatra or Italian opera, you can sample a fresh panini with prosciutto and mozzarella, or indulge in a homemade cannoli or gelati imported from Italy.

❹ **Mario Lanza Museum.** In this museum devoted to the famous tenor and Hollywood star (1921–59), you'll find thousands of photos, memorabilia, videocassette showings of Lanza's films, and souvenirs for sale. Lanza was supposedly moving a piano into the Academy of Music when he seized the opportunity to sing from its stage—and was first discovered. Arturo Toscanini said that Lanza had perhaps the greatest natural voice of the century. Lanza's birthplace, at 634 Christian Street, is a few blocks away.

✉ *712 Montrose St., Bella Vista/S. Philadelphia* ☎ *215/238–9691* 🌐 *www.mario-lanza-institute.org* 🎫 *Free* ⏲ *Mon.–Sat., 10–3.*

2 **Mummers Museum.** Even if you aren't in Philadelphia on New Year's Day, you can still experience this unique local institution and phenomenon. Famous for extravagant sequin-and-feather costumes and string bands, the Mummers spend the year preparing for an all-day parade up Market Street on January 1. The museum has costumes, photos of parades, and audiovisual displays of Mummerabilia. You can push buttons to compose your own Mummers medley, with banjos, saxophones, and xylophones, and you can dance the Mummers strut to the strains of "Oh, Dem Golden Slippers." A 45-inch screen shows filmed highlights of past parades.

Early English settlers brought to the Colonies their Christmastime custom of dressing in costume and performing pantomimes—the name Mummers derives from the German *mumme,* meaning "mask or disguise." In Philadelphia, families would host costume parties on New Year's Day; on January 1, 1876, the first individual groups paraded informally through the city. The parade caught on, and by 1901 the city officially sanctioned the parade and 42 Mummers clubs strutted for cash prizes.

These days, the Mummers also stage a summer Mummers Parade around July 4 (during the city's Welcome America! celebration); in late February they present the "Show of Shows" at the Spectrum. The latter is a chance to hear the original 16 string bands perform indoors. The museum presents free outdoor concerts (weather permitting) on most Tuesday evenings 8–10 from May to September. ✉ *1100 S. 2nd St., at Washington Ave., South Philadelphia* ☎ *215/336–3050* 🌐 *www.riverfrontmummers.com/museum.html* 🎫 *$3.50* ⏲ *Oct.–Apr., Tues.–Sat. 9:30–4:30, Sun. noon–4:30; May–Sept., Tues. 9:30–9:30, Wed.–Sat. 9:30–4:30, Sun. noon–4:30; closed Sun. July and Aug.*

UNIVERSITY CITY

University City is the portion of West Philadelphia that includes the campuses of the University of Pennsylvania, Drexel University, and the Philadelphia College of Pharmacy and Science. It also has the University City Science Center (a leading think tank), the Annenberg Center performing arts complex (part of the University of Pennsylvania), an impressive collection of Victorian houses, and a variety of moderately priced restaurants, movie theaters, stores, and lively bars catering to more than 32,000 students and other residents. The neighborhood stretches from the Schuylkill River west to 44th Street and from the river north to Powelton Avenue.

This area was once the city's flourishing western suburbs, where wealthy Philadelphians built grand estates and established summer villages. It officially became part of the city in 1854. Twenty years later the University of Pennsylvania moved its campus here from the center of the city. The university moved into many of the historic homes, and others were adopted by fraternities. There are still many privately owned, architecturally exciting properties, particularly on Locust, Spruce, and Pine

Arthur Ross Gallery 2
Fisher Fine Arts Library 3
Institute of Contemporary Art 1
University Museum of Archaeology & Anthropology . .4

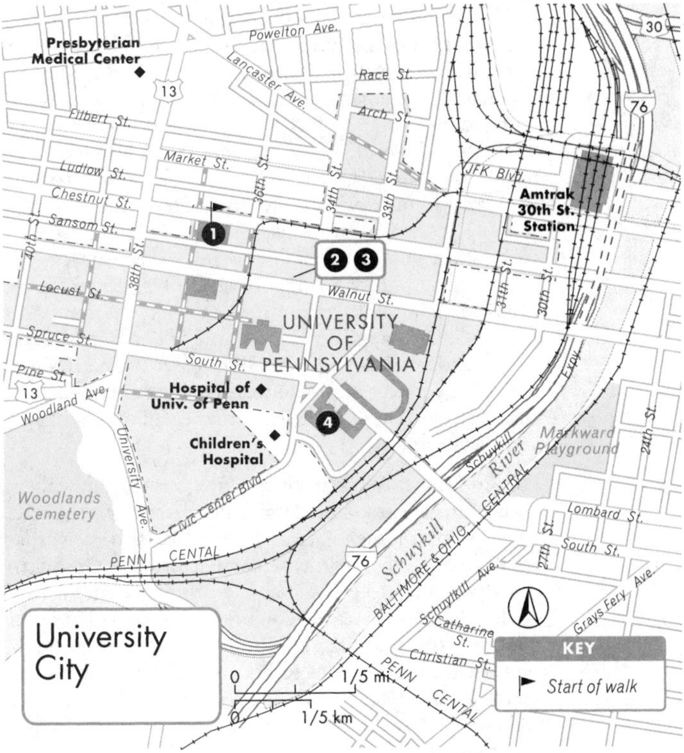

streets. Other areas of West Philadelphia beyond University City are, however, less prosperous today.

Penn has spruced up its campus with the Sansom Common development (between Walnut and Sansom streets, and 36th and 37th streets), which includes shops, a bookstore, and a hotel, the Inn at Penn. To promote the neighborhood's dining and arts scene, the University City District sponsors regular events, including a Friday night jazz series and restaurant weeks with specially priced meals (www.universitycitydistrict.com). Museums and galleries host special events the third Thursday of the month (4 PM–8 PM) and stay open late, and restaurants offer special discounts and activities. Metered parking is free after 5 PM and a shuttle bus makes a continuous loop around the neighborhood. **Penn's Information Center** (☎ 215/898–4636) is at 34th and Walnut streets.

Numbers in the text correspond to numbers in the margin and on the University City map.

a good walk

This walk through University City takes in the Ivy League campus of the University of Pennsylvania, where ivy really does cling to many buildings. Begin at the university's **Institute of Contemporary Art** ❶ ⚑, at 36th and Sansom streets. Walk east (down the hill) on Sansom Street to 34th Street and turn right (south). At 220 South 34th Street is the historic

Furness Building, which houses the **Arthur Ross Gallery** 2 and the **Fisher Fine Arts Library** 3. When you exit the building, you're in the heart of the University of Pennsylvania campus at the edge of College Green (Blanche Levy Park). You'll see a statue of Benjamin Franklin, who founded the university in 1740, in the middle of the green. To your right, the huge Van Pelt Library stretches from 34th Street to 36th Street. In front of it is Claes Oldenburg's *Broken Button.* To your left is College Hall, an administration building said to be the inspiration for the scary Addams House in cartoonist Charles Addams's work. Where the walk splits, stay right. Just west of 36th Street, the Annenberg School of Communications and the Annenberg Center are to the right; the famed Wharton School of Economics, to the left. As you pass the intersection of 37th Street, say hello to the statue of Ben Franklin sitting on a bench. A footbridge takes you over 38th Street (turn around for a good view of Center City) to Superblock, three high-rise student dormitories. Locust Walk ends at 40th Street with the dental school and a row of stores and restaurants.

Follow Locust Walk back to 37th Street and walk south (right) to Spruce Street. The Gothic sprawl ahead of you is the Quad, the university's first dorm buildings. Designed by Cope and Stewardson in 1895, the Quad became the prototype of the collegiate Gothic style prevalent in campuses coast to coast. These dormitory buildings—awash with gargoyles and gables—easily conjure up the England of everyone's dreams. South of the Quad on Hamilton Walk, you're smack back in the 20th century, thanks to Louis Kahn's Alfred Newton Richards Medical Research Laboratories building, a masterpiece by this important architect. Kahn, a brilliant teacher and architectural theorist, did not leave many completed buildings.

Head back to Spruce Street and turn right (east) to 33rd Street to explore the **University Museum of Archaeology and Anthropology** 4, which holds everything from mummies to Mayan artifacts.

TIMING University City is at its best when college is in session; the students rushing to classes give this area its flavor. Allow half an hour each in the Arthur Ross Gallery and the Institute of Contemporary Art, two hours in the University Museum, and an hour exploring the campus. If your time is limited, skip all but the University Museum, a don't-miss for the archaeologically inclined.

What to See

2 **Arthur Ross Gallery.** Penn's official art gallery showcases treasures from the university's collections and traveling exhibitions. The gallery shares its historic landmark building, designed by Frank Furness, with the **Fisher Fine Arts Library.** ✉ *220 S. 34th St., University City* ☎ *215/898–2083* 🌐 *www.upenn.edu/ARG* 🎫 *Free* 🕓 *Tues.–Fri. 10–5, weekends noon–5.*

3 **Fisher Fine Arts Library.** One of the finest examples remaining of the work of Philadelphia architect Frank Furness, this was the most innovative library building in the country when it was completed in 1890. It was the first library to separate the reading room and the stacks. Peek into the catalog room, dominated by a huge fireplace, and the reading room, with study

alcoves lit from the lead-glass windows above. The unusual exterior stirred controversy when it was built: note the terra-cotta panels, short heavy columns, and gargoyles on the north end. ✉ *220 S. 34th St., University City* ☎ *215/898–8325* 🌐 *www.library.upenn.edu/finearts* 🎫 *Free* ⏲ *Sept.–mid-May, Mon.–Thurs. 8:30 AM–midnight, Fri. 8:30–8, Sat. 10–8, Sun. noon–midnight; mid-May–late Aug., weekdays 9–7, closed weekends.*

need a break?

From 10 AM to 10 PM, you can refuel at **Moravian Cafes at Sansom Commons** (✉ 3409 Walnut St., University City), a food court with the requisite pizza, ice cream, steak sandwich, salad, and coffee counters. For something more gourmet, grab a stool at the sushi bar at the futuristic **Pod** (✉ 3636 Sansom St., University City ☎ 215/387–1803), where you can select your favorite raw fish from a conveyor belt.

1

❶ **Institute of Contemporary Art.** This museum, part of the University of Pennsylvania, has established a reputation for identifying promising artists and exhibiting them at a critical point in their careers. Among the artists who have had shows at ICA and later gone on to international prominence are Andy Warhol, Robert Mapplethorpe, and Laurie Anderson. ✉ *118 S. 36th St., at Sansom St., University City* ☎ *215/898–7108* 🌐 *www.icaphila.org* 🎫 *$6, free Sun. 11–1* ⏲ *Wed.–Fri. noon–8, weekends 11–5.*

★ ❹ **University Museum of Archaeology and Anthropology.** Rare treasures from the deepest jungles and ancient tombs make this one of the finest archaeological/anthropological museums in the world. The collection of more than a million objects, gathered largely during worldwide expeditions by University of Pennsylvania scholars, includes a 12-ton sphinx from Egypt, a crystal ball once owned by China's Dowager Empress, the world's oldest writing—Sumerian cuneiform clay tablets—and the 4,500-year-old golden jewels from the royal tombs of the kingdom of Ur. The museum's *Worlds Intertwined* galleries showcases its Greek, Roman, and Etruscan collections; the Etruscan collection is the only comprehensive exhibit of its kind in the United States. Children run to "The Egyptian Mummy: Secrets and Science" and to "Living in Balance: The Universe of the Hopi, Zuni, Navajo, and Apache." ✉ *33rd and Spruce Sts., University City* ☎ *215/898–4001* 🌐 *www.upenn.edu/museum* 🎫 *$8, free Sun.* ⏲ *Labor Day–Memorial Day, Tues.–Sat. 10–4:30, Sun. 1–5; Memorial Day–Labor Day, Tues.–Sat. 10–4:30.*

2

Manayunk, Germantown & Greater Philadelphia

WORD OF MOUTH

"[Try] Manayunk, a trendy renovated mill area north of center city. There are lots of cool shops, galleries, and good restaurants. It's impossible to park, but that won't be a problem if you take the train."

—lesliec1

"If you are into Renoir, the Barnes Foundation cannot be beat. It also has several other Impressionists and a good collection of African art. . . . Don't forget to reserve a timed ticket to visit and to park—the place is usually booked weeks in advance."

—PaulRabe

www.fodors.com/forums

By Joyce Eisenberg

WILLIAM PENN LAID OUT HIS ORIGINAL 2-square-mi city between the Delaware and Schuylkill rivers, and, as one might expect, most of the city's historic and cultural attractions sprung up within these boundaries. But over the next centuries, as Philadelphians moved away from the downtown area and stretched the city's borders to encompass 135 square mi, they made artistic and historical footprints that are farther away but worth following. You can find inspiration in heroic efforts past and present, whether you uncover the hiding places of runaway slaves at Germantown's Johnson House or watch 200 of the world's top bicyclists scale the steep Manayunk Wall at the Wachovia USPro Championship each June.

2

If you put the one point of your geometric compass on City Hall and the other on a radius 8 mi out, you'd encircle a number of neighborhoods that played an important role in the city's past. Manayunk, on the banks of the Schuylkill, was a working man's town where textile mills helped make Philadelphia one of the country's leading industrial cities in the mid-1800s. Farther from the river, Philadelphia's socialites built country homes in Germantown to escape disease and uncomfortable summers. In later years, their descendants traveled a little farther north along cobblestoned Germantown Avenue to Chestnut Hill to found an enclave with suburban sensibilities within city limits. While John Bartram cultivated his native plants in the meadows alongside the Schuylkill River in Southwest Philadelphia, Albert Barnes cultivated the aesthetic of his students at his art foundation and arboretum tucked away in Merion along the Main Line.

Extend the radius 16 mi from the center point, and you'll find some other riches. For John Pitcairn and the patrons of the Church of the New Jerusalem, Bryn Athyn's heavenly setting evoked the beauty of the Swedish countryside. In Northeast Philadelphia, exterminator Steve Kanya was after more earthly creatures, which he immortalized in his Insectarium.

Years ago, traveling to these outlying regions meant saddling up the horse and loading the wagon; today, you'll have to gas up the car or buy tokens for SEPTA. Even though the landscapes have changed, these spots are still worth the trip.

About the Restaurants

In Manayunk and Chestnut Hill, friendly neighborhood taverns, ethnic restaurants, and tiny storefront startups line Main Street and Germantown Avenue. Some longterm standard-bearers, like Jake's, earned Manayunk a star on the dining map. In summer, many of the restaurants set out tables for alfresco dining and people watching.

WHAT IT COSTS

	$$$$	$$$	$$	$	¢
AT DINNER	over $26	$20–$26	$14–$20	$8–$14	under $8

Prices are for one main course at dinner.

MANAYUNK

When this former mill town, rising dramatically up from the banks of the Schuylkill River, was at the height of its productivity, the European mill workers lived at the bottom of the steep hills and the company executives lived at the top. Today, it is lower Manayunk—along and intersecting with Main Street—that's the premier address in town. Just 7 mi northwest of Center City, Manayunk's more than 30 restaurants compete for attention, offering alfresco dining, creative menus, and valet parking. Many of the 80-plus stores are one-of-a-kind; among them are art galleries, antiques shops, and clothing boutiques. Popular bars and original music at Grape Street Philadelphia, a pub that has long been a live music destination, attract a postcollege crowd. This urban neighborhood, with its distinctive architecture, brick row houses, and narrow streets, is a good destination for a leisurely stroll with dinner and shopping; many stores stay open late.

In the mid-1800s, when Philadelphia was one of the nation's leading industrial cities, Manayunk prospered because of its many cotton mills, which provided raw material for the region's thriving paper and textile industries. Manayunk's canal, completed in 1819 to make navigable a difficult section of the river, provided water for the mills and transportation for the shipment of the finished goods. It allowed boats to travel 108 mi from Philadelphia to Pottsville. Mills lined both sides of the canal, and mules walked along the towpath pulling the canal boats.

During the Civil War the mills switched to wool textiles to produce blankets and uniforms for the troops. Soon after, Manayunk's mills closed because of competition from cheaper labor in the South, and the town's fortune declined. It took about 100 years for its luck to change. In the mid-1980s the neighborhood was designated a historic district. This new status provided a golden opportunity for business owners, who transformed the old mills into apartments and stores. Good fortune struck again in 1986, when the U.S. Pro Cycling championship picked Philadelphia as its home and made Manayunk's steep hill (now dubbed the "The Wall") the highlight of its route.

Manayunk has organized other special crowd-pleasing events. On the last weekend in June, the Manayunk Arts Festival lines Main Street with the largest outdoor arts and crafts show in the region. There's a Manayunk in Bloom festival each spring and a winter Holiday on Main event.

The canal towpath—part dirt and part wooden boardwalk—stretches between Main Street and the river, and you can access it behind Restoration Hardware. Old rail lines, textile mills, canal locks, and the ruins of the lock-tender's house are still visible. The Manayunk Development Corporation is planning a restoration of the canal, which would enable canoes and small boats to sail through.

The **Manayunk Development Corporation** (✉ 111 Grape St., Manayunk ☎ 215/482–9565 🌐 www.manayunk.com) can send you a visitors guide; its Web site lists special events, restaurants, and shops.

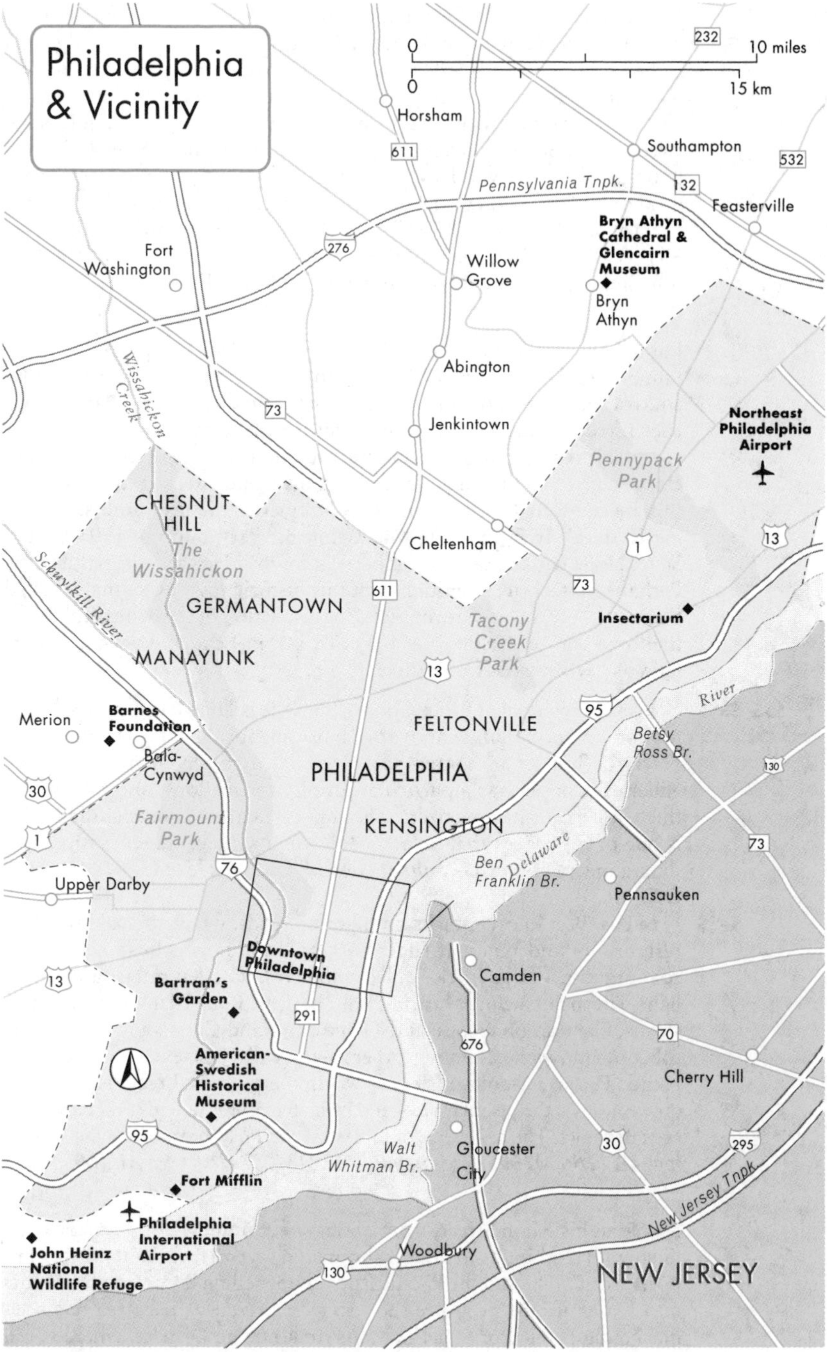
Philadelphia & Vicinity
0
10 miles
0
15 km
Horsham
Southampton
Feasterville
Pennsylvania Tnpk.
Bryn Athyn Cathedral & Glencairn Museum
Bryn Athyn
Fort Washington
Willow Grove
Abington
Jenkintown
Wissahickon Creek
Northeast Philadelphia Airport
Pennypack Park
CHESNUT HILL
The Wissahickon
Cheltenham
Schuylkill River
GERMANTOWN
Insectarium
Tacony Creek Park
MANAYUNK
Merion
Barnes Foundation
Bala-Cynwyd
FELTONVILLE
Betsy Ross Br.
River
PHILADELPHIA
Fairmount Park
KENSINGTON
Delaware
Ben Franklin Br.
Upper Darby
Pennsauken
Downtown Philadelphia
Camden
Bartram's Garden
American-Swedish Historical Museum
Cherry Hill
Walt Whitman Br.
Gloucester City
Fort Mifflin
New Jersey Tnpk.
Philadelphia International Airport
John Heinz National Wildlife Refuge
Woodbury
NEW JERSEY

GETTING HERE & GETTING AROUND

If you're driving from Center City, follow I–76 west (the Schuylkill Expressway) to the Belmont Avenue exit. Turn right across the bridge and right again onto Main Street and park. On weekends you'll be strolling with hundreds of visitors—and fighting with them for parking spaces. The town has been working to remedy that; there are parking lots between Main Street and the river (accessed along Main Street). Participating stores offer validation stickers for reduced parking rates. From 6 PM on, valet parking is available for evening diners and shoppers for $8. You can also take the SEPTA R6 (Norristown) train from Market East, Suburban Station, or 30th Street Station to the Manayunk Station (on Cresson Street) and walk downhill to Main Street.

Where to Eat

For many years, it would have been easy to update Manayunk's restaurant listings, because City Council, in an effort to keep development under control, put a moratorium on new restaurants and bars. That ban has been lifted, leaving the restaurant scene in flux. Jake's, the first and most successful restaurant on Main Street, is still top-notch. There's a good ethnic mix, including Thai, Japanese, Italian, and Greek, and two restaurants serve New Orleans cuisine. A number of the restaurants, including Kildare's Irish Pub, the Manayunk Brewery, and the 1903 United States Hotel Bar and Grill, are as popular for their bars as for their kitchens. Perhaps that's how it should be in this historic town: Originally called Flat Rock, for the rock formations in this section of the Schuylkill River, the town was rechristened Manayunk, a Leni-Lenape word that translates as "where we go to drink."

$$$–$$$$ Fodor's Choice ★

✕ **Jake's.** Owner-chef Bruce Cooper (his wife is Jake) has garnered a reputation for food that is innovative but somehow classic. The place displays the hottest in contemporary crafts, many from trendy nearby galleries. Cooper has a particular affinity for scallops, and transforms them into exquisite appetizers. The crab cakes are also outstanding. This is one of the places that helped Manayunk achieve its reputation as a dining mecca. ✉ *4365 Main St., Manayunk* ☎ *215/483–0444* ▭ *AE, DC, MC, V.*

$–$$

✕ **Le Bus.** Best known for its multigrain breads, which are sold to fancy restaurants and regional supermarkets, Le Bus is a bustling, homey restaurant in a large brick-walled room with wooden rafters and a skylight. The menu includes hearty soups; burgers; Long Island mussels; tasty salads, like salmon niçoise and Thai turkey; and Cuban and grilled Portobello sandwiches, among others—all really just excuses to eat the bread. The sweet-potato fries are worth the calories. Breakfast is served on weekdays; the popular weekend brunch features huevos rancheros and eggs Benedict. The few outdoor tables make a great post for people-watching. ✉ *4266 Main St., Manayunk* ☎ *215/487–2663* ▭ *AE, MC, V.*

Shopping

Manayunk's Main Street, from about street numbers 4400 to 3900, is lined with clothing stores, craft shops, and several merchants selling imports from Tibet and the Pacific Rim. Shops selling home and office furniture and accessories have the strongest presence. The area has been marketing its 30 stores as the Manayunk Design District, where you'll find custom, antique, contemporary, and traditional furnishings, lighting, and other design resources. Many stores stay open until 9 or 10 on Friday and Saturday nights. If you do come on a weekday, note that most stores don't open until noon.

Artesano. Craftsmen create staircases, balconies, beds, doors, and more with forged iron, along with door knockers, lamps and other accessories. The studio also allows customers to design their own iron works. ✉ *4443 Main St., Manayunk* ☎ *215/483–9273.*

Bias. This fashion-forward women's clothing boutique carries local designers and national talent; the collection and the shop interior is transformed four times a year with a seasonal theme. ✉ *4442 Main St., Manayunk* ☎ *215/483–8340.*

Gary P. Mann Design. Noted local gemologist and goldsmith Gary Mann creates elegant custom jewelry. The store is also known for its singular estate jewelry, carved jade and emerald pieces, and stack rings. ✉ *4349 Main St., Manayunk* ☎ *215/482–7051.*

Ligne Roset. The streamlined designs here have an international reputation but have recently gotten extra attention through appearances on *The Apprentice* and *Queer Eye for the Straight Guy.* The French company sells chic, contemporary furniture, rugs, and lighting. ✉ *4131 Main St., Manayunk* ☎ *215/487–2800.*

Sweet Violet. Gifts as pretty as the store's name await, including glassware, home accessories, and bath and body products. ✉ *4361 Main St., Manayunk* ☎ *215/483–2826.*

Why Be Board? You won't find any video games here. Instead, you'll be transported back to the days when families played board games and put puzzles together. The store has old favorites and award-winning games, kites, and undoubtedly some of your favorite childhood toys. ✉ *4439 Main St., Manayunk* ☎ *215/483–8800.*

GERMANTOWN & CHESTNUT HILL

In its transformation from Indian trail to toll road to main street, Germantown Avenue has woven a path through history. Once a rural farming village, Germantown is now decidedly urban, and the neighborhood once known for religious tolerance is today a model of racial integration. While wealthy Philadelphians, like the Wisters, Johnsons and Chews, lived peacefully along the "Great Road" until the British invaded; today's wealthy families live in Chestnut Hill, and the only invaders are tourists who come to shop and dine. It's a worthwhile pursuit, but so, too, is a visit to Germantown's historic homes, which have sheltered Quakers, government leaders, runaway slaves and inspired gardeners.

Germantown, about 6 mi northwest of Center City, has been an integrated, progressive community since 13 German Quaker and Mennonite families moved here in 1683 and soon welcomed English, French, and other European settlers seeking religious freedom. The area has a tradition of free thinking—the first written protest against slavery in America came from its residents. Today it houses a wealth of still-occupied and exceptionally well-preserved architectural masterpieces.

The Germantown area is rich in history. It was the site of Philadelphia's first gristmill (1683) and America's first paper mill (1690). The American Colonies' first English-language Bible was printed here (1743). By the time of the Revolution, Germantown had become an industrial town. In 1777 Colonial troops under George Washington attacked part of the British force here and fought the Battle of Germantown in various skirmishes. After the Revolutionary War Germantown became a rural retreat for wealthy city residents who could afford a "vacation home." The Deshler-Morris House was the summer White House where President Washington and his family resided in 1793 and 1794, when the yellow fever epidemic drove them from the city. For information on Germantown's historic attractions, visit ⊕ www.ushistory.org/germantown.

Farther northwest is Chestnut Hill. Although it's part of the city, Chestnut Hill is more like the classy suburbs of the Main Line. When Germantown's second railroad, the Chestnut Hill Line, began operation west of Germantown Avenue in 1884, it spurred the development of Chestnut Hill. Beyond cobblestone Germantown Avenue, lined with restaurants, galleries, and boutiques, you'll find lovely examples of Colonial Revival and Queen Anne houses. The Woodmere Art Museum is in this neighborhood. For information, contact the **Chestnut Hill Business Association** (✉ 8426 Germantown Ave., Chestnut Hill, 19118 ☎ 215/247–6696 ⊕ www.chestnuthillpa.com ⏲ Weekdays, 8:30–5, Sat. 10–4, Sun. noon–4).

In between Chestnut Hill and Manayunk is Mount Airy, a largely residential neighborhood that is often touted as a model of stable racial integration. The neighborhood has been revitalizing its business corridor. The anchor is the **Sedgwick Cultural Center** (✉ 7137 Germantown Ave., Mount Airy ☎ 215/248–9229 ⊕ www.sedgwickcenter.org), which offers a full calendar of live music, art exhibits, and family programs to "build community through the arts."

The best way to tour the area is by car. From Center City follow Kelly Drive to Midvale Avenue and turn right. Follow Midvale up the hill to Conrad Street and turn right, then make a left on Queen Lane, which ends at Grumblethorpe. You can also reach Germantown from Center City via SEPTA Bus 23; pick it up at 11th and Market streets and get off at Queen Lane.

a good drive

You can follow Germantown Avenue from lower Germantown north to Chestnut Hill. Many of the homes you'll see were built when Germantown Avenue was a dirt road; today it's lined with cobblestones. Begin your tour at **Stenton**, James Logan's manor just off of Germantown Avenue at Windrim Avenue and 18th Street. At Queen Lane is John Wister's **Grumblethorpe**, built from stones quarried on the property. A few blocks north on Germantown Avenue is Market Square, a park that was once the site of a prison and its stocks and a focal point for trade. Facing Market Square on your left is the **Deshler-Morris House**, with fine antiques and lovely gardens; diagonally across the square in a row of restored redbrick buildings is the **Germantown Historical Society**, which provides a good introduction to the houses in the area.

Drive north a half mile farther to the Quaker-style **Wyck House**, at the corner of Germantown Avenue and Walnut Lane. Just before Pastorius Street is the tiny, historic Germantown Mennonite Church. On this site in 1708 the Mennonites established their first church in the New World. The little log church was replaced in 1770 by the current building. Turn left on Tulpehocken Street; at Number 200 West is the Victorian Gothic **Ebenezer Maxwell Mansion**. Continue north on Germantown Avenue past the **Johnson House**, once a tannery, later a station on the Underground Railroad. At Number 6401 is **Cliveden**, an elaborate house at the end of a long, graceful driveway. Across the street is Upsala, a Federal-style home of the Johnson family (who also owned the Johnson House).

Adjacent to Germantown is the residential community of Mount Airy, and farther north, at the "top" of Germantown Avenue, is Chestnut Hill. The town's tony shopping district runs from Number 7900 to 8700. Half a mile north at Number 9201 is the **Woodmere Art Museum**, with works from the 19th and 20th centuries. From here, you could detour to **The Gardens of the Morris Arboretum** or the natural setting of the **Schuylkill Center for Environmental Education** to take a walk; both places are lovely at any time of year.

TIMING Each historic house has its own schedule, so it's difficult to coordinate your visit to include all the sights. However, you could catch five homes open on a Thursday afternoon and four on Saturday or Sunday afternoon. You could then head to Chestnut Hill for dinner. Avoid this trip in winter, when most of the homes are closed.

What to See

★ **Cliveden.** Its unique history and fine architecture combine to make Cliveden one of Germantown's treasures. It was built in 1763 by Benjamin Chew (1722–1810), a Quaker and Chief Justice of the Colonies. The area's most elaborate country house is a shining example of Georgian style, with Palladian windows and an elegant entrance hall with pedimented door frames. The home was occupied by the British during the Revolution. On October 4, 1777, Washington's unsuccessful attempt to dislodge the British resulted in his defeat at the Battle of Germantown. You can still see bullet marks on the outside walls. Today a museum that can be seen on a 45-minute guided tour, Cliveden occupies a 6-acre plot, with outbuildings and a barn converted into offices and a gift shop. Cliveden remained in the Chew family until 1972, when it was donated to the National Trust for Historic Preservation. ✉ *6401 Germantown Ave., Germantown* ☎ *215/848–1777* 🌐 *www.cliveden.org* 🎫 *$8* ⏲ *Apr.–Dec., Thurs.–Sun. noon–4.*

Deshler-Morris House. Known as the "Germantown White House," this is where President Washington lived and held Cabinet meetings during the yellow fever epidemic of 1793–94, making it the seat of government of the new republic for a short time. In October 1777, during the Battle of

Germantown, the house was the headquarters for British General Sir William Howe. The home features an ornate parlor, a dining room lined with Nanking china, and a tearoom with a table formerly owned by James Smith, a signer of the Declaration of Independence. As one of the many Germantown houses built flush with the road, it has enchanting side and back gardens. The house-museum, a part of Independence National Historical Park, is run by the National Park Service. ✉ *5442 Germantown Ave., Germantown* ☎ *215/596–1748* 🌐 *www.nps.gov/edal/dmhouse.htm* 🎟 *Free* ⏲ *Apr.–mid-Dec., Fri.–Sun. 1–4; other times by appointment.*

Ebenezer Maxwell Mansion. Philadelphia's only mid-19th-century house-museum is a Victorian Gothic extravaganza of elongated windows and arches. This gorgeous 1859 suburban villa has Philadelphia-made furniture and extensive period gardens. Its three-story tower is the incarnation of an old haunted house. ✉ *200 W. Tulpehocken St., Germantown* ☎ *215/438–1861* 🌐 *www.ushistory.org/germantown* 🎟 *$5* ⏲ *By appointment only for groups of 4 or more.*

★ **The Gardens at Morris Arboretum.** Begun in 1887 by siblings John and Lydia Morris and bequeathed to the University of Pennsylvania in 1932, this 166-acre arboretum typifies Victorian-era garden and landscape design with its romantic winding paths, a hidden grotto, tropical ferns in a fernery, and natural woodland. An eclectic retreat, the arboretum also holds a rose garden, English garden, Japanese garden, and meadows. It has 3,500 trees and shrubs from around the world, including one of the finest collections of Asian plants outside Asia. In summer and fall and at Christmas, the arboretum constructs an elaborate garden railway featuring G-scale trains and dozens of artful miniature buildings and props. The Chestnut Hill E or W commuter trains stop ½ mi away; Bus L stops at the corner of Hillcrest and Germantown avenues. ✉ *Hillcrest Ave. between Germantown and Stenton Aves., Chestnut Hill* ☎ *215/247–5777* 🌐 *www.upenn.edu/arboretum* 🎟 *$8* ⏲ *Apr.–Oct., weekdays 10–4, weekends 10–5 (open until 8 on Thurs. in summer); Nov.–Mar., daily 10–4; guided tours weekends at 2.*

Germantown Historical Society. The headquarters of the society has a historical and genealogical library and a museum showcasing noteworthy furniture, textile, and costume collections, from Colonial highboys and Peale paintings to Quaker samplers and mourning clothes. It's also an orientation point for anyone visiting the Germantown houses. ✉ *5501 Germantown Ave., Germantown* ☎ *215/844–0514* 🌐 *www.germantownhistory.org* 🎟 *Museum $5, museum and library $7.50* ⏲ *Tues.–Fri. 9–5, Sun. 1–5.*

Grumblethorpe. The blood of General James Agnew, who died after being struck by musket balls during the Battle of Germantown, stains the floor in the parlor of this Georgian house. Built by Philadelphia merchant and wine importer John Wister in 1744, Grumblethorpe is one of Germantown's leading examples of early-18th-century Pennsylvania-German architecture. The Wister family lived here for 160 years; on display are period furnishings and family mementos. ✉ *5267 Germantown Ave., Germantown* ☎ *215/843–4820* 🌐 *www.philalandmarks.org* 🎟 *$5* ⏲ *Apr.–mid-Dec., Tues., Thurs., and Sun. 1–4.*

off the beaten path

HISTORIC RITTENHOUSETOWN – North America's first paper mill was built here in 1690 by Mennonite minister William Rittenhouse. Over the next 150 years, 10 generations of his family lived on the site and operated the mill. His most famous offspring, born in 1732, was David Rittenhouse, astronomer, statesman, and first president of the U.S. Mint. You can stroll any time through these 30 picturesque acres along the Wissahickon; on summer weekends, the one-hour guided tour of the seven outbuildings gives insight into this self-sufficient industrial village, which is now a National Historic District. The visitor center has an introductory film and a model of the mill; special events include papermaking workshops, a family fun day, lantern tours, and an Easter egg hunt. ✉ *206 Lincoln Dr., Philadelphia* ☎ *215/438–5711* 🌐 *www.rittenhousetown.org* 🎫 *$5* ⏲ *Summer weekends, noon–4 (last tour at 3); Oct.–May, by appointment only.*

2

★ **Johnson House.** After bringing visitors through the hidden back entrance of this 1768 home, guides retrace the experience of slaves who found a haven here when the Johnson House was a key station on the Underground Railroad. They weave the story of the Johnson family, Quakers who worked to abolish slavery, with that of Harriet Tubman, who was sheltered here with runaway slaves and later guided them to freedom. Visitors see hiding places, including the third-floor attic, learn underground railroad code words, and view slavery artifacts, such as ankle shackles and collars. In 1777, the house was in the line of fire during the Battle of Germantown; the shutters still show the impact of the musket rounds. The home, now an Underground Railroad Museum National Historic Site, was one of the largest homes in Philadelphia—unusual for a modest Quaker family—and the oldest home in Germantown to be occupied year-round. ✉ *6306 Germantown Ave., Germantown* ☎ *215/438–1768* 🌐 *www.johnsonhouse.org* 🎫 *$5* ⏲ *Thurs. and Fri. 10–4 with tours by appointment, Sat. 1–4 with tours at 1:30, 2:30, and 3:30.*

Schuylkill Center for Environmental Education. This sanctuary consists of more than 500 acres of wildflowers, ferns, and thickets; ponds, streams, and woodlands; 6 mi of winding trails; and the 8-acre Pine Plantation. You may spot deer, hawks, Canada geese, red foxes, and other animals. Hands-on exhibits in the Discovery Museum explain the flora and fauna, and there are nature programs on weekends. The bookstore and gift shop follow the nature theme. Bus 27 stops at Henry and Port Royal Aves., 1 mi away. ✉ *8480 Hagy's Mill Rd., Roxborough* ☎ *215/482–7300* 🌐 *www.schuylkillcenter.org* 🎫 *$7* ⏲ *Mon.–Sat. 8:30–5, Sun. 1–5; trails close at 4:30.*

Stenton. While William Penn was away in England, his secretary, James Logan, managed the daily affairs of the colony. Logan, who went on to hold almost every important public office in the Colonies, designed the 1730 Georgian manor himself and named it for his father's birthplace in Scotland. He used it to entertain local luminaries and Native American tribal delegates; George Washington was a guest on his way to the Battle of Brandywine, and British General Howe claimed it for his headquarters during the Battle of Germantown. The Stenton mansion is filled with family and period pieces; the site also includes a kitchen wing, barn, and Colonial Revival garden. The guided 45-minute tour interprets the life of three generations of the Logan family and the life of the region from the 1720s through the American Revolution. ✉ *4601 18th St., Germantown* ☎ *215/329–7312* 🌐 *www.stenton.org* 🎟 *$5* ⏲ *Apr.–Dec., Tues–Sat. 1–4.*

Woodmere Art Museum. The art and artists of Philadelphia are showcased here, along with American and European art from the 19th and 20th centuries, in a fine collection of paintings and prints. Benjamin West, Frederick Church, and Pennsylvania impressionists such as Edward Redfield and Daniel Garber are represented. The museum also has a lovely collection of decorative arts, including tapestries, sculptures, porcelains, ivories, and Japanese rugs. ✉ *9201 Germantown Ave., Chestnut Hill* ☎ *215/247–0476* 🌐 *www.woodmereartmuseum.org* 🎟 *$5* ⏲ *Tues.–Sat. 10–5, Sun. 1–5.*

need a break?

Rollers Express-o (✉ 8341 Germantown Ave., Chestnut Hill ☎ 215/247–7715) is a casual, diner-style spot with satisfying breakfasts, such as homemade fruit-and-nut granola, three-grain pancakes, and hearty omelets. At lunch, there are crab cakes, potpies, and pies a là mode. It's open Tuesday through Sunday for breakfast and lunch.

Wyck. One of the most charming of Quaker-style houses, Wyck sheltered nine generations of the Wistar-Haines family between the 1690s and 1973. Their accumulated original furnishings are on display, along with ceramics, children's needlework, dolls, and other signs that this was a happy home. Outside is a garden of old roses, dating to the 1820s. Known as the oldest house in Germantown, Wyck was used as a British field hospital after the Battle of Germantown. The home was expanded over the years; its current form dates to 1824, when William Strickland made alterations. ✉ *6026 Germantown Ave., Germantown* ☎ *215/848–1690* 🌐 *www.wyck.org* 🎟 *$5* ⏲ *Apr.–mid-Dec., Tues., Thurs. noon–4:30, Sat. 1–4; or by appointment.*

Where to Eat

Germantown Avenue, from street numbers 7600 to 8700, is lined with restaurants catering to the local residents (this is, after all, their "Main Street") and people who come from the suburbs for shopping and dinner. Walk along the avenue until you find a restaurant that appeals to you—there are well-worn taverns, a vintage diner, cheese shops and bakeries, Middle Eastern and Asian restaurants, and ice cream and pizza parlors.

$$$–$$$$ ✕ **Osaka.** This recent addition to the Chestnut Hill dining scene has a contemporary, streamlined, split-level dining room, and a split personality to match. The sushi bar serves traditional and house-special maki, but it is the cooked food that is noteworthy. Chef Michael Fee, who spent time at Morimoto, prepares contemporary Asian dishes with a Korean accent. Try the duck breast confit with pickled red cabbage or the pan-seared scallops with bok choy and shiitake mushrooms. The staff is friendly and helpful, and the wine list has a great selection of cold sake. ✉ *8605 Germantown Ave., Chestnut Hill* ☎ *215/242–5900* ▭ *AE, D, MC, V* ⏲ *No lunch.*

$–$$ ✕ **Citrus.** At his tiny, eccentric BYOB restaurant, chef Chris Daher limits his menu to vegetarian and seafood dishes, but his creativity is endless. You could start off with fresh sardines or goat-cheese ravioli. Main courses include lasagna with white beans, Swiss chard, and pesto sauce; porcini-dusted scallops; and options for vegans. It's easiest to get a table midweek; the staff will take your name, send you across the street for a drink, and call you on your cell phone when it's your turn. On weekends, the 18-seat restaurant is impenetrable. This animal-loving café also features a bakery, where you'll find homemade dog biscuits along with the pecan pie. ✉ *136 Germantown Ave., Chestnut Hill* ☎ *215/247–8188* *BYOB* *Reservations not accepted* ▭ *No credit cards* ⏲ *Closed Sun. and Mon. No lunch.*

$–$$ ✕ **North By Northwest.** This Mount Airy nightspot is one of the best places for live music in Philadelphia. The music calendar is packed with local acts and national talent, along with salsa on Wednesdays (with free dance lessons), and jazz on Thursdays. The home-style cooking keeps the crowds happy. Lighter fare includes lamb burgers and prosciutto-and-arugula panini, while wild mushroom lasagna, tiger shrimp with creamy corn grits, and steak frites are heartier entrées. Original maple floors, exposed brick walls, and an original art deco bar give it a cozy feel. You can purchase advance tickets to music events and make your dinner reservation at the same time; or you can just stop by to eat. Check the Web site for upcoming events. ✉ *7165 Germantown Ave., Mt. Airy* ☎ *215/248–1000* 🌐 *www.nxnwphl.com* ▭ *AE, D, MC, V* ⏲ *Closed Mon. No lunch. No dinner Sun.*

Shopping

Like Philadelphia's Main Line, Chestnut Hill has an "old money" heritage, and some of the shops reflect that, with antique furniture; prints and rare books; Oriental rugs; and classic clothing stores, such as Talbots and Quelque Chose (selling Lilly Pulitzer clothing). These days, there's an artsy, hipper vibe mixed in, evident in the abundance of contemporary art galleries and clothing and accessories stores, like Artisans on the Avenue, Mango, and Jean-Jacques. Some national chains have set up shop on the mile-long stretch on Germantown Avenue that runs from the 7900 to 8700 blocks. But there are still plenty of singular stores—such as Bumble Beads, with accessories for jewelry-making; Barbara Russell Designs, which handcrafts needlepoint canvases; El Quetzal's handmade gfits; and the Happy Butterfly, with smocked dresses for girls and their dolls—to make this a worthwhile destination for shopping.

AROUND PHILADELPHIA

At the edges of the city limits—or just beyond—are some attractions that are well worth a drive, or long trek on public transportation. Five have Philadelphia addresses—south, southwest, and north of the downtown area—but are far enough away that Center City dwellers might consider them in another city altogether. Three spots are actually in the suburbs; the most notable being the famed Barnes Foundation in Merion on the Main Line. Farthest away are neighboring Glencairn Museum and the Bryn Athyn Cathedral, which could be visited on the way to Bucks County.

The American-Swedish Historical Museum is in the southern reaches of South Philadelphia. The Broad Street subway (you can pick it up just below the *Clothespin* sculpture at 15th and Market streets) can take you here. The *Clothespin* is also the pickup point for the No. 36 Trolley, which runs to Bartram's Garden, across the Schuykill in Southwest Philadelphia. Fort Mifflin and John Heinz National Wildlife Refuge at Tinicum are also in Southwest Philadelphia, near the airport. The Insectarium is a Northeast Philadelphia sight that's good, creepy fun.

What to See

American-Swedish Historical Museum. The Swedes settled the Delaware Valley in the mid-1600s before William Penn, but few traces remain other than Gloria Dei (Old Swedes') Church in Southwark and this museum. Modeled after a 17th-century Swedish manor house, the museum has 14 galleries that trace the history and contribution of Swedes in the United States. The John Ericsson Room honors the designer of the Civil War ironclad ship the *Monitor,* and the Jenny Lind Room contains memorabilia from the Swedish Nightingale's American tour of 1848–51. One exhibition details Alfred Nobel's career and the Nobel prize laureates who were honored during the past 100 years. Other rooms display handmade costumed Swedish peasant dolls, crafts, paintings, and drawings. To get here, you can pick up the subway just below the *Clothespin* sculpture, at 15th and Market streets. Take the Broad Street subway south to Pattison Ave. When you get out, cross Broad Street and walk five blocks west through the park to the museum. ✉ *1900 Pattison Ave., South Philadelphia* ☎ *215/389–1776* 🌐 *www.americanswedish.org* 🎟 *$6* ⏲ *Tues.–Fri. 10–4, weekends noon–4.*

Fodor's Choice ★ **Barnes Foundation.** It used to be pretty much a secret that one of the world's greatest collections of impressionist and postimpressionist art—175 Renoirs; 66 Cézannes (including his *Card Players*); 65 Matisses; plus masterpieces by van Gogh, Degas, Picasso, and others—was on view in the little town of Merion, 8 mi west of Center City. That was the way Albert C. Barnes wanted it. The son of a Philadelphia butcher who made millions by inventing Argyrol (used to treat eye inflammations), Barnes considered his art collection an educational tool, and until a 1961 court order the collection was open only to students of the educational institution he had chartered. Now that the trustees of Lincoln University have taken over, Barnes's public-be-damned attitude is a thing of the past. Recently, the Foundation was given permission by the court to relocate its gallery to a new building on the Benjamin Franklin Parkway, next to the Rodin Museum; the 12-acre arboretum and education center will remain at the Merion campus. Until about 2008, you can see the Gauguins, Tintorettos, and Degases displayed as they have always been: wallpapered floor-to-ceiling and cheek-by-jowl alongside household tools, Amish chests, and New Mexican folk icons. Reservations are required and

HIGH SOCIETY ON THE MAIN LINE

"OLD MAIDS NEVER WED AND HAVE BABIES PERIOD." *With this mnemonic, Philadelphians were taught to remember the westward-bound stops along the main line of the Pennsylvania Railroad: Overbrook, Merion, Narberth, Wynnewood, Ardmore, Haverford, Bryn Mawr, and after unnamed others, Paoli.*

In March 1823, the Pennsylvania legislature passed a charter for the construction of this, the state's first railroad, linking Philadelphia to Columbia via Lancaster, a distance of 82 miles. After the Civil War, genteel suburbs sprang up around the stations. The gracious estates with endless lawns and towering maples, the debutante balls and cricket clubs, were the province of wealthy families. Philadelphia's social elite were attracted by what was touted as the benefits of healthy, yet cultivated, country living.

The 1939 film Philadelphia Story, *a depiction of Main Line society life, starred Katharine Hepburn, a graduate of* ***Bryn Mawr College*** *(✉ 101 N. Merion Ave., Bryn Mawr ☎ 610/526–5000 ⊕ www.brynmawr.edu), the first college for women that offered B.A. degrees. Founded in 1885 and modeled after Cambridge and Oxford colleges, Bryn Mawr introduced the "collegiate Gothic" style of architecture to the United States. Nearby is the* ***Baldwin School*** *(✉ 701 W. Montgomery Ave., Bryn Mawr ☎ 610/525–2700 ⊕ www.baldwinschool.org), which Miss Florence Baldwin began in 1888 as a prep school for the college. The Baldwin campus includes a five-story 1892 chateau-style structure designed by Philadelphia architect Frank Furness. Furness also built the massive Victorian redbrick clubhouse at the* ***Merion Cricket Club*** *(✉ 325 Montgomery Ave., Haverford ☎ 610/642–5800 ⊕ www.merioncricket.com). In the early 1900s the club drew crowds of 25,000 spectators to its matches; today its Great Lawn also hosts croquet matches and tennis events.*

The main attraction of the Main Line is undoubtedly the ***Barnes Foundation,*** *home to Albert C. Barnes's staggering collection of impressionist and postimpressionist art, considered to be one of the world's finest. The opulent* ***Chanticleer*** *(✉ 786 Church Rd., Wayne ☎ 610/687–4163 ⊕ www.chanticleergarden.org) is a 35-acre pleasure garden circling a country estate; even the old tennis court has been transformed into a garden. Chanticleer is open April through October, Wednesday through Sunday 10–5 (until 8 Friday, May through August); admission is $5.*

Centuries before the socialites arrived, the Welsh Quakers settled on the Main Line on land granted by William Penn. Penn is said to have worshipped at the ***Merion Friends Meeting*** *(✉ 615 Montgomery Ave., Merion ☎ 610/664–4210), which is among the oldest Friends meeting houses in America. It was built between 1695 and 1704 in a Welsh-inspired architectural style. (Meetings for worship are Sunday at 11.) If you're lucky, Mother Divine herself will lead you on a fascinating tour of the well-preserved* ***Woodmont*** *(✉ 1622 Spring Mill Rd., Gladwyne ☎ 610/525–5598 ⊕ http://fdipmm.libertynet.org), headquarters of Father Divine's Peace Mission Movement, a progressive religious and social movement that was in its heyday in the 1930s. Father Divine is buried in a mausoleum on the grounds of this striking 1892 Gothic manor house, a National Historic Landmark that was built by a steel baron for a million dollars. Woodmont is free and open Sunday 1–5 April through October, with weekday tours by appointment. Modest dress is required.*

should be made at least 60 days in advance for the busiest months of April, May, October, and November, as admissions—and hours—are limited. If you don't arrive in time to join the limited first-come, first-served docent tours, opt for the $7 audioguide. SEPTA's Ardmore-bound 44 bus runs from 15th Street and Kennedy Boulevard to Old Lancaster Road and North Latches Lane half a block from the museum; or take SEPTA's R-5 train from 30th Street Station to the Merion Station stop, turn right on Merion Road and left on Latch's Lane, and walk ½ mi to the museum. ✉ *300 Latches La., Merion* ☎ *610/667–0290* 🌐 *www.barnesfoundation.org* 🎫 *$5* ⏲ *Sept.–June, Fri.–Sun. 9:30–5; July and Aug., Wed.–Fri. 9:30–5.*

Bartram's Garden. Begun in 1728 by the pioneering botanist John Bartram (1699–1777), this is America's oldest surviving botanical garden. Bartram, with his son William, introduced into cultivation more than 200 of our native plants; John's international reputation led to him being appointed the Royal Botanist for King George III. With stone columns and carvings by Bartram himself, the furnished 1728 Swedish farmhouse on the grounds reflects his unique vision of classical and Colonial architecture; it's a National Historic Landmark. The gardens include the nation's oldest ginkgo tree, a fragrant flower garden, and a riverside meadow. The trails extending to the Schuylkill River are part of the National Recreation Trails System. The 44-acre oasis is tucked into a heavily industrialized corner of Southwest Philadelphia. You can catch the No. 36 trolley in front of the *Clothespin*, at 15th and Market streets; the ride takes 20 minutes. Note that you can get a map to tour the gardens only when the house is open. ✉ *54th St. and Lindbergh Blvd., Southwest Philadelphia* ☎ *215/729–5281* 🌐 *www.bartramsgarden.org* 🎫 *$5 for house tour, $8 for house and garden tour, garden free* ⏲ *Garden: daily 10–5. House: Mar.–mid-Dec., Tues.–Sun. noon–4; tours at 12:10, 1:10, 2:10, and 3:10.*

★ **Bryn Athyn Cathedral.** At one of the most beautiful spots in the Philadelphia area, atop a hill overlooking the Pennypack Valley, stands a spectacular cathedral built in 12th-century Romanesque and 14th-century Gothic styles. The cathedral is the Episcopal seat of the Church of the New Jerusalem, a sect based on the writings of the Swedish scientist and mystic Emanuel Swedenborg (1688–1772). The main patrons of the church are descendants of John Pitcairn, an industrialist who made his fortune in paint and plate glass. Construction of the cathedral began in 1914 and went on for decades. It was built according to the medieval guild system: all materials—wood, metal, glass, stone—were brought to craftspeople at the site, and everything was fashioned by hand. The stained glass includes two colors, striated ruby and cobalt blue, found nowhere else in the Americas. From Center City, go north on Broad Street to Route 611, right on County Line Road, and south on Route 232 to the second traffic light; the cathedral will be on your right. ✉ *Rte. 232, Huntingdon Pike at Cathedral Rd., Bryn Athyn, 15 mi north of Center City* ☎ *215/947–0266* 🌐 *www.brynathyncathedral.org* 🎫 *Free* ⏲ *Tues.–Sun. 9:30–4; guides offer 30-min tours between 1 and 4 (sometimes preempted by special events); visitors welcome at services Sun. 9:30 (families with children) and 11 (adults).*

Fort Mifflin. Within this 49-acre National Historic Landmark, you can see cannons and carriages, officers' quarters, soldiers' barracks (which contain an exhibition called "Defense of the Delaware"), an artillery shed, a blacksmith shop, a bomb shelter, and a museum. Because of its Quaker origins, Philadelphia had no defenses until 1772, when the British began building Fort Mifflin. It was completed in 1776 by Revolutionary forces under General Washington. In a 40-day battle in 1777, 300 Continental defenders held off British forces long enough for Washington's troops to flee to Valley Forge. The fort was almost totally destroyed but was rebuilt in 1798 from plans by French architect Pierre Charles L'Enfant, who also designed the plan for Washington, D.C. In use until 1962, the fort has served as a prisoner-of-war camp, an artillery battalion, and a munitions dump. Special events include a reenactment of the siege of Fort Mifflin held on the second weekend in November. From Penn's Landing you can easily hop on I–95 to reach the fort; call for directions. ✉ *Island and Hog Island Rds., on the Delaware River near Philadelphia Int'l Airport, Southwest Philadelphia* ☎ *215/685–4167* 🌐 *www.fortmifflin.com* 🎫 *$6* 🕒 *Apr.–Nov., daily Wed.–Sun. 10–4.*

Glencairn Museum. The neo-Romanesque former home of Raymond and Mildred Pitcairn, built between 1928 and 1939, sits on a hill near Bryn Athyn Cathedral, the construction of which Raymond had supervised. A tour showcases the home's chapel, tower, and master bedroom, and the museum's art and artifacts that illuminate the history of religion; many of these were purchased as models for the craftsmen at work on the cathedral. On display are stained-glass windows from around 1200, a "spirit door" from an Egyptian tomb, and a marble statue of Minerva, along with other treasures representing ancient Egyptian, ancient Greek and Roman, Asian, medieval European, and Native American cultures. ✉ *1001 Cathedral Rd., Bryn Athyn* ☎ *267/502–2993* 🌐 *www.glencairnmuseum.org* 🎫 *$7* 🕒 *Open for tours by appointment, weekdays 9–5; Sat. 75–minute highlights tour at 11, 11:30, 12:30, and 1; reservations recommended.*

Insectarium. Even if you hate bugs, you'll love this ugly, yet beautiful collection of thousands of creepy crawlers—tarantulas, giant centipedes, assassin bugs, and metallic beetles that look like pieces of gold jewelry. There are more than 50 live species and mounted insects from around the world at this museum started by exterminator Steve Kanya. The 5,000-square-foot space has one of the largest butterfly and moth collections in North America, a working beehive, a tank filled with glow-in-the-dark scorpions, and a kitchen teeming with live cockroaches. Don't forget to check out the amazing bug gift shop (mounted insects, games, etc.) It's easier to drive here than to take public transportation; call the museum for directions, although you can pick up the subway in front of the *Clothespin*. By public transit: from 15th and Market Street Station take the Market-Frankford subway to the end (Bridge Street); transfer to SEPTA Bus 66 to Welsh Road. ✉ *8046 Frankford Ave., Northeast Philadelphia* ☎ *215/338–3000* 🌐 *www.insectarium.com* 🎫 *$5* 🕒 *Mon.–Sat. 10–4.*

John Heinz National Wildlife Refuge at Tinicum. More than 280 species of ducks, herons, egrets, geese, gallinules, and other birds have been spotted at this 1,200-acre preserve, the largest remaining freshwater tidal marsh in Pennsylvania. There are 8 mi of foot trails, an observation blind, an observation deck, boardwalks through the wet areas, and a canoe launch into the 4½-mi stretch of Darby Creek that runs through the preserve (it's the best way to see it, though you'll have to bring your own canoe). An environmental education center has a library, classrooms, and permanent and changing exhibits on wetlands, natural history, and regional wildlife. Bird-watchers can prepare for their visit by calling for recent sightings. The refuge is convenient to I–95, which you can pick up from Penn's Landing. Call for directions. ✉ *86th St. and Lindbergh Blvd., Southwest Philadelphia* ☎ *215/365–3118, 215/567–2473 bird-watching information* 🌐 *http://heinz.fws.gov* 🎫 *Free* 🕒 *Refuge, daily sunrise–sunset; visitor center, daily 8:30–4.*

Where to Eat

3

WORD OF MOUTH

"Breakfast at the Amish restaurant at Reading [Terminal] Market is wonderful. Get the baked grapefruit and try scrapple (but do NOT ask about ingredients until you try it)."

—Cassandra

"If you want to be in the 'scene,' go to Rittenhouse Square and have breakfast/brunch at either Rouge or Bleu. Grab a table by the window (or on the sidewalk, if the weather is nice), and people-watch."

—yk

www.fodors.com/forums

By Barbara Ann Rosenberg

BACK IN THE "DINING DARK AGES" when Philadelphia was known best for its "snapper" (turtle) soup and overstuffed Italian sandwiches (hoagies) and not much else, this was a difficult city to get excited about. Thankfully, those days are over. In fact, now the only thing that is difficult is choosing *where.* Whether you're in the mood to treat yourself to something fancy, sample innovative cuisine in one of several creative new spots, or just grab a quick bite, Philadelphia has an abundance of intriguing choices. A startling restaurant renaissance that put the city on the national culinary map began nearly 30 years ago and has been escalating ever since—both in the number and variety of places to eat. As each year passes, the tally of restaurants and the range of their cuisines have continued to mushroom—now Philadelphia's dining scene is truly international in scope.

Over the years, the city's restaurants have become more sophisticated in every way. Some have incorporated striking architectural details, providing backdrops as exciting as the food. The well-known Striped Bass spun the concept of what dining interiors should look like on its head by moving into a handsomely renovated brokerage house. Other restaurants followed, metamorphosing turn-of-the-last-century banks into trendy dining locations or building contemporary spaces designed for smashing visual impact.

Ethnic restaurants of nearly every persuasion, from Vietnamese and Malaysian to Jamaican and Cuban, have also enhanced the dining scene. Italian food, a stalwart in any city, has its own connotations here, ranging from South Philadelphia home style to restaurants that rate among the city's most elegant. And, despite people's mounting awareness of their cholesterol levels, steak houses have multiplied, both chain-affiliated and individually controlled. In keeping with a nationwide trend, hotel dining has improved significantly.

A good source for reasonably up-to-the-minute dining information is *Philadelphia,* a monthly magazine with restaurant listings. Two free weekly local papers, the *City Paper* and *Philadelphia Weekly,* also have restaurant reviews and numerous listings. These "freebies" are available in metal sidewalk dispensers on nearly every Center City street corner.

THE HISTORIC AREA, CHINATOWN & SOUTH PHILADELPHIA

The Historic Area has quite a concentration of restaurants, especially around Market Street. Smaller clusters appear in Society Hill and along South Street and in Chinatown. In addition to the fabulous Italian Market, South Philadelphia is a great place for cheap, hearty eats. Northern Liberties is a hike from Old City, and therefore not very convenient for a lunch stop, but the neighborhood's got a burgeoning nightlife scene—and funky restaurants to boot. Neighborhoods in this section are presented clockwise starting from the Historic Area.

3

Mealtimes Unless otherwise noted, the restaurants listed in this guide are open daily for lunch and dinner. Philadelphia doesn't keep late hours: restaurants usually close up by 10 PM on weekdays and stay open an hour or two later on weekends. As in many other cities, brunch has become a weekend ritual for work-weary patrons. Brunch is generally served from 11:30 to 2:30, with Sunday being the big day. Many of the top-notch hotels have outstanding (and expensive) brunches that are virtual extravaganzas. Of course, there are many casual, laid-back restaurants that are great for socializing with a not-so-early morning coffee—or Bloody Mary—in hand.

Reservations & Dress Reservations are noted only when they're essential or not accepted. Bear in mind that Philadelphia is becoming a well-attended convention city, so it's always wise to make reservations and to reconfirm when you get to town. (Le Bec-Fin and Buddakan are generally booked a month ahead for Saturday night.) Many restaurants that don't take reservations for small parties do so for larger groups.

Most of Philadelphia's restaurants can be classified as casual, but not, with the exception of inexpensive spots or the University City area, of the jeans and sneakers variety. Smart casual wear usually works except in the top hotel dining rooms and the most expensive places, where trendy chic is the norm. Dress is mentioned in reviews only when men are required to wear a jacket or a jacket and tie.

Wine, Beer & Spirits The legal drinking age in Pennsylvania is 21. Most large restaurants are licensed to served liquor, whereas smaller ones may have a bring-your-own policy. State-run liquor stores, called state stores, sell wine and other spirits. Beer is sold on a take-out basis by some bars and restaurants but is otherwise available only by the case from certain distribution centers.

Prices

	WHAT IT COSTS				
	$$$$	**$$$**	**$$**	**$**	**¢**
AT DINNER	over $26	$20–$26	$14–$20	$8–$14	under $8

Prices are for one main course at dinner.

Historic Area/Old City

Afghan

$ ✕ **Ariana.** Wall hangings, handsome rugs, and exotic clothing introduce patrons to the country of Afghanistan. The menu, too, is inviting, with straightforward descriptions of subtle, intriguingly seasoned dishes. Ap-

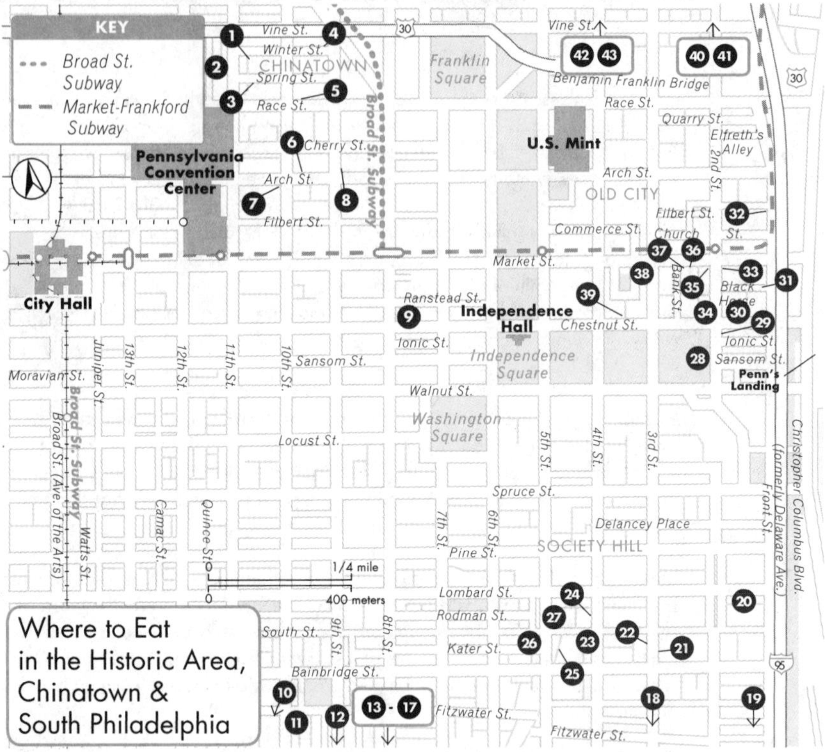

Where to Eat in the Historic Area, Chinatown & South Philadelphia

Historic Area/Old City

Ariana **29**
Bluezette **37**
Buddakan **39**
City Tavern **28**
Continental **33**
Cuba Libre **35**
Fork **38**
Morimoto **9**
Philadelphia Fish **34**
Plough and the Stars **30**
Radicchio Cafe **43**
Ristorante Panorama **32**
Tangerine **36**
Warmdaddy's **31**

Society Hill/South Street

Azafran **21**
Bistro Romano **20**
Django **24**
Hostaria da Elio **22**
Jim's Steaks **23**
Overtures **25**
South Street Souvlaki **26**
TiraMisu **27**

South Philadelphia

Café de Laos **10**
Cucina Forte **17**
Dmitri's **18**
La Lupe **12**
Morning Glory Diner **11**
Pastaria **13**
Pif **16**
The Saloon **15**
Tony Luke's **19**
Tre Scalini **14**

Chinatown

HK Golden Phoenix **5**
Joseph Poon **7**
Ocean Harbor **3**
Penang **6**
Rangoon **8**
Sang Kee **4**
Vietnam **1**
Vietnam Palace **2**

Northern Liberties

Aden **41**
Las Cazuelas **42**
Standard Tap **40**

petizers and side plates are delicious, and the rice-based offerings, often with tender lamb and chicken, are extraordinary. Check out the ultra-smooth rosewater-flavor *firney* (a milk-based pudding) for dessert. ✉ *134 Chestnut St., Old City* ☎ *215/922–1535* ▭ *AE, D, MC, V* ⊙ *No lunch Sun.*

American

$$$$ ✕ **City Tavern.** You can time-travel to the 18th century at this authentic re-creation of historic City Tavern, where the atmosphere suggests that founding fathers such as John Adams, George Washington, Thomas Jefferson, and the rest of the gang *might* have supped here (they didn't; the restaurant was built under the supervision of the National Park Service in 1994, to the specifications of the original 1773 tavern). The food—West Indies pepper pot soup, Martha Washington's turkey stew, honey pecan roast duckling—is prepared from enhanced period recipes and served on handsome Colonial-patterned china or pewter. ✉ *138 S. 2nd St., Old City* ☎ *215/413–1443* ▭ *AE, D, DC, MC, V.*

Contemporary

$$–$$$ ✕ **Fork.** Happy sounds emanate from the diners here—if you can hear them over the noise of the always lively bar patrons. A limited menu of tasty, attractively served food includes the moderately priced rack of lamb that arrives with potatoes and a green vegetable, or roast pork with multiple vegetables. There's usually a wait for a table but not always a place to wait comfortably. Sit as far back in the restaurant as possible to watch the folks at work in the open kitchen. ✉ *306 Market St., Old City* ☎ *215/625–9425* ▭ *AE, D, DC, MC, V* ⊙ *No lunch Sat.*

¢–$ ✕ **Continental Restaurant & Martini Bar.** Light fixtures fashioned like olives pierced with toothpicks are a tip-off to the theme at this cool watering hole. It's installed in a classic diner shell in the center of Old City's action. This is the first of Stephen Starr's trendy restaurants, where he serves lively (but not outré) food to people who know how to enjoy it. Don't miss the addictive Szechuan french-fried potatoes with hot-mustard sauce and the crispy calamari salad. ✉ *138 Market St., Old City* ☎ *215/923–6069* ▭ *AE, DC, MC, V.*

Fodor's Choice ★

Eclectic

$$–$$$$ ✕ **Buddakan.** With soaring walls softened by miles of fabric, this former post office has been transformed into a stylish restaurant. A 10-foot-tall gilded Buddha presides over the otherwise all-white space, seemingly approving of the mostly fusion food that pairs Asian ingredients with various cooking styles. Such relatively familiar dishes as chicken with cashews and tempura lump crab are superb. A long "community table" provides an opportunity to dine with anyone else fortunate enough to snag this center-stage space. Be prepared for major din as the evening wears on. ✉ *325 Chestnut St., Old City* ☎ *215/574–9440* *Reservations essential* ▭ *AE, DC, MC, V* ⊙ *No lunch weekends.*

Irish

$$–$$$ ✕ **Plough and the Stars.** The cheery first floor of a renovated bank feels like a genuine Irish pub. A long bar with a dozen spigots is invariably spouting several imported and a few local brews. In winter, patrons crowd around a blazing fireplace on stools set around small tables. It's possible to munch on good Irish smoked salmon on grainy bread while imbibing; you can also head to the upstairs dining room for some respite from the crush and choose from a panoply of worldly appetizers, salads, and main courses. ✉ *123 Chestnut St., enter on 2nd St., Old City* ☎ *215/733–0300* ▭ *AE, DC, MC, V.*

Italian

$$–$$$ ✕ **Ristorante Panorama.** The name refers to a lovely mural rather than a window view from this lively spot inside the Penn's View Inn. The restaurant has the largest wine cruvinet (storage system) in the country. Besides 120 wines by the glass, there's a huge selection of well-chosen bottles. You can sip them in Il Bar or in the main dining room. The food is authentic Italian—simple and hearty. The ambience is either noisy or animated, depending on your tolerance level. ✉, *14 N. Front St., Old City* ☎ *215/922–7800* ✍ *Reservations essential* ▭ *AE, DC, MC, V.*

$–$$ ✕ **Radicchio Cafe.** This tiny spot becomes loud and crowded as patrons arrive early and exchange their favorable comments about the food—linguini with calamari or scallops and shrimp, striped bass, tender lamb chops, and penne with crabmeat, to name a few. ✉ *402 Wood St., Old City* ☎ *215/627–6850* ✍ *Reservations not accepted* ▭ *MC, V* 🍷 *BYOB* ⊙ *No lunch weekends.*

Japanese

$$–$$$$ ✕ **Morimoto.** Stunningly expensive dishes created by celebrity chef Masaharu Morimoto (of the Food Network's *Iron Chef*) are served in an elegant, slightly futuristic setting. Tables and benches are made of hard white plastic. *Omakase* (tasting menus) are $40 at lunch and $80–$120 at dinner. Authentic and creative à la carte dishes include *toro* (tuna) with caviar and wasabi. ✉ *723 Chestnut St., Historic Area* ☎ *215/413–9070* ▭ *AE, D, DC, MC, V* ⊙ *No lunch Sun.*

Latin

★ $$ ✕ **Cuba Libre.** People who have been in Havana swear this place is a dead ringer. In any event, it is lovely, with balconies and fancy streetlights and even a leaded-glass window—on the interior. An entire menu is devoted to rum from everywhere in the Caribbean and Central and South America. There's some that's smooth enough to be mistaken for fine brandy and served in snifters. The appetizers, like lobster empanadas and crab cakes, taste fairly authentic; rice and black beans are served with just about everything, of course. It's lively and everyone seems to be having a good time. ✉ *10 S. 2nd St., Old City* ☎ *215/627–0666* ▭ *AE, D, DC, MC, V* ⊙ *No lunch.*

Moroccan

$$–$$$$ ✕ **Tangerine.** Although neither the interior nor the food are authentic Moroccan, there's enough of the genuine to make people feel as though they are in that beautiful, exotic country. Take the hundreds of candles twinkling in hundreds of niches. Take the *tagines* (cone-topped clay pots) that hold some of the oven-cooked dishes, and take the flavors of many of the richly spiced dishes and, somehow, the whole experience adds up to a trip to North Africa, in spirit, at least. Dishes are served family style.

ON THE MENU

Although Philadelphia is home to some of the most highly praised restaurants in the country, most of its specialties are decidedly down-to-earth.

The delicious cheese steak remains the best-known of Philly's food offerings. It's an artery-clogging combination of thinly sliced rib-eye steak, gooey cheese, and grilled onions and peppers, served on a fresh Italian roll. Hoagies, a Philadelphia spin on Italian sandwiches (called subs or heroes elsewhere), make quick, convenient, and highly filling lunches. Plump, salted, soft pretzels must be eaten with mustard to be the real deal.

An odd classic is snapper soup. The traditional recipe, made famous by Bookbinder's, involves adding turtle meat to a tomato-and-vegetable puree, flavored with herbs, garlic, and sherry.

Preserved duck with couscous and fruit is a good candidate. ✉ *232 Market St., Old City* ☎ *215/627–5116* ✍ *Reservations essential* ▭ *AE, DC, MC, V* ⏲ *No lunch.*

Seafood

$$–$$$ ✕ **Philadelphia Fish & Company.** Chef Anthony Bonnet is back in command of the adventurous, imaginative menu at this oasis for seafood lovers. The frequently changing items on the raw bar are outstanding. Outdoor dining and drinking take place in season on a deck that overlooks busy Chestnut Street and is good for people-watching—and traffic noise. ✉ *207 Chestnut St., Old City* ☎ *215/625–8605* ▭ *AE, D, DC, MC, V.*

Soul Food

$$–$$$ ✕ **Bluezette.** Looking very much like a work in progress with the steel structure climbing up the front, this ultramodern converted storefront serves soul food, Caribbean and Latin American style. No matter what taste of home people are looking for, it's all here. Fried chicken is always a winner; shrimp and grouper creole are special, as is the curried goat. There's also a top-drawer bar. ✉ *246 Market St., Old City* ☎ *215/627–3866* ▭ *AE, DC, MC, V* ⏲ *Closed Mon.*

$–$$ ✕ **Warmdaddy's.** This blues club also houses a creditable restaurant serving a full menu of sincere down-home cooking. The ribs and fried catfish are outstanding. ✉ *4 S. Front St., Old City* ☎ *215/627–8400* ▭ *AE, D, DC, MC, V* ⏲ *No lunch.*

Society Hill/South Street

Diners & Philly Food

¢ ✕ **Jim's Steaks.** You'll know when you're nearing Jim's when the scent of mountains of frying onions overwhelms your senses. Big, juicy, drippy sandwiches of Philly steaks—shaved beef piled high on long crusty rolls—come off the grill with amazing speed when the counter workers hit their stride; but be aware that no matter how hard you beg, they will not toast the rolls. Take extra napkins so you won't end up wearing your sandwich. Jim's is mostly take-out, but there are some tables and chairs upstairs. ✉ *400 South St., South Street* ☎ *215/928–1911* *Reservations not accepted* *No credit cards.*

Eclectic

$$–$$$ ✕ **Django.** An inspired young couple paired their skills to create this neighborhood haunt out of a storefront—food professionals and amateurs alike are intrigued. The regional European menu changes daily; you might find roasted duck, lemon-poached salmon, scallops, mussels, or a tender sirloin steak. Light, airy house-baked bread is charmingly served in plant pots. Furniture and tableware are simple and mismatched in an oh-so-chic way. ✉ *526 S. 4th St., South Street* ☎ *215/922–7151* *Reservations essential* *AE, DC, MC, V* *BYOB* *Closed Mon. No lunch.*

French

$$–$$$$ ✕ **Overtures.** The food isn't pure French, but the interpretations of chef Peter Lamlein are inspired. Although the menu changes periodically, there's always lavender-scented rack of lamb, a genuine winner. Among the stylish decorative touches are extravagant flower arrangements, trompe l'oeil paintings, and black-and-white floor tiles. ✉ *609–611 E. Passyunk Ave., off South St., South Street* ☎ *215/627–3455* *AE, DC, MC, V* *BYOB* *Closed Mon. No lunch.*

Fodor'sChoice ★

Greek

$–$$ ✕ **South Street Souvlaki.** The first thing you'll see is the large rotisserie, trumpeting the ubiquitous gyro—tasty slices of meat are stuffed inside a large fresh pita, with tangy yogurt and some exemplary fresh veggies. Other Greek specialties, such as stuffed grape leaves, moussaka, and, of course, souvlaki, round out the menu. ✉ *509 South St., South Street* ☎ *215/925–3026* *MC, V* *Closed Mon.*

Italian

$$–$$$ ✕ **Bistro Romano.** Copious portions of regional Italian cuisine are served in the brick-walled dining room of this early-18th-century granary. Don't miss the acclaimed Caesar salad prepared tableside by the genial owner, who thoroughly enjoys animated conversations with his guests. Tuesday-night lobster specials make the trip to the Society Hill area more than worthwhile. ✉ *120 Lombard St., South Street* ☎ *215/925–8880* *AE, D, DC, MC, V* *No lunch.*

$$–$$$ ✕ **TiraMisu Ristorante.** This is among the few restaurants in town that offer the exquisite dishes of Rome's Jewish community, which is why you'll find homemade matzos in your basket of Italian bread. A must-try is a special preparation of fried artichokes. The restaurant has an old-world elegance, including a piano bar. ✉ *528 S. 5th St., South Street* ☎ *215/925–3335* *AE, MC, V* *Closed Sun.*

$–$$$ ✕ **Hostaria da Elio.** The simple surroundings belie the sophistication of the chef, who prepares light-as-a-feather pastas with complex sauces.

Spinach gnocchi with homemade tomato sauce and gnocchi with Gorgonzola-cheese sauce are both excellent. Go early to avoid the crowds. ✉ *615 S. 3rd St., South Street* ☎ *215/925–0930* ▭ *AE, D, DC, MC, V* 🍷 *BYOB* ⏲ *Closed Mon.*

Latin

$–$$$ ✕ **Azafran.** No question that there's an artist at work here, indicated by the colorful paintings (sort of weird) and the delicious food (not at all weird, but certainly different). Pan-Latin is perhaps the best way to describe the menu that keeps patrons lined up every weekend. Empanadas, looking vaguely like egg rolls, are tops. There's outdoor dining in good weather. ✉ *617 S. 3rd St., South Street* ☎ *215/928–4019* ✍ *Reservations not accepted* ▭ *AE, DC, MC, V* 🍷 *BYOB* ⏲ *Closed Mon. No lunch.*

South Philadelphia

Diners & Philly Food

¢–$ ✕ **Morning Glory Diner.** The Morning Glory bills itself as a diner, and offers traditional touches such as big mugs of steaming coffee (although the mugs are pewter). But this popular place, transformed from a couple of storefronts, has its own idiosyncrasies: the big breakfasts come with mammoth homemade biscuits; if you want toast, you pay extra. Tasty turkey meat loaf, frequently topped off with homemade catsup, is a specialty. The accompanying fried potatoes, however, are often underseasoned and dull. Expect lines for weekend brunch. ✉ *735 S. 10th St., South Philadelphia* ☎ *215/413–3999* ▭ *No credit cards* ⏲ *No dinner Mon.*

¢ ✕ **Tony Luke's.** The location—nearly under I–95—earned such a reputation from truckers who stopped for huge beef or pork sandwiches with Italian greens and cheese that locals finally caught on and adopted the dinerlike establishment for their own. The lines are long, though they move quickly, and seating (outside only, under cover) is relatively scarce; still, people flock here from early morning to closing time for generous breakfasts and tasty sandwiches. For large orders, it's possible to call ahead for take-out. ✉ *39 E. Oregon Ave., South Philadelphia* ☎ *215/551–5725* ✍ *Reservations not accepted* ▭ *No credit cards* ⏲ *Closed Sun.*

French

$$–$$$ ✕ **Pif.** The quintessentially French food here benefits from proximity to the Italian Market. The owner selects his favorite ingredients there every morning. The menu changes daily, but it usually includes fresh fish. The frogs' legs and escargot appetizers get special attention. Authentic desserts are prepared by the owner's French wife. ✉ *1009 S. 8th St., Italian Market* ☎ *215/625–2923* ▭ *AE, D, DC, MC, V* 🍷 *BYOB* ⏲ *Closed Mon. No lunch.*

Italian

$$–$$$$ ✕ **Cucina Forte.** Chef Maria Forte turns out plenty of Italian classics, plus fanciful dishes such as Maria's Dream Soup (a mix of pork, chicken, and seafood with pasta), a true delight. A cream cake makes a delectable finish. Cucina Forte serves lunch by appointment only. ✉ *768 S. 8th*

St., South Philadelphia ☎ *215/238–0778* ▭ *AE, D, DC, MC, V* 🍷 *BYOB* ⏲ *Closed Mon.*

$$–$$$ ✕ **Pastaria at Franco and Luigi's.** Arias from classic operas, sung mostly by fresh-faced young singers who are in training or have done professional stints around Philadelphia and other cities, accompany somewhat unusual, but unquestionably Italian, dishes such as veal, shrimp, and scallops sautéed in scampi sauce over a bed of shredded radicchio. Reserve well in advance to ensure seating on weekends. ✉ *1547–49 S. 13th St., South Philadelphia* ☎ *215/755–8903* ▭ *AE* 🍷 *BYOB* ⏲ *Closed Mon. No lunch.*

$–$$$ ✕ **Tre Scalini.** "Three little steps" are exactly what it takes to enter this restaurant in South Philadelphia, a locus of down-home Italian. The food is more homey than trendy, but it's carefully prepared, including such unusual (for South Philadelphia) appetizers as a tangle of wild mushrooms, beautifully sautéed with garlic. Otherwise, pasta dishes—such as black pasta with prawns and crabmeat—are best. The main courses suffer by comparison. ✉ *1533 S. 11th St., South Philadelphia* ☎ *215/551–3870* ▭ *AE, MC, V* 🍷 *BYOB* ⏲ *Closed Mon.*

Mexican

¢–$ ✕ **La Lupe.** This homey little place on the edge of the Italian Market could not be more authentic in its flavors, and this fact is backed up by the presence of many Mexican-Americans on the weekends. Try the enchiladas *suizas,* which drip with genuine Mexican cheese. ✉ *1201 S. 9th St., Italian Market* ☎ *215/551–9920* ▭ *AE, D, MC, V* 🍷 *BYOB.*

Seafood

$–$$ ✕ **Dmitri's.** This no-frills eatery has developed quite a loyal following. The specialties, such as grilled octopus, have unmistakable flavors of lemon and garlic. Be forewarned: the wait for a table can be long. ✉ *795 S. 3rd St., Queen Village* ☎ *215/625–0556* ✍ *Reservations not accepted* ▭ *No credit cards* 🍷 *BYOB.*

Steak

$$$–$$$$ ✕ **The Saloon.** For many years this classic paneled restaurant has been a favorite among Philadelphia's most discerning diners, who enjoyed steaks and chops in more-than-generous portions and the always-true-to-their-roots Italian specialties. The superior quality of ingredients still shines, but with the help of an inspired chef, Gene Betz, a few more innovative twists sneak into the outstanding preparations, although not so many that they intrude on the sensibilities of the regulars. ✉ *750 S. 7th St., South Philadelphia* ☎ *215/627–1811* ▭ *AE* ⏲ *Closed Sun. No lunch Sat. and Mon.*

Thai

$–$$ ✕ **Café de Laos.** Wonderfully rendered *kalagas* (beaded and sequined wall hangings) set the tone at this elegant eatery. The staffers are often bedecked in elegant silk fabrics embroidered with gold thread. When you walk in the door you might think you've arrived in Southeast Asia, a feeling reinforced by the tasty, authentic Thai and Laotian food. ✉ *1117 South St., South Philadelphia* ☎ *215/647-1546* ▭ *MC, V.*

Chinatown

Burmese

$–$$ ✕ **Rangoon.** Burmese food is somewhat Chinese and somewhat Indian, with a touch of other tastes that make the mixture intriguing. The spring ginger salad and thousand-layer bread served with a potato-curry dipping sauce are both excellent. Portions are somewhat small, but because of the fullness of the flavors, diners usually leave satisfied. ⊠ *112 N. 9th St., Chinatown* ☎ *215/829–8939* ▭ *MC, V.*

Chinese

$–$$$ ✕ **Joseph Poon.** Named for its owner-chef, who created Chinese-Italian fusion, this contemporary restaurant decorated with jars of pasta is often the scene of special events, such as free weekly cooking classes. Peking duck pizza, Arch Street cioppino (fish in a black bean, bourbon, and ginger sauce), and fried spinach with five-spice powder and Parmesan are typical creations. Poon is also a celebrity master carver of fruits and vegetables, and his handiwork frequently decorates his plates. ⊠ *1002 Arch St., Chinatown* ☎ *215/928–9333* ▭ *AE, D, DC, MC, V* ⊙ *Closed Mon. No lunch weekends.*

¢–$$ ✕ **HK Golden Phoenix.** This restaurant, known for its authentic Hong Kong atmosphere, is where Chinatown really got started. Now it is a mecca for dim sum—China's answer to tapas—and the carts of many-flavored treats come flying around at lunchtime. Newcomers generally shy away from more unusual dishes like chicken feet. By and large, however, it is a favorite of veterans and novices alike, and the check is generally easy on the wallet. More familiar dishes are served in the evening. ⊠ *911 Race St., Chinatown* ☎ *215/629-4988* ▭ *AE, MC, V.*

¢–$$ ✕ **Ocean Harbor.** At lunch this restaurant resembles a Hong Kong–style teahouse. Carts filled with a dizzying array of dim sum fill the aisles. If you don't know what's in a particular dish, ask for a description—sometimes you get it. The clientele that crowds the restaurant at lunch is mainly Chinese. Evenings, when the menu features Cantonese, Mandarin, and Szechuan dishes, are quieter. There are plenty of vegetarian options. ⊠ *1023 Race St., Chinatown* ☎ *215/574–1398* ▭ *DC, MC, V.*

¢–$ ✕ **Sang Kee Peking Duck House.** Although the decor is getting a bit tired, Sang Kee continues to dish up delicious noodle soups. Egg or rice noodles come in different widths and are simmered with duck, pork, or beef brisket. If you wish, you can have your soup with both noodles *and* overstuffed, tender wontons. Other traditional foods, besides the house specialty duck, are carried from the kitchen with more speed than style. Beer is available. ⊠ *238 N. 9th St., Chinatown* ☎ *215/925–7532* ✍ *Reservations not accepted* ▭ *No credit cards.*

Malaysian

¢–$$ ✕ **Penang.** The juxtaposition of bamboo and exposed pipes is indicative of the surprising mix of flavors in this perennially busy restaurant. A taste of India creeps into a scintillating appetizer of handkerchief-thin crepes served with a small dipping dish of spicy chicken curry. Other preparations are redolent of flavors from several other Asian countries. Soups with various types of noodles are unusual, tasty, and filling.

⊠ *117 N. 10th St., Chinatown* ☎ *215/413–2531* ✍ *Reservations not accepted* ▭ *No credit cards.*

Vietnamese

¢–$ ✕ **Vietnam.** This popular restaurant next to a busy police station serves an extensive selection of Vietnamese dishes. Restaurateurs from much fancier establishments often find one another here, comparing notes on which dishes they find particularly tasty. The crisp spring rolls, squid with black bean sauce, and soups with rice noodles are good picks. Occasionally, however, it seems as if the chef might be "out to lunch." It's cheap enough, however, to forgive an occasional lapse without damaging the budget. ⊠ *221 N. 11th St., Chinatown* ☎ *215/592–1163* ▭ *No credit cards.*

¢–$ ✕ **Vietnam Palace.** Although Vietnam Palace is a bit more sophisticated than its neighbor, it's still up for grabs which of the two restaurants dishes up the more authentic grub. The menu here is lengthy, with soups, seafood, and fish entrées, and a whole page of vermicelli dishes. Reservations are recommended on weekends. ⊠ *222 N. 11th St., Chinatown* ☎ *215/592–9596* ▭ *AE, D, MC, V.*

Northern Liberties

American

$–$$ ✕ **Standard Tap.** This smoky, noisy restaurant is a Northern Liberties fixture, popular with young hipsters. The food, such as the duck confit salad and roasted beets, is decent, and undoubtedly the minimalist prices contribute to many folks' positive evaluation. There's brunch on Sunday. ⊠ *901 N. 2nd St., Northern Liberties* ☎ *215/238–0630* ✍ *Reservations not accepted* ▭ *AE, DC, MC, V* ⊙ *No lunch.*

Mediterranean

$–$$ ✕ **Aden.** This charming, funky restaurant turns out astonishing food from an open kitchen. The owners are a self-taught chef, Hadaar Nisimi, and his sister, Nurit, who serves as the restaurant's hostess. A grilled vegetable salad is a standout, and osso buco with barley risotto is a cornerstone of the menu. There's usually a selection of nicely prepared fish dishes. A pleasant garden is open in good weather. ⊠ *614 N. 2nd St., Northern Liberties* ☎ *215/627–9844* ▭ *AE, D, MC, V* *BYOB* ⊙ *No lunch weekends.*

Mexican

$ ✕ **Las Cazuelas.** This authentically Mexican family-run place is an anomaly in a rather industrial neighborhood. The colors, both inside and out, are warm and bright. The food is simple and rather gently spiced, apropos of the family's roots in the town of Puebla. Reservations are essential for groups larger than four. ⊠ *426–28 W. Girard Ave., Northern Liberties* ☎ *215/351–9144* ▭ *MC, V.*

CENTER CITY & WEST

There are a lot of restaurants to choose from in Center City. Many of them are high-price dazzlers like Le Bec-Fin, though the variety here is notable—dining can be a multicourse extravaganza or as simple as grabbing a falafel. Rittenhouse Square, naturally, also has its share of flash, with fewer budget options. Reliable choices are sparser up by Fairmount Park, but branch out again as you head west. In University City, you can enjoy the many affordable, funky eateries geared toward Penn students. There are also a few gems hidden off the Main Line.

Center City

Belgian

$–$$$ ✕ **Monk's Cafe.** Mussels are practically the national dish of Belgium. Whether steamed in classic style with wine and shallots or with cream, they are a high point at this casual, lively bar and restaurant. The fries that accompany them draw raves from the regulars who crowd the place. Burgers, too, are favorites. Add to these an outstanding assortment of Belgian specialty dishes and beers and you get the picture. ⊠ *264 S. 16th St., Center City* ☎ *215/545–7005* ✍ *Reservations not accepted* ▭ *MC, V* ⊙ *Closed Sun.*

Chinese

★ **$$–$$$$** ✕ **Susanna Foo.** The displays of exotic orchids and contemporary Chinese art provide a worthy setting for this nationally known restaurant. Foo has won many awards for her cuisine, which incorporates Western ingredients into traditional Chinese dishes. Favorites such as Hundred-Corner Crab Cakes are on the regular menu, and specials, such as foie gras, are offered from time to time. There's a full bar with imported beers and a pricey wine list. ⊠ *1512 Walnut St., Center City* ☎ *215/545–2666* ✍ *Reservations essential* ▭ *AE, DC, MC, V* ⊙ *No lunch weekends.*

Contemporary

★ **$$$$** ✕ **The Grill.** Don't let the unassuming name fool you: this place is everything you'd expect from a restaurant in the Ritz-Carlton Philadelphia. You'll find a sophisticated, eclectic menu designed by one of the city's outstanding chefs. Foie gras and grilled quail are two of the best starters. Main courses include such choices as a superb veal chop and rack of baby lamb. There's a dessert buffet on Friday and Saturday nights that sends patrons sighing with pleasure. ⊠ *10 S. Broad St., Center City* ☎ *215/735–7700* ✍ *Reservations essential* 👔 *Jacket required* ▭ *AE, D, DC, MC, V* ⊙ *No lunch weekends.*

$$$–$$$$ ✕ **Bliss.** Multi-talented chef Francesco Martorella exercises his imagination in this somewhat stark space—think of it as a blank canvas that allows him to create wonderful dishes ranging from pan-seared sirloin with potato puree gratin to stir-fried red-chili prawns. The patrons, many of them music stars from the nearby Academy of Music, are drawn to this place where the chef is clearly in command and enjoys his position. An early crowd gives way to a more sophisticated group as the evening wears on and more and more bottles from the excellent wine list are poured. ⊠ *220-224 S. Broad St. Center City* ☎ *215/731-1100* ✍ *Reservations essential* ▭ *AE, D, DC, MC, V* ⊙ *Closed Sun.*

$$$–$$$$ ✕ **Founders.** At this elegant top-floor restaurant in the historic Park Hyatt Philadelphia at the Bellevue, tuxedoed waiters bring your meal in covered silver trays. Arched windows give stunning views of Center City. The out-

Center City

Alma de Cuba **21**
Astral Plane **27**
Black Sheep **25**
Bliss **36**
Brasserie Perrier **22**
Capital Grille **39**
Caribou Cafe **45**
Deux Cheminées **44**
Ernesto's 1521 Cafe **26**
Founders **37**
The Grill **40**
Il Portico **32**
Jamaican Jerk Hut **28**
Le Bec-Fin **30**
Los Catrines **23**
McCormick & Schmick's **41**
Monk's Cafe **24**
Morton's of Chicago **38**
Palm **37**
!Pasion! **35**
Petite Passion **11**
Reading Terminal Market **42**
Samosa **43**
Sansom Street Oyster House **33**
Striped Bass **34**
Susanna Foo **31**
Vetri **29**
Zanzibar Blue **37**

Rittenhouse Square

Bleu **20**
Devon Seafood Grill **18**
Friday Saturday Sunday **13**
Genji **16**
Lacroix **14**
Prime Rib **19**
Rouge **17**
Smith & Wollensky **15**

Ben Franklin Parkway & Art Museum Area

Delmonico's **4**
Figs **3**
Fountain **5**
London Grill **2**
Museum Restaurant **1**

University City

Marigold Kitchen **12**
Nan **7**
Pod **9**
Tandoor India **10**
Thai Singa House **6**
White Dog Café **8**

standing Sunday brunch is amazing in bounty and variety. Jackets are required for dinner Friday and Saturday. ✉ *200 S. Broad St., Center City* ☎ *215/790–2814* ▭ *AE, DC, MC, V* ⏲ *No dinner Sun. and Mon.*

$–$$$$ ✕ **Astral Plane.** This charming townhouse is filled with mementos from more romantic eras. It was a hangout for stage and screen folk passing through town, and their favorite dishes still pepper the menu. Favorites include macadamia-encrusted sea bass and chicken stuffed with prosciutto and fresh mozzarella. The host's welcome is extraordinary and the locals who have adopted the restaurant for many years set a casual, funky tone. ✉ *1708 Lombard St.* ☎ *215/546-6230* ▭ *MC, V* ⏲ *No dinner Sun.*

$$–$$$ ✕ **Friday Saturday Sunday.** Although the menu (like the decor) is somewhat dated, the finished product is generally pleasing. Entrées are simple compared with today's inventive fusion cuisines—grilled tuna steak, chicken Dijon, filet mignon—but will nonetheless leave you feeling satisfied. One of the restaurant's pluses is the policy of charging just $10 above cost for wine. ✉ *261 S. 21st St., Center City* ☎ *215/546–4232* ✍ *Reservations essential* ▭ *AE, DC, MC, V* ⏲ *No lunch Sat.–Mon.*

$$–$$$ ✕ **Zanzibar Blue.** Known primarily as an upscale lounge drawing some of the top names in jazz, this low-lit boîte in the Park Hyatt Philadelphia at the Bellevue is reminiscent of Parisian clubs. The eclectic food is prepared by long-standing star chef Al Paris; there's delicious mango-barbecued king shrimp scampi and cider-glazed double-cut pork chops. The short ribs are extraordinary. The Sunday brunch features top-notch jazz along with eggs and other brunch specialties. ✉ *200 S. Broad St., Center City* ☎ *215/732–5200* ▭ *AE, D, DC, MC, V* ⏲ *No lunch.*

$–$$ ✕ **Petite Passion.** You can eat like a king at paupers' prices at this intimate 50-seat restaurant inside the Art Institute of Philadelphia. On Wednesday and Thursday the four-course lunch is $10; the six-course dinner, $20. The menu changes weekly, depending on what's fresh in the market and what inspires the culinary arts students and instructors. ✉ *2300 Market St., Center City* ☎ *215/405–6766* ✍ *Reservations essential* ▭ *No credit cards* ⏲ *Closed Fri.–Tues.*

Eclectic

★ ¢ ✕ **Reading Terminal Market.** A long-standing landmark, the Reading Terminal Market contains a profusion of stalls, shops, lunch counters, and food emporiums in a huge indoor market. You can choose from numerous raw ingredients and prepared foods—Chinese, Greek, Mexican, Japanese, Thai, Middle Eastern, Italian, and Pennsylvania Dutch, to name a few. Food options include an extensive salad bar, hoagie and cheese steak shops, a deli, a bakery, a sushi bar, and an outstanding ice cream counter. Get here early to beat the lunch rush. Hours are 8–6. ✉ *12th and Arch Sts., Center City* ☎ *215/922–2317* ⏲ *Closed Sun.*

French

$$$$ ✕ **Deux Cheminées.** This restaurant occupies two 19th-century mansions filled with Oriental rugs, oil paintings, and objets d'art that create a supremely romantic setting. The French-style food on the $85 prix-fixe menu is classic in style and presentation. Signature dishes include rack of lamb with truffle sauce and a rich crab bisque with Scotch.

The service here is truly solicitous. ✉ *1221 Locust St., Center City* ☎ *215/790–0200* 💳 *AE, DC, MC, V* ⏲ *Closed Sun. and Mon. No lunch.*

$$$$ Fodor'sChoice ★ ✕ **Le Bec-Fin.** For many years this outpost of cuisine from Lyon, with gold-colored walls and gleaming crystal chandeliers that resemble those at Versailles, set a stratospherically high standard for Philadelphia. There is still sufficient acclaim to require an advance reservation of a month or more to garner a table on Saturday night. The popular *galette de crab* (a sublime crab cake) is a signature appetizer. Do save room for the magnificent dessert cart. If dinner is out of your price range, it's possible to indulge in an amazing three-course lunch for $45. Le Bar Lyonnais—down a flight of stairs from the main dining room—is a small, charming space that features the chef's specialty dishes for more affordable prices. ✉ *1523 Walnut St., Center City* ☎ *215/567–1000* *Reservations essential* *Jacket required* 💳 *AE, D, DC, MC, V* ⏲ *Closed Sun.*

$$$–$$$$ ✕ **Brasserie Perrier.** Another work by Georges Perrier, owner of Le Bec-Fin, this exuberant, Americanized version of a brasserie has an art deco ambience with silvery ceilings and plush banquettes. Chef Chris Scarduzio's cuisine is modern French, with Italian and Asian influences. Try the crispy black sea bass with black truffle sauce. Weekly plats de jour include Alsacian *choucroute* (duck served with sausage and sauerkraut) and braised lamb shank. At lunch, a $26 prix-fixe three-course meal is served along with an à la carte menu. ✉ *1619 Walnut St., Center City* ☎ *215/568–3000* 💳 *AE, DC, MC, V* ⏲ *No lunch Sun.*

$$–$$$$ ✕ **Caribou Cafe.** From the sidewalk seating to the bistro fare (mussels, sausages, and steak frites), chef Olivier de St. Martin has created an authentic spot for Francophiles. The vintage posters over the bar reinforce the atmosphere. A menu of French aperitifs puts neophytes in the mood to enjoy the kitchen's creations. Duck confit is a favorite. ✉ *1126 Walnut St., Center City* ☎ *215/625–9535* 💳 *AE, DC, MC, V.*

Indian

¢–$ ✕ **Samosa.** This lunch and dinner buffet will please even the strictest vegetarians. The Sikh family that runs Samosa clearly enjoys its loyal clientele, who return to the table again and again to savor the tasty, but never too spicy, dishes. There are always delicious samosas (triangle-shape pastries filled with potatoes and peas), perfectly cooked basmati rice, and the best veggies in the market. Desserts are super-sweet. No liquor is allowed on the premises. ✉ *1214 Walnut St., Center City* ☎ *215/545–7776* 💳 *MC, V.*

Irish

$–$$ ✕ **Black Sheep.** Converted from a private club with blacked-out windows, this Dublin-style pub has been packing them in for rivers of Irish draft and kitchen specialties. Fish-and-chips could have been produced on the "auld sod," and the malt vinegar to sprinkle over it all does little to dampen the crisp crust. The first-floor bar is noisy and spirited, but the mood gets a bit quieter as you climb the steps to the dining room. ✉ *247 S. 17th St., Center City* ☎ *215/545–9473* *Reservations not accepted* 💳 *AE, D, DC, MC, V.*

Italian

$$$–$$$$ ✕ **Vetri.** Chef Mark Vetri blew into town from New York, where his cooking had garnered all sorts of kudos. This tiny space was formerly home to such stellar restaurants as Le Bec-Fin. The magic of the location seems to be working again as Vetri's deft hands turn out such specialties as feather-light green gnocchi, shellfish soup, and a strange-sounding but exquisite dessert known as chocolate polenta soufflé. Saturday dinner is limited to a five-course tasting menu for $65 or a seven-course tasting menu for $90. Some complain that the portions are too small. ✉ *1312 Spruce St., Center City* ☎ *215/732–3478* ✍ *Reservations essential* ▭ *AE, DC, MC, V* ⊙ *Closed Sun. No lunch.*

$$–$$$$ ✕ **Il Portico.** This elegant restaurant is next door to flashy Le Bec-Fin, so it doesn't get the attention it deserves. Service is excellent, as is the food: beef carpaccio, black *tagliolini* (long, flat pasta) with salmon in a brandy sauce, chicken breast stuffed with fontina cheese and Parma ham, and a simple pasta sautéed with broccoli and sausage. Some dishes are a bit pricey. ✉ *1519 Walnut St., Center City* ☎ *215/587–7000* ✍ *Reservations essential* ▭ *AE, MC, V* ⊙ *No lunch weekends.*

$–$$$ ✕ **Ernesto's 1521 Cafe.** A devoted clientele has helped transform this simple café into a sophisticated bistro. The location across from the Kimmel Center hasn't hurt, either. The food is creative, with hints of French and other cuisines mingling with the standard Italian flavors. The fried calamari, for example, is served with mango chutney. The vegetable Napoleon satisfies vegetarians; carnivores might prefer the braised lamb or one of the seafood dishes. Desserts made by the owner's mother are outstanding. A lighter menu is available after 8 PM. ✉ *1521 Spruce St., Center City* ☎ *215/546–1521* ▭ *MC, V* ⊙ *Closed Mon. No dinner Sun.*

Jamaican

$–$$ ✕ **Jamaican Jerk Hut.** The scintillating flavors of Jamaica taste at least as good as on their original turf. That's because of chef Nicola Shirley, who applies her culinary school training to the dishes of her homeland. Pork or chicken jerk is lovingly tended over an authentic pit; the curries and *roti* (pancakes with fillings such as curried chickpeas or chicken) are exemplary. This tiny storefront is primarily take-out, but you can eat in a charming back garden when the weather permits. ✉ *1436 South St., Center City* ☎ *215/545–8644* ▭ *No credit cards* ⊙ *Closed Sun.*

Japanese

$$–$$$ ✕ **Genji.** When it opened in University City, this restaurant helped kick off the craze for Japanese cuisine. At its Center City location, it continues to cater to the cult of those who love fine raw (and cooked) fish. Spare and utterly Japanese, it has a loyal following. ✉ *1720 Sansom St., Center City* ☎ *215/564–1720* ▭ *AE, D, DC, MC, V* ⊙ *No lunch weekends.*

Latin

$$–$$$$ ✕ **¡Pasion!** The rich red entryway sets the tone for the culinary passion inside. A tented ceiling floats over flower-covered walls. Argentine chef Guillermo Pernot's food draws on his intimacy with several South American and Caribbean cuisines, and he certainly doesn't hold back on the intensity of any of the seasonings. Chilean sea bass is cooked with wild mushrooms and tamarind sauce; the stunning sampler plate of ceviche is a specialty. ✉ *211 S. 15th St., Center City* ☎ *215/875–9895* ▭ *AE, D, DC, MC, V* ⊙ *No lunch.*

$$–$$$$ ✕ **Alma de Cuba.** A bit of scrolled ironwork greets diners, who have to traipse up one or two flights of stairs to get to the action. A bar that pulsates with Cuban music lets everyone know this is a happening place. But the decor is evocative of—what? Bare brick walls and a lot of black paint don't say much about Cuba. The food contains a few genuine dishes, such as *lechon asado* (crispy roasted baby pig) and shrimp ceviche, all prepared by chef Douglas Rodriguez. Although oysters are not generally considered Cuban, they are a knockout here. Bring a flashlight if you want a shot at reading the menu. ✉ *1623 Walnut St., Center City* ☎ *215/988–1799* ▭ *AE, DC, MC, V* ⏲ *No lunch weekends.*

Mexican

★ **$$–$$$$** ✕ **Los Catrines.** Chef Carlos Molina makes this a destination for anyone in the mood for Mexican food. Authentic south-of-the-border dishes such as *chiles rellenos* (moderately spicy poblano peppers stuffed with cheese or ground meat), and *posole* (pork and hominy stew). The dining room features Mexican glassware and colorful ceramics. You can choose from a dozen different Mexican beers and 52 types of tequila. ✉ *1602 Locust St., Center City* ☎ *215/546–0181* ▭ *AE, DC, MC, V* ⏲ *Closed Sun. No lunch Sat.*

Seafood

$$$$ ✕ **Striped Bass.** This striking restaurant opened with a bang in 1994, then struggled to keep its panache. It managed to re-emerge as a stellar entry with Alfred Portale at the helm and Christopher Lee running the kitchen. The focus is innovative fish and seafood dishes, and there is an extensive raw bar of pristine shellfish. A spectacular 16-foot sculpture of a leaping striped bass continues to hang over the exhibition kitchen, setting the tone for anyone confused about the current thrust of the restaurant. But the rest of the room has a more sophisticated look, with subdued upholstery on the ultra-contemporary chairs and enormous stunning barrel-shaped crystal chandeliers. ✉ *1500 Walnut St., Center City* ☎ *215/732–4444* ✍ *Reservations essential* ▭ *AE, DC, MC, V* ⏲ *No lunch Sat.*

$$–$$$$ ✕ **Sansom Street Oyster House.** This restaurant has the most authentic "fish house" feeling in the city, almost like no-nonsense places in Boston. The Mink family, who ran the place since time immemorial, left as their legacy the huge collection of antique oyster plates that decorate the walls. Chef Cary Neff searches out the freshest seafood and then prepares it simply and expertly. There's always a whole fish on the daily changing menu, cooked to perfection. If crispy bronzino, a farm-raised Mediterranean fish, is being served, give it a try. There's an active raw bar at the front of the restaurant. ✉ *1516 Sansom St., Center City* ☎ *215/567–7683* ▭ *AE, D, DC, MC, V* ⏲ *Closed Sun.*

$$ ✕ **McCormick & Schmick's Seafood Restaurant.** "Big, bold, and beautiful" might be the best way to describe this fish house, especially when you're talking about the ceiling with its remarkable art deco chandeliers. There are more than 40 daily specials brought in from many ports, such as Maine (lobsters) and Chile (sea bass). Of course, there are oysters galore. The food is prepared by a knowledgeable kitchen crew and served by a well-trained staff. ✉ *1 S. Broad St., Center City* ☎ *215/568–6888* ▭ *AE, D, DC, MC, V* ⏲ *No lunch weekends.*

BRING YOUR OWN, BUDDY

W **HEN PHILADELPHIA RESIDENTS** *make plans to go out for Italian food, somebody is certain to ask, "Is it BYOB?" The 10% tax on alcoholic beverages purchased in restaurants, which is on top of the regular 7% tax on meals, has made bringing one's own bottle of wine more and more popular. It's a great deal, as most places don't charge for corking your bottle or for supplying glasses.*

One favorite trattoria with a BYOB policy is ***Hosteria da Elio*** *(✉ 615 S. 3rd St., South Street ☎ 215/925–0930), brainchild of Elio Sgambati. A native of Rome, the chef has an idiosyncratic style that his patrons appreciate. His gnocchi, either green or white, is a must, as is the light, rich Italian wedding cake. And the long list of specials your server recites never disappoints.*

Cucina Forte *(✉ 768 S. 8th St., South Philadelphia ☎ 215/238–0778) is a quiet place—except on Saturday nights, when it is impossible to hear your friends across the table. Maria Forte is a talented chef who one night dreamed about a soup that she later cooked up for her guests. The soup is replicated more or less faithfully each night, except when she decides to stray from the original recipe. It doesn't matter which of several variations are served, since the soup is always delicious. Glasses are provided in several sizes and one of them is generally acceptable for the wine of the evening.*

Trattoria Prima Donna *(✉ 1506 Spruce St., Center City ☎ 215/790–0171) is an anomaly: the restaurant has a full bar with both wine and spirits, but notes at the bottom of its menu that patrons are also "free to bring their own wine." And there's no corkage charge. Strange, but welcome. This location, around the corner from the Kimmel Center, the city's main music venue, makes it popular. Don't miss the meat cannelloni.*

Steak

$$$–$$$$ ✕ **Morton's of Chicago.** This classic steak house attracts many visitors familiar with its outposts in other cities, as well as a devoted coterie of local business executives. Etched glass and wood paneling provide a semblance of privacy in the large dining room, and there's an intimate

CloseUp

WHERE TO REFUEL AROUND TOWN

For those times when all you want is a quick bite—and you just can't face another cheese steak or slice of pizza—consider these alternatives.

Cosi: *This specialist in pancetta sandwiches satisfies office workers and tourists alike with beguilingly crisp crusts and a variety of tasty fillings. Pleasant desserts round out the menu.*

Italian Market: *At 9th and Christian are a few lunch spots featuring hot pork and tripe sandwiches in addition to many varieties of hoagies. If you prefer fish, Anastasio's Fish Market at 9th and Washington also serves lunch and dinner.*

Street Vendors: *A number of lunch carts in Center City offer ethnic food, including Chinese, Japanese, Middle Eastern, and Italian, as well as the more standard hot dogs, hamburgers, and fresh fruit. In University City, the block between 37th and 38th on Sansom Street has various ethnic vendors catering to Penn students.*

stand-up bar. The house specialty, a 24-ounce porterhouse, puts the most determined carnivore to the test. Pristine whole fish and lobsters are priced by the pound. ✉ *1411 Walnut St., Center City* ☎ *215/557–0724* ▭ *AE, DC, MC, V* ⊙ *No lunch.*

$$–$$$$ ✕ **Capital Grille.** It's only fair to question whether this is a restaurant or an art gallery. When you first enter the stunning dining room, you'll find walls covered with exquisitely framed paintings and pedestals bearing bronze statues. Steaks and chops come in two sizes: large and larger. A baby lobster (about a pound) makes an excellent appetizer along with the requisite green salad and shrimp cocktail. The wine cellar is ample and fairly priced for a selection of excellent bottles. ✉ *1338 Chestnut St., at Broad St., Center City* ☎ *215/545–9588* ▭ *AE, D, MC, V* ⊙ *No lunch weekends.*

$$–$$$$ ✕ **Palm.** The city's branch of this celebrated chain holds forth in a beige space off the lobby of the Park Hyatt at the Bellevue. The steak-house ambience comes complete with bare floors, harried waiters, and huge steaks, chops, and salads whizzing by. Nearly in the shadow of City Hall, this is deal-making territory, and local movers and shakers are frequently seen chatting at lunch and dinner. Caricatures of local legends hang on the walls, and it's fun to match up the diners with their likenesses. The flavorful New York strip steak is fine at dinner, and the stupendous steak sandwich (*no* relation to a cheese steak) is a lunchtime value. ✉ *200 S. Broad St., Center City* ☎ *215/546–7256* ▭ *AE, D, DC, MC, V* ⊙ *No lunch weekends.*

Rittenhouse Square

Contemporary

$$$$ ✕ **Lacroix.** Jean-Marie Lacroix, the former chef at the Four Seasons, has become head honcho of the kitchen at the Rittenhouse Hotel. Here he has introduced a new twist on the prix-fixe—build a three-course, four-course, or five-course meal from any items from the menu and pay $55, $65, or $75. Pumpkin soup with warm leek flan and fried shallots, beef tenderloin with bone marrow ravioli, and Alaskan halibut with veal stew are just some of the choices. ✉ *210 W. Rittenhouse Sq., Rittenhouse Square* ☎ *215/790–2533* ⚠ *Reservations essential* ♔ *Jacket required* ▭ *AE, D, DC, MC, V.*

$$–$$$$ ✕ **Rouge.** A jewel box of a restaurant, Rouge is very much a "meet and greet" kind of place. Ladies who lunch love it—as do wheelers and dealers with offices in the neighborhood—both for midday repast and a chance to meet for drinks at the busy bar or one of the sidewalk or window tables overlooking Rittenhouse Square. The martinis are large, but food portions can sometimes be small. The tuna tartare is excellent, as are the steak frites and herb-roasted chicken. Many regulars opt for the outstanding hamburger. ✉ *205 S. 18th St., Rittenhouse Square* ☎ *215/732–6622* ⚠ *Reservations not accepted* ▭ *AE, MC, V.*

$–$$$ ✕ **Bleu.** This lively café with its hand-painted French-inspired murals is the sister restaurant to Rouge, at the other end of a dynamic block facing Rittenhouse Square. The menu features gorgeous salads filled with exotic ingredients and a blockbuster hamburger-and-french-fries combo. In pleasant weather you can enjoy the moving panorama of people walking and cycling past the square by sitting at the open windows or snagging an increasingly difficult-to-obtain sidewalk table. ✉ *227 S. 18th St., Rittenhouse Square* ☎ *215/545–0342* ⚠ *Reservations not accepted* ▭ *AE, DC, MC, V.*

Seafood

$$–$$$$ ✕ **Devon Seafood Grill.** Once you get past the crowded bar (it's so popular with young singles that it's nearly impossible to get in the door on Fridays), you enter a quintessential fish house with all the classic dishes and then some. Lobster in several sizes is always on the menu and generally available in all of them, beautifully cooked to order. Hot biscuits delivered to the table are runaway favorites. ✉ *225 S. 18th St., Center City* ☎ *215/546–5940* ▭ *AE, DC, MC, V.*

Steak

$$$–$$$$ ✕ **Smith & Wollensky.** Adjacent to the Rittenhouse Hotel, this lively outpost of a New York classic steak house is on two levels—a café-type bar on the 1st floor and a traditional dining room upstairs. The restaurant serves a typical steak-house menu with some unique variances: all the steaks are dry-aged on the premises, a roasted pork shank is a permanent menu special, and a 28-ounce Cajun rib eye is the runaway favorite of locals. A baby lobster is a delightful appetizer. ✉ *210 Rittenhouse Sq., Rittenhouse Square* ☎ *215/545–1700* ▭ *AE, D, DC, MC, V.*

★ **$$–$$$$** ✕ **Prime Rib.** The glamorous atmosphere and clubby feel immediately make you aware that you're in for some serious eating. Habitués (of whom there are many) admire the gigantic slabs of dry-aged prime beef, glistening fresh seafood (also served in more than generous portions), addictive baked potato skins, and other sit-up-and-take-notice dishes that keep this handsome restaurant hopping. ✉ *Warwick Hotel, 1701 Locust St., Center City* ☎ *215/772–1701* ⚠ *Reservations essential* ♔ *Jacket required* ▭ *D, MC, V* ⊙ *No lunch weekends.*

Ben Franklin Parkway/Art Museum Area

Contemporary

$$$$ Fodor'sChoice ★ ✕ **Fountain.** Dining here is a cosmopolitan experience, blending pleasant, polished service with elegant appointments. The peak of the experience, however, is unquestionably the food, with such dishes as soup with smoked salmon and celeriac, and sautéed Hawaiian onaga fillet with porcini mushroom ragout. Chef Martin Hamann and his staff are constantly experimenting to create culinary excitement that changes with the seasons. The restaurant is tucked away off the lavish but understated lobby of the Four Seasons—a culinary oasis for travelers and a favorite dining location for well-heeled locals. Especially popular is the Sunday brunch, a knockout in bounty, elegance—and price. ✉ *1 Logan Sq., Benjamin Franklin Parkway/Museum Area* ☎ *215/963–1500* *Reservations essential* *Jackets required* *AE, D, DC, MC, V.*

$$$ ✕ **Museum Restaurant.** The venerable Philadelphia Museum of Art gives visitors an opportunity to feed their bodies while nourishing their souls at lunch as well as at Wednesday dinner and Sunday brunch. The restaurant is bright, white, and hung with a rotating display of paintings. The Chef's Table, a buffet with unlimited returns, artfully arranges foodstuffs such as ham, salmon, green beans, Parmesan toasts, crisp salads, and a fine cheese board. ✉ *26th St. and Benjamin Franklin Pkwy., Benjamin Franklin Parkway/Museum Area* ☎ *215/684–7990* *AE, DC, MC, V* *Closed Mon. No dinner Thurs.–Tues.*

$$–$$$ ✕ **London Grill.** Serving modern takes on old favorites, such as sea scallops poached in lobster oil with potato blinis, this longtime favorite keeps locals interested with its seasonally changing menus, which are imaginative and consistently good. So, too, is the bar food; mussels, wings, and quesadillas are popular. ✉ *2301 Fairmount Ave., Fairmount* ☎ *215/978–4545* *AE, D, DC, MC, V* *No lunch Sat.*

Mediterranean

$$–$$$ ✕ **Figs.** A large fig tree sets the tone for this simple restaurant. Some Moroccan specialties are woven through the menu. Otherwise, the flavors of the Mediterranean permeate. Kebabs are tasty; usually there's a good *tagine* (stew of meat or poultry simmered with vegetables, olives, garlic, and spices) on the menu. ✉ *2501 Meredith St., Fairmount* ☎ *215/978–8440* *No credit cards* *BYOB* *Closed Mon.*

Steak

$$–$$$$ ✕ **Delmonico's.** This restaurant has such a sophisticated atmosphere that patrons dress up—you rarely see people wearing jeans or even khakis. Leopard-print carpeting and dark-wood booths complete the picture. The dry aged steaks satisfy those who come to this out-of-the-way location for the pleasure of chef Vincent Alberici's individual touches that dress up the otherwise ordinary steak house menu. Lobster bisque is a house specialty, and the kitchen also shines with unique vegetable and seafood presentations. ✉ *Hilton Philadelphia City Avenue, 4200 City Ave., City Line Avenue* ☎ *215/879-4000* *AE, D, DC, MC, V.*

University City

Contemporary

$$–$$$ ✕ **White Dog Cafe.** The restaurant specializes in organic foods such as grass-fed beef and trout with a hazelnut crust. Seasonings can be overly ambitious, so choose carefully. Vegetarians can find plenty to please them here. The small, lively bar has a number of American beers on tap and in bottles; the wine list, too, is all-American. ✉ *3420 Sansom St., University City* ☎ *215/386–9224* ▭ *AE, D, DC, MC, V.*

$$ ✕ **Marigold Kitchen.** Just about every dish at this simple eatery bears the stamp of the current chef. Workaday ingredients like chicken livers take on an original twist when served in delicious croquettes. Plain-Jane desserts like bread pudding become exotic when made with pumpernickel and chocolate. The atmosphere, typified by golden-oak furniture, is unremarkable. ✉ *501 S. 45th St., West Philadelphia* ☎ *215/222-3699* ▭ *AE, DC, MC, V* ⏲ *Closed Mon.*

Eclectic

★ $$ ✕ **Nan.** Long before "fusion" was an official foodie term, the inspired chef here took a wholly different approach to his native Thai cuisine, pairing it with French ingredients and techniques. As a result, you're just as likely to find escargot on the menu as chicken *saté.* Others have followed suit, but Nan is still bewitching diners with an intoxicating mix of flavors: salmon with lemongrass, pork cooked with thyme and dried fruits, and pheasant with tamarind, to name just a few. The simple three-course lunch is a bargain; the fruit tart is ethereal. ✉ *4000 Chestnut St., University City* ☎ *215/382–0818* ▭ *AE, MC, V* 🍷 *BYOB* ⏲ *Closed Sun. and Mon.*

$–$$ ✕ **Pod.** The futuristic atmosphere of this restaurant (all-white tables and chairs and enveloping booths whose lighting changes color with the touch of a button) is a fitting setting for food with strong Asian overtones that ultimately defies precise description. The sushi conveyor is an entertaining touch. Dim sum, stir fry, and crab pad thai share the menu with entrées such as crispy scallion chicken, wasabi-crusted filet mignon, and the amusingly named "Lobzilla," a 3-pound lobster served with risotto and soba noodle salad. There's an extensive sake bar—you can get it warm or cold. Reservations are essential on the weekend. ✉ *3636 Sansom St., University City* ☎ *215/387–1803* ▭ *AE, DC, MC, V* ⏲ *No lunch weekends.*

Indian

$–$$$ ✕ **Tandoor India.** Although the ambience is not particularly elegant in this student-oriented restaurant, there's a full range of delicious foods cooked in the *tandoor* (super-hot clay oven) as well as other dishes prepared in conventional pots and pans. There's a bargain-price buffet at lunch and dinner and a full range of other authentic North and South Indian specialties served à la carte. ✉ *106 S. 40th St., University City* ☎ *215/222–7122* ▭ *AE, D, DC, MC, V* 🍷 *BYOB.*

Thai

$ ✕ **Thai Singa House.** Simple and unprepossessing, this pleasant family-run Thai outpost cooks all the usual Thai dishes as well as an array of more unusual ones (for this country, at least), including venison and wild boar. Pad thai is particularly well prepared, with a fine meld of flavors. The family is fun to talk with, and the proprietor and his wife are helpful both to novices and to experts exploring unfamiliar dishes on the menu. ✉ *3939 Chestnut St., University City* ☎ *215/382–8001* 💳 *AE, D, DC, MC, V.*

BEYOND DOWNTOWN PHILADELPHIA

Manayunk, Germantown & Chestnut Hill

For full reviews of the restaurants in these neighborhoods, *see* Chapter 2, Manayunk, Germantown & Chestnut Hill.

$$$–$$$$ ✕ **Jake's.** ✉ *4365 Main St., Manayunk* ☎ *215/483–0444.*

$$$–$$$$ ✕ **Osaka.** ✉ *8605 Germantown Ave., Chestnut Hill* ☎ *215/242–5900.*

$–$$ ✕ **Citrus.** ✉ *136 Germantown Ave., Chestnut Hill* ☎ *215/247–8188.*

$–$$ ✕ **Le Bus.** ✉ *4266 Main St., Manayunk* ☎ *215/487–2663.*

$–$$ ✕ **North By Northwest.** ✉ *7165 Germantown Ave., Mt. Airy* ☎ *215/248–1000.*

Main Line

French

$$$–$$$$ ✕ **Georges.** This restaurant looks as if it were transported brick by brick from Provence. Table settings reflect the warm colors of southern France. The bouillabaisse (a fish and shellfish soup) is true to its origins; the ultimate representative of the region is the *salade niçoise,* made with fresh rather than canned tuna, and tiny, tasty olives. Gravlax, mysteriously called here *fondant de saumon,* is cut in thick chunks rather than slices; it's sumptuous. The wine list includes a number of reasonable bottles, including some from Provence. ✉ *Spread Eagle Village, 503 W. Lancaster Ave., Wayne* ☎ *610/964–2588* 💳 *AE, D, DC, MC, V* ⏲ *No lunch weekends.*

Mediterranean

★ **$$–$$$$** ✕ **Bianca.** The subtle atmosphere of the restaurant is a perfect backdrop for its exquisite food, making it worth a trip from downtown Philadelphia. Award-winning chef Dominique Filoni produces sauces that are somehow rich without being full of fat. Indulge in stellar slow-cooked dishes such as luscious caramelized short ribs. Desserts, once a disappointment, have improved to meet the main-course standards. ✉ *24 N. Merion Ave., Bryn Mawr* ☎ *610/527–7700* 💳 *AE, D, DC, MC, V* ⏲ *No lunch.*

Thai

$–$$ ✕ **Lemon Grass Thai.** With occasional deviations (mostly the lunchtime specials), the Thai food here is about as authentic as you can get in town. It's conscientious in its presentation, but down-to-earth enough to be a favorite among Penn students. Pad thai with baby shrimp is among the most popular choices. ✉ *3626 Lancaster Ave., West Philadelphia* ☎ *215/222–8042* 💳 *AE, D, DC, MC, V* ⏲ *No lunch weekends.*

Where to Stay

4

WORD OF MOUTH

"The Penn's View Inn is a really pretty hotel . . . The area is perfect for walking on a Sunday and having brunch in one of the many restaurants along that street. You can walk over to the Liberty Bell and the lovely park where it resides. . . ."

—ScarlettK

"If Thom from *Queer Eye for the Straight Guy* were to decorate a hotel, it would look like [the Hotel Sofitel Philadelphia]. The room walls and closets paneled in honey-colored wood, the carpets and fabrics of wonderful patterns and colors, and the marble bathroom with a rimless shower were all a visual treat. . . ."

—Alicia

www.fodors.com/forums

By Bernard Vaughan

FROM HISTORIC DIGS WITH FOUR-POSTER BEDS to grand hotels serving room-service foie gras, Philadelphia has lodgings for every style of travel. Thanks to the Pennsylvania Convention Center and a hotel-building boom in the late 1990s, some mid-price chains have moved into town or have spruced up their accommodations. If you have greater expectations, you need look no further than the city's handful of swank hotels, each with its own gracious character.

Budget, moderate, and luxury properties are spread throughout the downtown area. The Historic Area, on the east side of downtown, centers on Independence Hall and extends to the Delaware River, and is a good base for sightseeing. Old City and Society Hill lodgings are also convenient for serious sightseeing; Society Hill is the quietest of the three areas. For business-oriented trips, Center City encompasses the heart of the downtown business district, centered around Broad and Market streets, and Rittenhouse Square hotels are also nearby.

If you prefer to keep your distance from the tourist throngs, check out the Benjamin Franklin Parkway–Museum Area along the parkway from 16th Street to the Philadelphia Museum of Art. There are also a couple of hotels in University City—just across the Schuylkill River in West Philadelphia and close to the University of Pennsylvania and Drexel University—a 5- to 10-minute drive or taxi ride from Center City. Additional hotels are clustered near Philadelphia International Airport, about 8 mi south (a 20-minute drive) of Center City. Four are in the City Line Avenue area, west of downtown. Other options can be found in outlying areas, including Valley Forge, and Lancaster and Bucks counties.

Historic Area, Old City & Society Hill

$$$–$$$$ **Hyatt Regency at Penn's Landing.** The theme here is "room with a view." The first hotel to open on the banks of the Delaware River offers dramatic river views from both back and front rooms of the 22-story tower. The 4th-floor fitness center overlooks the city and the waterfront; after you swim in the indoor pool, you can lounge on the outdoor terrace. Likewise, Keating Restaurant has both indoor seating and alfresco dining on a deck above the river. The guest rooms are contemporary and well sized; Business Plan rooms include laptop computers and fax machines. ✉ *201 S. Columbus Blvd., Penn's Landing 19106* ☎ *215/928–1234 or 800/233–1234* 📠 *215/521–6600* 🌐 *www.pennslanding.hyatt.com* *337 rooms, 13 suites* *Restaurant, café, room service, in-room safes, cable TV, in-room broadband, indoor pool, health club, sauna, bar, business services, meeting rooms, car rental, free parking, parking (fee)* 💳 *AE, D, DC, MC, V.*

$$$–$$$$ **Omni Hotel at Independence Park.** An ornate fireplace dominates the breathtaking marble lobby of this towering hotel in the historic district. Enjoy cocktails in the adjoining lounge, where floor-to-ceiling windows overlook an expansive lawn and city streets. The spacious rooms all have views of the greenery but are otherwise undistinguished. All are decorated in pretty floral prints and have sleeper sofas. Children are treated to complimentary cookies and milk. This is a pleasant base for visiting

Facilities Assume that all rooms have private baths unless otherwise noted. Assume that hotels operate on the **European Plan** (EP, with no meals) unless we specify that they use the **Continental Plan** (CP, with a Continental breakfast), **Breakfast Plan** (BP, with a full breakfast), **Modified American Plan** (MAP, with breakfast and dinner), or the **Full American Plan** (FAP, with all meals).

Reservations Even with the large number of hotel rooms, sometimes it's difficult to find a place to stay, so advance reservations are advised. Philadelphia has no real off-season, but many hotels offer discount packages for weekends, when the demand from business travelers and groups subsides. Besides substantially reduced rates, these packages often include an assortment of freebies, such as breakfast, parking, cocktails, and the use of exercise facilities. Tickets to popular museum shows have become part of many packages, too. Most downtown hotels charge an average of $15 a day for parking, but some include it in the rate.

Prices We always list the facilities that are available, but we don't specify whether they cost extra. When pricing accommodations, always ask what's included and what costs extra.

WHAT IT COSTS

	$$$$	$$$	$$	$	¢
FOR 2 PEOPLE	over $240	$190–$240	$140–$190	$90–$140	under $90

Prices are for a standard double room.

the nearby art galleries and cafés, as well as the Liberty Bell, Independence Hall, and other sights. ✉ *4th and Chestnut Sts., Old City 19106* ☎ *215/925–0000 or 800/843–6664* 🖷 *215/925–1263* 🌐 *www.omnihotels.com* *147 rooms, 3 suites* *Restaurant, room service, in-room data ports, in-room safes, minibars, cable TV, Wi-Fi, indoor pool, exercise equipment, health club, hot tub, massage, spa, bar (with entertainment), lobby lounge, shop, laundry service, concierge, business services, Internet, parking (fee), no-smoking rooms, no-smoking floors* ▭ *AE, D, DC, MC, V.*

$$–$$$$ **Sheraton Society Hill.** Convenient to downtown sights, this Colonial-style building is two blocks from Penn's Landing, three blocks from Head House Square, and four blocks from Independence Hall. Framed by archways, the pleasant atrium lobby is flooded with natural light during the day and lighted by wrought-iron lanterns at night. Rooms are done in restful shades of blue or green; the 4th-floor rooms facing east toward the Delaware River have the best views. The glass ceiling over the indoor pool provides an outdoor feel year-round. ✉ *1 Dock St., Society*

Hill 19106 ☎ 215/238–6000 or 800/325–3535 🖷 215/922–2709 🌐 www.sheraton.com ⇨ 365 rooms, 14 suites ♁ 2 restaurants, room service, in-room data ports, some refrigerators, cable TV with movies and video games, indoor pool, wading pool, gym, health club, hot tub, massage, sauna, bar, laundry service, concierge, Internet, business services, meeting rooms, airport shuttle (fee), parking (fee), some pets allowed, no-smoking floors ▭ AE, D, DC, MC, V.

$–$$$ **Best Western Independence Park Hotel.** Surrounded by key historic sites as well as many nightlife options, this five-story hotel is in the middle of things. Built in 1856, it has been run as a hotel since 1988. The high-ceiling guest rooms are modern but have a few period touches. Deluxe rooms have parlors and king-size beds. Continental breakfast is served in a glass atrium, and afternoon tea is available in the lobby. A wine and cheese reception is held every Wednesday at 5:30. ✉ *235 Chestnut St., Old City 19106 ☎ 215/922–4443 or 800/624–2988 🖷 215/922–4487 🌐 www.independenceparkinn.com ⇨ 36 rooms ♁ In-room data ports, cable TV, business services, meeting rooms, parking (fee), some pets allowed (fee), no-smoking rooms ▭ AE, D, DC, MC, V 🍴 CP.*

$–$$$ **Holiday Inn Historic District.** This hotel lies within what is billed as the country's "most historic square mile," within a block and a half of the Liberty Bell and Independence Hall. The eight-story hotel with rooftop pool was refurbished in 1999, but is already looking tired in the lobby and hallways. The rooms are still pleasant, and this is still a bargain. ✉ *4th and Arch Sts., Old City 19106 ☎ 215/923–8660 or 800/843–2355 🖷 215/923–4633 🌐 www.holiday-inn.com/phlhistoric ⇨ 364 rooms, 7 suites ♁ Restaurant, dining room, room service, cable TV with movies and video games, in-room data ports, WiFi, pool, exercise equipment, bar, lounge, shops, laundry facilities, Internet, business services, parking (fee) ▭ AE, D, DC, MC, V.*

$$ Fodor'sChoice ★ **Penn's View Inn.** This cosmopolitan little hotel in a refurbished 19th-century commercial building on the fringe of Old City has its own brand of urban charm. The owner is a well-regarded Italian-born restaurateur and also runs Ristorante Panorama, the downstairs eatery, and Il Bar, with perhaps the best wine cellar in the city. Accommodations are comfortable and rather European looking, with Chippendale-style furniture, floral wallpaper, and queen beds; four larger rooms have fireplaces, whirlpool baths, and views of the Delaware River. Rooms facing the street can be noisy. ✉ *14 N. Front St., Old City 19106 ☎ 215/922–7600 or 800/331–7634 🖷 215/922–7642 🌐 www.pennsviewhotel.com ⇨ 50 rooms, 2 suites ♁ Restaurant, dining room, room service, in-room data ports, some in-room hot tubs, some refrigerators, cable TV, in-room broadband, wine bar, concierge, business services, meeting rooms, airport shuttle, parking (fee), no-smoking rooms ▭ AE, DC, MC, V 🍴 CP.*

$–$$ **Thomas Bond House.** This bed-and-breakfast sits in the heart of Old City. Built in 1769 by a prominent local physician, the four-story Georgian house has undergone a faithful, meticulous restoration of everything from its molding and wall sconces to the woodwork and flooring. Rooms have reproduction period furnishings (there are also a few antiques), including four-poster beds, and two have marble fireplaces. In keeping with the Colonial theme, some rooms are a tad cold in winter.

Continental breakfast is served weekdays; a full breakfast is served on weekends. ✉ *129 S. 2nd St., Old City 19106* ☎ *215/923–8523 or 800/845–2663* 🖷 *215/923–8504* 🌐 *www.winston-salem-inn.com/philadelphia* *10 rooms, 2 suites* *Cable TV, business services, parking (fee); no smoking* ▭ *AE, MC, V* *CP.*

¢–$$ **Comfort Inn at Penn's Landing.** The reasonable price is the main attraction at this 10-story hotel. Tucked among several busy streets, the location has more noise than charm—but if you have a room on an upper floor facing the river, you'll enjoy a good view of the Benjamin Franklin Bridge lit up at night. A bar helps enliven the small, nondescript lobby. The courtesy van service to Center City is a nice plus. ✉ *100 N. Columbus Blvd., Penn's Landing 19106* ☎ *215/627–7900 or 800/228–5150* 🖷 *215/238–0809* 🌐 *www.comfortinn.com* *185 rooms, 2 suites* *In-room data ports, in-room safes, cable TV, Wi-Fi, bar, lobby lounge, laundry service, business services, meeting rooms, airport shuttle, parking (fee), no-smoking rooms* ▭ *AE, D, DC, MC, V* *CP.*

¢ **Bank Street Hostel.** This independently owned hostel is downtown's best bargain. It's on the edge of the historic district in a 140-year-old factory that has been combined with two neighboring buildings. Dormitory-style rooms, segregated by gender, have enough bunk beds to accommodate 70 people. Guests often gather around the pool table and watch nightly videos in the common area. The facility is a member of Hostelling International. ✉ *32 S. Bank St., Old City 19106* ☎ *215/922–0222 or 800/392–4678* 🖷 *215/922–4082* 🌐 *www.bankstreethostel.com* *70 beds* *Kitchen, billiards; no room phones, no room TVs* ▭ *No credit cards.*

Center City

★ $$$$ **Ritz-Carlton Philadelphia.** You'll feel like you're checking into the Pantheon when you enter this neoclassical hotel set in a century-old bank building. Sixty thousand square feet of Georgian white marble are sparsely decorated with palms, classical statues, and well-chosen antiques. Sixteen Ionic columns ascending the height of nine stories dwarf the lobby lounge, and natural light cascades through the oculus of the 140-foot dome ceiling. Guest rooms done in a warm caramel-and-brown color scheme are less grandiose—and surprisingly small—but offer good views of the city. The Club rooms, on the top four floors, feature upgraded amenities, a dedicated concierge, and complimentary food in the hand-carved, walnut-panel Ritz-Carlton Club, which has breathtaking views of the north, east, and south sides of the city. ✉ *10 S. Broad St., Center City 19107* ☎ *215/523–8000 or 800/241–3333* 🖷 *215/523–8002* 🌐 *www.ritzcarlton.com* *303 rooms, 36 suites* *2 restaurants, room service, in-room data ports, in-room safes, minibars, cable TV with movies, in-room broadband, gym, bar, laundry service, concierge, Internet, business services, travel services, parking (fee), some pets allowed, no-smoking floors* ▭ *AE, D, DC, MC, V.*

$$$$ Fodor's Choice ★ **Westin Philadelphia.** If luxurious accommodations and plenty of shopping are your top priorities, you're not going to beat the Westin. The 15-story structure sits between the twin blue towers of Liberty Place and

Historic Area, Old City & Society Hill ▼

Bank Street Hostel **34**
Best Western Independence Park **36**
Comfort Inn Penn's Landing **32**
Holiday Inn Historic District **31**
Hyatt Regency Penn's Landing **39**
Omni Independence Park **35**
Penn's View Inn **33**
Sheraton Society Hill **38**
Thomas Bond House **37**

Center City ▼

Alexander Inn **24**
Courtyard Philadelphia Downtown **27**
Crowne Plaza City Center **10**
Doubletree **21**
Hampton Inn **29**
Holiday Inn Express Midtown **22**
Hotel Sofitel **15**
Latham **14**
Loews Philadelphia **25**
Marriott Residence Inn . . **28**
Park Hyatt at the Bellevue **20**
Philadelphia Marriott . . . **26**
Philadelphia Travelodge . **30**
Ritz-Carlton **23**

Westin 16

Rittenhouse Square ▼

Radisson Plaza Warwick .13

The Rittenhouse 11

Rittenhouse Square B&B . .12

Benjamin Franklin Parkway/ Museum Area ▼

Best Western Center City . .1

Embassy Suites 8

Four Seasons 6

Hotel Windsor 9

Wyndham Franklin Plaza . .7

University City ▼

The Gables 17

Inn at Penn 18

Sheraton University City .19

City Avenue ▼

Chamounix Mansion 3

Hilton Philadelphia City Avenue 2

Holiday Inn City Line 5

Homewood Suites City Avenue 4

Airport District ▼

Four Points by Sheraton .41

Hilton Philadelphia Airport 43

Holiday Inn Philadelphia Airport 42

Philadelphia Airport Marriott 44

Sheraton Suites, Philadelphia Airport 40

near the Shops at Liberty Place, where you'll find more than 70 stores, boutiques, and restaurants. Rooms are decorated in what can be called luxury Colonial. Breakfronts full of gorgeous china and fine paintings set the tone in the public areas. The top-notch fitness center features video monitors on each treadmill. But if you plan on working out, sightseeing, shopping—or even just leaving the room, for that matter—the hotel's signature, aptly named "Heavenly Bed" can make it a herculean effort. ✉ *99 S. 17th St., at Liberty Pl., Center City 19103* ☎ *215/563–1600 or 800/937–8461* 📠 *215/567–2822* 🌐 *www.westin.com/philadelphia* *275 rooms, 15 suites* *Restaurant, room service, in-room safes, minibars, cable TV, cable TV with movies and video games, in-room data ports, in-room broadband, Wi-Fi, exercise equipment, health club, massage, bar, lobby lounge, babysitting, children's programs (ages 2–11), laundry service, concierge, concierge floor, Internet, business services, meeting rooms, airport shuttle, parking (fee), some pets allowed, no-smoking rooms* 💳 *AE, D, DC, MC, V.*

$$$–$$$$ **Loews Philadelphia Hotel.** Topped by the red neon letters PSFS (referring to the former tenant, Pennsylvania Savings Fund Society), this 1930s building was the country's first skyscraper in the ultramodern international style. With an attitude that is decidedly contemporary, the hotel has guest rooms that are equipped with cordless phones and data ports. There are three levels of concierge rooms with a private library and lounge. The lobby lounge and Sole Food, an eclectic, fusion seafood restaurant, are both art deco in style. A 15,000-square-foot state-of-the-art fitness center includes a sauna, steam room, and indoor lap pool. ✉ *1200 Market St., Center City 19107* ☎ *215/627–1200 or 800/235–6397* 📠 *215/231–7305* 🌐 *www.loewshotels.com* *581 rooms, 35 suites* *Restaurant, room service, in-room data ports, in-room safes, minibars, cable TV with movies and video games, in-room broadband, indoor pool, gym, health club, sauna, bar, lounge, babysitting, children's programs (ages 3-12), laundry service, concierge floors, Internet, business services, convention center, parking (fee), some pets allowed* 💳 *AE, D, DC, MC, V.*

$$$–$$$$ Fodor's Choice ★ **Park Hyatt Philadelphia at the Bellevue.** A Philadelphia institution for almost a century, the elegant Bellevue sparkles. Starting with the champagne toast when you check in, a stay here is all about luxury. The spacious rooms are done in light, bright prints and have the high ceilings and moldings typical of older buildings. Founders, the posh restaurant, has views of the city from its 19th-floor perch; The Barrymore Room, topped by a 30-foot stained-glass dome, is great for tea and cocktails. Bliss offers eclectic American and Asian-influenced cuisine in a serene setting smack in the middle of Broad Street's theater district. The hotel's lower floors have been transformed into shopping (including Tiffany's and Ralph Lauren). ✉ *Broad and Walnut Sts., Center City 19102* ☎ *215/893–1234 or 800/233–1234* 📠 *215/732–8518* 🌐 *www.parkhyatt.com* *133 rooms, 39 suites* *6 restaurants, food court, room service, in-room fax, in-room data ports, in-room safes, some kitchens, minibars, cable TV with movies and video games, in-room DVDs, in-room broadband, Wi-Fi, indoor pool, hair salon, hot tub, massage, sauna, spa, bar, lobby lounge, shops, babysitting, laundry service, concierge, Internet, business services, parking (fee), no-smoking rooms* 💳 *AE, D, DC, MC, V.*

$$$–$$$$ **Philadelphia Marriott.** This bustling convention hotel—the biggest in Pennsylvania—fills an entire city block. It has so many corridors that sometimes even the staff gets lost. For an intrinsically impersonal type of place, the Marriott tries hard to meet special needs; it also offers some of the lowest rates in its price category. The five-story lobby atrium has a water sculpture, piano music (live and taped), and greenery (real and fake). The more than 1,400 guest rooms are brightly decorated; half come with two queen beds, the rest with kings. You can request, at no additional cost, one of the 250 "rooms that work," with adjustable desks and extra lighting and outlets. The hotel has recently added a sushi bar and coffee shop. ✉ *1201 Market St., Center City 19107* ☎ *215/625–2900 or 800/228–9290* 📠 *215/625–6000* 🌐 *www.philadelphiamarriott.com* *1,408 rooms, 76 suites* *3 restaurants, coffee shop, room service, in-room data ports, some in-room hot tubs, some kitchenettes, some refrigerators, cable TV with movies and video games, in-room broadband, indoor pool, wading pool, exercise equipment, health club, hair salon, hot tub, spa, bar, 2 lobby lounges, sports bar, shop, laundry facilities, laundry service, concierge, business services, meeting rooms, parking (fee), some pets allowed, no-smoking floors* 💳 *AE, D, DC, MC, V.*

$$–$$$$ **Courtyard Philadelphia Downtown.** This hotel is in the historic City Hall Annex, and the original brass, copper, and bronze details on the elevators and staircases have been lovingly refinished. It's across the street from its sister property, the Philadelphia Marriott; both provide easy access to the Pennsylvania Convention Center. The hotels share some facilities—meeting rooms, for example. Each of the pleasant, comfortable guest rooms is decorated in muted shades of red, green, and gold, and has a full-size desk. ✉ *21 N. Juniper St., Center City 19107* ☎ *215/496–3200 or 800/321–2211* 📠 *215/496–3696* 🌐 *www.marriott.com* *498 rooms, 21 suites* *Restaurant, room service, in-room data ports, cable TV with movies, in-room broadband, indoor pool, gym, lobby lounge, laundry facilities, laundry service, concierge, Internet, business services, meeting rooms, airport shuttle (fee), parking (fee), no-smoking floors* 💳 *AE, D, DC, MC, V.*

★ **$$–$$$$** **Hotel Sofitel Philadelphia.** In the middle of the city's French Quarter, this luxury hotel has more of a hip feeling than some of its stuffier Federal-style neighbors. The simplicity of Shaker quilts inspired the lobby floor, done in seven types of granite and marble. Shades of brown, gold, green, and blue hues give the rooms a warm, tranquil feel. There are large desks and stylish furniture in the living areas. Spacious bathrooms include glass-enclosed showers and oversize tubs. Chez Colette, the trademark brasserie, pays homage to the famous writer—vintage French advertisements decorate the walls. ✉ *120 S. 17 St., Center City 19103* ☎ *215/569–8300 or 800/763–4835* 📠 *215/569–1492* 🌐 *www.sofitel.com* *306 rooms, 69 suites* *Restaurant, room service, in-room data ports, in-room safes, minibars, cable TV, in-room broadband, Web TV, gym, lobby lounge, concierge, Internet, meeting rooms, parking (fee), some pets allowed, no-smoking rooms* 💳 *AE, D, DC, MC, V.*

$$–$$$$ **Marriott Residence Inn.** Originally the Market Street National Bank, this building from the 1920s has had its art deco facade beautifully restored. (The rooms remain mostly Marriott.) You can choose between studios or one- or two-bedroom suites; all have full kitchens, living rooms, and work areas. Novel amenities include grocery shopping (give your shopping list to the staff, and they'll pick up items for you) and complimentary dinner Monday to Thursday. A hot breakfast is also included daily. Across from City Hall, this hotel is close to all major downtown destinations. ✉ *1 E. Penn Sq., corner of Market and Juniper Sts., Center City 19107* ☎ *215/557–0005 or 800/331–3131* 📠 *215/557–1991* 🌐 *www.residenceinn.com* *269 suites* *Dining room, in-room data ports, kitchens, cable TV with movies and video games, in-room broadband, indoor pool, gym, dry cleaning, laundry facilities, concierge, Internet, business services, meeting rooms, parking (fee), some pets allowed (fee), no-smoking floors* 💳 *AE, D, DC, MC, V* 🍴 *BP.*

$$–$$$ **Crowne Plaza Philadelphia City Center.** This 25-floor hotel is a short walk from Rittenhouse Square. The generous guest rooms have a contemporary red color scheme. Rooms on the Club Level have complimentary Bath & Body Works products and share a lounge. The Elephant & Castle serves indifferent British food but is a convenient place for a drink. There is also a "quiet floor" that bans children and tour groups and housekeeping dares not enter between 9 PM and 10 AM. ✉ *1800 Market St., Center City 19103* ☎ *215/561–7500 or 800/227–6963* 📠 *215/561–4484* 🌐 *www.crowneplaza.com* *445 rooms, 2 suites* *Restaurant, coffee shop, room service, in-room data ports, cable TV with movies and video games, in-room broadband, pool, gym, bar, shop, laundry facilities, laundry service, concierge, Internet, business services, airport shuttle, parking (fee), no-smoking floors* 💳 *AE, D, DC, MC, V.*

$$–$$$ **Doubletree Philadelphia.** The hotel's sawtooth design ensures that each room has a peaked bay window with an eye-popping 180-degree view. Rooms on the east side look out toward the Delaware River. The four-story atrium lobby lounge observes one of the busiest corners of Philly's theater district, directly across the street from the handsome Academy of Music. Guest rooms are decorated in earth tones and have modern furnishings. Café Academy has unusually good contemporary food and pleasant service. The upscale Standing O Bar & Bistro serves lighter fare. ✉ *Broad St. at Locust St., Center City 19107* ☎ *215/893–1600 or 800/222–8733* 📠 *215/893–1664* 🌐 *www.doubletree.com* *434 rooms, 5 suites* *2 restaurants, room service, in-room data ports, cable TV with movies and video games, in-room broadband, indoor pool, exercise equipment, health club, hot tub, sauna, spa, racquetball, bar, lobby lounge, shop, laundry service, concierge, concierge floor, Internet, business services, meeting rooms, parking (fee), some pets allowed, no-smoking rooms* 💳 *AE, D, DC, MC, V.*

$$–$$$ **Latham.** Doormen clad in elegant vests and riding boots welcome you at this small, elegant boutique hotel. The rooms, done up in traditional hunter green or contemporary black and tan, are furnished with marble-top bureaus, Louis XV–style writing desks, and full-wall mirrors; bathrooms have marble showers. The full-service restaurant, Jolly's, serves breakfast, lunch, and dinner; the adjoining retro Redhead Lounge echoes with piano music in the evening. This is a great location for the itinerant shopper—rooms overlooking Walnut Street have the best view of the colorful shopping district. ✉ *135 S. 17th St., Center City 19103*

☎ 215/563–7474 or 877/528–4261 ⎙ 215/568–0110 🌐 www.lathamhotel.com ⇝ 138 rooms, 1 suite ♁ Restaurant, room service, in-room data ports, cable TV, Wi-Fi, gym, laundry service, concierge, Internet, business services, meeting rooms, parking (fee), no-smoking rooms ▭ AE, D, DC, MC, V 🍴 EP.

$–$$ **Alexander Inn.** The nicely refurbished rooms at this small hotel have an art deco feel. The property is close to the Pennsylvania Convention Center, the Avenue of the Arts, and most downtown attractions. It has a largely gay clientele, and is near some of the city's gay bars. ✉ *12th and Spruce Sts., Center City 19107* ☎ *215/923–3535 or 877/253–8466* ⎙ *215/923–1004* 🌐 *www.alexanderinn.com* ⇝ *48 rooms* ♁ *Cable TV with movies, in-room data ports, in-room broadband, gym, concierge, Internet, business services, meeting rooms, parking (fee), no-smoking rooms* ▭ *AE, D, DC, MC, V* 🍴 *CP.*

$–$$ **Hampton Inn.** This hotel bills itself as the "best value hotel in Center City" and backs it up with a gym, business center, and complimentary Continental breakfast, where, weather permitting, guests can enjoy their coffee and pastry on a patio on 13th Street. Rooms have walk-in closets with full-length mirrors and spacious bathrooms with long marble countertops. The hotel is a short walk away from the Convention Center, Reading Terminal Market, and Chinatown. ✉ *1301 Race St., Center City 19107* ☎ *215/665–9100 or 800/426–7866* ⎙ *215/665–9200* 🌐 *www.hamptoninn.com* ⇝ *250 rooms, 20 suites* ♁ *Cable TV with movies, in-room data ports, in-room broadband, indoor pool, gym, hot tub, laundry facilities, Internet, business services, meeting rooms, parking (fee), some pets allowed, no-smoking floors* ▭ *AE, D, DC, MC, V* 🍴 *CP.*

$–$$ **Holiday Inn Express Midtown.** What this hotel lacks in frills it more than makes up for with its central location, free access to a nearby health club, and complimentary breakfast bar. All rooms have contemporary furnishings and a light floral motif as well as large work desks and ironing boards. The location is excellent: one block from the Broad Street subway, near the theater and shopping district, and three blocks from the Pennsylvania Convention Center. ✉ *1305 Walnut St., Center City 19107* ☎ *215/735–9300 or 800/564–3869* ⎙ *215/732–2682* 🌐 *www.himidtown.com* ⇝ *168 rooms* ♁ *Cable TV with movies and video games, Wi-Fi, pool, laundry service, Internet, business services, meeting rooms, parking (fee), some free parking, no-smoking rooms* ▭ *AE, D, DC, MC, V* 🍴 *CP.*

¢–$$ **Philadelphia Travelodge.** On the edge of Chinatown, this small hotel has a location as good as many other downtown hotels but charges much less. There's not much in the way of amenities, but the bare-bones accommodations are fine for a brief stay. Rooms are done in a green-and-beige color scheme and have small bathrooms (a separate sink and mirror are in the bedroom). All rooms have work areas with high-speed Internet access. A skylight from the 4th-story ceiling floods the corridors with natural light. ✉ *1227–1229 Race St., Center City 19107* ☎ *215/564–2888 or 800/578–7878* ⎙ *215/564–2700* 🌐 *www.travelodge.com* ⇝ *50 rooms* ♁ *In-room data ports, cable TV with movies, in-room broadband, parking (fee), no-smoking rooms* ▭ *AE, D, MC, V* 🍴 *CP.*

Rittenhouse Square

★ **$$$$** **The Rittenhouse.** This small luxury hotel takes full advantage of its location on Rittenhouse Square; the restaurant and many of the rooms overlook the city's famous park. The 33-story building's sawtooth design gives the guest rooms unusual shapes, with nooks and alcoves. Each room has a large marble bathroom with a TV; many have whirlpool tubs. Posh amenities include three telephones, an entertainment center tucked into an armoire, high-speed Internet, and king-size beds. The management is deeply involved in community affairs, and promotes local artists at the 3rd-floor Satellite Gallery, and with the placement of original art throughout the hotel. Chef Jean-Marie Lacroix's restaurant puts a sumptuous French spin on local ingredients. ✉ *210 W. Rittenhouse Sq., Rittenhouse Square 19103* ☎ *215/546–9000 or 800/635–1042* 📠 *215/732–3364* 🌐 *www.rittenhousehotel.com* *87 rooms, 11 suites* *3 restaurants, tea shop, room service, in-room data ports, in-room fax, some kitchenettes, minibars, some microwaves, cable TV with movies and video games, in-room broadband, indoor pool, gym, health club, hair salon, massage, sauna, spa, bar, shops, babysitting, dry cleaning, laundry service, concierge, business services, parking (fee), some pets allowed, no-smoking floors* 💳 *AE, D, DC, MC, V.*

$$–$$$ Fodor's Choice ★ **Rittenhouse Square Bed & Breakfast.** Tucked away on a small street near Rittenhouse Square, this refined, European-style mansion offers the luxury of a large hotel in an intimate space on the 4th floor. Every room has its own personality, with Louis XVI–inspired chairs, vintage mirrors, skylighted whirlpool baths, Chippendale-style tables, and neoclassical rugs. You can also rent the entire mansion for special occasions, as many celebrities have done to protect their privacy. A wine reception is held daily from 5 to 7 in the lobby, where you can relax on fauteuil-style chairs or play a game of chess. ✉ *1715 Rittenhouse St., Rittenhouse Square 19103* ☎ *215/546–6500 or 877/791–6500* 📠 *215/546–8787* 🌐 *www.rittenhousebb.com* *8 rooms, 2 suites* *Cable TV with movies, in-room data ports, concierge, Internet, parking (fee); no kids under 12, no smoking* 💳 *AE, D, DC, MC, V* 🍴 *CP.*

$–$$ **Radisson Plaza Warwick Hotel.** An elegant marble lobby welcomes you to this landmark 1929 Renaissance–style hotel. The pleasant and bright guest rooms, all decorated in floral motifs, come in three distinct categories—standard, deluxe, and the exclusive Plaza Club Level accommodations. All rooms have large desks, high-speed Internet service, and free newspaper delivery. The hotel is around the corner from Rittenhouse Square. ✉ *1701 Locust St., Center City 19103* ☎ *215/735–6000 or 800/333–3333* 📠 *215/790–7766* 🌐 *www.radisson.com/philadelphiapa* *516 rooms, 29 suites* *2 restaurants, coffee shop, room service, in-room data ports, some in-room safes, cable TV with movies, in-room broadband, exercise equipment, gym, hair salon, bar, babysitting, laundry service, concierge floors, Internet, business services, meeting room, airport shuttle (fee), parking (fee), some pets allowed, no-smoking rooms* 💳 *AE, D, DC, MC, V* 🍴 *CP.*

LODGING ALTERNATIVES

Apartment Rentals

If you want a home base that's roomy enough for a family and comes with cooking facilities, consider a furnished rental. These can save you money, especially if you're traveling with a group. Home-exchange directories sometimes list rentals as well as exchanges. ***Almost Like Home*** *(☎ 610/935–0935 🌐 www.almostlikehome.net) is a good local resource for furnished suites, apartments, and houses.*

B&Bs

Bed-and-breakfasts in Philadelphia can be appealing for a number of reasons, such as a warm welcome or antiques-filled rooms. These sometimes (but not always) less expensive alternatives to hotels offer considerable diversity, depending on amenities. Breakfasts range from simple to hearty to elegant. Be aware that some B&Bs welcome children and pets, but others do not. A number of B&Bs are listed in this chapter, and reservation services can help you find others in or near the center of the city or in a variety of other neighborhoods from urban to rural.

Bed and Breakfast Connections–Philadelphia *(📫 Box 21, Devon 19333 ☎ 610/687–3565 or 800/448–3619 🌐 www.bnbphiladelphia.com) represents more than 100 inspected host homes and inns, including a Colonial town house, a converted barn, and a farmhouse on the Main Line. Properties are in Philadelphia, Valley Forge, the Brandywine Valley, and Bucks and Lancaster counties.*

Home Exchanges

If you would like to exchange your home for someone else's, join a home-exchange organization, which will send you its updated listings of available exchanges for a year and will include your own listing in at least one of them. It's up to you to make specific arrangements. ***HomeLink International*** *(📫 Box 47747, Tampa, FL 33647 ☎ 813/975–9825 or 800/638–3841 📠 813/910–8144 🌐 www.homelink.org) charges $98 for a one-year membership.* ***Intervac U.S.*** *(📫 Box 590504, San Francisco, CA 94159 ☎ 800/756–4663 📠 415/435–7440 🌐 www.intervacus.com) has a $93 yearly fee, which includes one catalog and online access.*

Hostels

Hostels provide dormitory-style accommodations for less than you'd pay to park your car at a downtown hotel. They also offer a sense of adventure and a chance to share living, eating, and sleeping quarters with travelers from all over the world. Contact the ***American Youth Hostel Regional Office and Travel Center*** *(✉ 1210 Sansom St., Center City ☎ 215/925–6004) for information and recommendations.*

Hostelling International (HI) *(✉ American Youth Hostels, 733 15th St. NW, Suite 840, Washington, DC 20005 ☎ 202/783–6161 📠 202/783–6171 🌐 www.hiayh.org) is the umbrella group for a number of national youth-hostel associations. Membership in any HI national hostel association, open to travelers of all ages, allows you to stay in HI-affiliated hostels at member rates. A one-year membership is $25 for adults (C$26.75 in Canada, £9.30 in the U.K., $30 in Australia, and $30 in New Zealand). Members have priority if the hostel is full.*

Benjamin Franklin Parkway/Museum Area

$$$$ Fodor's Choice ★ **Four Seasons.** On the outskirts of the finance district, this landmark is within walking distance of the Philadelphia Museum of Art and the department stores along Walnut Street. Furnishings are in the formal Federal style—just right for Philadelphia. The staff indulges you (with in-room exercise equipment and nonallergenic pillows), your children (with milk and cookies at bedtime), and your pet (with fresh-baked dog biscuits and Evian water served in a silver bowl). Other amenities include limousine service within Center City. Rooms on the hotel's north side offer the best views of the Greek Revival public library and family court, Logan Circle, and the Cathedral of Saints Peter and Paul. The Fountain Restaurant is one of the best in town and the Swann Lounge one of the liveliest at cocktail time. ✉ *1 Logan Sq., Benjamin Franklin Parkway/Museum Area 19103* ☎ *215/963–1500 or 800/332–3442* 📠 *215/963–9506* 🌐 *www.fourseasons.com/philadelphia* *364 rooms, 102 suites* *2 restaurants, café, room service, in-room data ports, some in-room faxes, in-room safes, minibars, cable TV, cable TV with movies and video games, in-room broadband, indoor pool, gym, health club, hot tub, massage, sauna, spa, steam room, bar (with entertainment), shops, babysitting, laundry service, concierge, business services, meeting rooms, parking (fee), some pets allowed, no-smoking floors* 💳 *AE, D, DC, MC, V.*

$$$–$$$$ **Embassy Suites.** On Logan Square, this hotel puts you within walking distance of Boathouse Row and the Philadelphia Museum of Art. Suites have separate living rooms with sofa beds, work-dining areas, and private balconies—many with stunning views of nearby Fairmount Park. Business suites have work desks and ergonomic chairs. A cooked-to-order breakfast is served every morning, and an evening reception—with complimentary beer, wine, and light snacks—is served daily from 5:30 to 7:30. ✉ *1776 Benjamin Franklin Pkwy., Benjamin Franklin Parkway/Museum Area 19103* ☎ *215/561–1776 or 800-362–2779* 📠 *215/963–0122* 🌐 *www.embassysuites.com* *288 rooms* *Restaurant, room service, microwaves, refrigerators, in-room data ports, cable TV with movies and video games, in-room broadband, Web TV, health club, sauna, bar, dry cleaning, laundry service, Internet, meeting rooms, parking (fee), no-smoking floors* 💳 *AE, D, DC, MC, V* *BP.*

$$$–$$$$ **Hotel Windsor.** This 24-story all-suites hotel caters to corporate business travelers as well as to vacationing families. Nearly all of the building is reserved for nonsmokers. Easily recognizable by its cylindrical shape, the hotel is within easy walking distance of downtown shopping and the four museums along the parkway. The suites are nicely furnished and have fully equipped kitchens; many have balconies. There are two restaurants on the ground floor: the family-owned Peacock on the Parkway serves international fare, and Asia on the Parkway serves French-style Asian cuisine. ✉ *1700 Benjamin Franklin Pkwy., Benjamin Franklin Parkway/Museum Area 19103* ☎ *215/981–5678 or 877/784–8379* 📠 *215/981–5684* 🌐 *www.windsorhotel.com* *110 suites* *2 restaurants, in-room data ports, kitchens, kitchenettes, cable TV, in-room broadband, pool, health club, hair salon, bar, shops, laundry facilities,* *laundry service, concierge, business services, meeting rooms, parking (fee), no-smoking rooms* ▭ *AE, D, DC, MC, V* ||◎| *CP.*

$$–$$$$ **Wyndham Franklin Plaza.** Although it's a popular convention hotel—a 70-foot atrium lobby sets the appropriate tone for business meetings—the Wyndham also caters to both business and leisure travelers with a variety of added amenities, such as oversize desks and cordless phones. The hotel also features a new business center with laptop computers. Rooms, decorated in soft greens, have full-length mirrors and Herman Miller ergonomic chairs. The hotel also has a private health club. ✉ *17th and Race Sts., Benjamin Franklin Parkway/Museum Area 19103* ☎ *215/448–2000 or 800/822–4200* 🖷 *215/448–2864* 🌐 *www.wyndham.com* *757 rooms, 19 suites* *2 restaurants, room service, in-room data ports, some in-room safes, some kitchenettes, some refrigerators, cable TV with movies and video games, in-room broadband, Wi-Fi, tennis courts, indoor pool, gym, health club, hair salon, hot tub, massage, basketball, racquetball, squash, bar, laundry service, concierge, Internet, business services, meeting rooms, parking (fee), no-smoking rooms* ▭ *AE, D, DC, MC, V.*

¢–$ **Best Western Center City.** Close to the Philadelphia Museum of Art and the Rodin Museum, this old-timer was renovated a few years ago but is still a bit tired. Rooms come with all the basics, including coffeemakers, ironing boards, and spacious work areas. The best views are from rooms facing south toward the downtown skyline. ✉ *501 N. 22nd St., Benjamin Franklin Parkway/Museum Area 19130* ☎ *215/568–8300 or 800/528–1234* 🖷 *215/557–0259* 🌐 *www.bestwestern.com* *179 rooms, 4 suites* *Restaurant, in-room data ports, cable TV, Wi-Fi, pool, exercise equipment, gym, bar, sports bar, shop, laundry service, business services, meeting rooms, free parking, some pets allowed, no-smoking rooms* ▭ *AE, D, DC, MC, V.*

University City

$$–$$$$ **Inn at Penn.** Near the University of Pennsylvania, this hotel is a welcome sight for anyone needing to stay in University City. The hotel, which has a grand staircase in the lobby, has created a warm atmosphere. Twenty-first–century amenities abound in the guest rooms: two phone lines, two-tiered work areas, digital temperature control, and high-speed Internet. There's also a small fitness room. The Penne Restaurant features regional Italian cuisine and an extensive wine list. Remember that rates rise at certain times, including graduations. ✉ *3600 Sansom St., University City* ☎ *215/222–0200 or 800/445–8667* 🖷 *215/222–4600* 🌐 *www.theinnatpenn.com* *238 rooms, 8 suites* *Restaurant, room service, in-room data ports, in-room safes, minibars, cable TV with movies and video games, in-room broadband, Wi-Fi, Web TV, gym, lounge, babysitting, laundry service, concierge, business services, meeting rooms, parking (fee), no-smoking rooms* ▭ *AE, D, DC, MC, V.*

$$–$$$$ **Sheraton University City.** With plush beds and oversized chairs, spacious work areas and three types of in-room Internet access, this hotel offers a practical balance of luxury and practicality. Sizable guest rooms feature small sitting areas with tables good for coffee or meals. Like the

CloseUp

WITH CHILDREN?

MOST HOTELS IN PHILADELPHIA allow children under a certain age to stay in their parents' room at no extra charge, but others charge for kids as extra adults; be sure to find out the cutoff age for children's discounts. Babysitting services are offered at several upscale hotels. In hotels where they are not offered, the front desk or concierge may provide referrals.

*The **Hyatt Regency at Penn's Landing** (✉ 201 S. Columbus Blvd., Penn's Landing ☎ 215/928–1234 or 800/233–1234 🌐 www.hyatt.com) welcomes children with a kid's guide to fun in Philadelphia and offers 10 child-proof suites.*

*The **Loews Philadelphia Hotel** (✉ 1200 Market St., Center City ☎ 215/627–1200 or 800/235–6397 🌐 www.loewshotels.com) offers half-price deals for adjoining rooms, book and game rentals, and supervised children's activities.*

Inn at Penn across the street, it is within walking distance of 30th Street Station, the University of Pennsylvania, Drexel University, and, on a nice day, downtown Philadelphia. ✉ *3549 Chestnut St., 19104* ☎ *215/387–8000 or 877/459-1146* 📠 *215/387–7920* 🌐 *www.sheraton.com/universitycity* ⇨ *325 rooms, 19 suites* ♨ *Restaurant, coffee shop, room service, in-room data ports, some in-room fax, cable TV with movies and video games, in-room broadband, Web TV, pool, gym, bar, shop, babysitting, laundry service, concierge, business services, Internet, meeting rooms, parking (fee), some pets allowed* ▭ *AE, D, DC, MC, V* 🍽 *EP.*

$–$$ **The Gables.** Built in 1889 for a prominent doctor and his family, this ornate mansion is a wonderful place for a B&B. The 1st-floor parlor and entryway feature natural cherry and chestnut wood, and the guest rooms have oak floors with elaborate inlays of mahogany, ash, and cherry. In the dining room, guests are served a hot breakfast. An idyllic wraparound porch is perfect for reading a morning paper. One room has a glass-enclosed sitting porch, and two have working fireplaces. The owners—who live in the building—are avid collectors of Victoriana, so just about every knickknack or piece of furniture is more than a century old. ✉ *4520 Chester Ave., 19143* ☎ *215/662–1918* 📠 *215/662–1918* 🌐 *www.gablesbb.com* ⇨ *9 rooms, 1 suite* ♨ *In-room data ports,* *cable TV, in-room VCRs, Wi-Fi, library, Internet, free parking; no smoking* ▭ *AE, D, MC, V* 🍽 *BP.*

City Line Avenue

If you prefer to stay outside downtown, City Line Avenue is a 10-minute ride on the Schuylkill Expressway to Center City under favorable conditions; however, the expressway is frequently heavily congested at rush hour.

$$–$$$$ **Hilton Philadelphia City Avenue.** One of the city's most popular spots for weddings and bar mitzvahs, this hotel has an elegant marble lobby with grand chandeliers. Guest rooms have one king- or two queen-size beds, and, for restless kids, Sony Playstation consoles. Business-class rooms feature access to a concierge lounge and complimentary cocktails and hors d'oeuvres. Delmonico's specializes in aged prime beef. ✉ *4200 City Ave., City Line Avenue 19131* ☎ *215/879–4000 or 800/445–8667* 📠 *215/878–3068* 🌐 *www.philadelphiacityavenue.hilton.com* *209 rooms, 10 suites* *Restaurant, room service, in-room safes, in-room data ports, cable TV with movies and video games, Wi-Fi, indoor pool, gym, bar, lounge, shop, dry cleaning, concierge, concierge floor, Internet, business services, meeting rooms, parking (fee), no-smoking floors* ▭ *AE, D, DC, MC, V* 🍽 *BP.*

$–$$$ **Homewood Suites Philadelphia City Avenue.** For an extended business trip, this hotel built in 2005 might be your best bet. Built adjacent to the Hilton City Avenue, this all-suites hotel shares its neighbor's restaurant and bar but stands apart with its in-room comforts, including fully stocked kitchens with imported marble countertops. Too busy to go shopping? Give the staff a shopping list and they'll deliver your order to your room. A complimentary hot breakfast is served daily, and evening drinks are served Monday to Thursday. Rooms get ample natural light and most offer a tranquil view of the Philadelphia skyline 5 mi away. ✉ *4200 City Ave., City Line Avenue 19131* ☎ *215/966–3000 or 800-225–5466* 📠 *215/966–3020* 🌐 *homewoodsuites.hilton.com* *122 suites* *Restaurant, in-room data ports, kitchens, microwaves, in-room safes, cable TV with movies and video games, in-room DVDs, in-room broadband, Wi-Fi, indoor pool, gym, bar, lounge, shop, laundry facilities, concierge floor, business services, meeting rooms, parking (fee), no-smoking rooms* ▭ *AE, D, DC, MC, V* 🍽 *BP.*

$–$$ **Holiday Inn City Line.** This eight-story hotel is a good value in a choice location—like its neighbors, it is close to downtown as well as trendy Manayunk. Guest rooms look fresh with taupe walls and peach-colored rugs. In the lobby you can sink into an overstuffed easy chair and watch swimmers in the glass-enclosed pool, which, with the canopy removed, becomes an outdoor pool in summer. ✉ *4100 Presidential Blvd., City Line Avenue 19131* ☎ *215/477–0200 or 800/642–8982* 📠 *215/473–5510* 🌐 *www.hi-cityline.com* *337 rooms, 3 suites* *Restaurant, in-room data ports, cable TV with movies, Wi-Fi, pool, gym, lounge, laundry facilities, laundry service, concierge, Internet, business services, meeting rooms, car rental, free parking, no-smoking floors* ▭ *AE, D, DC, MC, V.*

¢ **Chamounix Mansion.** This is the cheapest place to stay in Philadelphia—$15 a night if you're an American Youth Hostel member, $18 if you're not. The restored 1802 Federal-style country estate is loaded with character. Flags line the entrance hall; rooms are styled after an 1850 country villa and walls are decorated with old maps, sketches, and paintings. There's a self-service kitchen. Chamounix Mansion is a 15-minute walk from a bus stop; call for directions. ✉ *3250 Chamounix Dr., W. Fairmount Park 19131* ☎ *215/878–3676 or 800/379–0017* 🖷 *215/871–4313* 🌐 *www.philahostel.org* *10 rooms for 80 people, with shared baths* *Bicycles, lounge, recreation room, laundry facilities, Internet; no room phones, no room TVs* 💳 *MC, V* ⊗ *Closed Dec. 15–Jan. 15.*

Airport District

A 20-minute drive or taxi ride from most sightseeing and entertainment, these hotels about 8 mi south of Center City are somewhat less expensive than those downtown.

$$$ **Sheraton Suites, Philadelphia Airport.** A glass-wall elevator whisks you to your floor at this all-suites hotel, where interior balconies overlook the light-filled atrium lobby. Most accommodations have a king-size bed in the bedroom and a queen-size sofa bed in the living room, two telephones, and two remote-control televisions. All rooms have extras that delight business travelers, such as complimentary daily newspapers. ✉ *4101 Island Ave., Airport District 19153* ☎ *215/365–6600 or 800/937–8461* 🖷 *215/492–9858* 🌐 *www.sheraton.com* *251 suites* *Restaurant, in-room data ports, kitchenettes, minibars, refrigerators, cable TV with movies and video games, indoor pool, gym, hot tub, sauna, basketball, volleyball, bar, lobby lounge, business services, meeting room, airport shuttle, no-smoking rooms* 💳 *AE, D, DC, MC, V.*

$$–$$$ **Philadelphia Airport Marriott.** This sprawling hotel has a walkway connecting it directly to Terminal B at Philadelphia International Airport. Guest rooms have blue-and-green color schemes. Three-quarters of the rooms have voice mail, data ports, and a speakerphone. Weekend packages are a good value. ✉ *1 Arrivals Rd., Airport District 19153* ☎ *215/492–9000 or 800/228–9290* 🖷 *215/492–6799* 🌐 *www.marriott.com* *419 rooms, 5 suites* *Restaurant, coffee shop, room service, cable TV with movies and video games, Web TV, indoor pool, gym, lounge, shop, laundry facilities, laundry service, concierge, Internet, business services, meeting rooms, free parking, parking (fee), no-smoking floors* 💳 *AE, D, DC, MC, V.*

$$ **Four Points by Sheraton.** Although this hotel is surrounded by highways and is across the street from the airport, it's a quiet place. The five-story L-shape building has pleasant, spacious rooms with two double beds or one queen-size bed and a chaise. ✉ *4101 Island Ave., Airport District 19153* ☎ *215/492–0400 or 800/325–3535* 🖷 *215/492–9858* 🌐 *www.fourpoints.com* *177 rooms* *Restaurant, café, room service, in-room data ports, cable TV with movies and video games, in-room broadband, pool, health club, lounge, laundry facilities, laundry service, business services, meeting rooms, airport shuttle, no-smoking rooms* 💳 *AE, D, DC, MC, V.*

$$ Hilton Philadelphia Airport. During the week this hotel attracts mostly business travelers, but weekends bring vacationing couples who appreciate the substantially lower rates. Rooms are spacious, with sitting areas and work desks; furnishings are made of cherry hardwood. One of the older airport hotels, it has remained pleasant and quiet. ✉ *4509 Island Ave., Airport District 19153* ☎ *215/365–4150 or 800/445–8667* 🖷 *215/937–6382* 🌐 *www.hilton.com* *331 rooms, 3 suites* *Restaurant, room service, in-room data ports, cable TV with movies and video games, in-room broadband, indoor pool, exercise equipment, gym, health club, hot tub, bar, sports bar, shop, laundry service, business services, meeting rooms, airport shuttle, free parking, some pets allowed* 💳 *AE, D, DC, MC, V.*

$ **Holiday Inn Philadelphia International Airport.** The lobby sets a traditional tone, with green marble, gold-trimmed furniture, and fireplaces. The slightly oversize guest rooms have pastel color schemes. There are often good weekend rates. The hotel is 3 mi south of the airport. ✉ *45 Industrial Hwy., Rte. 291, Essington 19029* ☎ *610/521–2400 or 800/843–2355* 🖷 *610/521–1605* 🌐 *www.holiday-inn.com* *308 rooms* *Restaurant, in-room data ports, cable TV with movies and video games, outdoor pool, gym, lounge, shop, laundry facilities, concierge, Internet, business services, airport shuttle, free parking, no-smoking floors* 💳 *AE, D, DC, MC, V.*

Nightlife & the Arts

5

WORD OF MOUTH

"Head to Old City, which is the area between Front and 5th streets, and between Race and Chestnut . . . Some of the more popular (trendy) [bars] are Glam, 32 °, the bar at Cuba Libre, Continental, Plough and the Stars . . . there are many more so I'm sure that just by walking around the area you'll find ones that suit your taste."

—Mcat

"[The Continental Restaurant and Martini Bar] is a fun place to go with a group either for drinks or meals. The atmosphere is upscale fun–kind of like George Jetson meets James Bond. Recommended!"

—Dave from Philly

www.fodors.com/forums

By Piers Marchant

PHILADELPHIA HAS A RHYTHM OF ITS OWN. Whether you're listening to the Philadelphia Orchestra while picnicking on the lawn at the Mann Center for the Performing Arts, or having a jazz brunch at Zanzibar Blue, you'll soon be caught up in that rhythm. Of course, Philly holds a special place in pop music history. *American Bandstand,* hosted by Dick Clark, began here as a local dance show. When it went national in 1957, it gave a boost to many hometown boys, including Fabian, Bobby Rydell, Frankie Avalon, and Chubby Checker. The city's rock-and-roll tradition began in 1955 with Bill Haley and the Comets. In the 1970s the Philadelphia Sound—a polished blend of disco, pop, and rhythm and blues—came alive through Kenny Gamble and Leon Huff; its lush sound has been kept alive by chart toppers such as Hall and Oates, Patti LaBelle, Boyz II Men, and rapper/actor Will Smith, as well as newer acts, notably Jill Scott, Eve, and Pink.

There's no shortage of live entertainment, ranging from the Philly Pops to the Mellon Jazz Festival. There are also summer concerts of popular and classical music at the Robin Hood Dell East and at Fairmount Park's Mann Center for the Performing Arts. Huge rock groups stop in Philadelphia on their national tours, playing at the Wachovia Center; the Keswick Theatre, in suburban Glenside; or the Tweeter Center in Camden, New Jersey. Smaller bands hit great venues like the TLA on South Street, the Trocadero in Chinatown, and Philly's newest and brightest venue, the wonderful World Cafe Live—home of WXPN's famed radio broadcast—in University City.

This is a city of neighborhoods, and you can find entertainment in all of them. From Broadway shows at the Forrest Theater to performance art and poetry readings at the Painted Bride, there's always something new to explore. The city's Avenue of the Arts cultural district on North and South Broad streets is one significant sign of the new energy in town. Of the arts facilities on the avenue, some are long-standing, such as the stunning Academy of Music and the Merriam Theater; others, including the Wilma Theater and the Prince Music Theater, are more recent additions. Adding further excitement to the Avenue of the Arts is the $255-million Kimmel Center for the Performing Arts, the spectacular home of the Philadelphia Orchestra.

Depending on the time of year, you might also be able to take part in city-wide arts festivals like the renowned International Film Festival in spring or the cutting-edge Fringe Festival in autumn. On a lighter note, you can relax by partying at clubs along the Delaware River or checking out some of the city's fine jazz.

Bars and clubs can change hands or go out of business faster than a soft pretzel goes stale. Many places are open until 2 AM; cover charges vary from free to about $12. Some may not be open every night, so call ahead. A few places do not accept credit cards, so carry some cash. For current information check the entertainment pages of the *Philadelphia Inquirer,* the *City Paper,* and *Philadelphia* magazine.

NIGHTLIFE

You can listen to a chanteuse in a chic basement nightclub, dance 'til 2 AM in a smoky bistro, or sip cocktails in any number of swank lounges. South Street between Front and 9th streets is still hip, with one-of-a-kind shops, bookstores, galleries, restaurants, and bars that attract the young and the restless in droves. Today, however, those in the know head to the trendy bars and clubs of Old City, where the crowd is a bit more chic and upscale, or to the emerging artist enclave of Northern Liberties. Over the past few years Main Street in Manayunk, in the northwest section of the city, has also arrived as a fashionable nightlife destination. More than a dozen clubs line the Delaware River waterfront, most near the Benjamin Franklin Bridge. Besides its club scene, Philadelphia also has larger venues—and draws big names—for rock, pop, and jazz concerts.

Bars & Brew Pubs

Azure. This restaurant serves vegan- and vegetarian-friendly fare, though meat is also on the menu. The vibrant bar draws locals, who pour in for stylish cocktails and a full range of heady brews. ✉ *931 N. 3rd St., Northern Liberties* ☎ *215/629–0500* 🌐 *www.azurerestaurant.net.*

The Bards. A lively and authentic Irish pub, the Bards has an Irish crowd, Irish food, full-bodied beers, and great Irish music sessions on Sunday evenings from 7 to 10. ✉ *2013 Walnut St., Rittenhouse Square* ☎ *215/569–9585.*

Black Sheep. This handsome pub is just off Rittenhouse Square in a refurbished town house with a Mission-style fireplace on the main floor and a quiet smoke-free dining room on the upper level. Beer lovers can choose from nearly a dozen local and imported brews on tap, and many more by the bottle. Bring an appetite, too: the impressive kitchen cooks up delicious comfort food like fish-and-chips and shepherd's pie. ✉ *247 S. 17th St., Rittenhouse Square* ☎ *215/545–9473.*

★ **Copa, Too.** Attracting an interesting swath of clientele—everyone from ratty hipsters to proto yuppies—the joint gets quite crowded during its after-work happy hour. Besides margaritas and some of the best burgers in the city, the bar offers a vast selection of beers—some 100 varieties are available on tap and by the bottle. ✉ *263 S. 15th St., Center City* ☎ *215/735–0848.*

Dirty Frank's. Frank is long gone, but this place is still dirty, cheap, and a Philadelphia classic. An incongruous mixture of students, artists, journalists, and resident characters crowd around the horseshoe-shape bar and engage in friendly mayhem. ✉ *347 S. 13th St., Center City* ☎ *215/732–5010.*

Fergie's Pub. This cozy taproom is a comfortable spot for a burger and a brew. Downstairs there's a fun jukebox with samplings from Sinatra to U2; upstairs, on Tuesday and Thursday, there's always an action-packed round of Quizzo, a team trivia game. ✉ *1214 Sansom St., Center City* ☎ *215/928–8118.*

★ **New Wave Café.** To its devoted Queen Village clientele, the New Wave is more than just the place to wait for a table at Dmitri's, the always crowded seafood restaurant across the street. The regulars come to this long, narrow bar a few blocks off South Street to unwind with a local Yuengling beer, play a game of darts, and enjoy a surprisingly innovative and oft-changing menu, including flat-bread pizzas, grilled tuna, and homemade gnocchi. ✉ *784 S. 3rd St., Queen Village* ☎ *215/922–8484* 🌐 *www.newwavecafe.com.*

★ **Royal Tavern.** In the wilds of the Bella Vista neighborhood, the Royal serves both nouveau hipsters and entrenched locals with equal aplomb. Beer—both local and imported—is abundant, but so are fine mixed drinks and better-than-average comfort food. To top it off, there's a thoroughly exhilarating jukebox. ✉ *937 E. Passyunk Ave., Bella Vista* ☎ *215/389–6694.*

SoMa. The clever name—referring to the Old City location south of Market Street—sets the tone at this below-street-level hip bar–cum–dance club. SoMa has a small bar at the back, upholstered couches along the walls, and lighting best described as intimate. ✉ *33 S. 3rd St., Old City* ☎ *215/413–3892.*

★ **Southwark.** This place is a throwback to the days before martinis had to be chocolate. That isn't to say the excellent bartenders can't fashion you a fancy, newfangled drink (in fact, the key lime martini is pretty fabulous), just that you won't necessarily need one, sitting up against the simple-yet-elegant bar. The food—consider it "French countryside"—is also excellent. ✉ *701 S. 4th St., Queen Village* ☎ *215/238–1888.*

Fodor's Choice ★ **Standard Tap.** With its dimly lighted interior, cherrywood bar, and jukebox—not to mention up to 13 beers on tap each night—this neighborhood fixture is prime for conversation, people-watching, or simply sipping your brew. It also has surprisingly good food. ✉ *901 N. 2nd St., Northern Liberties* ☎ *215/238–0630.*

Woody's. Philadelphia's most popular gay bar is spread over two levels, offering several bars—with monitors playing music videos and campy moments from TV shows and movies—and a large dance floor upstairs. On Sundays, two-steppers take over the place for country dancing; on other nights the music is a mix of techno and dance tracks. ✉ *202 S. 13th St., Center City* ☎ *215/545–1893* 🌐 *www.woodysbar.com.*

Comedy Clubs

Comedy Sportz. Anything goes during this once-a-week night of improvisational comedy. There are two shows every Saturday at the Playground at the Adrienne Theater, and the audience is always welcome to participate. ✉ *2030 Sansom St., Rittenhouse Square* ☎ *877/985–2844* 🌐 *www.comedysportz.com.*

Laugh House. This 250-seat club offers an open-mike night on Wednesday and showcases local and national acts Thursday through Sunday. ✉ *221 South St., South Street* ☎ *215/440–4242.*

Dance Clubs

32°. A self-described "luxe lounge" in Old City, the place has Euro-pretensions throughout—in fact, it even accepts Euros as currency. Sleek, modern, and—indeed—luxurious, it serves fine booze by the bottle and rents private lockers where you can store your unfinished spirits. DJs spin a blend of house, hip-hop, and R & B grooves. ✉ *16 S. 2nd St., Old City* ☎ *215/627–3132* 🌐 *www.32lounge.com.*

700 Club. In the heart of the happening Northern Liberties scene, the 700 Club remains a smoky, no-frills type of joint. The ground floor bar gives way upstairs to an even smokier living room–type lounge where area DJs tear up the dance floor. The non-hip need not apply: you'll find more ripped jeans and '70s-theme T-shirts here than leopard-print spandex or gold lamé halter tops. ✉ *700 N. 2nd St., Northern Liberties* ☎ *215/413–3181.*

Dave & Buster's. Call this an amusement park for the somewhat grown-up. A short list of what's going on—besides music and dancing—includes two restaurants, five bars, pool tables, pinball and video games, just-for-fun blackjack and poker, and a virtual reality shooting game. An outdoor deck overlooks the Delaware River. ✉ *Pier 19 N, 325 N. Columbus Blvd., Penn's Landing/Delaware Avenue* ☎ *215/413–1951* 🌐 *www.daveandbusters.com.*

★ **Five Spot.** This sleek throwback to the era of the supper club is frequented by a stylish retro crowd that enjoys a stiff martini and knows how to swing its way around a dance floor. There's live music (big band, Latin, and swing) Tuesday to Thursday, and DJs on Friday and Saturday. Latin dance lessons are given at 9 on Thursday. ✉ *5 S. Bank St., Old City* ☎ *215/574–0070* 🌐 *www.thefivespot.com.*

Fluid. This small dance club atop the Latest Dish restaurant is nearly hidden behind an unmarked door on an alley just off 4th Street near South. Once inside, follow the funky stairwell to the 2nd floor, where you'll hear a mix of hip-hop, rap, and techno spun by some of the city's best DJs. ✉ *613 S. 4th St., South Street* ☎ *215/629–0565* 🌐 *www.fluidnightclub.com.*

Polly Esther's and Culture Club. The music and decor of the '70s and '80s take center stage at this hot spot, part of a national chain. The bar is painted to look like the Partridge family's bus, *Charlie's Angels* photographs adorn one wall, and there's a *Saturday Night Fever*–style disco floor. It's open Thursday through Saturday. ✉ *1201 Race St., next to the Pennsylvania Convention Center, Center City* ☎ *215/851–0776* 🌐 *www.pollyesthers.com.*

Shampoo. This giant, two-story space is teeming with revelry. The dance floors are generously spread out amid the eight bars. Be sure to visit the infamous outdoor groove garden—replete with hot tub. Friday brings in one of the city's best gay dance parties, Saturday usually involve visiting DJs spinning plenty of house and techno. ✉ *417 N. 8th St., Northern Liberties* ☎ *215/922–7500* 🌐 *www.shampooonline.com.*

Tritone. For those seeking some offbeat adventure, this joint, in a refurbished area of upper South Street, is a hipster's dream. During any given week it offers eclectic live music, cutting-edge DJs, and a full menu of special events, including Wednesday Jukebox Night, Soul Sundays, and a variety of performance artists and musicians. ✉ *1508 South St., Center City West* ☎ *215/545–0475* 🌐 *www.tritonebar.com.*

Jazz, Blues & Cabaret

Philadelphia has a rich jazz and blues heritage that includes such greats as the late, legendary jazz saxophonist John Coltrane and current players like Grover Washington Jr. That legacy continues today in clubs around town. The Mellon Jazz Festival in June is a popular event.

Chris' Jazz Café. This intimate hangout off the Avenue of the Arts showcases top local talent Monday through Saturday in a cigar- and pipe-friendly environment. ✉ *1421 Sansom St., Center City* ☎ *215/568–3131* 🌐 *www.chrisjazzcafe.com.*

Philadelphia Clef Club of Jazz & Performing Arts. Dedicated solely to jazz, including its history and instruction, the organization has a 200-seat cabaret-style theater for concerts. ✉ *736–738 S. Broad St., Center City* ☎ *215/893–9912* 🌐 *www.clefclubofjazz.8m.com.*

★ **Warmdaddy's.** This rustic, down-home blues club and restaurant, owned by the people who run Zanzibar Blue, serves up live blues and southern cuisine every night of the week. ✉ *4 S. Front St., at Market St., Old City* ☎ *215/627–8400 reservations, 215/627–2500 hrs and upcoming performances* 🌐 *www.warmdaddys.com.*

★ **Zanzibar Blue.** A hip restaurant and bar adjoins the hottest jazz room in town. The best local talent plays on weeknights; nationally known names take the stage on weekends. There's a jazz brunch on Sunday from 11 to 2 for $22.95 per person. ✉ *Downstairs at the Bellevue, Broad and Walnut Sts., Center City* ☎ *215/732–4500* 🌐 *www.zanzibarblue.com.*

Lounges

Fodor'sChoice ★ **Brasserie Perrier.** The bar and banquette at this modern deco bistro, owned by Georges Perrier of Le Bec-Fin fame, attract a sophisticated, after-work crowd. ✉ *1619 Walnut St., Center City* ☎ *215/568–3000* 🌐 *www.brasserieperrier.com.*

★ **Continental Mid-Town.** A more audacious incarnation of the Old City staple, the Mid-Town offers much the same as the original but does so on two floors of ambient gorgeousness. A full menu and two bars serve the overflowing crowds of trendy folks looking for the next big thing. Hey, they've found it. ✉ *1801 Chestnut St., Center City West* ☎ *215/567–1800* 🌐 *www.starr-restaurant.com.*

Continental Restaurant & Martini Bar. This retro former diner draws a hip, twentysomething crowd to its swank setting for cocktails and a tapas-style dinner menu. The design, including lots of stainless steel and lighting fixtures resembling olives stabbed with toothpicks, is worth checking out. ✉ *138 Market St., Old City* ☎ *215/923–6069* 🌐 *www.starr-restaurant.com.*

Happy Rooster. The boys once ruled this venerable, upscale roost—house rules prohibited unescorted women from sitting at the bar. Today, under owner Rose Parrotta, anyone is free to relax at the handsome rosewood bar accented by brass lanterns. Those seeking more privacy may wish to enjoy a cocktail at one of the cozy booths. In either case, be sure to sample a well-prepared dish from the ever-changing blackboard menu—choices might include a classic Caesar salad, a deluxe burger with fries, or mahimahi fillet in a gingery butter sauce. It's closed Sunday. ✉ *118 S. 16th St., Center City* ☎ *215/963–9311* 🌐 *www.thehappyrooster.com.*

★ **Il Bar.** The wine bar at Panorama, a northern Italian restaurant in the Penn's View Inn, stands out for its 120-bottle selection, daily tastings, curved bar, and romantic atmosphere. It's open seven nights a week, with a separate entrance from the restaurant. ✉ *14 N. Front St., Old City* ☎ *215/922–7800* 🌐 *www.pennsviewhotel.com.*

Inn Philadelphia. This meticulously restored Colonial-style restaurant on a quaint side street is best appreciated for its warm, convivial lounge. It's a good place to stop for a cocktail before dinner or a nightcap on your way home. Live piano music is a plus on weekends, and there's seating in the "secret garden" in warmer months. ✉ *251 S. Camac St., Center City* ☎ *215/732–8630* 🌐 *www.innphiladelphia.com.*

Library Lounge. Handsome and wood-paneled, this space on the 19th floor of the venerable Park Hyatt at the Bellevue harkens to the days when gentlemen left the ladies behind to retire to the library; today all are welcome. So, too, are cigars. Oriental carpets, shelves lined with leather-bound volumes, and a roaring fire complete the scene. ✉ *Broad and Walnut Sts., Center City* ☎ *215/893–1234.*

The Rotunda and the Vault. Under the soaring, 140-foot-high rotunda of this former bank building, refashioned as the Ritz-Carlton Philadelphia, is an elegant lobby bar with marble floors and overstuffed couches—a gracious spot to have a before- or after-dinner cocktail or indulge in a fattening dessert. Just off the lobby is the handsome Vault, a smaller bar specializing in champagnes and fine brandies; here, cigar smoking is more than welcome—it's expected. ✉ *10 S. Broad St., Broad and Chestnut Sts., Center City* ☎ *215/523–8000.*

Fodor's Choice ★ **Swann Lounge.** Melodious jazz and luscious desserts are served on Friday and Saturday nights in this extremely elegant lounge in the Four Seasons. You can dance to the trio's music in between sampling confections from the Viennese-style dessert buffet. A Sunday brunch with contemporary jazz and big band music is also offered. ✉ *18th St. and Benjamin Franklin Pkwy., Center City* ☎ *215/963–1500.*

Tank Bar. This bar is tucked away on the 2nd floor of Friday, Saturday, Sunday, a longtime Rittenhouse Square neighborhood restaurant. Tiny white lights, strategically placed mirrors, and a tank full of exotic tropical fish add just the right touches of comfort and sophistication. ✉ *261 S. 21st St., Rittenhouse Square* ☎ *215/546–4232.*

Twenty Manning. The intimate lounge area and sleek bar at this chic Rittenhouse Square restaurant-bar make for great people-watching. You'll see a mix of downtown professionals, artistic types, and couples on first dates. Wear something black to feel most at home. ✉ *261 S. 20th St., Rittenhouse Square* ☎ *215/731–0900* 🌐 *www.twentymanning.com.*

Rock, Pop & Folk Music

Electric Factory. Named in honor of the original Electric Factory, which opened in 1968 and hosted acts ranging from Jimi Hendrix to the Grateful Dead, this newer incarnation occupies a cavernous former warehouse just north of Center City and presents mainly alternative rock

NIGHTLIFE MOVES NORTH

GENTRIFICATION HAS BROUGHT NORTHERN LIBERTIES *much more than skyrocketing rents—a nightclub and restaurant renaissance is afoot in this neighborhood, which spans from Spring Garden Street to Girard Avenue, and from Delaware Avenue to 6th Street. The neighborhood still has an industrial, working-class feel, though much of the area's old industry—including printing, textiles, and metalworking—is long gone. How do you get hip to the scene? Check the* City Paper *or* Philadelphia Weekly *for events. The* ***Northern Liberties Neighborhood Association*** *(☎ 215/627–6562 🌐 www.northernliberties.org) also has information.*

The neighborhood has no shortage of eats and libations. ***The Abbaye*** *(✉ 3rd St. and Fairmount Ave., Northern Liberties ☎ 215/627–6711) is a neighborhood bar that serves five kinds of Belgian beer.* ***North Third*** *(✉ 801 N. 3rd St., Northern Liberties ☎ 215/413–3666 🌐 www.norththird.com) is a casual bar and lounge with varied entertainment from Thursday through Saturday—usually live music ranging from acoustic rock and blues to jazz and funk, short films, or comedy shows. The* ***Ministry of Information*** *(✉ 449 Poplar St., Northern Liberties ☎ 215/925–0999) is a popular joint for local hipsters (of which there are an abundance). The bar features many draught options, a good jukebox, and a couple of well-used pool tables.*

There's plenty of musical diversity at ***Transit*** *(✉ 600 Spring Garden St., Northern Liberties ☎ 267/258–1321 🌐 www.transitnightclub.com), where you'll hear house, techno, and funk. The sprawling space hosts "Making Time," a semi-regular confluence of DJs from all over the Northeast. The 100-year-old* ***Ortlieb's Jazz Haus*** *(✉ 847 N. 3rd St., Northern Liberties ☎ 215/922–1035 🌐 www.ortliebsjazzhaus.com) has music every night of the week; Tuesday and Sunday nights include a jam session for local musicians.*

bands. It has a capacity of about 2,500, but that number mostly refers to standing room; the main concert area doesn't have seats, although you can sit down at a balcony bar and watch the proceedings from there. ✉ *421 N. 7th St., Northern Liberties* ☎ *215/568–3222* 🌐 *www.electricfactory.com.*

Grape Street Philadelphia. The former pub, long a Philly live music staple, expanded into the comparatively cavernous space once occupied by a nightclub. The new venue still maintains its live-music chops, bringing in everyone from DJ Jazzy Jeff to The Roots. ✉ *4100 Main St., Manayunk* ☎ *215/483–7084* 🌐 *www.grapestreet.com.*

The Khyber. Small and loud, this Old City spot has lots of action. The music is all live, including alternative and rock performed by national and local talent. With more than 100 brands of beer, it has one of the best selections in town. The Khyber is open Monday to Saturday. ✉ *56 S. 2nd St., Old City* ☎ *215/238–5888.*

Theatre of Living Arts. The TLA, a former independent movie house, is a South Street institution that helped launch John Waters's film career; it was also the longtime home of the *Rocky Horror Picture Show.* Today the TLA presents concerts by a range of rock, blues, and adult alternative acts, including such diverse artists as Lucinda Williams and

The Libertines. ✉ *334 South St., South Street* ☎ *215/922–1011* 🌐 *www.thetla.com.*

Tin Angel Acoustic Café. Local and national musicians hold forth at a 105-seat acoustic cabaret above the Serrano restaurant (patrons get preferred seating). You can sit at candlelight tables or at the bar and hear music from blues to folk. ✉ *20 S. 2nd St., Old City* ☎ *215/928–0978* 🌐 *www.tinangel.com.*

Trocadero. This spacious rock-and-roll club in Chinatown occupies a former burlesque house where W. C. Fields and Mae West performed. A lot of the old decor remains: mirrors, pillars, and balconies surround the dance floor. Most every up-and-coming band that's passing through Philly plays here to an under-thirty crowd. On other nights local DJs play for dance parties. On Monday, it hosts a popular movie series. ✉ *1003 Arch St., Center City/Chinatown* ☎ *215/922–5483* 🌐 *www.thetroc.com.*

World Cafe Live. A welcome entrant into Philly's burgeoning music scene, the café houses the eponymous WXPN-FM broadcast, which features such acoustic and world-beat contemporary artists as Hothouse Flowers and Solas. The café also has two theaters—the largest of which, Downstairs Live, seats up to 500—and two restaurants. ✉ *3025 Walnut St., University City* ☎ *215/222–1400* 🌐 *www.worldcafelive.com.*

THE ARTS

Of all the performing arts, it's music for which Philadelphia is most renowned and the Philadelphia Orchestra of which its residents are most proud. Considered one of the world's best symphony orchestras, it rose to fame under the batons of former conductors Leopold Stokowski, Eugene Ormandy, and Riccardo Muti. The orchestra's present home is the cello-shape Verizon Hall at the Kimmel Center for the Performing Arts. The 2,500-seat hall is the centerpiece of the performing arts center at Broad and Spruce streets—a dynamic complex housed under a glass-vaulted roof. Orchestra concerts during the September–May season are still among the city's premier social events. If you can get tickets, go. You'll see some of the city's finest performers in an opulent setting, with many Philadelphians dressed to match the occasion. The Opera Company of Philadelphia and the Pennsylvania Ballet perform at the orchestra's former home, the venerable Academy of Music, built in 1857 and modeled after Milan's La Scala opera house.

Until the early 1980s Philadelphia was considered an important tryout town for theatrical productions headed to New York. (Today, due to high production costs, few Broadway shows even have out-of-town tryouts on that scale.) But the rich theatrical tradition continues here. The city serves as a major stop for touring productions of shows from *Les Misérables* to *Rent,* and the local theater scene, which supports more than two dozen regional and local companies, is thriving.

Information & Tickets

For current performances and listings, the best guides to Philly's performing arts are the "Guide to the Lively Arts" in the daily *Philadelphia Inquirer,* the "Weekend" section of the Friday *Inquirer,* and the "Friday" section of the *Philadelphia Daily News.* Two free weekly papers, the *City Paper* and the *Philadelphia Weekly,* have extensive listings of concerts and clubs; they are available free in news boxes all over downtown.

The **Independence Visitor Center** (✉ 6th St. between Market and Arch, Independence Hall ☎ 215/965–7676 🌐 www.gophila.com/nightlife) is open daily 8:30 to 5 and has information about performances.

UpStages (✉ 1412 Chestnut St., Center City ☎ 215/569–9700 🌐 www.princemusictheater.org/upstages.html) has tickets for many cultural events. Discount tickets, often reduced up to 50%, are offered on the day of the performance. **TicketMaster** (☎ 215/336–2000 🌐 www.ticketmaster.com) sells tickets to rock concerts and other performing arts events.

Prices for performing arts events vary widely. Tickets for rock or pop concerts range from $10 or $15 for a small venue such as the Tin Angel or lawn seats at the Mann Center, to $75 and up for good seats at the Wachovia Center to see the Rolling Stones; theater tickets can go from $15 for local productions to $70 for touring productions of Broadway shows; Philadelphia Orchestra tickets range anywhere from $10 for the amphitheater to $120 or more for the best box seats.

Classical Music

Chamber Orchestra of Philadelphia. Directed by Ignat Solzhenitsyn, this prestigious group—formerly known as Concerto Soloists of Philadelphia—performs chamber music from September to June at the Perelman Theater at the Kimmel Center for the Performing Arts. ✉ *Broad and Spruce Sts., Center City* ☎ *215/790–5800, 215/545–5451 concert information* 🌐 *www.chamberorchestra.org.*

Curtis Institute of Music. The gifted students at this world-renowned music conservatory give free recitals several times a week from October through May at 8 PM. All of its students are on full scholarships; its alumni include such luminaries as Leonard Bernstein, Samuel Barber, and Anna Moffo. The recital hotline lists events. The school also has an opera, alumni recital, and symphony orchestra series. ✉ *1726 Locust St., Rittenhouse Square* ☎ *215/893–5261 hotline, 215/893–7902 ticket office* 🌐 *www.curtis.edu/html/10000.shtml.*

★ **Peter Nero and the Philly Pops.** Grammy-winning pianist and conductor Peter Nero leads an orchestra of local musicians in programs that swing from Broadway to big band, or from ragtime to rock and roll, with ease. The six-concert series is presented at the Kimmel Center for the Performing Arts from October to May. ✉ *Broad and Spruce Sts., Center City* ☎ *215/546–6400* 🌐 *www.phillypops.com.*

Philadelphia Chamber Music Society. From October to May, the society presents more than 60 concerts featuring nationally and internationally known musicians. The schedule is packed with a piano, vocal, and chamber music series, a special events and jazz series, and string recitals. Performances are held in the Perelman Theater at the Kimmel Center for the Performing Arts, at the Pennsylvania Convention Center, and at other locations in the city. ☎ *215/569–8587 information, 215/569–8080 box office* 🌐 *www.philadelphiachambermusic.org.*

★ **Philadelphia Orchestra.** The world-renowned ensemble performs at Verizon Hall at the Kimmel Center for the Performing Arts September to May. In summer the orchestra stages a concert series at the Mann Center for the Performing Arts. Christopher Eschenbach took the musical reigns in 2003 and has continued the phenomenal success the orchestra has seen under its six previous musical directors. ✉ *Broad and Spruce Sts., Center City* ☎ *215/893–1999* 🌐 *www.philorch.org.*

Concert Halls

★ **Academy of Music.** Modeled after Milan's La Scala opera house and completed in 1857, the Academy of Music was the Philadelphia Orchestra's home for its first century. The academy is now home to the Opera Company of Philadelphia and the Pennsylvania Ballet; the schedule is filled out with performances by major orchestras, theatrical and dance touring companies, and solo artists. It's worth the price of admission to experience the academy's lavish, neo-baroque interior, with its red velvet seats, gilt, carvings, murals on the ceiling, and huge crystal chandelier. ✉ *Broad and Locust Sts., Center City* ☎ *215/893–1999* 🌐 *www.academyofmusic.org.*

Annenberg Center. The performing arts complex on the University of Pennsylvania campus has four stages, from the 120-seat Studio to the 962-seat Zellerbach Theater. Something's always going on—including productions of musical comedy, drama, dance, and children's theater. ✉ *3680 Walnut St., University City* ☎ *215/898–3900* 🌐 *www.pennpresents.org.*

Keswick Theatre. This 1,250-seat former vaudeville house with fine acoustics hosts rock, jazz, and country music concerts as well as musicals. ✉ *Easton Rd. and Keswick Ave., Glenside* ☎ *215/572–7650* 🌐 *www.keswicktheatre.com.*

Fodor'sChoice ★ **Kimmel Center for the Performing Arts.** This striking new complex evokes Philadelphia's traditional redbrick structures, while making a contemporary design statement. The 450,000-square-foot facility by architect Rafael Viñoly includes the 2,500-seat cello-shape Verizon Hall, the more intimate 650-seat Perelman Theater, a café and restaurant, a gift shop, rooftop terrace, and public plaza—all topped by a dramatic glass-vaulted roof. Along with its resident companies, such as the Philadelphia Orchestra, the Chamber Orchestra, and the American Theater Arts for Youth, the center presents touring orchestral, jazz, and dance performances. ✉ *Broad and Spruce Sts., Center City* ☎ *215/893–1999* 🌐 *www.kimmelcenter.org.*

Mann Center for the Performing Arts. Pops, jazz, contemporary music, Broadway theater, opera, dance, and Shakespeare are presented in this open-air amphitheater in Fairmount Park from May through September. From late June through July, the Philadelphia Orchestra is in residence, along with noted soloists and guest conductors. International food booths and a tented buffet restaurant offer dinner before the show. ✉ *W. Fairmount Park, near 52nd St. and Parkside Ave., Fairmount Park/W. Philadelphia* ☎ *215/893–1999* 🌐 *www.manncenter.org.*

Painted Bride Art Center. By day it's a contemporary art gallery showing bold, challenging works. By night it's a multidisciplinary, multicultural performance center, with performance art, prose and poetry readings, folk and new music, jazz, dance, and avant-garde theater. The gallery is open Tuesday–Saturday noon–6. ✉ *230 Vine St., Old City* ☎ *215/925–9914* 🌐 *www.paintedbride.org.*

Robin Hood Dell East. The Dell is the site for rhythm-and-blues and soul music concerts on Monday and Wednesday evenings in July and August. ✉ *Strawberry Mansion Dr., E. Fairmount Park, Strawberry Mansion* ☎ *215/685–9560.*

Tweeter Center. Formerly known as the E-Centre, the Tweeter Center, across the Delaware River in Camden, New Jersey, programs everything from symphonies to rock and roll in an adaptable space. The indoor section ranges from 1,600 to 7,000 seats; the lawn seats 12,000. Shows include major rock and pop acts as well as touring musicals and children's theater. ✉ *1 Harbor Blvd., Camden, NJ* ☎ *856/365–1300 ticket information and directions* 🌐 *www.tweetercenter.com/philadelphia.*

Wachovia Spectrum and Wachovia Center. Rock concerts are often staged in these enormous sports facilities on the south side of the city, each of which holds more than 16,000 fans. Recent headliners have included U2 and Eric Clapton; monster truck competitions, wrestling matches, and circuses are also on the calendar. ✉ *S. Broad St. and Pattison Ave., off I–95, South Philadelphia* ☎ *215/336–3600* 🌐 *www.comcast-spectacor.com.*

Music Festivals

Mellon Jazz Festival. A series of concerts and events (mostly free or cheap) are presented throughout the year at different locations around the city. Look for top names in jazz, such as Pat Martino, Wynton Marsalis, and Chick Corea. ☎ *215/893–1955* 🌐 *www.mellon.com/jazz.*

Philadelphia Folk Festival. First held in 1962, the oldest continuously running folk festival in the country takes place each year for three days during the last week in August. Doc Watson, Taj Mahal, Joan Baez, and Judy Collins are just a few of the artists who have performed here. ✉ *Old Pool Farm, near Schwenksville* ☎ *215/242–0150 or 800/556–3655* 🌐 *www.folkfest.org.*

Dance

Dance Celebration/Next Move Series. Modern dance takes the stage at this Annenberg Center series, which presents works by local, national, and internationally known companies. Recent seasons have featured Dance-Brazil, Dance Theatre of Harlem, and Paul Taylor Dance Company, among others. ✉ *3680 Walnut St., University City* ☎ *215/636–9000* 🌐 *www.annenbergcenter.org.*

★ **Pennsylvania Ballet.** Artistic Director Roy Kaiser leads the company through a season of classic favorites and new works; they dance on the stage of the Academy of Music. Their annual *Nutcracker* production is a holiday favorite. ✉ *Broad and Locust Sts., Center City* ☎ *215/551–7000* 🌐 *www.paballet.org.*

Philadelphia Dance Company. This modern dance troupe, also known as Philadanco, is recognized for its innovative performances that forge contemporary and classical forms with the traditions of other cultures. Its home is the Perelman Theater at the Kimmel Center for the Performing Arts. ✉ *Broad and Spruce Sts., Center City* ☎ *215/387–8200* 🌐 *www.kimmelcenter.org.*

Film

The Bridge: Cinema de Lux. Looking for wireless Internet and a frothy cappuccino along with your popcorn and movie? This high-tech movie theater–entertainment center on the University of Pennsylvania's campus features such upscale amenities as concierge service, rocking recliner seats, advance ticketing, and a full-service bar and restaurant. The Media Immersion Room, with six plasma screens, includes work from Penn's film and animation students. ✉ *40th and Walnut Sts., University City* ☎ *215/386–3300* 🌐 *www.thebridgecinema.com.*

International Gay & Lesbian Film Festival. Organized by Theatre of Living Arts Video founder Raymond Murray, who has written several books on film, this festival is held annually in early July in venues around the city. ☎ *215/733–0608* 🌐 *www.phillyfests.com.*

International House. I-House on the University of Pennsylvania campus presents an international film series throughout the year and also sponsors the popular Philadelphia Festival of World Cinema. ✉ *3701 Chestnut St., University City* ☎ *215/387–5125.*

Philadelphia Festival of World Cinema. This 12-day event in May is filled with screenings, seminars, and events attended by critics, scholars, filmmakers, and cinema buffs. It's held at various venues around the city. ☎ *215/733–0608* 🌐 *www.phillyfests.com.*

Ritz Five, Ritz at the Bourse, and Ritz East. These are the finest movie theaters in town for independent and foreign films. All three have comfortable seats, clean surroundings, first-rate sound systems, and courteous audiences and staff. ✉ *Ritz Five, 214 Walnut St., Society Hill* ✉ *Ritz at the Bourse, 4th St. north of Chestnut St., Independence Hall* ✉ *Ritz East, 2nd St. between Chestnut and Walnut Sts., Old City* ☎ *215/925–7900* 🌐 *www.ritzfilmbill.com.*

The Roxy. Philly's classic film repertory house offers a unique mix of new and classic films. ✉ *2023 Sansom St., Rittenhouse Square* ☎ *215/923–6699.*

Sharon Pinkenson Film Project. Based at the Prince Music Theater—and named after the energetic head of the city's film office who is credited with raising the city's cinematic profile through films like *Philadelphia* and *The Sixth Sense*—this film series offers a mix of classic and contemporary films and documentaries, with an emphasis on works by local filmmakers. ✉ *1412 Chestnut St., Center City* ☎ *215/972–1000 or 215/569–9700* 🌐 *www.princemusictheater.org.*

United Artists Main Street 6 Theatre. Manayunk has a multiplex to complement its shopping and dining options. ✉ *3720 Main St., Manayunk* ☎ *215/482–6230.*

United Artist Riverview Plaza. Showing first-run commercial releases, this renovated cinema is a modern, 19-screen multiplex. ✉ *1400 S. Columbus Blvd., Penn's Landing/Delaware Avenue* ☎ *215/755–2219.*

Opera

AVA Opera Theatre. The resident artists at the Academy of Vocal Arts, a four-year, tuition-free vocal training program, present four or five fully staged opera productions during their October to May season. They are accompanied by the Chamber Orchestra of Philadelphia and perform at various venues in and around the city. ✉ *1920 Spruce St., Rittenhouse Square* ☎ *215/735–1685* 🌐 *www.avaopera.org.*

Opera Company of Philadelphia. The company stages five productions a year between October and May, at the Academy of Music; some operas have international stars. All performances are in the original language, with English supertitles above the stage. ✉ *Broad and Locust Sts., Center City* ☎ *215/893–3600 or 215/732–8400* 🌐 *www.operaphilly.com.*

Savoy Company. The oldest Gilbert and Sullivan company in the country stages one G & S operetta each May or June at the Academy of Music and at Longwood Gardens in Kennett Square. ☎ *215/735–7161* 🌐 *www.savoy.org.*

Theater

The Adrienne. The main stage, once home to the prestigious Wilma Theater, now houses two up-and-coming theatrical groups, **1812 Productions** (☎ 215/592–9560) and **InterAct Theatre** (☎ 215/568–8077). The Second Stage offers improv comedy and hosts productions from visiting theater companies. ✉ *2030 Sansom St., Rittenhouse Square* ☎ *215/569–9700.*

Arden Theatre Company. The Arden, formed in 1988, is known for premiering new works and offering a mix of classic drama, comedy, and musicals, with a special affinity for the works of Stephen Sondheim; the company has won many local Barrymore Awards. Recent productions have included *Picasso at the Lapin Agile, Sweeney Todd,* and *Fences.* Its home is in Old City. ✉ *40 N. 2nd St., Old City* ☎ *215/922–8900* 🌐 *www.ardentheatre.org.*

Brick Playhouse. This small theater group, with a space that seats 70, develops and produces new works by local playwrights and performance artists. ✉ *2034 Sansom St., Center City West* ☎ *215/592–1183* 🌐 *www.thebrickplayhouse.org.*

Forrest Theatre. The Forrest is the place to catch Broadway blockbusters in Philadelphia. About eight high-profile shows are presented each season, including such Broadway smashes as *The Phantom of the Opera, The Tale of the Allergist's Wife,* and *A Night with Dame Edna.* ✉ *1114 Walnut St., Center City* ☎ *215/923–1515* 🌐 *www.forrest-theatre.com.*

Freedom Theatre. The oldest and most active African-American theater in Pennsylvania is nationally renowned. Performances are scheduled from September through June. ✉ *1346 N. Broad St., N. Philadelphia* ☎ *215/978–8497or 215/765–2793* 🌐 *www.freedomtheatre.org.*

Merriam Theater. Built in 1918 as the Shubert, the ornate 1,688-seat theater has showcased many stage greats, including Al Jolson, Helen Hayes, Katharine Hepburn, Sammy Davis Jr., Angela Lansbury, and Sir Laurence Olivier. Now owned by the University of the Arts and named after a local benefactor, the lavishly decorated Merriam hosts a full schedule of national tours of Broadway shows, modern dance companies, and solo performers, from the magicians Penn & Teller to tap dancer Savion Glover. ✉ *250 S. Broad St., Center City* ☎ *215/732–5446.*

Philadelphia Theatre Company. Philadelphia and world premieres of works by contemporary American playwrights are performed here. The company also produces Stages, a program showcasing new plays by American playwrights. ✉ *1714 Delancey St., at Plays and Players, Rittenhouse Square* ☎ *215/985–0420* 🌐 *www.phillytheatreco.com.*

Prince Music Theater. Formerly known as the American Music Theater Festival, this organization has renovated an old movie theater and named it in honor of legendary Broadway director-producer Harold Prince. The theater presents original musicals and a cabaret series with national acts, including Andrea Marcovicci and Patti LuPone. The organization is also home to the Sharon Pinkenson Film Project, a venue for independent film. ✉ *1412 Chestnut St., Center City* ☎ *215/569–9700* 🌐 *www.princemusictheater.org.*

Society Hill Playhouse. For more than 40 years, this small off-Broadway–style theater, just off South Street, has mounted original plays. Their *Lafferty's Wake,* a musical about a rowdy Irish funeral service, played for four years. The main stage is for contemporary works; the Second Space Cabaret Theater has musical comedies. ✉ *507 S. 8th St., Society Hill* ☎ *215/923–0210* 🌐 *www.societyhillplayhouse.com.*

★ **Walnut Street Theatre.** Founded in 1809, this is the oldest English-language theater in continuous use in the United States. The schedule includes musicals, comedies, and dramas in a lovely 1,052-seat auditorium where almost every seat is a good one. Smaller stages showcase workshop productions of new plays and are rented by other theater companies. ✉ *9th and Walnut Sts., Center City* ☎ *215/574–3550* 🌐 *www.wstonline.org.*

Wilma Theater. Under artistic director Blanka Zizka, the Wilma has gained favorable critical notices for innovative presentations of American and European drama. Its season runs from September to June. ✉ *Broad and Spruce Sts., Center City* ☎ *215/546–7824* 🌐 *www.wilmatheater.org.*

Sports & the Outdoors

6

WORD OF MOUTH

"The Phillies' Citizens Bank Ballpark is awesome—great seats and great food. Try to get an afternoon game. Our seats are in the left field lower level, and you can't beat it. If you want to talk to the players they're only 10 yards away. Of course in Philly, we only yell at the players!"

—sunriseway

"You could also rent bikes or rollerblades and spend some time getting fresh air and seeing the fall color on the drives in Fairmount Park."

—elle

www.fodors.com/forums

By Bernard Vaughan

PHILADELPHIANS ARE PERHAPS THE MOST OUTRAGEOUS, most dedicated sports fans in the country. They possess a notorious reputation for boorishness—booing Santa Claus, applauding opposing teams' injuries—but this is merely a front for fragile hearts continually betrayed over the years by their beloved but faltering teams. Years are not marked by the changing of the seasons for Philadelphia sports fans. They are marked by whatever sport is in season: the Eagles, 76ers, and Flyers keep them busy from fall through spring, where the Phillies step in for those long summer afternoons.

But Philadelphians don't just watch sports. After a 1999 national survey deemed them the fattest city dwellers in America, the city took action, sponsoring numerous fitness programs. The multitude of bikers, runners, and rollerbladers you'll see on the streets will disprove Philly's portly reputation, as will the always-crowded gyms and health clubs scattered throughout the city.

On weekend mornings (7–noon) from April through October, the West River Drive is closed to car traffic, making this a prime spot for sports enthusiasts. In the afternoons, only the section from the Sweetbriar Cutoff to the East Falls Bridge is closed. Breathtaking trails for running, biking, and hiking interweave Fairmount Park. Walking along Forbidden Drive, a gravel trail along the Wissahickon Creek, you'll understand why artists from Thomas Eakins to Edgar Allan Poe felt inspired to immortalize the park in their work. Shafts of sunlight filter through the trees, while birdcalls complement the dense chorus of crickets bellowing from the mossy woods.

Baseball

Since 2004, the **Philadelphia Phillies** have played in **Citizens Bank Park** (✉ 11th St. and Pattison Ave., South Philadelphia ☎ 215/463–1000 ⊕ www.philadelphiaphillies.com). The season runs from April to October. Tickets range from $15 to $40.

The minor-league **Camden River Sharks,** a member of the independent Atlantic League, play May through September at **Campbell's Field** (✉ 401 N. Delaware Ave., Camden ☎ 856/963–2600 or 866/742–7579) in New Jersey, across the Delaware River from Penn's Landing. Tickets are $6–$12.

Basketball

Philadelphia consistently produces first-rate basketball prospects, and vigorous, competitive pickup games can be found at hundreds of courts around the city.

Fodor's Choice ★ The **Philadelphia 76ers** play at the **Wachovia Center** (✉ Broad St. at I–95, South Philadelphia ☎ 215/339–7676 ⊕ www.76ers.com) from November to April. Tickets are $15–$105.

Collegiate Big Five basketball (✉ Big Five Office, The Palestra, 235 S. 33rd St., University City ☎ 215/898–4747) features teams from LaSalle, St.

Joseph's, Temple, the University of Pennsylvania, and Villanova. The season runs from December to March.

Biking

One popular treat for cyclists is to ride the paved path along the east side of the **Schuylkill River,** cross East Falls Bridge, and return on the west side of the river. The path begins behind the Philadelphia Museum of Art and is parallel to Kelly Drive. This 8-mi loop is about an hour of casually paced biking. Fodor'sChoice ★ **Forbidden Drive,** a 5½-mi dirt-and-gravel bridle path along a stream in the Wissahickon, in the northwestern section of Fairmount Park, is a great ride.

The **Bicycle Club of Philadelphia** (✉ Box 30235, 19103 🌐 www.phillybikeclub.org) organizes rides, from afternoon outings to week-long events.

Bike Line (✉ 1028 Arch St., Art Museum ☎ 215/923–1310) rents bikes for $25–$35 per day for weekday rides. Prices go up to $45–$60 per day on the weekends. Bike rentals, as well as in-line skate rentals, are available year-round at **Drive Sports** (✉ Eastern end of Boathouse Row, near the art museum, Benjamin Franklin Parkway/Museum Area ☎ 215/232–7368). Weather permitting, it's open daily 11–7.

ON THE SIDELINES One of the world's top biking events, the **Wachovia U.S. Pro Cycling Championship** (☎ 610/676–0390 🌐 www.procyclingtour.com) is held each June. The 156-mi race starts and finishes at Benjamin Franklin Parkway. Highlights include the infamous Manayunk Wall, a steep hill in the Manayunk section of the city.

Boxing

★ The **Blue Horizon** (✉ 1314 N. Broad St., N. Philadelphia ☎ 215/763–0500 🌐 www.legendarybluehorizon.com) has unofficially been deemed the premier boxing venue in the country. It holds only 1,200 people—small in comparison to Madison Square Garden or Caesars Palace—but every seat is close to the action, and Philly boxing fans have always made up for the small crowd by making extra noise. The club's reputation for being rather grungy has changed after a $3-million renovation. Twice-monthly fights in the refurbished venue feature a groundbreaking technology: sensors placed in boxer's gloves to measure the accuracy of punches, facilitating more accurate decisions. General admission seats are $38 and ringside views go for $44. VIP tickets range from $60 to $125.

J. Russell Peltz has been a major Philadelphia-area promoter for more than 25 years. **Peltz Boxing Promotions** (✉ 2501 Brown St. ☎ 215/765–0922 🌐 www.peltzboxing.com) occasionally holds bouts in Atlantic City and at the **Wachovia Center** (✉ Broad St. and Pattison Ave. ☎ 215/336–3600).

Fishing

On the banks of Wissahickon Creek and Pennypack Creek you can find good trout fishing; call **Fairmount Park** (☎ 215/685–0000) for information. Both creeks are stocked for the mid-April–December season. You'll need a license ($17 for Pennsylvania residents, $35 for nonresidents), available at local sporting goods stores.

Football

Fodor'sChoice ★ The **Philadelphia Eagles** can be seen in action at their new state-of-the-art facility, Lincoln Financial Field (✉ 11th St. and Pattison Ave., South Philadelphia ☎ 267/570–4000 🌐 www.philadelphiaeagles.com) from September through January. The stadium has a grass playing field and holds up to 68,000 fans. Many of the best seats go to season-ticket holders; individual tickets are $55–$70.

Philadelphia Soul, one of arena football's top franchises, plays at the Wachovia Center from late January through May (✉ Broad St. and Pattison Ave. ☎ 215/636–0421 🌐 www.philadelphiasoul.com)

Golf

Philadelphia has six 18-hole courses that are open to the public. Cobb's Creek is the most challenging; Roosevelt is the easiest.

For golfers who love lots of action, **Cobb's Creek and Karakung** (✉ 7200 Lansdowne Ave., W. Philadelphia ☎ 215/877–8707) are two adjacent courses. Cobb's Creek plays in and around the creek itself, making for lovely vistas and challenging shots. Karakung has hilly fairways and smaller greens. Both are par 71. Greens fees are $29 weekdays, $33 weekends and holidays.

Franklin D. Roosevelt (✉ 20th St. and Pattison Ave., South Philadelphia ☎ 215/462–8997) is a flat, relatively easy par 69. Greens fees are $18–$22 weekdays, $18–$26 weekends.

J. F. Byrne (✉ 9500 Leon St., N.E. Philadelphia ☎ 215/632–8666), a short but challenging course with small greens and water on six holes, is rated par 67. Greens fees are $24 weekdays, $28 weekends.

With Frankford Creek running through it, **Juniata** (✉ L and Cayuga Sts., Juniata ☎ 215/743–4060) is an impressive par 66. Greens fees are $18.25 weekdays, $22.50 weekends.

Tree-lined fairways make **Walnut Lane** (✉ 800 Walnut La., Roxborough ☎ 215/482–3370), a short (4,500 yards) course, into a fairly challenging par 62. Greens fees are $18–$21 weekdays, $22–$25 weekends.

Outside Philadelphia, the privately owned **Valley Forge Golf Club** (✉ 401 N. Gulph Rd., Valley Forge, King of Prussia ☎ 610/337–1776), near Valley Forge National Historic Park, is open to the public. Trees, doglegs, and small greens make this course (6,266 yards, par 71) a challenging one. Greens fees are $20 weekdays, $30 weekends.

Health Clubs & Spas

Some downtown gyms and health clubs allow nonmembers to purchase day passes or weeklong memberships. **Pennsport Athletic Club** (✉ 325 Bainbridge St., Queen Village ☎ 215/627–4900), around the block from trendy South Street, has an indoor pool, four racquetball courts, spinning classes, rock-climbing facilities, and three weight rooms available for $15 a day with proof of membership to another health club. **Rittenhouse Square Fitness Club** (✉ 2002 Rittenhouse Sq., Rittenhouse Square ☎ 215/985–4095) features Nautilus and Kaiser circuit equipment and is within walking distance of the heart of the financial district. Day passes cost $10; a weekly pass is $25. **12th Street Gym** (✉ 204 S. 12th St., Center City ☎ 215/985–4092) offers more than 50 of the most challenging fitness classes in the city, as well as a full-size basketball court and a sundeck, for $20 daily or $59 weekly.

Philadelphia has no shortage of trendy day spas offering the latest and greatest in relaxation.

Pileggi on the Square. Located between Society Hill and Old City, this spa-salon is within walking distance of prime sightseeing and shopping areas. Duck in to the renovated town house for the spa pedicure, during which feet are soaked in sea rock eucalyptus oil, then massaged with sea serum before being wrapped in a hot towel to soften the skin. The similarly luxurious spa manicure includes a paraffin wax treatment and hand massage. *✉ 717 Walnut St., Society Hill ☎ 215/627–0565 🌐 www.pileggionthesquare.citysearch.com.*

Reset Wellness Spa. Day spa facilities and health care services combine to offer a full range of treatments from microderm abrasion to chiropractic care. Choose from 15 different facials and massages, including the "Reset System" deep tissue massage. Reset has the city's only Alpha Environmental Capsule, a full-body relaxation capsule utilizing vibratory massage, aromatherapy, music, and heat. There are two locations; the Camac Street spa is in a renovated bathhouse and has an impressive art gallery. *✉ 1704 Walnut St., Center City ☎ 215/732–2050 ✉ 201 S. Camac St., Center City ☎ 215/893–9934.*

The Spa at Four Seasons. The 80-minute Philadelphia Freedom Hot Towel Infusion combines deep massage with steaming hot towels steeped in aromatic herbs. Body treatments include a rosemary citron sea salt scrub and the signature massage—an 80-minute odyssey using a medley of massage techniques meant to symbolize the four seasons. *✉ 1 Logan Sq., Benjamin Franklin Parkway/Museum Area ☎ 215/405–2815 Ext. 2575 🌐 www.fourseasons.com/philadelphia.*

Terme Di Aroma. Hanging vines of pothos and philodendron escort you through the lobby into the dim, cozy interior lined with Syrian vases and antique Egyptian doors. Although the name pays a nod to the ancient Mediterranean practices of meditation and healing offered here, you'll also find Asian-influenced treatments, such as Thai massage, and aromatherapy thrown in for good measure. Notable services include the prenatal massage, hot stone therapy, and the Shiatsu massage—a combination of stretches and acupressure. ✉ *32 N. 3rd St., Old City* ☎ *215/829–9769* 🌐 *www.termediaroma.com.*

★ **Toppers Spa.** Flowers and perfumes permeate this spotless, labyrinthine spa. In the Solarium, a greenhouselike pagoda brimming with plants and natural light, you can enjoy a Lakota Indian–influenced Raindrop Therapy Massage in which essential oils are dripped onto the spine and followed up by a full spine massage. Other services include the hydrotherapy rejuvenation—the ultimate in tub time. ✉ *117 S. 19th St., Rittenhouse Square* ☎ *215/496–9966* 🌐 *www.topperspa.com.*

Hiking

There are 25 mi of fine solo walks or hikes in **Fairmount Park** (☎ 215/685–0000 🌐 www.phila.gov/fairpark) and 54 mi in the unspoiled Wissahickon, a northern section of the park. Despite the bucolic quality of these areas, it's important to remember that you are in an urban setting and should take appropriate precautions. If you're alone, keep to the main paths along Kelly Drive and West River Drive, or consider joining a hiking group.

You can meet hikers at the **Batona Hiking Club** (☎ 215/233–0916 🌐 http://members.aol.com/batona) on Sunday morning at a central Philadelphia location (such as Broad and Arch streets) and carpool to hiking areas within a two-hour drive of the city, including the Appalachian Trail, the Delaware Water Gap, and the New Jersey Pine Barrens. Hikes range from 7 to 12 mi and tend to be more strenuous than those of other clubs.

The Department of Recreation sponsors the **Wanderlust Hiking Club** (☎ 215/424–8510 🌐 www.phila.gov/recreation/parks/wanderlust). Relatively easy hikes of 5 to 8 mi, many through Fairmount Park and Pennypack Park, begin every Saturday afternoon at 1:30. Check the "Weekend" section of the Friday *Philadelphia Inquirer* for weekly locations.

Hockey

The **Philadelphia Flyers** hit the ice at the **Wachovia Center** (✉ Broad St. at I–95, South Philadelphia ☎ 215/952–7300) from October to April. Tickets are $23–$85.

The energetic **Philadelphia Phantoms,** the city's minor-league hockey team, are the Flyers' AHL affiliate. You can see them at the **Wachovia Spectrum** (✉ Broad St. and Pattison Ave., South Philadelphia ☎ 215/465–4522) from October through April. Tickets cost $14–$18.

Horseback Riding

Of the numerous bridle paths coursing through Philadelphia, the most popular are the trails of the Wissahickon in the northwest, Pennypack Park in the northeast, and Cobb's Creek Park in the southwest. **Ashford Farm** (✉ River Rd., Lafayette Hill ☎ 610/825–9838 🌐 www.ashfordfarm.com), just over the northwestern border of the city, has lessons for $40–$60 per hour.

ON THE SIDELINES Thoroughbred racing takes place at **Philadelphia Park** (✉ 3001 Street Rd., Bensalem ☎ 215/639–9000 🌐 www.philadelphiapark.com). Post time is usually 12:25, Saturday–Tuesday year-round.

Ice-Skating

You can skate outdoors—with the Delaware River and Benjamin Franklin Bridge as a backdrop—daily from November to March at the **Blue Cross RiverRink** (✉ Festival Pier, Columbus Blvd. at Spring Garden St., Penn's Landing ☎ 215/925–7465 🌐 www.riverrink.com). Admission is $5 to $6. You can skate indoors at the **University of Pennsylvania Ice Rink at the Class of 1923 Arena** (✉ 3130 Walnut St., University City ☎ 215/898–1923), which is open to the public from September through the first week of April. Admission is $5.50 weekdays, $6.50 weekends.

In-Line Skating

In-line skating enthusiasts can take to the narrow city streets for high-flying, but safe—helmets are mandatory—10- to 12-mi treks. You can meet skaters of the **Landskaters Inline Skate Club** (🌐 www.landskaters.org) April through October on the steps of the Philadelphia Museum of Art on Sunday at 10 AM, Tuesday at 7 PM, and the second Saturday of each month at 7 PM.

Jogging

Joggers can be seen on streets all over the city, but probably no area is favored more than Kelly and West River drives, a scenic 8-mi route along the Schuylkill River. Then, of course, there are the steps of the art museum itself, host to Rocky-like runners who raise their arms in salute during early morning jaunts.

From dawn to dusk, the south walkway of the **Benjamin Franklin Bridge** provides a tough but rewarding 3½-mi round-trip run with a terrific view of the Delaware River waterfront. **Fairmount Park** (☎ 215/685–0000)—especially along the river drives and Wissahickon Creek—is a natural for joggers and runners. Forbidden Drive along the Wissahickon offers more than 5 mi of soft-surface trail along a picturesque creek in a secluded valley. Only runners, walkers, bikers, and horses can use the trail—motor vehicles aren't allowed.

Pennypack Park (✉ Pine Rd. and Bloomfield Ave., N.E. Philadelphia ☎ 215/214–2524 or 215/685–0000), in the northeast section of the city, has an 8-mi macadam trail along Pennypack Creek. Those interested in the ultimate in running—through wide-open spaces on bike trails, horse trails, and grassy hills and dales—have to head outside Philadelphia to **Valley Forge National Historical Park.**

The **Northeast Roadrunners of Philadelphia** (☎ 215/343–7908 🌐 www.erols.com/runadvte) has more information about jogging and running in the city.

ON THE SIDELINES The **Broad Street Run** (☎ 215/683–3594 🌐 www.broadstreetrun.com), a 10-miler down Broad Street, is a May event.

CloseUp

PHILADELPHIA'S OTHER LEGACY

ASK A LOT OF PEOPLE WHAT THEY KNOW ABOUT PHILADELPHIA *and after a brief mention of the Liberty Bell, they'll probably bring up the boxing epic Rocky. Indeed, Philadelphia has played a vital role in the history of boxing. The city has hosted many memorable bouts and produced countless "Philadelphia fighters," a signature breed known for more than 100 years as tenacious, crowd-pleasing scrappers.*

In the 1880s, saloons owned by ex-bare-knuckle fighters had unlicensed bouts in their back rooms; venues such as the Ariel club were hosting regular matches by the 1890s. Prizefighting was illegal until 1884, so matches were deemed six-round exhibitions in which no decision was rendered. Gamblers outwitted the law by consulting newspaper verdicts the next day.

Outdoor boxing started in 1914 and continued for more than 40 years. Most memorable was the mythical 1926 battle between two "outsiders," or non-Philadelphians: heavyweight champion Jack Dempsey versus Gene Tunney at Sesquicentennial Stadium. Tunney upset the "Manassa Mauler" in a 10-round decision beneath a relentless rainstorm as 120,000 people watched.

The 1920s saw Philadelphia fighters rise to contention in nearly every weight class, and the onset of the Depression in the 1930s failed to hinder Philadelphia's boxing scene. Jewish brawler Lew Tendler, Strawberry Mansion's Harry Blitman, the masterful Tommy Loughran, and Big George Godfrey were feared throughout the boxing world. Midget Wolgast—at 5 feet, 3 inches and 108 pounds—was one of the all-time greats of the flyweight division, and there was the colorful "Two-Ton" Tony Galento, a 5-foot, 9-inch, 240-pounder whose diet and training were primarily focused on beer drinking. Convention Hall opened in 1932, and hosted such historic fights as Steve "Hurricane" Hamas's upset over Germany's legendary boxer Max Schmeling.

Camden's Jersey Joe Walcott was the region's first heavyweight champ, but he lost to Rocky Marciano in 1952 in what Herman Taylor, a Philly promoter and icon for nearly 70 years, called "the greatest heavyweight fight I ever looked at." Sonny Liston was based in North Philly from 1958 to 1962, and Joe Frazier—who would go on to beat Muhammad Ali—first put on his gloves in Philadelphia.

Although Rocky brought Philly boxing to the national consciousness, the city lost its standing for major boxing events in the 1980s, when casinos in Atlantic City, New Jersey began to draw the big matches. But the culture of boxing continues in such venues as the legendary Blue Horizon, and storied gyms such as Champ's and Joe Frazier's continue to produce good, old-fashioned "Philadelphia fighters."

— Bernard Vaughan

Penn Relays (✉ Franklin Field, 33rd and Spruce Sts. ☎ 215/898–6145) is one of the world's oldest and largest amateur track meets with more than 350 races and events.

The **Philadelphia Distance Run** (🌐 www.runphilly.com) is the country's premier half-marathon, with more than 7,000 runners completing a 13-

mi course through downtown and along the Schuylkill River. Other competitions in this September event include a walk and a children's run.

The **Philadelphia Marathon** (☎ 215/685–0054 🌐 www.philadelphiamarathon.com) runs through Center City and along the Schuylkill River and is held the Sunday before Thanksgiving.

Lacrosse

The **Philadelphia Wings,** an indoor lacrosse team, has won several major indoor Lacrosse League championships in recent years. The team plays at the **Wachovia Center** (✉ Broad St. at I–95, South Philadelphia ☎ 215/389–9464); the season runs from January through March. Tickets cost $18–$27.

Rock Climbing

Go Vertical (✉ 950 North Penn St., Northern Liberties ☎ 215/928–1800 🌐 www.govertical.com) is one of the largest rock-climbing gyms on the East Coast, with 48-foot-high walls, 58 climbing ropes, and more than 200 climbing routes for all levels of expertise. Day passes range from $12 to $15.

Livezy Rock in Fairmount Park is a favorite of local climbers. Inexperienced climbers shouldn't attempt to tackle the rock alone. The parks department (☎ 215/685–0000) has information on organized climbs.

Rowing

The placid Schuylkill River, the elegant Boathouse Row, the annual regattas, and a climate that allows an average of 360 rowing days a year all make Philadelphia the rowing capital of the world. From February to October you can watch single and team races out on the river, usually from 5 AM to dusk. Dozens of major meets are held here, including ★ the largest college rowing event in the country, the **Dad Vail Regatta** (☎ 215/542–1443 🌐 www.dadvail.org). This May event includes up to 500 sculls from more than 100 colleges. Free shuttle buses for spectators provide transportation from remote parking areas. More than 1,000 rowers compete in the **Independence Day Regatta** (☎ 302/479–9294), held around July 4. The May **Stotesbury Cup Regatta** (☎ 302/479–9294) includes more than 3,200 students from 120 schools.

Soccer

Philadelphia Kixx, the city's first national professional soccer team, draws crowds of exuberant fans to the **Wachovia Spectrum** (✉ Broad St. and Pattison Ave., South Philadelphia ☎ 888/888–5499). You can catch the team in action from October through April; tickets are $10–$25.

Swimming

A pristine, Olympic-size indoor pool is available at the **Christian Street YMCA** (✉ 1724 Christian St., South Philadelphia ☎ 215/735–5800 🌐 www.ymcaphilly.org) for only $5, from 7 AM to 8:30 PM weekdays, and until 4 PM on Saturday. The YMCA is about a 10-minute walk south from Rittenhouse Square.

After doing laps in the 25-meter indoor pool at the **12th Street Gym** (✉ 204 S. 12th St., Center City ☎ 215/985–4092 🌐 www.12streetgym.com), you can relax on a poolside lounge chair. The staffers pride themselves on keeping the pool spotless. Day passes are $20.

From Memorial Day weekend through September, **Philadelphia Sports Club** (✉ 220–250 S. 5th St., Society Hill ☎ 215/592–8900 🌐 www.philadelphiasports.com) opens a large outdoor pool for swimming laps or just cooling off. The L-shape pool is surrounded by an extensive sundeck furnished with lounge chairs; lifeguards are usually on duty. Day passes are $25.

Tennis

Fairmount Park has more than 100 free public courts, but many players must bring their own nets. Courts are first-come, first-served. Call the **Department of Recreation** (☎ 215/683–3650 or 215/685–0000) for information.

Among the main courts is **Chamounix Tennis Courts** (✉ Chamounix Dr. off Belmont Mansion Dr., Fairmount Park W.). The **West Park Tennis Courts** (✉ George's Hill near 52nd and Parkside, Fairmount Park W.) are adjacent to the Mann Center, West Fairmount Park.

Shopping

7

WORD OF MOUTH

"Shopping on Walnut Street from Broad (14th) to Rittenhouse Square (20th) is nice but very high-end. South Street can get a little crazy at night and lots of young people go there, but the shops are funky and fun. Another great area for shopping is Antique Row on Pine Street between 12th and 9th Streets."

—erinj1977

"Take a walk to Lord and Taylor on Market Street and see the fountain and lights display. They run it about every half hour or so in the main concourse of the store."

—schmerl

www.fodors.com/forums

By Laura Knowles Callanan

HOMEY MEETS HAUTE IN PHILADELPHIA. You'll find it all here—funky artwork and highbrow housewares, fine jewels, and haute couture. Indeed, Philadelphia has spawned some influential fashion retailers. Nationally known clothing designer Paula Hian works out of a studio in Manayunk. The Urban Outfitters chain was born in a storefront in West Philadelphia. Its sophisticated sister, Anthropologie, also has its roots in Philadelphia. Lagos, the popular high-end jewelry line, was founded here, and all items are still produced locally. High-fashion boutiques Joan Shepp, Knit Wit, and Plage Tahiti, all in the Rittenhouse Square area, are well regarded by locals for designer clothing and accessories.

Some of the most spirited shopping in town is also pleasing to the palate. The indoor Reading Terminal Market and the outdoor Italian Market are bustling with urban dwellers buying groceries and visitors in search of the perfect Philadelphia cheese steak. Equally welcoming is the city's quaint, cobblestone Antiques Row, the three-block stretch of Pine Street crammed with shops selling everything from estate jewelry to stained glass and rare books. Also worth a trip is Jewelers' Row, the oldest and second-largest diamond district in the country.

Most stores accept traveler's checks and Visa, MasterCard, and American Express. Policies on personal checks vary. Pennsylvania has a 6% sales tax, and the city adds another 1%. However, these taxes do not apply to clothing, medicine, and food bought in stores.

For more information on shopping in Manayunk, Germantown, and Chestnut Hill, *see* Chapter 2, Manayunk, Germantown & Greater Philadelphia.

Shopping Districts & Malls

Pine Street from 9th Street to 12th Street has long been Philadelphia's **Antiques Row.** The three-block area has dozens of antiques stores and curio shops, many specializing in expensive period furniture and Colonial heirlooms.

Across the street from the Liberty Bell is the **Bourse** (✉ 21 S. 5th St., between Market and Chestnut Sts., Independence Hall ☎ 215/625–0300), an elegantly restored 1895 commodities exchange building. The six-story skylighted atrium contains a few fun shops catering to tourists, such as Best of Philadelphia, as well as a festive international food court.

The **Chestnut Street Transitway,** which extends from 8th to 18th streets, is somewhat seedy after dark but buzzes with urban vitality during the day. It has stores that sell rare and used books, custom tailors, sporting goods stores, and inexpensive trendy clothing stores.

Franklin Mills Mall (✉ off I–95 at Exit 24, Rte. 63, Woodhaven Rd., N. E. Philadelphia ☎ 215/632–1500) is a bargain lover's paradise spanning 1.7 million square feet, with 200 stores and two food courts. Discount outlet stores include Ann Taylor Loft, Nordstrom Rack, Off Fifth–Saks Fifth Avenue Outlet, and Last Call Neiman Marcus. The mall, about 20 mi from downtown, is nearly a mile in length, and the park-

Philadelphia makes the old new again with its plethora of antiques and art and crafts galleries. Use these themed shopping itineraries as guides for exploration by foot or bus. For further information about these stores, refer to the individual listings.

Antiques Begin your shopping in the high-end shops on Pine Street between 9th and 12th streets, long known as Antiques Row. **M. Finkel & Daughter** (✉ 936 Pine St., Center City) is known for furniture and needlework from the late 18th and early 19th centuries. **G. B. Schaffer Antiques** (✉ 1014 Pine St., Center City) carries stained glass, silver, and a large selection of paintings and prints. Walk five blocks north to Chestnut Street, which is lined with mostly urban-inspired, inexpensive clothing and variety stores. Continue west to **Freeman's** (✉ 1808 Chestnut St., Rittenhouse Square), an auction house one block from the upscale Shops at Liberty Place. Freeman's, the oldest building designed specifically for an auction house, spans six floors. Explore the store's specialty departments, which include fine American and European art and rare books and prints. Nearby you'll find plenty of places to stop for a quick bite. Walk a block south on 19th Street to Rittenhouse Square and stroll through the park for a taste of the good life in the city. A number of antiques shops can be found in the elegant area surrounding the park. Visit **Metro Antiques** (✉ 257 S. 20th St., Rittenhouse Square), between Locust and Spruce streets, for sterling silver, period jewelry, and decorative collectibles. **Niederkorn Silver** (✉ 2005 Locust St., Rittenhouse Square) specializes in decorative items such as antique silver picture frames.

Art & Crafts Galleries Philadelphia is an excellent hunting ground for arts and crafts, particularly in the heart of Center City and in Old City. Begin downtown, with Chestnut and Walnut, two major shopping streets. Between 16th and 18th streets you'll find some wonderful galleries specializing in contemporary art, such as **Schmidt/Dean Gallery** (✉ 1710 Sansom St., Rittenhouse Square), which presents paintings by local artists. **Works on Paper** (✉ 1611 Walnut St., Rittenhouse Square) is well regarded for its selection of modern prints. You can find contemporary art in trendy Old City as well, by venturing down Chestnut Street by foot or bus to 3rd Street. For a great selection of contemporary prints head to **The Works** (✉ 303 Cherry St., Old City). **Snyderman Gallery,** on the top floor at the same address, sells beautiful handmade furniture and glass pieces.

---

ing lot holds almost 9,000 cars. Be sure to pick up a map to help you navigate the mall, which is arranged in color-coded sections.

A block north of Chestnut Street is Philadelphia's landmark effort at urban-renewal-cum-shopping, the **Gallery at Market East** (✉ Market St. between 8th and 11th Sts., Center City ☎ 215/925–7162), America's first enclosed downtown shopping mall. The four-level glass-roof structure near the Pennsylvania Convention Center contains 150 mid-price retailers. It includes 40 food outlets and one department store, **Strawbridge's** (☎ 215/629–6000), which has somewhat higher-quality merchandise. Strawbridge's, now part of the May Company chain, is homegrown; it was founded by prominent local businessmen Justus C. Strawbridge and Isaac Clothier.

If you want local color, nothing compares with South Philadelphia's **Italian Market.** On both sides of 9th Street from Christian Street to Washington Avenue and spilling out onto the surrounding blocks, hundreds of outdoor stalls and indoor stores sell spices, cheeses, pastas, fruits, vegetables, and freshly slaughtered poultry and beef, not to mention household items, clothing, shoes, and other goods. It's crowded and filled with the aromas of everything from fresh garlic to imported salami. The vendors can be less than hospitable, but the food is fresh and the prices are reasonable. Food shops include the Spice Corner, Di Bruno Brothers House of Cheese, Claudio's, and Talluto's Authentic Italian Foods. Fante's is well known for cookware. The market's hours are Tuesday–Saturday 9–5:30; some vendors open earlier, and others close around 3:30. Some shops are open Sunday from 9:30 to 12:30.

Jewelers' Row, centered on Sansom Street between 7th and 8th streets, is one of the world's oldest and largest markets of precious stones: more than 350 retailers, wholesalers, and craftspeople operate here. The 700 block of Sansom Street is a brick-paved enclave occupied almost exclusively by jewelers.

Lord & Taylor (✉ surrounded by 13th, Juniper, Market, and Chestnut Sts., Center City ☎ 215/241–9000) displays the chain's classic merchandise in the spacious former John Wanamaker department store, a Philadelphia landmark. Its focal point is the nine-story grand court with its 30,000-pipe organ—the largest ever built—and a 2,500-pound statue of an eagle, both remnants of the 1904 Louisiana Purchase Exposition in St. Louis. During Christmastime, the space is filled with families and office workers gazing (and listening) in awe at the store's legendary holiday sound-and-light show and organ performances.

For browsing, visit the historic and hip neighborhood of **Manayunk.** This former mill town along the Schuylkill River is crammed with art galleries and clothing boutiques, and with one-of-a-kind stores selling everything from clocks and crystals to board games and Balinese artifacts. Alfresco dining, lively bars, and stay-open-late shops make this a great evening destination. For more information, *see* Chapter 2, Manayunk, Germantown & Greater Philadelphia

Market Place East (✉ Market St. between 7th and 8th Sts., Center City ☎ 215/592–8905), across from the Gallery, is in a historic building saved from the wrecker's ball at the 11th hour. The century-old former Lit Brothers department store went through a $75-million renovation to emerge as an office building with a five-level atrium full of moderately priced stores and restaurants.

Once a commercial waterfront district, **Old City** (✉ Front to 5th Sts. and Chestnut to Vine Sts., Old City ☎ 215/440–7000) is home to all things artsy. Lofts, art galleries, furniture stores, and unique home decor shops line the streets; there are also the requisite trendy clothing and shoe stores. After dark, young professionals and students (many live in area warehouses and factories converted into apartment buildings) flock to the area's bars and clubs. Some of Philadelphia's most innovative restaurants can also be found here. One of the best times to explore Old City's gallery scene is during First Friday. As the name implies, on the first Friday of each month, from 5 PM to 9 PM, Old City galleries are open to the public. Many offer refreshments, and the street scene becomes quite festive by dark.

Fodor'sChoice ★ Serious shoppers will want to make a trip to **The Plaza & The Court at King of Prussia** (✉ U.S. 202 at the Schuylkill Expressway, King of Prussia ☎ 610/265–5727 Plaza, 610/337–1210 Court), the largest retail shopping complex on the East Coast. The two malls are an elegant place to stroll and shop; there are nearly 400 specialty shops and eight department stores, including Nordstrom, Neiman Marcus, Bloomingdale's, and Crate & Barrel. The mall is about 20 mi from downtown; SEPTA Bus 124 or 125 runs here from 17th Street and John F. Kennedy Boulevard.

Fodor'sChoice ★ The roots of the **Reading Terminal Market** (✉ 12th and Arch Sts., Center City ☎ 215/922–2317) date to 1892, when the Reading Railroad commissioned a food bazaar to be built in the train shed's cellar as part of its grand expansion plans. Stroll amid the bustling stalls and you'll see and smell old and new culinary delights. Amish merchants sell baked goods and produce straight from the farm alongside vendors offering the latest gourmet vegetarian dishes, artisan breads, and sushi. Vendors also sell exotic spices, flowers, crafts, jewelry, clothing, and cookbooks. Eighty-six merchants are represented here, but try not to miss Amish-owned Fisher's Soft Pretzels for piping hot, freshly rolled soft pretzels; Bassetts Ice Cream, America's oldest ice cream makers; Metropolitan Bakery, for hearty breads and light pastries; and the Down Home Diner for affordable Southern-style fare. The market is open Monday through Saturday, from 8 AM to 6 PM. The Amish vendors are open Wednesday through Saturday.

Fodor'sChoice ★ Shop-'til-you-droppers make a beeline for **Rittenhouse Row,** the area between Broad and 21st streets, and Spruce and Market streets. Stroll down Walnut Street between Rittenhouse Square and Broad Street for the greatest concentration of swanky stores and tony boutiques, art galleries, and jewelers. On 18th Street in the block north of Rittenhouse Square, you'll find a sidewalk vendor selling handmade Peruvian shawls, street artist Joe Barker painting watercolors of Philadelphia cityscapes, and a shop—Scoop de Ville—that sells homemade chocolate and custom-blended frozen yogurt.

At 16th and Chestnut streets is the upscale **Shops at Liberty Place** (✉ 1625 Chestnut St., Center City ☎ 215/851–9055). The complex features a food court and popular stores, including Ann Taylor Loft, Aveda, Benetton, the Coach Store, J. Crew, and the Body Shop. More than 60 stores and restaurants are arranged in two circular levels within a strikingly handsome 90-foot glass-roof atrium.

The elegant **Shops at the Bellevue** (✉ Broad and Walnut Sts., Center City) include Polo–Ralph Lauren, with the designer's classic styles; the chic clothes of Nicole Miller; Tiffany & Co.; Origins bath and body products; and a Williams-Sonoma cookware store. A downstairs food court is bustling at lunchtime; several upscale restaurants in the historic building, which also houses an elegant hotel, are popular in the evening.

For some of the most entertaining people-watching in the city, head to **South Street,** just south of Society Hill. Pierced and tattooed teens vie for space with moms wheeling strollers on this bustling strip from Front Street near the Delaware River to 9th Street. More than 300 unusual stores—high-fashion clothing, New Age books, music and health food, avant-garde art galleries, and 100 restaurants—line the area. Most shops are open in the evening. You'll find a few of the national chains, but 95% of the stores are locally owned, selling things you won't find in the mall back home.

Specialty Stores

Antiques

Many dealers in higher-price wares cluster on Antiques Row—Pine Street between 9th and 12th streets. Some less expensive shops, carrying newer treasures such as '50s and '60s designs, are clustered off South Street, on Bainbridge Street between 4th and 9th streets. Call to check hours, as dealers may open late or be closed a few days a week.

Architectural Antiques Exchange. Victorian embellishments from saloons and apothecary shops, stained and beveled glass, gargoyles, and advertising memorabilia entice shoppers here. ✉ *715 N. 2nd St., Northern Liberties* ☎ *215/922–3669.*

Calderwood Gallery. Art nouveau and art deco furniture, glass, and bronze tempt discerning collectors at this fine establishment. ✉ *1622 Spruce St., Rittenhouse Square* ☎ *215/546–5357.*

★ **Freeman's.** This is not only the city's most prominent auction house, but also America's oldest (founded in 1805). An estate sale is held the first Wednesday of each month; free appraisal days (no reservations required) are scheduled for the third Wednesday of each month. Specialty departments include fine paintings, fine American and European furniture and decorative arts, 20th-century design, and rare books and prints. Freeman's auctioned one of the original fliers on which the Declaration of Independence was printed and posted throughout the city. It sold for $404,000 in 1968. ✉ *1808 Chestnut St., Rittenhouse Square* ☎ *215/563–9275.*

G. B. Schaffer Antiques. Fine 18th-, 19th-, and early-20th-century American furnishings, stained glass, silver, porcelain, paintings, and prints are the specialties here. ✉ *1014 Pine St., Center City* ☎ *215/923–2263.*

★ **M. Finkel & Daughter.** Late-18th- and early-19th-century American furniture, needlework, samplers, and folk art make this an important outpost for Americana buffs. ✉ *936 Pine St., Center City* ☎ *215/627–7797.*

Metro Antiques. The store displays a wide variety of objects: sterling silver pieces, art deco jewelry, bar glassware, and African masks and statues. ✉ *257 S. 20th St., Rittenhouse Square* ☎ *215/545–3555.*

Niederkorn Silver. A fine selection of silver items, including jewelry, pieces for the desk and dresser, and a nice selection of baby silver, makes this a worthwhile stop. ✉ *2005 Locust St., Rittenhouse Square* ☎ *215/567–2606.*

South Street Antiques Market. This indoor market about half a block below South Street holds the stalls of 25 dealers who sell everything from furniture, paintings, and stained glass to jewelry and '50s collectibles. It's closed Monday and Tuesday. ✉ *615 S. 6th St., South Street* ☎ *215/592–0256.*

Vintage Instruments. Antique strings and woodwinds are displayed here; the store specializes in violins and also carries American fretted instruments, such as banjos, guitars, and mandolins. ✉ *1529 Pine St., Center City* ☎ *215/545–1100.*

W. Graham Arader. This is the flagship store of a highly respected chain that stocks the world's largest selection of 16th- to 19th-century prints and maps, specializing in botanicals, birds, and the American West. ✉ *1308 Walnut St., Center City* ☎ *215/735–8811.*

Art & Crafts Galleries

For current shows in Philadelphia's numerous galleries, see the listings in *Philadelphia* magazine or the "Weekend" section of the Friday *Philadelphia Inquirer.* Many galleries are near Rittenhouse Square; others are on South Street or scattered about downtown. For the hottest gallery scene, however, head to Old City.

★ **American Pie Contemporary Crafts.** An eclectic mix of handcrafted jewelry, blown glass, and Judaica is displayed here. Artists from around the country are represented, including the innovative craftsman Sticks, who makes personalized hand-painted wood pieces. The staff is especially knowledgeable and helpful. ✉ *718 South St., South Street* ☎ *215/922–2226.*

Clay Studio. A nonprofit organization runs the gallery and conducts classes as well as an outreach program to inner-city schools. There are clay works and pottery by well-known artists; the gallery has juried shows and group exhibits. ✉ *139 N. 2nd St., Old City* ☎ *215/925–3453.*

David David Gallery. American and European paintings, drawings, and watercolors from the 16th to the 20th centuries are on display. ✉ *260 S. 18th St., Rittenhouse Square* ☎ *215/735–2922.*

★ **Fabric Workshop and Museum.** A nonprofit arts organization runs this center and store dedicated to creating new work in fabric and other materials, working with emerging and nationally and internationally recognized artists. ✉ *1315 Cherry St., Center City* ☎ *215/568–1111.*

Fleisher Ollman Gallery. You'll find fine works by 20th-century self-taught American artists here. ✉ *1616 Walnut St., Suite 100, Rittenhouse Square* ☎ *215/545–7562.*

Gross McCleaf Gallery. This is a good place to see works by both prominent and emerging artists, with an emphasis on Philadelphia painters. ✉ *127 S. 16th St., Rittenhouse Square* ☎ *215/665–8138.*

Helen Drutt. This gallery presents contemporary American and European artists, with a focus on ceramics and jewelry. ✉ *1721 Walnut St., Rittenhouse Square* ☎ *215/735–1625.*

I. Brewster. The specialty here is contemporary paintings and prints by such artists as Salvador Dalí, Peter Max, Marc Chagall, Louis Icart, Erté, Andy Warhol, Pablo Picasso, and Roy Lichtenstein. ✉ *1628 Walnut St., Rittenhouse Square* ☎ *215/731–9200.*

Locks Gallery. Shows present works by an impressive assortment of contemporary regional, national, and international painters, sculptors, and mixed-media artists. ✉ *600 Washington Sq. S, Washington Square* ☎ *215/629–1000.*

Muse Gallery. Established in 1978 by the Muse Foundation for the Visual Arts, Muse Gallery is an artist's cooperative committed to increasing the visibility of local artwork and presenting experimental work in a variety of media. ✉ *60 N. 2nd St., Old City* ☎ *215/627–5310.*

Newman Galleries. The works at this gallery range from 19th-century paintings to contemporary lithographs and sculpture. It's strong on 20th-century painters from the Bucks County area. ✉ *1625 Walnut St., Rittenhouse Square* ☎ *215/563–1779.*

Nexus Foundation for Today's Art. A group of artists started this nonprofit organization in 1975. The emphasis is on experimental art as well as new directions in traditional media. ✉ *137 N. 2nd St., Old City* ☎ *215/629–1103.*

Schmidt/Dean Gallery. Contemporary paintings, sculpture, prints, and photographs are shown; the specialty is work by Philadelphia artists. ✉ *1710 Sansom St., Rittenhouse Square* ☎ *215/569–9433.*

School Gallery of the Pennsylvania Academy of the Fine Arts. Stop here to see rotating exhibits of works by faculty, alumni, and students in the school's attractively renovated building near the Pennsylvania Convention Center. ✉ *1301 Cherry St., Center City* ☎ *215/972–7600.*

Schwarz Gallery. American and European paintings of the 18th to 20th century are the focus, with an emphasis on Philadelphia artists. ✉ *1806 Chestnut St., Rittenhouse Square* ☎ *215/563–4887.*

Snyderman Gallery. One-of-a-kind handmade furniture pieces and glass objects are displayed on the 1st floor of this Old City gallery. ✉ *303 Cherry St., Old City* ☎ *215/238–9576.*

The Works. The basement level of this Old City gallery showcases contemporary American crafts in wood, fiber, ceramics, and metals. ✉ *303 Cherry St., Old City* ☎ *215/922–7775.*

Works on Paper. The contemporary prints here have won the gallery a reputation as one of the city's best. ✉ *1611 Walnut St., Rittenhouse Square* ☎ *215/988–9999.*

Bookstores

★ **AIA Bookstore & Design Center.** Run by the Philadelphia chapter of the American Institute of Architects (AIA), this shop specializes in books on architectural theory, building construction, interior design, and furnishings. It also sells architectural drawings and watercolors, blueprint posters, international magazines, home furnishings, and unusual gifts. ✉ *117 S. 17th St., Center City* ☎ *215/569–3188.*

Giovanni's Room. Focusing on books dealing with gay, lesbian, and feminist topics, this well-regarded store stocks an extensive inventory and sponsors many author appearances. ✉ *345 S. 12th St., Center City* ☎ *215/923–2960.*

Joseph Fox. This small bookstore specializes in art, architecture, and design. ✉ *1724 Sansom St., Rittenhouse Square* ☎ *215/563–4184.*

Penn Bookstore. The 60,000-square-foot store, operated by Barnes & Noble, is the largest academic bookstore in the United States. Highlights include tomes from the University of Pennsylvania faculty, loads of Penn-insignia clothing and memorabilia, a multimedia section, and a children's reading room. You'll also find a Starbucks and the requisite best-sellers. ✉ *3601 Walnut St., University City* ☎ *215/898–7597.*

Robin's Bookstore. Not the biggest bookstore in town, but this is definitely the sentimental favorite of devotees of literature, poetry, and minority studies. Third-generation bookseller Larry Robin has been working in Center City for nearly 60 years. The city's oldest independent bookstore was started by his grandfather in 1936. Book fans are drawn to the frequent readings and book signings by local authors, poets, and free-thinkers. ✉ *108 S. 13th St., Center City* ☎ *215/735–9600.*

Whodunit. The city's only store specializing in mysteries, spy stories, and adventure books also stocks out-of-print mysteries and general-interest books. Co-owner Art Bourgeau has published six mysteries and a nonfiction book on mystery writing. ✉ *1931 Chestnut St., Rittenhouse Square* ☎ *215/567–1478.*

RARE & USED BOOKS

Bauman Rare Books. An antiquarian bookstore with volumes dating as far back as the 15th century, this is a treasure trove for collectors in the fields of law, science, literature, travel, and exploration. Bauman's also has a print and map collection. ✉ *1215 Locust St., Center City* ☎ *215/546–6466.*

Hibberd's. Rare and used books, remainders, and a large selection of unusual art books are the sizable draws for book aficionados. ✉ *1306 Walnut St., Center City* ☎ *215/546–8811.*

Cameras & Photographic Equipment

Mid-City Camera. This major stock house carries a large line of darkroom equipment and all major camera brands in all formats. It also buys and sells used cameras and has a service department and rentals. ✉ *1316 Walnut St., Center City* ☎ *215/735–2522.*

Roth Camera Repairs. If you have camera trouble, here's the place to go. The store prides itself on extra-quick service. ✉ *1015 Chestnut St., Jefferson Bldg. lobby, Room 102, Center City* ☎ *215/922–2498.*

Clothing

CHILDREN'S CLOTHING

Born Yesterday. This shop is filled with unique clothing and toys for haute tots. Specialties include handmade goods, imported fashions, and styles not available elsewhere. ✉ *1901 Walnut St., Rittenhouse Square* ☎ *215/568–6556.*

Children's Boutique. The store carries a look between conservative and classic in infant to preteen clothes and shoes. You can buy complete wardrobes, specialty gifts, and handmade items. An extensive toy department carries the latest in kiddie crazes. ✉ *1702 Walnut St., Rittenhouse Square* ☎ *215/732–2661.*

Kamikaze Kids. Unique designer fashions for infants to preteens are showcased in a child-friendly atmosphere, with cloud-painted walls and play areas. ✉ *527 S. 4th St., South Street* ☎ *215/574–9800.*

MEN'S & WOMEN'S

Banana Republic. The well-known chain's Philadelphia flagship store is set in a grand building that once housed the Manufacturer's and Banker's Club. Men's and women's clothing, shoes, and accessories are stylish, modern, and versatile. ✉ *1401 Walnut St., Center City* ☎ *215/751–0292.*

Burberrys Ltd. Newly remodeled, this British-owned establishment was named after Thomas Burberry, who designed the trench coat in the mid-1850s. Men and women will find classic British raincoats, overcoats, sport coats, and cashmere sweaters. The signature tan, red, and black plaid is a classic and covers everything from trench coats to bikinis. ✉ *1705 Walnut St., Rittenhouse Square* ☎ *215/557–7400.*

Hats in the Belfry. Pass by this bright corner shop and you'll be tempted to try on a hat from the huge window display. Go funky or fancy, casual or classic—you'll find hats to suit each and every whim. ✉ *245 South St., South Street* ☎ *215/922–6770.*

Nicole Miller. You'll find loads of this successful designer's quirky scarves, boxer shorts, and ties at eponymous boutiques in Center City and Manayunk. Women's collections include simple and elegant sportswear, evening wear, and handbags in beautiful colors. ✉ *Shops at the Bellevue, Broad and Walnut Sts., Center City* ☎ *215/546–5007* ✉ *4249 Main St., Manayunk* ☎ *215/930–0307.*

Polo/Ralph Lauren. The city's entry in the Lauren retail empire of classically styled apparel carries the designer's women's, men's, and home collections. ✉ *Shops at the Bellevue, Broad and Walnut Sts., Center City* ☎ *215/985–2800.*

Urban Outfitters. What started out as a storefront selling used jeans to students in West Philadelphia is now a trendsetting chain on campuses across the country. Three floors showcase an eclectic array of hip clothing, unusual books, and funky housewares that can go from the dorm room to the family room. ✉ *1627 Walnut St., Rittenhouse Square* ☎ *215/569–3131.*

Zipperhead. For almost 20 years this has been the alternative clothing landmark for the spiked-hair-and-nose-ring set. Offerings here include motorcycle jackets, rock band T-shirts, and hard-to-find body jewelry for those hard-to-pierce places. ✉ *407 South St., South Street* ☎ *215/928–1123.*

MEN'S CLOTHING

Allure. Classic and stylish Italian clothing draws a cosmopolitan crowd. Brioni, Pal Zileri, Verri, Donna Karan, and Canali are some of the designers here. ✉ *4255 Main St., Manayunk* ☎ *215/482–5299.*

★ **Boyds.** The largest single-store men's clothier in the country has nine shops that present the traditional English look, avant-garde Italian imports, and dozens of other styles and designers, from Armani to Zegna. The store has departments for extra tall, large, and short men; formal wear; and shoes; and there's an excellent café for lunch, free valet parking, and 60 tailors on the premises. Women will find a small selection of high-quality designer clothes, too. ✉ *1818 Chestnut St., Rittenhouse Square* ☎ *215/564–9000.*

Brooks Brothers. This is the oldest men's clothing store in America, founded in New York in 1818. You'll find business attire appropriate for Monday morning through casual Friday, as well as brightly colored weekend wear and country club couture. ✉ *1513 Walnut St., Center City* ☎ *215/564–4100.*

Wayne Edwards. Stylish without being intimidating, the store carries exclusive lines of classic contemporary clothing from Italy, Japan, France, and the United States. Designers include Postman, Vestimenta, and Armani. ✉ *1525 Walnut St., Center City* ☎ *215/731–0120.*

WOMEN'S CLOTHING

Anthropologie. Three floors of an elegant Rittenhouse Square building are brimming with lush colors, floral patterns, and vintage and ethnic-inspired styles that offer a departure from the ordinary. The 3rd floor offers romantic lingerie and racks of sale items. Pretty jewelry, stylish shoes and handbags, and other accessories add an enchanting femininity to fashion. Head downstairs for an array of home decor, including glassware, pottery, pillows, and mirrors. ✉ *1801 Walnut St., Rittenhouse Square* ☎ *215/568–2114.*

Asta De Blue. This funky boutique is set in a brownstone off Rittenhouse Square. Find upbeat contemporary clothing, jewelry, accessories, and gifts. Key collections include Zelda, Harari, Lilith, and Tse. The owners say they have the largest collection of Arche footwear outside Manhattan. ✉ *265 S. 20th St., Rittenhouse Square* ☎ *215/732–0550.*

Jacques Ferber. Since 1879, this famed furrier has been offering high-style furs, shearlings, outerwear, and accessories that make a fashion statement. ✉ *1708 Walnut St., Rittenhouse Square* ☎ *215/735–4173.*

★ **Joan Shepp.** Cutting-edge fashion is displayed in a setting reminiscent of a New York loft. Notable designers include Chloe, mui mui, Yohji Yamomoto, Dries Van Noten, and Jean-Paul Gaultier, and shoes by Prada. ✉ *1616 Walnut St., Rittenhouse Square* ☎ *215/735–2666.*

★ **Knit Wit.** High-fashion clothes and accessories from sportswear to cocktail dresses are the focus here. Alberta Ferretti, Blue Marine, Piazza Sempione, and Paul Smith are among the designs. ✉ *1718 Walnut St., Rittenhouse Square* ☎ *215/564–4760.*

Lele Design. Body-conscious styles and gorgeous fabrics are local designer Lele Tran's trademarks. Customers select samples from the racks, with alterations provided if needed. You can also make adaptations to existing styles for a custom design. ✉ *207 S. 13th St., Center City* ☎ *215/546–5975.*

Paula Hian Designs. The striking black-and-white banner outside this local designer's Manayunk showroom hints at the sophisticated style within. Hian's showroom features her modern, minimalist fashions, including sportswear, evening wear, and knitwear. Hian designs some of the fabrics; others are imported from France and Italy. Appointments are suggested, especially for custom work. ✉ *106 Gay St., Manayunk* ☎ *215/487–3067.*

Plage Tahiti. This leading showcase for promising young high-fashion designers carries a wide selection of chic and charming swimwear and designs by Theory, Womyn, Bluegirl, and Seven. ✉ *128 S. 17th St., Center City* ☎ *215/569–9139.*

Public Image. Trendy clothing is the focus of this Manayunk boutique. Designers include Anna Sui, Vivienne Tam, and Nanette Lepour. A sister accessories store next door carries accoutrements by Kate Spade, Stella Pace, and many others. ✉ *4390 Main St., Manayunk* ☎ *215/482–4008.*

Discount Shopping

Cambridge Clothing Factory Outlet. This is a manufacturers' outlet for men, with 10 national brands starting at 40% off retail. Out-of-towners can get immediate alterations. ✉ *1520 Sansom St., 2nd fl., Center City* ☎ *215/568–8248.*

Daffy's. Housed in an attractive Egyptian deco–style building, Daffy's carries higher-end American and European designs for men, women, and children at 40%–75% off retail (sometimes even more with special markdowns). Be forewarned: patience is a virtue here. Carefully rummage through the racks and be sure to head directly to the 5th floor to find amazing bargains on women's designer fashions and evening wear by Moschino or Jean-Paul Gaultier. ✉ *1700 Chestnut St., Center City* ☎ *215/963–9996.*

Dan's Cancellation Shoes. Shrewd shoppers come here for Ferragamo slingbacks, Prada sneakers, or Fendi sandals for a fraction of their retail price. Racks of shoes in sizes 4 to 14 line this store, where affordability supplants ambience. ✉ *1733 Chestnut St., Center City* ☎ *215/922–6622.*

Food

The Italian Market is a classic Philly experience and the Reading Terminal Market is a city gem, but you'll also find smaller specialty stores that sell fine cheese, chocolate, caviar, and more.

Caviar Assouline. Looking for a delicious gift? This stylish store carries imported and American caviar, smoked seafood, truffles, foie gras, Valrhona chocolate, and more. If you can't decide, pick up a catalog and order from home. ✉ *505 Vine St., Old City* ☎ *215/627–3511* ✉ *Reading Terminal, 12th Arch St., Center City* ☎ *215/629–9200* ✉ *Shoppes at Liberty Place, 17th St., Center City* ☎ *215/972–1616.*

Chef's Market. Enter this food emporium and you'll be tempted by luscious displays brimming with Brie, Jarlsburg, and fontina (and 100 other varieties of cheese), decadent homemade desserts like crème brûlée and tiramisu, and savory entrées and side dishes. Packaged items include 150 varieties of imported jams, 40 olive oils, and 60 flavored vinegars. ✉ *231 South St., South Street* ☎ *215/925–8360.*

Di Bruno Bros. There are two locations to tempt the palate—the original one in the Italian Market and the hipper one in Rittenhouse Square. DiBruno's is a mecca for cheese lovers—the store carries more than 300 different varieties from around the world, as well as some housemade kinds. You'll also find barrels of olives, imported olive oils, Abbruzze sausage, and balsamic vinegar that's been aged for 75 years. The staff is very knowledgeable and will provide friendly advice on storage, preparation, and serving ideas. Ask for recipes and samples. ✉ *109 S. 18th St., Rittenhouse Square* ☎ *215/665–9220* ✉ *930 S. 9th St., South Philadelphia* ☎ *215/922–2876.*

Maron Fine Chocolates. America's oldest independent retail candy store, opened by Swiss candy maker Conrad Maron in 1850, is thriving in its new location near Rittenhouse Square. This family-run confectionery's specialties include chocolate-dipped fruits, truffles, sugar-free items, and molded chocolates. Sweet tooth still not satisfied? Maron also has an ice cream parlor, Scoop de Ville, in the rear of the store. Choose from an extensive list of decadent toppings to create a custom-blended treat. ✉ *1734 Chestnut St., Rittenhouse Square* ☎ *215/988–9992.*

Gifts & Souvenirs

Best of Philadelphia. A former commodities exchange office houses this fun spot for inexpensive souvenirs: on display are more than 100 different items, from Ben Franklin key chains to miniature Liberty Bells. ✉ *Bourse Bldg., 21 S. 5th St., Independence Hall* ☎ *215/629–0533.*

The Black Cat. This University City gift store with a social conscience is in connecting brownstone row houses next to its sister business, the White Dog Café. Most products are made from recycled or other earth-friendly materials. Look for journals, picture frames, and photo albums covered in handmade paper. ✉ *3426 Sansom St., University City* ☎ *215/386–6664.*

Holt's Cigar Company. Stogie aficionados make a point of stopping by this cigar emporium, whose Philadelphia roots date back more than 100 years. The shop features a comfortable smoking lounge and one of the nation's largest walk-in humidors. Find private label Ashton cigars, a wide array of smoking accessories and humidors, and writing instruments from Mont Blanc, Waterman, and Cross. ✉ *1522 Walnut St., Center City* ☎ *215/732–8500.*

Morgan's Cauldron. You'll find everything for the discriminating witch—bells, books, candles, incense, tarot cards, ritual robes, capes, and long dresses (black only). ✉ *509 S. 6th St., South Street* ☎ *215/923–5264.*

Scarlett Alley. Owned and operated by Mary Kay Scarlett and her daughter Liz, this delightful shop at the corner of 3rd and Race features an ever-changing assortment of unique jewelry, housewares, and stationery, as well as toys, soaps, and teas. Items are displayed on furniture designed and handcrafted by Richard Scarlett, Liz's father; it's also for sale or custom order. ✉ *241 Race St., Old City* ☎ *215/592–7898.*

Touches. Upscale shoppers come to this attractive shop for its handmade shawls, purses, belts, unusual jewelry, and children's gifts. ✉ *225 S. 15th St., Center City* ☎ *215/546–1221.*

Xenos Candy and Gifts. Asher chocolates and Philly souvenirs from key chains to T-shirts are stocked here, near the sites of the historic district. ✉ *231 Chestnut St., Old City* ☎ *215/922–1445.*

Home Decor

Flotsam and Jetsam. Run by two interior designers, this colorful, bright store showcases styles that juxtapose the old and new. Modern metal and glassware is displayed alongside restored antiques and found objects from around the world. Take note of the gorgeous hand-painted floors and vibrant walls. About 75% of the store's crafts, art, furniture, and accessories is designed locally. ✉ *149 N. 3rd St., Old City* ☎ *215/351–9914.*

Ten Thousand Villages. Woven rugs, pottery, carvings, and other handcrafted gifts made by skilled artisans in 32 countries such as Kenya, Thailand, and India make this fair trade store a favorite for innovative gifts with a social conscience. ✉ *1122 Walnut St., Center City* ☎ *215/574–2008.*

Usona. Furniture and accessories are what the owner calls "global modern," reflecting a fusion of different styles, periods, and materials. Accent pieces, like picture frames and mirrors, are interesting and affordable. ✉ *113 S. 16th St., Center City* ☎ *215/496–0440.*

Housewares & Accessories

Fante's. One of the nation's oldest gourmet supply stores has the largest selection of coffeemakers and cooking equipment in the United States. Family owned since 1906, Fante's is famous for oddball kitchen gadgets such as truffle shavers and pineapple peelers; restaurants and bakeries all over the country and overseas order from the store. It's in the Italian Market, so you can combine a visit here with other food shopping. ✉ *1006 S. 9th St., Italian Market* ☎ *215/922–5557.*

Foster's Urban Homeware. Quirky and useful home accessories are displayed in this spacious store with a cool, industrial-hip flavor. A sister operation, a cookware purveyor, is in the Reading Terminal Market. ✉ *124 N. 3rd St., Old City* ☎ *267/671–0588.*

Kitchen Kapers. From one store in South Jersey, this family business has grown to be one of the largest independent kitchenware stores in the United States. This is a good source for fine cookware, French copper, cutlery, coffees, and teas. ✉ *213 S. 17th St., Center City* ☎ *215/546–8059.*

Williams-Sonoma. High-quality cookware, appliances, glassware, dishes, and interesting gadgets like ergonomic potato peelers and asparagus shavers bring out the gourmand in anyone. Seasonally decorated in bright colors like summery limes and lemons or autumnal golds and reds, the shop has food samples, cooking demonstrations, and shelves of gorgeously photographed cookbooks. ✉ *Shops at the Bellevue, Broad and Walnut Sts., Center City* ☎ *215/545–7392.*

Jewelry

Jewelry shoppers in search of antique and contemporary pieces have many options in Philadelphia. The stores lining Jewelers' Row can provide one-stop shopping, but also look for unique pieces in galleries, antique shops, and boutiques.

★ **Halloween.** If the sheer quantity of baubles crammed into this tiny shop doesn't take your breath away, the gorgeous, one-of-a-kind designs will. Shelves, drawers, displays, and even the 2nd-floor balcony overflow with rings, necklaces, earrings, bracelets, pins, and much more, ranging from classic pearls to mystical amber. Owner Henri David (who designs some pieces) is well known for his lavish and outrageous Halloween fetes. He'll do custom work, such as creating mates for single earrings. ✉ *1329 Pine St., Center City* ☎ *215/732–7711.*

Harry Sable. Harry "King of the Wedding Bands" Sable has been selling diamond rings, gold jewelry, and watches for more than 50 years. ✉ *122 S. 8th St., Historic Area* ☎ *215/627–4014.*

J. E. Caldwell. A local landmark since 1839, the store is adorned with antique handblown crystal chandeliers by Baccarat, making it as elegant as the jewels it sells. Along with traditional and modern jewelry, Caldwell has one of the city's largest selections of gifts from Waterford and Reed & Barton. ✉ *1339 Chestnut St., Center City* ☎ *215/864–7800.*

Jack Kellmer Co. Fine jewelry, imported stones, and elegant watches are displayed in a grand building that once housed a bank. The store's dramatic entranceway, 50-foot vaulted ceiling, travertine marble walls, and Colonial-inspired brass chandeliers are the perfect setting for precious stones and unique creations. ✉ *717 Chestnut St., Center City* ☎ *215/627–8350.*

★ **Lagos–The Store.** Lagos jewelry, sold in upscale department stores, gets top billing here. All pieces are handcrafted and designed in Philadelphia by Ann and Steven Lagos. Aficionados are thrilled by the selection, including the Diamond and Caviar, Glacier Deco, and Delta Pearl designs. ✉ *1735 Walnut St., Rittenhouse Square* ☎ *215/567–0770.*

Richard Kenneth. Jewelry from the late-Georgian, Victorian, art nouveau, art deco, and '40s-retro periods are what you'll find at this shop near Rittenhouse Square. Kenneth specializes in repairs and appraisals. ✉ *202 S. 17th St., Rittenhouse Square* ☎ *215/545–3355.*

Scriven. Designer Keith Scriven started selling handmade jewelry from a corner of his art gallery. When customers were wowed by the designs, Scriven knew it was time to open a separate store. His spare, elegant shop showcases his signature bold designs, formed from precious metals and precious and semiprecious stones. The intricate "Angela" link necklace is exquisite. ✉ *1602 Spruce St., Center City* ☎ *215/545–8820.*

Tiffany & Co. This is the local branch of the store, famous for its exquisite gems, fine crystal, and china, and, of course, its signature blue gift box. ✉ *Shops at the Bellevue, 1414 Walnut St., Center City* ☎ *215/735–1919.*

Luggage & Leather Goods

Robinson Luggage. This shop at Broad and Walnut carries moderate to expensive brands of luggage, leather, and travel accessories. The selection of briefcases and attaché cases is the largest in the Delaware Valley. ✉ *201 S. Broad St., Center City* ☎ *215/735–9859.*

Music

Sound of Market Street. The knowledgeable staff and impressive selection make this, the largest independent music store in Philadelphia, a music lover's paradise. There's an extensive gospel section as well as a full room of jazz. Reggae, R & B, hip-hop, and rap are also well represented. ✉ *15 S. 11th St., South Philadelphia* ☎ *215/925–3150.*

Theodor Presser. The best selection of sheet music in Center City draws musicians from far and wide. The store specializes in classical but also carries pop and will special order anything. ✉ *1718 Chestnut St., Rittenhouse Square* ☎ *215/568–0964.*

Tower Records. Open 9 AM to midnight 365 days a year, Tower stocks more than 250,000 CDs and tapes—the largest selection in the city. The Avenue of the Arts (Broad Street) location has an extensive classical section. ✉ *100 S. Broad St., Center City* ☎ *215/568–8001* ✉ *610 South St., South Street* ☎ *215/574–9888.*

Perfumes & Cosmetics

Bluemercury. Makeup and skin-care junkies can get their fix at this sleek shop featuring products from Aqua di Parma, Bliss, Bumble & Bumble, Fresh, Trish McEvoy, Laura Mercier, and many others. In the back of the store, spa services are offered in a serene setting. ✉ *1707 Walnut St., Rittenhouse Square* ☎ *215/569–3100.*

Francis Jerome. This high-end makeup boutique stocks an array of hard-to-find products from lines such as T. LeClerc, Paula Dorf, Murad, Molton

Brown, and B. Kamins. The friendly staff pampers you with customized facials and other beauty treatments. ✉ *124 S. 19th St., Rittenhouse Square* ☎ *215/988–0440.*

Kiehl's Since 1851. Step inside this store and you'll feel like you are in an old-world apothecary—with a sleek, modern twist. The staff is friendly and helpful and knows everything about the extensive line of natural lotions, balms, and cosmetics. Generous samples let you try them out. ✉ *1737 Walnut St., Rittenhouse Square* ☎ *215/636–9936.*

Parfumerie Douglas Cosmetics. A wide selection of major brands of perfume, cosmetics, and beauty accessories is found here. ✉ *Shops at Liberty Pl., 1625 Chestnut St., Center City* ☎ *215/569–0770* ✉ *3603 Walnut St., University City* ☎ *215/222–2366.*

Shoes

Aerosoles. You'll find all looks from sporty to dressy at this store, whose stylish, comfortable line comes in a rainbow of colors from lavender to marigold. ✉ *1700 Walnut St., Rittenhouse Square* ☎ *215/546–5407.*

Bottino. Men's shoes are the stars here, all handmade and imported from Italy. Some very big feet get shod here, including those of regular customers, among them Michael Jordan. ✉ *121 S. 18th St., Rittenhouse Square* ☎ *215/854–0907.*

Danielle Scott, Ltd. This boutique is a destination for anyone in search of high-end stilettos, mules, and sandals straight off the runway. Noteworthy designers include Jimmy Choo, Robert Clergerie, Dolce and Gabbana, and Marc Jacobs. The store also carries jewelry and handbags. ✉ *1718 Walnut St., Rittenhouse Square* ☎ *215/545–9800.*

Head Start Shoes. Floor-to-ceiling windows showcasing a huge selection of Italian shoes and boots beckon to shoppers passing by this hip shop. Inside you'll find women's, men's, and children's footwear in the trendiest styles. ✉ *126 S. 17th St., Rittenhouse Square* ☎ *215/567–3247.*

Sherman Brothers Shoes. This discount retailer of men's shoes has name-brand merchandise and excellent service. The store stocks extra-wide and extra-narrow widths, as well as sizes up to 16. ✉ *1520 Sansom St., Center City* ☎ *215/561–4550.*

Sporting Goods

City Sports. Besides sports equipment from in-line skates to bike helmets, the store carries plenty of brand-name active wear and its own line of clothing. ✉ *1609 Walnut St., Center City* ☎ *215/985–5860.*

Eastern Mountain Sports. Outdoorsmen and -women will find a large selection of clothing and equipment for activities like running, skiing, camping, and boating. Located on the University of Pennsylvania campus, the shop features an in-store rock-climbing wall. Equipment rentals are available. ✉ *130 S. 36th St., University City* ☎ *215/386–1020.*

The Original I. Goldberg. This store is hip and practical, with an emphasis on sporting apparel and camping gear. Goldberg's is crammed with government-surplus, military-style clothing, jeans and work clothes, unusual footwear, and exclusive foreign imports. Rummaging here is a sport in itself. ✉ *1300 Chestnut St., Center City* ☎ *215/925–9393.*

Rittenhouse Sports. Its focus is on gear for triathlon sports—running, swimming, and cycling—but the store also stocks shoes for aerobics and other activities. ✉ *1729 Chestnut St., Rittenhouse Square* ☎ *215/569–9957.*

Wine & Liquor

Pennsylvania liquor stores are state operated. State stores (as they're known) are generally open Monday and Tuesday 11–7, Wednesday–Saturday 9–9. You may find chilled beer at delis and gourmet shops.

Wine and Spirits Shoppe. This shop carries one of the best selections of fine wines and liquors in the city. ✉ *1913 Chestnut St., Rittenhouse Square* ☎ *215/560–4215.*

8

Side Trips from Philadelphia

The Brandywine Valley & Valley Forge

WORD OF MOUTH

"Take the tour at Winterthur–a huge old Du Pont castle of a mansion, now an outstanding museum of the decorative arts. . . . There's a great multistory courtyard inside the mansion–with the entire facade of an old building on each side. Very attractive grounds to stroll in, too."

—johncharles

"Another highlight of the area is the Brandywine River Museum . . . which features paintings by N. C., Andrew, and Jamie Wyeth. Also nearby is a Simon Pearce glassblowing facility, where you can view the glass blowing and then head upstairs for a lovely lunch or dinner overlooking the Brandywine River."

—Rumrita1

www.fodors.com/forums

By Joyce Eisenberg

IT'S EASY TO EXPAND YOUR VIEW of the Philadelphia area by taking one or more day trips to destinations that are within an hour's drive of the city. Head southwest and in 30 minutes you can be immersed in a whole new world—or make that "worlds." First you can see the verdant hills and ancient barns of the Brandywine Valley, home to three generations of Wyeths and other artists inspired by the rural landscapes outside their windows. Then you can visit the extravagant realm of du Pont country, including Pierre S. du Pont's resplendent Longwood Gardens, whose summer fountain displays are world-renowned, and Winterthur, an important repository of American decorative furnishings, over the border in Delaware. Or you can explore the Revolutionary War battlefield of Brandywine at Chadds Ford. These attractions are year-round favorites of Philadelphians, and area bed-and-breakfasts and inns make the Brandywine appealing as an overnight or weekend trip and as a day excursion.

The historical park at Valley Forge adds another dimension to the revolutionary story that began in Independence Hall. Not far away, the town called King of Prussia dates to that period, but is now primarily synonymous with shopping, thanks to its huge upscale mall. It's just a half hour from Philadelphia and easily accessible by public transportation.

About the Restaurants & Hotels

It seems that most restaurants in the Brandywine Valley and Valley Forge regions serve Continental-American cuisine, with creative contemporary touches at the better establishments. Most also present local specialties—fresh seafood from the Chesapeake Bay and dishes made with Kennett Square mushrooms. As an added pleasure, some of the region's best restaurants are in restored Colonial and Victorian homes.

Many of the region's accommodations may be considered bed-and-breakfasts because of their intimate atmosphere, but they are far from the typical B&B—which is usually a room in a private home—and are more accurately characterized as inns or small hotels.

WHAT IT COSTS

	$$$$	$$$	$$	$	¢
RESTAURANTS	over $26	$20–$26	$14–$20	$8–$14	under $8
HOTELS	over $240	$190–$240	$140–$190	$90–$140	under $90

Restaurant prices are for one main course at dinner. Hotel prices are for two people in a standard double room.

THE BRANDYWINE VALLEY

You'll probably experience a strong sense of déjà vu during a journey to the Brandywine Valley. While creating some of the most beloved works in 20th-century American art, Andrew Wyeth made the valley's vistas instantly recognizable. Using colors quintessentially Brandywine—the earthen brown of its hills, the slate gray of its stone farmhouses, and the dark green of its spruce trees—the famous American realist captured its unostentatiously beautiful personality. He also inspired many people to flock to this valley and fall in love with its peaceful byways. Today, new housing developments continuously crop up and the main highway, U.S. 1, is lined with strip malls and gas stations. Yet, places off the main paths make you feel you have discovered a tucked-away treasure.

The Brandywine Valley actually incorporates parts of three counties in two states: Chester and Delaware counties in Pennsylvania and New Castle County in Delaware. Winding through this scenic region (about 25 mi southwest of Philadelphia), the Brandywine River flows lazily from West Chester, Pennsylvania, to Wilmington, Delaware. Although in spots it's more a creek than a river, it has nourished many of the valley's economic and artistic endeavors.

The valley is also the site of one of the more dramatic turns in the American Revolution, the Battle of Brandywine, and a fascinating museum dedicated to helicopters. Antiques shops, fine restaurants, and cozy country inns dot the region. Your best bet is to rent a car and explore on your own.

If you start early enough, and limit your time at each stop, you can tour the valley's top three attractions—the Brandywine River Museum, Longwood Gardens, and Winterthur—in one day. If you have more time to spend in the valley, you can visit additional sites in Pennsylvania and then move on to Wilmington.

Kingdom of the du Ponts

Although paintings of the Wyeth family distilled the region's mystery, it was the regal du Pont family that provided more than a bit of its magnificence, recontouring the land with grand gardens, mansions, and mills. Their kingdom was established by the family patriarch, Pierre-Samuel du Pont, who had escaped with his family from post-Revolutionary France and settled in northern Delaware. The Du Pont company was founded in 1802 by his son Éleuthère Irénée (E. I.), who made the family fortune, first in gunpowder and iron and later in chemicals and textiles.

E. I. and five generations of du Ponts lived in Eleutherian Mills, the stately family home on the grounds of a black-powder mill that has been transformed into the Hagley Museum. The home, from which Mrs. Henry du Pont was driven after accidental blasts at the powder works, was closed in 1921. Louise du Pont Crowninshield, a great-granddaughter of E. I., restored the house fully before opening it to the public. Louise's relatives were busy, too. Henry Francis du Pont was filling his country estate, Winterthur, with furniture by Duncan Phyfe, silver by Paul Revere, splendid decorative objects, and entire interior woodwork fittings salvaged from homes built between 1640 and 1860.

Pierre S. du Pont (cousin of Henry Francis) devoted his life to horticulture. He bought a 1,000-acre 19th-century arboretum and created Longwood Gardens, where he entertained his many friends and relatives. Today 350 acres of the meticulously landscaped gardens are open to the public. Displays range from a tropical rain forest to a desert; acres of heated

Historic Landmarks

Brandywine Battlefield is where General Washington and his troops met defeat at the hands of the British in 1777, forcing them to retreat to Valley Forge for a brutal winter encampment. Both areas are now home to large public parks with a wealth of historic artifacts and information about the region's part in the American Revolution. Brandywine also features two restored Quaker farmhouses. At Valley Forge, you can stroll through the 3,600-acre grounds, take the self-guided auto tour, or hike on one of 6 mi of biking-jogging paths.

Shopping

There are many shops, galleries, and boutiques scattered throughout the region, but the massive King of Prussia Mall is unquestionably the locus of willing shoppers. The mall houses some 365 stores, including the fashionable (Kenneth Cole, Diesel, and DKNY), the trendy (Versace and Kate Spade), and the familiar (Borders, Brookstone, and The Body Shop). Forty restaurants and eight major department stores (from Sears to Neiman Marcus) round out this shopping extravaganza.

Gardens

Some of America's most spectacular botanical sights, including the renowned Longwood Gardens, are in the Brandywine area. While touring the Hagley Museum and Library, as well as nearby Winterthur, take time to step outside and appreciate the gorgeous natural backgrounds designed to complement the architecture. The grounds of Rockwood, a rural Gothic manor in Wilmington, Delaware, have splendid landscaping.

Spring is the most obvious time to visit these glorious oases, but other seasons can be rewarding, too: Longwood Gardens, a treat at any time of year, has one of the world's largest conservatories, and Rockwood has a similarly stunning, though smaller, Victorian cast-iron-and-glass garden room. At the Brandywine River Museum, the Brandywine Conservancy's Wildflower and Native Plant Gardens are a riot of fall colors, as are the grounds surrounding the French-inspired parterres of the Hagley Museum and Library. Winterthur's Enchanted Woods is a whimsical children's garden.

---

conservatories, where flowers are in bloom year-round, create eternal summer. Pierre also built the grand Hotel du Pont, adjacent to company headquarters, in downtown Wilmington. No expense was spared; more than 18 French and Italian craftspeople labored for two years, carving, gilding, and painting. Alfred I. du Pont's country estate, Nemours, was named after the family's ancestral home in north-central France. It encompasses 300 acres of French gardens and a mansion in Louis XVI style.

Wyeth Country

Although Andrew Wyeth is the most famous local artist, the area's artistic tradition began long before, when artist-illustrator Howard Pyle started a school in Wilmington in 1900. He had more than 100 students, including Andrew's father, N. C. Wyeth; Frank Schoonover; Jessie Willcox Smith; Maxfield Parrish; and Harvey Dunn. It was this tradition that inspired Andrew and his son Jamie.

In 1967 local residents formed the Brandywine Conservancy to prevent industrialization of the area and pollution of the river; their actions included significant land purchases. In 1971 the organization opened the Brandywine River Museum in a preserved 19th-century gristmill. It celebrates the Brandywine School of artists in a setting much in tune with their world.

Numbers in the text correspond to numbers in the margin and on the Brandywine Valley map.

West Chester

30 mi west of Philadelphia.

The county seat of Chester since 1786, this historic mile-square city holds distinctive 18th- and 19th-century architecture, with fine examples of Greek Revival and Victorian styles. A small but vital downtown has shopping possibilities as well as restaurants and bars serving everything from classic American fare to the latest microbrews. Fine examples of classical architecture, including the Chester County Courthouse and Market Street Station, can be found near the intersection of High and Gay streets. The town is also home to one of the area's most visited attractions, the QVC Studios, in an industrial park off U.S. 202.

★ 1 **QVC Studio Park.** This is the world's largest electronic retailer, which in one year alone answered 180 million phone calls, shipped more than 120 million packages, and netted more than $4.8 billion in sales. On a one-hour guided tour of the company headquarters you can catch a glimpse of its round-the-clock live broadcast from five studio views and see how QVC products make the route from testing to sale. The tour is designed for ages six and up and begins on the hour. If you want to be part of a studio audience for a live broadcast, call to make a reservation; it's free. The studio is wheelchair accessible. ✉ *1200 Wilson Dr.* ☎ *800/600–9900* 🌐 *www.qvctours.com* 🎫 *Tours $7.50* ⏲ *Daily 10–4.*

★ 2 **American Helicopter Museum & Education Center.** Ever since Philadelphian Harold Pitcairn made the first rotorcraft flight in 1928, the Southeastern Pennsylvania area has been considered the birthplace of the helicopter industry. In fact, two of the three major U.S. helicopter manufacturers trace their roots to this region. This heritage is showcased here, and you can learn about and climb aboard nearly three dozen vintage and modern aircraft that reflect the copter's historic roles in war and rescue missions, in agriculture, and in police surveillance. ✉ *1200 American Blvd.* ☎ *610/436–9600* 🌐 *www.helicoptermuseum.org* 🎫 *$6* ⏲ *Wed.–Sat. 10–5, Sun. noon–5.*

Chester County Historical Society. The society's architectural complex, known as the History Center, includes a former opera house where Buffalo Bill once performed. Galleries tell about the region's settlers and the decorative furniture they crafted. A hands-on history lab lets you churn butter and dress up in a hoop skirt. The society's collection of

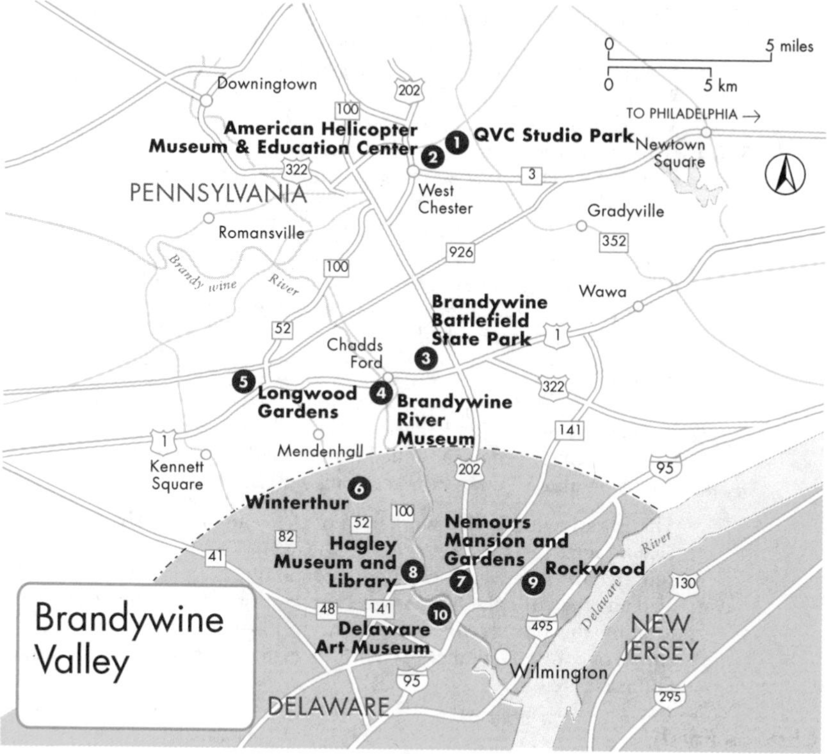

American cross-stitch samplers is extensive; in the museum shop you can get everything you need to start stitching yourself. ✉ *225 N. High St.* ☎ *610/692–4800* 🌐 *www.chestercohistorical.org* *$5* ⏲ *Mon.–Sat. 9:30–4:30.*

Where to Eat

$$$$ **Fodor's Choice ★** ✕ **Dilworthtown Inn.** Fresh seafood from the Chesapeake Bay, osso buco, and rack of lamb are among the entrées at this longtime area favorite for romantic dining; the New Zealand lobster tail and the chateaubriand are big enough to share. The 15 dining rooms of this elegant 1754 country inn are carefully restored and decorated with antiques and Oriental rugs. The wine cellar, one of the region's best, stocks more than 800 vintages, including a merlot and a chardonnay bottled exclusively for the inn. Men should wear jackets. ✉ *1390 Old Wilmington Pike, Dilworthtown, south of West Chester* ☎ *610/399–1390* 🌐 *www.dilworthtown.com* 💳 *AE, D, DC, MC, V* ⏲ *No lunch.*

★ $$–$$$ ✕ **High Street Caffe.** Massive mirrors and silver beaded lighting fixtures create a fun and sexy vibe at this small café. Everything here is done up in the color purple—walls, tablecloths, and even the coffee mugs. The staff in the kitchen and dining room are attentive to details. Louisiana smoked alligator sausage and crawfish tails in a spicy barbecue sauce are popular starters. Jambalaya, étouffée, and po'boys are traditional French Quarter entrées; more exotic fare includes surf-and-turf scampi and seafood linguine. There's live jazz Friday to Sunday night. ☒ *322 S. High St.* ☎ *610/696–7435* 🌐 *www.highstreetcaffe.com* 💳 *AE, MC, V* ⊙ *Closed Mon. No lunch weekends* *BYOB.*

$–$$$ ✕ **Iron Hill Brewery.** An old Woolworth's building with tin ceilings and maple floors has been converted into a bustling restaurant and pub. Jamaican jerk pork and Louisiana barbecued shrimp are two of the creatively prepared entrées. Light fare includes chili, chicken-and-sausage gumbo, and Santa Fe chicken pizza baked in a wood oven. True to the name, the eatery also brews a large variety of beers and ales. In warm weather the outdoor tables provide a nice spot for people-watching. ☒ *3 W. Gay St.* ☎ *610/738–9600* 🌐 *www.ironhillbrewery.com* 💳 *AE, D, DC, MC, V.*

Shopping

Baldwin's Book Barn (☒ 865 Lenape Rd. ☎ 610/696–0816 🌐 www.bookbarn.com) is a book lover's dream. This off-the-beaten-path bookstore in a converted barn is filled with more than 300,000 used and rare books on almost every subject, along with historic maps and prints.

The Brandywine Valley workshop of the renowned Irish glassblower **Simon Pearce** (☒ 1333 Lenape Rd. (Rte. 52) ☎ 610/793–0949 🌐 www.simonpearce.com) is stocked with original glass and pottery. There's also an area with glassblowing demonstrations, and a restaurant overlooking the Brandywine River. The food—served on Simon Pearce china, of course—is American with an Irish accent, including beef-and-Guinness stew.

Chadds Ford

11 mi south of West Chester, 30 mi southwest of Philadelphia.

A Revolutionary War battlefield park and a museum celebrating area artists make this historic town appealing. There are some pretty side roads to explore as well.

In a restored barn, the **Chaddsford Winery** (☒ U.S. 1 ☎ 610/388–6221 🌐 www.chaddsford.com) offers tastings and tours of its wine-making facilities.

❸ **Brandywine Battlefield State Park** is near the site of the Battle of Brandywine, where British general William Howe and his troops defeated George Washington on September 11, 1777. The Continental Army then fled to Chester, leaving Philadelphia vulnerable to British troops. The visitor center has displays about the battle that are a good introduction to the area's history. On the site are two restored Quaker farmhouses that once sheltered Washington and General Lafayette. The 50-acre park is a fine place for a picnic. ☒ *U.S. 1* ☎ *610/459–3342* 🌐 *www.ushistory.org/brandywine* 🎫 *Park free, house tours $5* ⊙ *Mar.–Nov., Tues.–Sat. 9–5, Sun. noon–5; Dec.–Feb., Thurs.–Sat. 9–5, Sun. noon–5.*

❹ Fodor'sChoice ★ In a converted Civil War–era gristmill, the **Brandywine River Museum** showcases the art of Chadds Ford native Andrew Wyeth, a major American realist painter, as well as his father, N. C. Wyeth, illustrator of many children's classics; and his son, Jamie. The collection also emphasizes still lifes, landscape paintings, and American illustration, with works by such artists as Howard Pyle and Maxfield Parrish. The glass-wall lobby overlooks the river and countryside that inspired the Brandywine School. The museum uses a system of filters, baffles, and blinds to direct natural light. Outside the museum, you can visit a garden with regional wildflowers and follow a 1-mi nature trail along the river.

The N. C. Wyeth House and Studio, where N. C. painted and raised his children, is open part of the year. The 1911 home, set on a hill, holds many of the props N. C. used in creating his illustrations. His daughter, Carolyn, lived and painted here until 1994. You can also tour the Kuerner Farm, just a mile away. Andrew discovered it on a walk when he was 15; he used the farm's landscape, buildings, and animals as the subjects of many of his best-known paintings. A shuttle takes you from the museum to the house or to the farm for a 60-minute guided tour. Reservations for the tours can be made two weeks in advance. ✉ *U.S. 1 and Rte. 100* ☎ *610/388–2700 information, 610/388–8326 reservations* 🌐 *www.brandywinemuseum.org* 🎟 *$8 museum, $5 house, $5 farm* ⏲ *Museum daily 9:30–4:30; house and farm Apr.–Nov., Wed.–Sun. 10–3:15.*

Where to Stay & Eat

$$$ ✕ **Chadds Ford Inn.** Washington's officers slept in this 1736 inn before the Battle of Brandywine. It served as a lively rest stop on the Wilmington–Philadelphia–Lancaster commerce route. Visitors today dine on regional American cuisine in a Colonial-style dining room warmed by stone hearths. Entrées such as veal medallions with wild mushrooms, pork tenderloin stuffed with figs, and Maryland crab cakes are served in generous portions. Sunday brunch is popular. The inn is across the highway from the Brandywine River Museum. ✉ *U.S. 1 and Rte. 100* ☎ *610/388–7361* 💳 *AE, DC, MC, V* ⏲ *Closed Mon.*

$ ✕ **Hank's Place.** Locals flock to this wood-paneled outpost for hearty breakfast specials, such as shiitake mushroom omelets and eggs Benedict topped with chipped beef. Hank's is also open for home-style lunches and dinners (come early, as it closes at 7 PM). The meat loaf, chicken potpie, fresh fish, and deep-fried Kennett Square mushrooms beckon. The strawberry pie and apple dumplings are specialties. ✉ *U.S. 1 and Rte. 100* ☎ *610/388–7061* 💳 *No credit cards* ⏲ *No dinner Sun.–Mon.*

$–$$ 🏨 **Brandywine River Hotel.** Near the Brandywine River Museum and the Chadds Ford Inn, this two-story hotel has tasteful Queen Anne–style furnishings, classic English chintz, and floral fabrics that create a homey bed-and-breakfast feeling. Suites have fireplaces and whirlpool baths. Afternoon tea with homemade cookies and a plentiful Continental breakfast with fresh fruit and homemade muffins are included; wine and beer are available in the lobby's cash bar. Request a room that overlooks the surrounding pasture. ✉ *U.S. 1 and Rte. 100, 19317* ☎ *610/388–1200* 📠 *610/388–1200* 🌐 *www.brandywineriverhotel.com* 🛏 *29 rooms, 10 suites* 🛎 *Dining room, some refrigerators, cable TV, gym, lobby lounge, shops, business services, meeting room, some pets allowed* 💳 *AE, D, DC, MC, V* 🍽 *CP.*

Kennett Square

7 mi west of Chadds Ford.

Kennett Square is where mushroom cultivation began in the United States. By the mid-1920s, 90% of the nation's mushrooms were grown in southeastern Pennsylvania. The town celebrates its heritage with its annual Mushroom Festival in September. Most visitors come to visit Longwood Gardens, a lovely spot about 3 mi northeast of Kennett Square. The town itself, with its Victorian-era homes lining the tree-lined streets, is also worth a visit; there are shops, galleries, and restaurants along East State Street between Broad and Union.

5 Fodor's Choice ★ **Longwood Gardens** has established an international reputation for its immaculate, colorful gardens full of flowers and blossoming shrubs. In 1906 Pierre S. du Pont (1870–1945) bought a simple Quaker farm and turned it into the ultimate early-20th-century estate garden. Seasonal attractions include magnolias and azaleas in spring; roses and water lilies in summer; chrysanthemums in fall; and camellias, orchids, and palms in winter. You can stroll in the Italian water garden or explore a meadow full of wildflowers on the garden's 350 acres. Bad weather is no problem, as 4 acres of exotic foliage, cacti, ferns, and bonsai plants are housed in heated conservatories. Outdoors is the Bee-aMazed Children's Garden, with a honeycomb maze, queen bee throne, and small splashing fountains; a large indoor children's garden is slated to open in 2006. The spectacular illuminated fountain displays on Tuesday, Thursday, and Saturday evenings in summer are very popular; the gardens stay open until 10. The cafeteria (open year-round) and dining room (closed January–March) serve varied, reasonably priced meals. ✉ *U.S. 1* ☎ *610/388–1000* 🌐 *www.longwoodgardens.org* 🎟 *$14, $10 on Tues.* ⏲ *Apr.–Oct., daily 9–6; Nov.–Mar., daily 9–5; plus some evenings in summer and Thanksgiving–Christmas.*

Where to Stay & Eat

$–$$$ ✕ **Half Moon Restaurant & Saloon.** Eclectic eats like crab nachos and Caesar salad with blackened alligator typify this lively spot. The restaurant maintains much of its original 1920s allure with an expansive white-tile floor and original tin ceilings, but there's nothing historic about the menu, which is vast and most definitely modern. A rooftop deck for outdoor dining, live music on Thursday and Saturday nights, top-shelf tequilas, and more than 30 beers on tap—including hand-pulled English-style beers—make Half Moon a popular nightspot. ✉ *108 W. State St.* ☎ *610/444–7232* 🌐 *www.halfmoonrestaurant.com* 💳 *AE, D, MC, V* ⏲ *Closed Sun.*

★ $–$$$ ✕ **Sovana Bistro.** Chef Nicholas Farrell transforms local and organic ingredients into satisfying meals at this rustic restaurant, which is part French bistro and part Italian trattoria. Hand-cut pappardelle pasta in a Bolognese sauce, grilled porcini-crusted pork tenderloin, and apple tarts with cheddar crusts are stars on the seasonal menu. Though a lunch of a grilled ham-and-cheese sandwich and tomato soup might sound mundane, it is anything but: the ham is imported, the mozzarella and bread are made in-house, and the tomato soup is roasted and drizzled with basil-infused oil. The wood-oven pizzas, breads, and pastries are sold in an adjacent café, which also has breakfast items. ✉ *696 Unionville Rd.* ☎ *610/444–5600* 🌐 *www.sovanabistro.com* *Reservations not accepted* ▭ *AE, MC, V* ⏲ *No lunch Sun.* *BYOB.*

$ ✕ **Taqueria Moroleón.** The portions are huge and the food is authentic at this cantina named after the owner's hometown in Mexico. This strip-mall restaurant's red, yellow, and blue walls hung with sombreros and piñatas provide a colorful backdrop for a menu of fajitas and enchiladas, complemented by dishes like deep-fried red snapper with avocado salad, and skirt steak simmered with tender cactus and cheese. The low prices and friendly service make this popular place. ✉ *New Garden Shopping Center, 345 Scarlet Rd., just south of W. Baltimore Pike* ☎ *610/444–1210* ▭ *D, DC, MC, V* *BYOB.*

$$–$$$ **Fairville Inn.** This bed-and-breakfast, halfway between Longwood Gardens and Winterthur, has bright, airy rooms furnished with Queen Anne and Hepplewhite reproductions and dramatic white-draped canopy beds. The main house, built in 1857, has a striking living room with a fireplace. Rooms in the carriage house and springhouse have decks; those in the latter have a sweeping view down to the pond. The Fairville serves a complimentary breakfast, which often includes homemade pancakes or Belgian waffles, and an afternoon tea with home-baked cookies. ✉ *506 Rte. 52 (Kennett Pike), Mendenhall 19317* ☎ *610/388–5900* *610/388–5902* 🌐 *www.fairvilleinn.com* *13 rooms, 2 suites* *Dining room, cable TV, business services. No kids under 12, no smoking* ▭ *AE, D, MC, V* *BP.*

$–$$$ **The Inn at Whitewing Farm.** Near Longwood Gardens, this 1700s Pennsylvania farmhouse is on 43 tranquil rolling acres dotted with horses and cows. On the grounds are five houses for guests, including a gatehouse suite, a renovated stable and hay barn, and a house by a swan-filled pond which is stocked for catch-and-release fishing. Comfortable bedrooms are elegantly decorated in the greens, burgundies, and pale yellows of the English hunt style, and all have marble-floor baths. In good weather, complimentary country breakfast (including stuffed French toast or pancakes with raspberry sauce) is served on the terrace. Tea and cordials are a treat in the afternoon. ✉ *370 Valley Rd., 19348* ☎ *610/388–2664* *610/388–3650* 🌐 *www.whitewingfarm.com* *7 rooms, 3 suites* *Dining room, cable TV, tennis court, pool, hot tub, billiards; no smoking* ▭ *No credit cards* *BP.*

Fodor's Choice ★

Wilmington

15 mi southeast of Kennett Square.

Delaware's commercial hub and largest city has handsome architecture—with good examples of styles such as Federal, Greek Revival, Queen Anne, and art deco—and abundant cultural attractions. Wilmington began in 1638 as a Swedish settlement and later was populated by employees of various du Pont family businesses and nearby poultry ranches. The four-block Market Street Mall marks the city center and is distinguished by the Grand Opera House. The four-story theater, built by the Masonic Order in 1871, has a white cast-iron facade in French Second Empire style to mimic the old Paris Opera. The adjoining Giacco Building houses a smaller theater and art galleries. Outside Wilmington's compact city center are several outstanding museums, including some that are legacies of the du Ponts.

Henry Francis du Pont (1880–1969) housed his 85,000 objects of American decorative art in a sprawling nine-story country estate called 6 **Winterthur.** Today the collection, displayed in 175 rooms in the original mansion, is recognized as one of the nation's finest. To sample the collection, you can choose among different one-hour, theme discovery tours—such Elegant Entertaining—and two-hour tours that delve into ceramics, textiles, or furniture. No children under 8 are allowed except on the daily family tour, which is open to all but geared to kids ages 4 to 12. The museum also has galleries with permanent displays and changing exhibitions of antiques and crafts that you can study at your own pace. Surrounding the estate are 982 acres of landscaped lawns and naturalistic gardens, which you can visit on a 30-minute narrated tram ride or on your own. The Enchanted Woods is a fantasy-theme 3-acre children's garden with an 8-foot-wide bird's nest, a faerie cottage with a thatched roof, and a troll bridge. A gift shop and cafeteria, which serves Sunday brunch, are also on the grounds. ✉ *Rte. 52, 5 mi south of U.S. 1* ☎ *302/888–4600* 🌐 *www.winterthur.org* 🎟 *$20–$30* ⏲ *Tues.–Sun. 10–5.*

Fodor's Choice ★

7 For a look at how the very wealthy lived, visit **Nemours Mansion and Gardens,** a 300-acre country estate built for Alfred I. du Pont in 1910. This modified Louis XVI château showcases 102 rooms of European and American furnishings, rare rugs, tapestries, and art dating to the 15th century. The gardens, reminiscent of those at Versailles, are landscaped with fountains, pools, and statuary. The estate can be seen only on guided two-hour tours. Visitors must be at least 12 years old. Note: the mansion is undergoing a two-year restoration, and is slated to reopen in early 2007. ✉ *1600 Rockland Rd., between Rte. 141 and U.S. 202* ☎ *302/651–6912* 🌐 *www.nemoursmansion.org.*

The **Wilmington Public Library,** catercorner to the Hotel du Pont, holds a wonderful bounty among its shelves: 14 of 17 canvases, plus the jacket and endpaper paintings, done by N. C. Wyeth in 1920 to illustrate Daniel Defoe's *Robinson Crusoe.* ✉ *10th and Market Sts.* ☎ *302/571–7400* 🌐 *www.wilmlib.org* ⏲ *Mon.–Thurs. 9–8, Fri. and Sat. 9–5.*

A restored mid-19th-century mill community on 235 landscaped acres ★ 8 along the Brandywine River, the **Hagley Museum and Library** provides an enlightening look at the development of early industrial America. This is the site of the first of the du Pont family's black-powder mills. Live demonstrations depict the dangerous work of the early explosives industry. "Du Pont Science and Discovery" traces the company's evolution and displays a NASCAR car and a space suit. Admission includes a narrated bus tour through the powder yards with stops at Eleutherian Mills, the 1803 Georgian-style home furnished by five generations of du Ponts, and a French Renaissance–style garden. Allow about two hours for your visit. The coffee shop is open for lunch except in winter.

✉ *Rte. 141 between Rte. 100 and U.S. 202* ☎ *302/658–2400* 🌐 *www.hagley.org* 🎟 *$11* ⏲ *Mar. 15–Dec., daily 9:30–4:30; Jan.–Mar. 14, weekends 9:30–4:30; winter tours, weekdays at 1:30.*

9 **Rockwood,** a quietly elegant English-style country house and a fine example of rural Gothic architecture, stands in contrast to the opulent, French-inspired du Pont homes in the area. Built in 1851 by Joseph Shipley, a Quaker banker, the house is now a museum filled with 19th-century decorative arts and furnishings. Additionally, the 72-acre public grounds feature 2½ mi of paved, lighted trails. Tours are given on the hour 10–3. Rockwood hosts a summer concert series, an ice cream festival, and a Christmas festival. ✉ *610 Shipley Rd.* ☎ *302/761–4340* 🌐 *www.rockwood.org* 🎟 *Free* ⏲ *Grounds daily dawn–10 PM; mansion and café daily 7–5.*

10 A treat for art lovers, the **Delaware Art Museum** moved into a splendid new 85,000-square-foot building in 2005. The lighted roofline changes colors according to the celestial calendar, and Dale Chihuly's Persian Window installation draws attention to the entrance. The museum's holdings include a good collection of paintings by Howard Pyle (1853–1911), a Wilmington native known as the "father of American illustration," as well as works by his students N. C. Wyeth, Frank Schoonover, and Maxfield Parrish. Other American artists represented are Benjamin West, Winslow Homer, Edward Glackens, and Edward Hopper. The museum also has the largest American collection of 19th-century English pre-Raphaelite paintings and decorative arts and a children's interactive gallery. *The Crying Giant,* by Tom Otterness, is one of the highlights of the 9-acre Sculpture Park. ✉ *2301 Kentmere Pkwy.* ☎ *302/571–9590* 🌐 *www.delart.org* 🎟 *$10* ⏲ *Tues. and Thurs.–Sat. 10–4, Wed. 10–8, Sun. noon–4.*

Where to Stay & Eat

$$$–$$$$ ✕ **821.** Leather banquettes, slate floors, and soft amber lighting contribute to the Mediterranean ambience at this restaurant across from the Grand Opera House. The highly inventive changing menu may include crispy duck confit with Gorgonzola polenta or braised short ribs with parsnip puree, but the constant is fresh local ingredients prepared with French and Italian influences. The *shiatta* (flatbread encrusted with sundried cherries) is a specialty. The small and large plate choices are meant for sharing tapas-style, as are the desserts. If you can't decide, there are four- and six-course tasting menus paired with wines. ✉ *821 Market St.* ☎ *302/652–8821* 🌐 *www.restaurant821.com* 💳 *AE, D, DC, MC, V* ⏲ *Closed Sun. No lunch.*

★ **$$$–$$$$** ✕ **Green Room.** For years people have celebrated special occasions in the Hotel du Pont's main restaurant. Its gold-encrusted hand-etched plaster ceiling, massive Spanish chandeliers, and tall French windows have added to the Edwardian splendor. Such delicacies as venison loin chop and wild rockfish—recipes blending the traditional with the contemporary—can be savored on china by Versace. Dinner is accompanied by impeccable service and jazz piano. The three-course tasting menu changes daily. You can soak up the ambience at a reduced price at the weekday lunch buffet. The Sunday brunch is extravagant and wonderful. Jackets are required on weekend evenings. ✉ *Hotel du Pont, 11th and Market Sts.* ☎ *302/594–3154* 🌐 *www.dupont.com/hotel/dining green.htm* ✍ *Reservations essential* ▭ *AE, D, DC, MC, V.*

★ $$$–$$$$ ✕ **Krazy Kat's.** Oil paintings of regal felines watch over diners at this plushly furnished restaurant on the grounds of the Inn at Montchanin Village, between Kennett Square and Wilmington. Leopard-print chairs and soft lighting round out the atmosphere of elegance with a grin. The unique setting and creative menu draw regulars from Philadelphia and beyond, who come for crab bisque, crab cakes, and filet mignon, as well as apple-walnut bread pudding. ✉ *Inn at Montchanin Village, Rte. 100 and Kirk Rd.* ☎ *302/888–4200* 🌐 *www.montchanin.com/krazykats.html* ▭ *AE, D, DC, MC, V* ⏲ *No lunch weekends.*

$$–$$$$ ✕ **Deep Blue.** Ultramodern, airy, and convivial, this bar and bistro contrasts with the formal Hotel du Pont across the street. Seared ahi tuna rubbed with Chinese spices, crab-crusted wild salmon, and poached lobster tail with gnocchi are a few of the imaginatively seasoned and beautifully presented dishes. The raw bar has more than a dozen types of oysters; the bar has a wide selection of microbrews on tap. There's live music Friday and Saturday nights. The $30 three-course pretheater menu ensures that you'll be on time at the nearby Grand Opera House. ✉ *111 W. 11th St.* ☎ *302/777–2040* 🌐 *www.deepbluebarandgrill.com* ▭ *AE, D, DC, MC, V* ⏲ *Closed Sun. No lunch weekends.*

$$$$ 🏨 **Hotel du Pont.** Built in 1913 by Pierre S. du Pont, this luxury hotel in downtown Wilmington has hosted everyone from Charles Lindbergh to John F. Kennedy. The elegant 12-story building radiates an old-world feel. The lobby has a spectacular carved, gilded, and painted ceiling, polished marble walls, and Queen Anne and Chippendale furnishings. The walls display more than 700 original works of art, including Wyeths and Schoonovers. The spacious guest rooms have a contemporary French flair, with soothing monochrome color schemes and earthy textures. The Green Room is known for its marvelous Sunday brunch. ✉ *11th and Market Sts., 19801* ☎ *302/594–3100 or 800/441–9019* 🖷 *302/594–3108* 🌐 *www.hoteldupont.com* 🛏 *206 rooms, 11 suites* ♨ *Restaurant, cafeteria, room service, in-room safes, Internet, minibars, cable TV with movies, golf privileges, gym, sauna, hair salon, massage, bar, lobby lounge, theater, business services, airport shuttle; no-smoking floors* ▭ *AE, D, DC, MC, V.*

★ $$–$$$$ 🏨 **Inn at Montchanin Village.** This small luxury hotel includes 11 painstakingly restored 19th-century cottages that once housed workers at the nearby mills. Each elegant room is decorated with oil paintings, reproductions of antique furniture, and four-poster or canopy beds covered with Frette linens. All have kitchenettes and luxurious marble baths; some have porches with wicker rockers. The great room, where evening hors d'oeuvres are served, has overstuffed chairs, game tables, and a stone hearth that stretches from floor to ceiling. About 10 minutes from downtown Wilmington, this inn is nestled in a series of peaceful gardens intersected with landscaped walkways. ✉ *Rte. 100 and Kirk Rd., Montchanin 19710* ☎ *302/888–2133 or 800/269–2473* 🖷 *302/888–0389* 🌐 *www.montchanin.com* 🛏 *12 rooms, 16 suites* ♨ *Restaurant,* *picnic area, room service, in-room safes, in-room data ports, some in-room hot tubs, kitchenettes, cable TV, in-room VCRs, gym, lobby lounge, concierge, business services, meeting rooms; no smoking* ▭ *AE, D, DC, MC, V.*

Brandywine Valley A to Z

BUS TRAVEL

From Philadelphia, Greyhound Lines operates out of the terminal at 10th and Filbert streets, just north of the Market East commuter rail station. There are about six daily departures to the Wilmington terminal at 101 North French Street. The trip takes one hour.

Greyhound Lines ☎ 215/931-4075 or 800/231-2222 ⊕ www.greyhound.com.

CAR TRAVEL

Take U.S. 1 south from Philadelphia; the Brandywine Valley is about 25 mi from Philadelphia, and many attractions are on U.S. 1. To reach Wilmington, pick up U.S. 202 south just past Concordville or take I–95 south from Philadelphia.

TOURS

Colonial Pathways organizes full-day bus tours through the Brandywine Valley. American Heritage Landmark Tours offers a variety of trips for larger groups. Brandywine Outfitters rents out both canoes and kayaks and offers a range of scenic trips on the Brandywine River.

American Heritage Landmark Tours ✉ 14 Anthony Dr., Malvern 19355 ☎ 610/647-4030 ⊕ www.ahltours.com. **Brandywine Outfitters** ✉ 2096 Strasburg Rd., Coatesville 19320 ☎ 610/486-6141 or 800/226-6378 ⊕ www.canoepa.net. **Colonial Pathways** Box 879, Chadds Ford 19317 ☎ 610/388-2654 ⊕ www.colonialpathways.com.

TRAIN TRAVEL

Amtrak has frequent service from Philadelphia's 30th Street Station to Wilmington's station at Martin Luther King Jr. Boulevard and French Street on the edge of downtown. It's a 25-minute ride.

The Southeastern Pennsylvania Transportation Authority's R2 commuter train has hourly departures to Wilmington from Philadelphia's Suburban, 30th Street, and Market East train stations. The trip takes one hour.

Amtrak ☎ 800/872-7245 ⊕ www.amtrak.com. **SEPTA** ☎ 215/580-7800 ⊕ www.septa.com.

VISITOR INFORMATION

The three visitors bureaus listed below publish free seasonal guides with listings for dining, lodging, and attractions, as well as a calendar of events. These are available at attractions and hotels. The **Visitor Center** (✉ 300 Greenwood Rd., Kennett Square ☎ 800/228-9933) at the entrance to Longwood Gardens is operated by the Chester County Conference and Visitors Bureau. It's open daily 10–6.

Chester County Conference and Visitors Bureau ✉ 400 Exton Square Pkwy. Exton 19341 ☎ 610/280-6145 or 800/228-9933 ⊕ www.brandywinevalley.com **Delaware County's Brandywine Conference and Visitors Bureau** ✉ 1 Beaver Valley Rd., Chadds Ford 19317 ☎ 610/565-3679 or 800/343-3983 ⊕ www.brandywinecvb.org. **Greater**

Wilmington Convention and Visitors Bureau ✉ 100 W. 10th St., Wilmington, DE 19801 ☎ 302/652-4088 or 800/489-6664 🌐 www.visitwilmingtonde.com.

VALLEY FORGE

The monuments, markers, huts, and headquarters in Valley Forge National Historical Park illuminate a decisive period in U.S. history. The park, with its quiet beauty that seems to whisper of the past, preserves the area where George Washington's Continental Army endured the bitter winter of 1777–78. The 225th anniversary of this "Philadelphia Campaign" was marked in 2002 with reenactments and living-history events at several Valley Forge historic sites. Scheduled to open in late 2007, the American Revolution Center at Valley Forge will exhibit the largest collection of Revolutionary War–era artifacts and documents ever assembled.

Other nearby attractions are the Mill Grove Audubon Center, once the home of naturalist John James Audubon; the studio and residence of craftsman Wharton Esherick; and King of Prussia mall.

Numbers in the text correspond to numbers in the margin and on the Valley Forge map.

Valley Forge

20 mi northeast of downtown Philadelphia.

A major site of the Revolutionary War is near the suburban village of Valley Forge. The town was named because of an iron forge built in the 1740s.

★ ❶ **Valley Forge National Historical Park,** administered by the National Park Service, is the location of the 1777–78 winter encampment of General George Washington and the Continental Army. Stop first at the Valley Forge Welcome Center to see the 18-minute orientation film (shown every 30 minutes) and view exhibits. You can pick up a map for a 10-mi self-guided driving tour of the attractions in the 3,600-acre park; an audio tour costs $10 for tapes and $12 for CDs. From June to October, the park offers a bus tour with a taped narration for $15.50 per person. Stops include reconstructed log huts of the Muhlenberg Brigade and the National Memorial Arch, which pays tribute to the soldiers who suffered through the brutal winter. Other sites are the bronze equestrian statue of General Anthony Wayne, in the area where his Pennsylvania troops were encamped; Artillery Park, where the soldiers stored their cannons; and the Isaac Potts House, which served as Washington's headquarters.

The park is quiet today, but in 1777 the army had just lost the nearby battles of Brandywine, White Horse, and Germantown. While the British occupied Philadelphia, Washington's soldiers were forced to endure horrid conditions here—blizzards, inadequate food and clothing, damp quarters, and disease. Although no battle was fought at Valley Forge, 2,000 soldiers died here.

The troops did win one victory that winter—a war of will. The forces slowly regained strength and confidence under the leadership of Prussian drillmaster Friedrich von Steuben. In June 1778 Washington led his

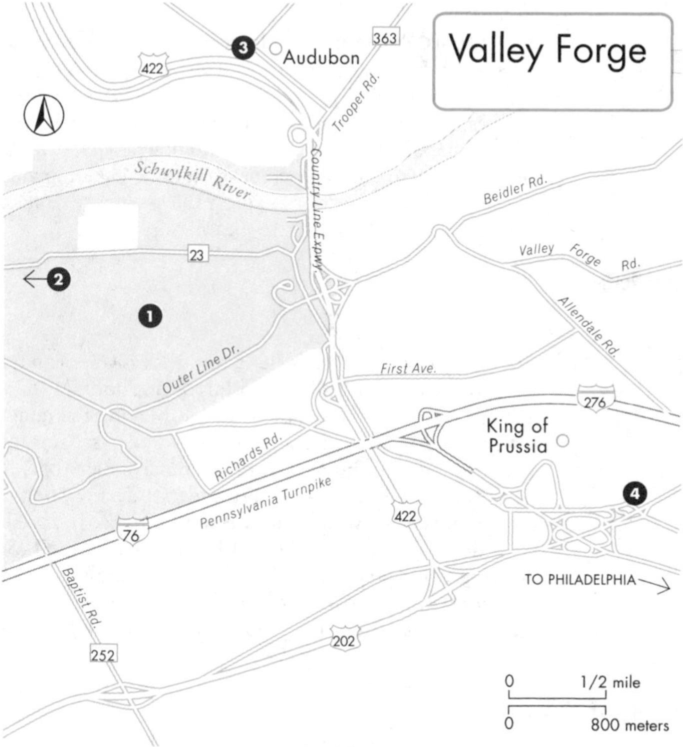

troops away from Valley Forge in search of the British. Fortified, the Continental Army was able to carry on the fight for five years more.

The park contains 6 mi of jogging and bicycling paths and hiking trails, and you can picnic at any of three designated areas. A leisurely visit to the park takes no more than half a day. ✉ *Rte. 23 and N. Gulph Rd.* ☎ *610/783–1077* 🌐 *www.nps.gov/vafo* 🎫 *Park free; Washington's headquarters $3 Apr.–Nov., free Dec.–Mar.* 🕒 *Park: daily 6 AM–10 PM; welcome center daily 9–5.*

2 The **Wharton Esherick Museum** preserves the former home and studio of the "Dean of American Craftsmen." Best known for his sculptural furniture, Esherick (1887–1970) shaped a new aesthetic in decorative arts by bridging art with furniture. The museum, recently designated as a National Historic Landmark, houses 200 examples of his work—paintings, woodcuts, furniture, and wood sculptures. The studio, in which everything from the light switches to the spiral staircase is hand-carved, is one of his monumental achievements. The museum is 2 mi west of Valley Forge National Historical Park. Reservations are required for the hourly tours. On weekdays, a minimum of five people is required for a tour. ✉ *1520 Horseshoe Trail* ☎ *610/644–5822* 🌐 *www.levins.com/esherick.html* 🎫 *$9* 🕒 *Mar.–Dec., Sat. 10–5, Sun. 1–5.*

Shopping

The **Chapel Cabin Shop,** (✉ Alongside the Washington Memorial Chapel on Rte. 23 ☎ 610/783–0576 🌐 www.washingtonmemorialchapel.org) is staffed primarily by volunteers from the parish, who make the cakes, candies, and jams that are sold here. Proceeds help keep the privately owned chapel afloat. You'll also find fine pewter, Colonial art, and souvenirs related to the American Revolution. The shop includes a tiny luncheonette—and outdoor picnic tables—where you can enjoy daily specials, such as Martha's 16-Bean Soup.

Audubon

2 mi north of Valley Forge.

❸ The **Mill Grove Audubon Center** was the first American home of Haitian-born artist and naturalist John James Audubon (1785–1851). Built in 1762, the house is now a museum displaying the major works of this renowned American naturalist, including his paintings of birds and wildlife, and an original copy of his massive *Birds of America*. The attic has been restored to a studio and taxidermy room. The National Audubon Society, which runs the museum, has restored these treasures and added others. Mill Grove is located within the 175-acre Audubon Wildlife Sanctuary, which has 5 mi of hiking trails. ✉ *Audubon and Pawlings Rds.* ☎ *610/666–5593* 🌐 *www.montcopa.org/historicsites* 🎫 *Free* ⏲ *Museum Tues.–Sat. 10–4, Sun. 1–4; grounds Tues.–Sun. dawn–dusk.*

King of Prussia

5 mi southeast of Audubon.

Shopping is a main draw in this busy suburban town. For lunch or an afternoon of browsing, head to the **King of Prussia Mall,** one of the nation's largest shopping complexes. Comprising two main buildings—the Plaza and the Court—the mall contains more than 40 restaurants, 365 shops and boutiques, and eight major department stores, including Bloomingdale's, Nordstrom, and Neiman Marcus. The Pavilion, the most recent addition to the existing complex, has a collection of perennial favorites, including Morton's of Chicago, the Bamboo Club, Borders, and H&M. ✉ *U.S. 202 at the Schuylkill Expressway, 160 N. Gulph Rd.* ☎ *610/265–5727* 🌐 *www.kingofprussiamall.com* ⏲ *Mon.–Sat. 10–9:30, Sun. 11–7.*

❹ Fodor'sChoice ★

Where to Stay & Eat

$$$$ ✕ **Savona.** Strikingly attractive and thoroughly refined in taste and ambience, this restaurant, with its outstanding Riviera-influenced cuisine, is a destination for many people from the surrounding suburbs, corporate types, and, yes, Center City folks, too. Every appointment is in place: gorgeous tableware and other lavish touches of various sorts. The lobster risotto is exquisite, as is the roast squab. The wine list is extensive and creative, and the service is thoughtful and professional. ✉ *100 Old Gulph Rd., Gulph Mills* ☎ *610/520–1200* 💳 *AE, DC, MC, V* ⏲ *No lunch.*

$$–$$$$ ✕ **California Café.** This stylish bistro in the Plaza at King of Prussia doesn't feel like a mall restaurant. The seasonal American dishes show

Southwestern and Asian influences, evident in the mussels in a lemongrass and coconut milk broth and the herb fettuccine with seared chicken and Szechuan black bean sauce. You can order a full dinner, a small plate, or a pizza made in the wood-burning oven. The lunchtime bento box sampler and the "three-way" dinner with chile rellenos, lamb chops, and calamari are good choices. Wines by the glass and unusual cocktails—like blood-orange mojitos and key-lime martinis—provide what the eatery terms "liquid therapy." ✉ *160 N. Gulph Rd.* ☎ *610/354–8686* 🌐 *www.californiacafe.com* ▭ *AE, D, MC, V.*

$–$$ **Crowne Plaza Valley Forge.** You can shop 'til you drop at the King of Prussia Mall right across the street and then sleep soundly in the pillow-top beds with plush duvets and piles of pillows. An extreme makeover gave this stylish hotel a skylit marble-floor lobby and extensive conference space. Guests can use the nearby Bally Total Fitness health club. The hotel has a free shuttle to the mall. ✉ *260 Mall Blvd., 19406* ☎ *610/265–7500* 📠 *610/254–0666* 🌐 *www.crowneplazavalleyforge.com* *215 rooms, 10 suites* *Restaurant, cable TV with movies, Internet, in-room data ports, lobby lounge, concierge floor, business services, convention center; no-smoking floors* ▭ *AE, D, DC, MC, V* *EP.*

Valley Forge A to Z

BUS TRAVEL

The Southeastern Pennsylvania Transportation Authority's Bus 125 leaves from 13th and Market streets (twice an hour starting at 5:15 AM) for King of Prussia (including The Plaza & The Court) and continues on to Valley Forge National Historical Park.

SEPTA ☎ 215/580-7800 🌐 www.septa.com.

CAR TRAVEL

Take the Schuylkill Expressway (I–76) west from Philadelphia to Exit 327 (Mall Boulevard). Make a right onto Mall Boulevard and a right onto North Gulph Road. Follow the road 1½ miles to Valley Forge National Historical Park. Mall Boulevard also provides easy access to The Plaza & The Court shopping complex.

TOURS

The self-driven Valley Forge National Historical Auto-Tour can be purchased from the Welcome Center ($10 tape, $12 CD).

Valley Forge Welcome Center ✉ Rte. 23 and N. Gulph Rd. ☎ 610/783-1077 🌐 www.nps.gov/vafo.

VISITOR INFORMATION

The Valley Forge Country Funline has information about special events and exhibits.

Valley Forge Convention and Visitors Bureau ✉ 600 W. Germantown Pike, Suite 130, Plymouth Meeting 19462 ☎ 610/834-1550 or 800/441-3549 🌐 www.valleyforge.org. **Valley Forge Country Funline** ☎ 610/834-8844.

9 Bucks County

WORD OF MOUTH

"[New Hope] is . . . still a lovely place to spend a weekend. There is ample shopping, great people watching, a small playhouse, . . . [and] a train ride which will take you all over the countryside. There is an old barge ride with mules (very nostalgic). [The town] has some gorgeous scenery, and wonderful restaurants."

—diann

"Check out the Wedgwood Inn–close to Peddler's Village and Doylestown. We've stayed there and LOVE it—it is also kid-friendly. At Peddler's Village, there is a place called Giggleberry Fair–carousel and other kid-friendly things. A nice stop after the adults get their fill of shopping in little boutique shops."

—lisabees

www.fodors.com/forums

By Andrea Lehman

BUCKS COUNTY, about an hour's drive northeast of Philadelphia, could have remained 625 square mi of sleepy countryside full of old stone farmhouses, lush hills, and covered bridges if it hadn't been discovered in the '30s by New York's Beautiful Brainy People. Such luminaries as writers Dorothy Parker and S. J. Perelman and lyricist Oscar Hammerstein II bought country homes here, a short drive from Manhattan. Pulitzer prize–and Nobel prize–winning author Pearl S. Buck chose to live in the area because it was "a region where the landscapes were varied, where farm and industry lived side by side, where the sea was near at hand, mountains not far away, and city and countryside were not enemies." Author James A. Michener, who won the 1947 Pulitzer prize for his *Tales of the South Pacific,* was raised and worked in Doylestown. The region quickly gained a nickname: the Genius Belt.

Over the years Bucks County has been known for art colonies and antiques, summer theater, and country inns. Cookie-cutter housing developments are now planted where grain once grew, however. It's not unusual to find suburban sprawl and hyper-development adjacent to an old clapboard farmhouse or ancient stone barn. Yet many areas of central and upper Bucks County remain as bucolic as ever—a feast of lyrical landscapes, with canal and river vistas, rolling hills, and fertile fields. Driving back roads is one of the county's pleasures, and making your way through quiet little towns, stopping at historic sites, checking out little antiques shops, and staying overnight in an appealing inn make for a classic weekend getaway.

A Bit of History

Named after England's Buckinghamshire, Bucks County was opened to European settlement by William Penn in 1681 under a land grant from Charles II. The county's most celebrated town, New Hope, was settled in the early 1700s and, together with its neighbor across the river, Lambertville, New Jersey, was called Coryell's Ferry. (One of the original gristmills is now the home of the Bucks County Playhouse.) The town was the Pennsylvania terminal for stagecoach traffic and Delaware River ferry traffic. Barges hauled coal along the 60-mi Delaware Canal until 1931.

Commerce built up New Hope, but art helped sustain it. An art colony took root in the late 19th century and was revitalized in the 1930s by theater folk and more recently with the arrival of galleries and artists from around the country. Doylestown's James A. Michener Art Museum, showcasing 19th- and 20th-century American art, now has a satellite location in New Hope.

Exploring Bucks County

Many Bucks County sights are along two corridors: U.S. 202, which connects Doylestown and New Hope, and Route 32, which winds its way from Pennsbury Manor north through pretty villages such as Erwinna. You'll also want to explore the quiet roads leading off these traffic-filled thoroughfares.

Although you can see the major attractions in a daylong whirlwind tour of Bucks County, many people plan overnight stays at some of the prettiest inns in the Mid-Atlantic region. A number of houses and mills, some dating back to a half century before the Revolution, are now excellent restaurants and bed-and-breakfasts. A hearty meal, blissful sleep, and a day spent driving leisurely along River Road are what make visits to Bucks County most enjoyable.

Among the leading destinations is New Hope, a hodgepodge of old stone houses, narrow streets and alleys, pretty courtyards, and busy restaurants. Summer weekends can be frantic here, with traffic jams and motorcycle fleets along Main Street and shoppers thronging the tiny boutiques and galleries. The Delaware Canal threads through town, and you can glide lazily along it in a mule-pulled barge. Or you can stroll across a bridge spanning the Delaware River to Lambertville, New Jersey, a postcard-perfect small town known for its antiques shops and galleries.

Doylestown, the county seat, was an important coach stop during the 18th century. Today the town is best known as the home of Henry Chapman Mercer, curator of archaeology at the University of Pennsylvania Museum, master potter, self-taught architect, writer of Gothic tales, and notable eccentric. When Mercer died in 1930, he left behind a magnificently bizarre castle named Fonthill, an equally bizarre museum displaying 50,000 implements and tools, and a pottery and tile works that still makes Mercer tiles.

The county is also a repository of Colonial history. Among the most interesting sites is Pennsbury Manor, a reconstruction of the Georgian-style mansion William Penn built in the late 1600s. On the banks of the Delaware, the 500-acre Washington Crossing Historic Park is situated where the general and his troops crossed the icy river on Christmas night 1776 to surprise the Hessian mercenaries at Trenton, New Jersey.

The Delaware River and the canal that follows its path are used for canoeing, kayaking, and fishing. Thousands float down the river each year in inner tubes or rubber rafts. Joggers, hikers, bicyclists, cross-country skiers, and horseback riders take full advantage of the canal towpath—at least those sections that are open.

About the Restaurants

Bucks County has no regional specialties to call its own, but you can discover some sophisticated restaurants as well as casual country spots. What makes dining here special are the enchanting settings, ranging from a French-style auberge to Colonial-era manor. Fine meals of French or American fare are served in restored mills, pre-Revolutionary taverns, stagecoach stops, small cafés, and elegant Victorian mansions. In summer and fall, it's best to make reservations for weekend dining.

About the Hotels

Bucks County has relatively limited lodging options for families; larger inns, hotels and motels, and campgrounds are the best bets. There are numerous choices for couples: accommodations ranging from modest to elegant can be found in historic inns, small hotels, and B&Bs. Most

It's entirely possible to visit Bucks County as a day trip from Philadelphia, but a few days more allow you to sample many of the area's pleasures.

Numbers in the text correspond to numbers in the margin and on the Bucks County map.

If you have **1 day**

Start in **Doylestown** 9 at Fonthill, the fantastic mansion built by local Renaissance man Henry Chapman Mercer. As lunchtime approaches, wend your way along U.S. 202, stopping at any antiques shops displaying wares along the roadside, usually indicating they're open for business. Have lunch in **New Hope** 5, take a quick stroll through town to check out the eclectic boutiques and gracious historic buildings, and then head north on River Road for a stirring drive along the Delaware River up to **Lumberville** 12 or **Erwinna** 14. Have dinner at one of the inns in these towns.

If you have **2 days**

At your starting point in **Washington Crossing Historic Park** 4, you can see where George Washington set off across the river with his troops on that fateful Christmas night in 1776. Then drive up River Road to **New Hope** 5 and have lunch, perhaps outside. In the afternoon head west to explore Mercer Mile in **Doylestown** 9 and return to New Hope to spend the night at an inn. On Day 2, check out the antiques shops across the river in **Lambertville** 6 and then drive upriver in Pennsylvania on River Road for about 17 mi. Stop to stretch your legs along the way with a stroll on the scenic Delaware Canal towpath. Have dinner and spend the night at an inn in **Erwinna** 14 or **Kintnersville** 16.

If you have **3 days**

Drive up River Road to **Erwinna** 14. In season—roughly from May to October—even the mildly athletic might enjoy a canoe (tube in hot weather) trip south on the Delaware River, beginning at the rental facility in **Point Pleasant** 13. As an alternative, take a stroll or bike ride on the river's bucolic towpath north of Point Pleasant.

On Day 2, drive downriver to **New Hope** 5 for breakfast. Shop and see the town, then head west on U.S. 202. Visit the museums on Mercer Mile in **Doylestown** 9. Another choice is to spend the afternoon at Peddler's Village in **Lahaska** 7. Consider dinner and window-shopping just across the river from New Hope in **Lambertville** 6.

History buffs can fill their plate on the third day by starting out with a tour of the pre-Revolutionary village of **Fallsington** 2 and **Pennsbury Manor** 3, William Penn's country retreat, both near Morrisville in the southern part of the county. Drive north along the river in the afternoon, and you'll end up at **Washington Crossing Historic Park** 4, where a walk through the glorious parkland can easily occupy the rest of the day.

hostelries include breakfast in their rates. Reserve early—as much as three months ahead for summer and fall weekends. Many accommodations require a two-night minimum stay on weekends and a three-night minimum on holiday weekends. Many inns prohibit or restrict smoking. Because some inns are historic homes furnished with fine antiques, the owners may not allow children or may have age restrictions.

WHAT IT COSTS

	$$$$	$$$	$$	$	¢
RESTAURANTS	over $26	$20–$26	$14–$20	$8–$14	under $8
HOTELS	over $240	$190–$240	$140–$190	$90–$140	under $90

Restaurant prices are for one main course at dinner. Hotel prices are for two people in a standard double room in high season.

Timing

Spring, summer, or fall—each time of year has its own pleasures and seasonal festivals. Summer and fall weekends are especially busy, so make reservations well ahead and be ready for some crowds; a weekday trip could be more relaxing. Winter has its appeal here, too, especially around the holidays; the snow-covered fields are lovely.

Langhorne

25 mi northeast of Philadelphia.

❶ Families come to the Oxford Valley Mall for **Sesame Place**, a water-based theme park based on the popular children's show. Sesame Place is mostly for kids 2 to 10, who come to crawl, climb, and jump; float, slide, and splash; and meet, greet, and perhaps hug the ageless Big Bird and his friends. Though there are plenty of dry-land activities, the highlights of the park—especially on a hot summer day—are the water rides, including the popular Rambling River and Sky Splash (which are just what they sound like). As befits a park for preteen thrill-seekers, the roller coaster—Vapor Trail—is modest by theme park standards, but it's got more than enough excitement for its riders. Other kid favorites are the daily parades and shows and Sesame Neighborhood, a replica of the beloved TV street. ✉ *100 Sesame Rd., off Oxford Valley Rd. near U.S. 1 at I–95* ☎ *215/752–7070* 🌐 *www.sesameplace.com* 🎟 *$39.95* ⏲ *Late May–early Sept., daily; early May and mid-Sept.–late Oct., weekends; hrs vary.*

Fallsington

❷ *2 mi east of Langhorne.*

The pre-Revolutionary village of Fallsington displays more than 300 years of American architecture, from a simple 17th-century log cabin to the Victorian excesses of the late 1800s. Ninety period homes are found in the village, which is listed on the National Register of Historic Places.

Three historic buildings—a 17th-century log cabin and an 18th-century tavern and house—have been restored and opened for guided tours by

Antiques The bargain-priced treasures that made Bucks County an antiques-hunter's paradise are now few and far between, but there's still lots of good antiquing here. You'll find antiques shops tucked here and there, but especially along U.S. 202 between Doylestown and New Hope and in New Hope itself. Across the bridge in Lambertville, New Jersey, dozens more shops carry such treasures as armoires from Provence, Depression glass, and vintage 20th-century toy rocket ships, and south of Lambertville, a large flea market draws scores of antiques hounds. Shops are generally open on weekends, with weekday hours by appointment only: it's best to call first.

Covered Bridges Eleven working covered bridges are all that remain of the 36 originally built in Bucks County. Although the romantically inclined call them "kissing bridges" or "wishing bridges," the roofs were actually intended to protect the supporting beams from the ravages of the weather. The bridges are examples of the lattice-type construction of overlapping triangles, without arches or upright beams. They are delightful to stumble upon, but if you're serious about seeing them, contact the Bucks County Conference and Visitors Bureau. Locations of the bridges are listed in its visitors guide and marked on its map.

Taking to the Towpath One of the best ways to experience the beauty of Bucks is to stroll along the grassy towpath of the Delaware Canal, one of Pennsylvania's most scenic byways. Dotted with fieldstone bridge-tender houses and clapboard toll-collector offices—now private studios and homes—and shaded by magnificent trees, the path runs parallel to the Delaware River and River Road. Constructed in 1832 to allow access for coal barges, the canal and towpath are known today as the Delaware Canal State Park. Until a catastrophic flood in 2005 washed out many sections, the towpath was a favorite for biking, hiking, and jogging, as well as cross-country skiing in winter. At the time of writing, the only sections scheduled to be reopened are those between Point Pleasant and Upper Black Eddy, between Washington Crossing and Morrisville, and north of New Hope to Centre Bridge.

Vintage Bucks County Though Napa and Sonoma may not be quaking in their boots just yet, Buck's County's vineyards are a growing industry, thanks to well-drained limestone soil and a relatively moderate climate. As a result, wine-tasting is catching on as a local pursuit. Seven county wineries make up the Bucks County Wine Trail (www.buckscountywinetrail.com), and wine lovers pay them visits for tastings and tours, not to mention buying a bottle or case. You can make touring the vineyards an activity by itself, or combine winery visits with sightseeing. The Bucks County Conference & Visitors Bureau has organized Fruits of Our Labor excursions that pair stops at wineries with visits to parks and museums.

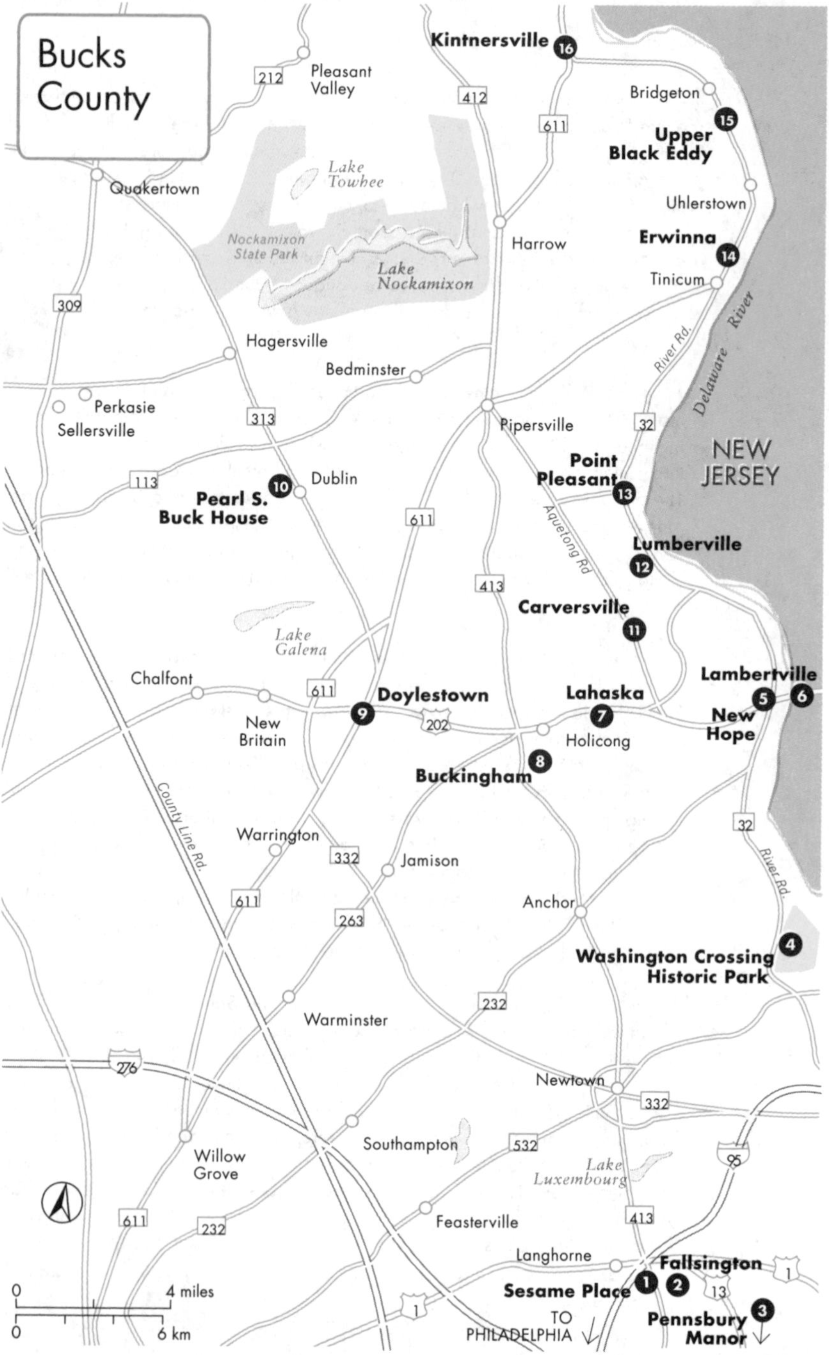
Bucks County
Kintnersville 16
Pleasant Valley
Bridgeton
Upper Black Eddy 15
Lake Towhee
Quakertown
Uhlerstown
Erwinna 14
Harrow
Nockamixon State Park
Lake Nockamixon
Tinicum
River Rd.
Delaware River
Hagersville
Bedminster
Perkasie
Sellersville
Pipersville
NEW JERSEY
Point Pleasant 13
Dublin
Pearl S. Buck House 10
Aquetong Rd
Lumberville 12
Carversville 11
Lake Galena
Chalfont
Doylestown 9
Lahaska 7
Lambertville 6
New Hope 5
New Britain
Holicong
Buckingham 8
County Line Rd.
Warrington
Jamison
River Rd.
Anchor
Washington Crossing Historic Park 4
Warminster
Newtown
Southampton
Willow Grove
Lake Luxembourg
Feasterville
Langhorne
Fallsington 2
Sesame Place 1
Pennsbury Manor 3
TO PHILADELPHIA
0 4 miles
0 6 km
212
412
611
309
313
32
113
611
413
611
202
332
611
263
232
276
332
532
95
611
232
413
1
13
1

Historic Fallsington. Make sure to call ahead for an appointment. ✉ *4 Yardley Ave., off Tyburn Rd. W* ☎ *215/295–6567* 🌐 *www.historicfallsington.org* 🎫 *$5* ⏲ *Mid-May–Oct., Tues.–Sat. 10:30–3:30; Nov.–mid-May, Tues.–Fri. 10:30–3:30.*

Morrisville

3 mi east of Fallsington.

3 On a gentle rise 150 yards from the Delaware River, **Pennsbury Manor** is a 1939 reconstruction of the Georgian-style mansion William Penn built in the 1680s. Living-history demonstrations on 43 of the estate's original 8,400 acres provide a glimpse of everyday life in 17th-century America. The property, including formal gardens, orchards, an icehouse, a smokehouse, and a bake-and-brew house, helps paint a picture of the life of an English gentleman 300 years ago. The plantation also shows that although history portrays Penn as a dour Quaker, as governor of the colony he enjoyed the good life by importing the finest provisions and keeping a vast retinue of servants. These extravagances led to financial difficulties that resulted in Penn spending nine months in a debtor's prison. Though you can wander about the grounds on your own, the house can be seen only on a tour. One Sunday a month in the warm weather there are special programs devoted to historic trades, such as open-hearth cooking or beer brewing. To get here, follow the blue-and-yellow historical markers. As you pass the landfill, you might wonder if you're going in the right direction, but don't worry. Past some of the not-so-nice aspects of the 21st century are some interesting parts of the 17th century. ✉ *400 Pennsbury Memorial Rd., between Morrisville and Bristol* ☎ *215/946–0400* 🌐 *www.pennsburymanor.org* 🎫 *$5* ⏲ *Grounds Tues.–Sat. 9–5, Sun. noon–5. Tours late Mar.–Nov., Tues.–Fri. at 10, 11:30, 1:30, and 3:30, Sat. at 11, 12:30, 2, and 3:30, Sun. at 12:30, 1:30, 2:30, and 3:30; Dec.–mid-Mar., Tues.–Sat. at 11 and 2, Sun. at 2.*

Washington Crossing Historic Park

4 *7 mi north of Fallsington.*

It was from the site of what is now **Washington Crossing Historic Park,** that on Christmas night in 1776 General Washington and 2,400 of his men crossed the Delaware River, attacked the Hessian stronghold at Trenton, and secured a much-needed victory for the Continental army. Today park attractions, including historic houses and memorials, are divided between the Lower Park and Upper Park.

In the Lower Park, at Routes 32 and 532, the Visitors Center displays a reproduction of Emanuel Leutze's famous 1851 painting of the crossing (the original hangs in the Metropolitan Museum of Art in New York). Here you can purchase tickets for guided tours of the Lower Park. You can tour the McConkey Ferry Inn, where tradition has it that Washington and his staff had Christmas dinner while waiting to cross the river. You can also see replicas of Durham boats, used in that fateful crossing, and visit some of the early-19th-century buildings of Taylorsville.

In the Upper Park, 125-foot-tall Bowman's Hill Tower, about 5 mi north of the visitors center, offers a commanding view of the Delaware River. An elevator takes you up the 1931 tower, which is open seasonally. A half mile farther north, the Thompson-Neely House, an 18th-century miller's house, and the Thompson-Neely gristmill offer tours that tell of life in Bucks County during and after the American Revolution. The house was used as a hospital during the 1776–77 encampment of Washington's army. Some Revolutionary soldiers are buried near the home.

The 100-acre **Bowman's Hill Wildflower Preserve** (☎ 215/862–2924) showcases hundreds of species of wildflowers, trees, shrubs, and ferns native to Pennsylvania. Take the guided tour (offered April through October) or follow any of the short well-marked trails. The park holds special events throughout the year, including a reenactment of the crossing in December. ✉ *Rte. 32* ☎ *215/493–4076* 🎫 *Grounds free, tour and tower $5* ⏲ *Park Tues.–Sat. 9–5, Sun. noon–5; tours Tues.–Sat. at 9, 10, 11, 1, 2, 3, and 4; Sun. at noon, 1, 2, 3, and 4.*

On a 200-year-old estate near where Washington crossed the Delaware, the family-run **Crossing Vineyards** mixes vintage charm with modern wine-making techniques. Despite a nod to the rustic (a beam ceiling in the tasting room and gift shop), the old gambrel-roofed barn feels fresh and upscale. In a 15- to 20-minute tasting, the staff lets you know what to expect from the different types of wines. Ask to see Lucy and Ethel, the computerized press and crusher-destemmer, respectively. Concerts are offered in summer. ✉ *1853 Wrightstown Rd., off Rte. 532* ☎ *215/493–6500* 🌐 *www.crossingvineyards.com* 🎫 *$5* ⏲ *Daily noon–6.*

Where to Eat

$–$$ ✕ **Café Marcella.** This charming eatery is nestled under the trees along River Road between the two sections of Washington Crossing Historic Park. Dine on regional Italian dishes made with fresh ingredients in either of two cozy dining rooms or a glassed-in porch. All the classics are here—fettuccine Alfredo, pasta alla Bolognese, and *frutti di mare frá diavolo* (pasta with shrimp, clams, scallops, and mussels sautéed with crushed red peppers)—but quite possibly better than you remember them. If Washington had dined here, he might have stayed in Pennsylvania. ✉ *1253 River Rd.* ☎ *215/321–8789* 💳 *AE, MC, V* 🍷 *BYOB* ⏲ *No lunch.*

New Hope

❺ *8 mi north of Washington Crossing Historic Park, 40 mi northeast of Philadelphia.*

The cosmopolitan village of New Hope attracts artists, shoppers, and lovers of old homes—and hordes of day-trippers, motorcyclists, and backpackers on summer weekends. It's also one of the East Coast's most popular weekend getaways among gays and lesbians. The town, listed on the National Register of Historic Places, is easy to explore on foot; the most interesting sights and stores are clustered along four blocks of Main Street and on the cross streets—Mechanic, Ferry, and Bridge streets—which lead to the river. Some parts of town are older than others. As you might guess from their names, Ferry Street dates back to colonial times; Bridge Street is Victorian.

The **Parry Mansion,** a stone house built in 1784, is notable because the furnishings reflect decorative changes from 1775 to the Victorian era—including candles, whitewashed walls, oil lamps, and wallpaper. Wealthy lumber-mill owner Benjamin Parry built the house, which was occupied by five generations of his family. ✉ *S. Main and Ferry Sts.* ☎ *215/862–5652* 🌐 *www.parrymansion.org* 🎟 *$5* ⏲ *May–Dec., weekends 1–5.*

need a break?

Don't mind a little butterfat in your mid-shopping break? You've got two excellent options along Main Street. Grab a cup of coffee and a yummy pastry or light meal at **C'est la Vie** (✉ 20 S. Main St. ☎ 215/862–1956), where you can eat at tables overlooking the river. **The Last Temptation** (✉ 115 S. Main St. ☎ 215/862–3219) dishes up delicious ice cream. You can blend in M&Ms and other decadent delights.

The **James A. Michener Art Museum,** an outpost of the larger museum in Doylestown, houses changing exhibits as well as a multimedia tribute to a dozen Bucks County artists, including Pearl S. Buck, Oscar Hammerstein II, Moss Hart, and Edward Hicks. ✉ *500 Union Sq.* ☎ *215/862-7633* 🌐 *www.michenermuseum.org* 🎟 *$5* ⏲ *Jan.–Mar., Wed.–Sun. 11–5; Apr.–Dec., Tues.–Sun. 11–5.*

Beginning in 1832, coal barges plied the Delaware Canal. Today the canal is a state park, and you can ride a mule-pulled barge from the **Delaware River Canal Boat Company.** The hour-long narrated excursion travels past Revolutionary-era cottages, gardens, and artists' workshops. A barge historian–folk singer is aboard the 80-passenger boat. ✉ *New and S. Main Sts.* ☎ *215/862–0758* 🌐 *www.onthecanal.net and www.canalboats.com* 🎟 *$10* ⏲ *May–Oct., daily noon, 1:30, 3, 4:30.*

The **New Hope & Ivyland Rail Road** makes a 9-mi, 50-minute scenic round-trip between New Hope and Lahaska. The passenger train, pulled by an authentic steam locomotive or vintage diesel, crosses a trestle used in the rescue scenes in silent films like *The Perils of Pauline.* The New Hope depot is an 1891 Victorian gem. Special events, which require reservations, include dinner trips on Saturday evenings and holiday excursions in December. ✉ *W. Bridge and Stockton Sts.* ☎ *215/862–2332* 🌐 *www.newhoperailroad.com* 🎟 *$11* ⏲ *Mid-June–Oct., daily; Nov., Fri.–Sun.; Dec., Thurs.–Sun.; Jan.–mid-June, weekends and holidays; daily departure times vary.*

Where to Stay & Eat

★ $$$$ ✕ **La Bonne Auberge.** One of Bucks County's most elite and expensive restaurants, La Bonne Auberge serves classic French cuisine in a pre-Revolutionary farmhouse. The Terrace Room has a modern French country ambience. Some specialties are sautéed Dover sole with capers and rack of lamb. The five-course table d'hôte menu, available Thursday evenings in addition to the regular menu, is a bargain. The restaurant is in a residential development called Village 2. ✉ *Village 2 off Mechanic St.* ☎ *215/862–2462* *Reservations essential* *Jacket required* *AE, D, MC, V* *Closed Mon.–Wed. No lunch.*

$$–$$$$ ✕ **Martine's.** Reminiscent of an English pub (with French overtones) with its beam ceiling, plaster-over-stone walls, and fireplace, Martine's has an eclectic, seasonally changing menu that might include filet mignon *au poivre* (with peppercorn sauce), rack of lamb, and steamed seafood mélange. Don't miss the French onion soup. Outdoor dining is on a small patio. ✉ *7 E. Ferry St.* ☎ *215/862–2966* *AE, MC, V.*

$$–$$$$ ✕ **Odette's.** In 1961 Parisian Odette Myrtil Logan converted a former canal lock house into a restaurant. The atmosphere is French country bistro; the cuisine, updated Continental, with a menu that changes seasonally and includes such choices as porcini-dusted tuna and grilled lamb chops. Sunday brunch is buffet-style. Be sure to request a table with a river view. Entertainment consists of a nightly session around the piano bar, legendary among local show-tune buffs, plus regular appearances by nationally known cabaret performers. ✉ *247 S. River Rd.* ☎ *215/862–2432* *AE, DC, MC, V* *Closed Tues.*

$$–$$$ ✕ **Havana Bar and Restaurant.** Grilled specialties enhance the American regional and contemporary cuisine at Havana. Typical menu items are a 10-ounce garlic and Brie burger with balsamic-glazed onions, mushroom and shallot risotto, and molasses and black-pepper salmon. The bar is enlivened by jazz, blues, and dance bands from Tuesday through Sunday and by karaoke on Monday. The view of Main Street is ideal for people-watching, especially from the partly covered outdoor patio. ✉ *105 S. Main St.* ☎ *215/862–9897* *www.havananewhope.com* *AE, D, DC, MC, V.*

$$–$$$ ✕ **Mother's.** Still one of New Hope's most popular dining spots after 30 years, Mother's mixes good food (apple-walnut salad, crab *con queso*, roast duck, and homemade soups), a warm atmosphere, and a fun-loving staff. You can eat in a quaint room of brick and wood overlooking Main Street or in the more private and cozy back dining room. Don't forget dessert; Mother's is known for it. ✉ *34 N. Main St.* ☎ *215/862–5857* *www.mothersnewhope.com* *AE, D, MC, V.*

$–$$$ ✕ **Triumph Brewing Company.** The smell of hops outside alerts you to the focus of this restaurant and brew pub. Shiny vats glisten through windows on the far wall of the bar, while brick walls and exposed beams and ductwork add to the industrial feel. Food ranges from burgers, burritos, and fish-and-chips to pan-seared black bass and lamb shank braised in amber ale. Wash everything down with the seven-beer sampler. There's live music Fridays, Saturdays, and some Wednesdays. ✉ *400 Union Sq.* ☎ *215/862–8300* *AE, D, DC, MC, V.*

★ $$–$$$ ✕ **Mansion Inn.** Even though busy Main Street is just steps away from the massive front door, there's a feeling of calm inside this 1865 Second Empire–style inn. The decor is not all Victoriana, however. A peek past the arched doorways into the clubby front salon or sunny yellow dining room reveals the eclectic decor. Upstairs guest rooms feature some antiques, such as four-poster beds, along with comfortable upholstered pieces. Suites have fireplaces, and some have whirlpools. The restaurant ($$–$$$$; closed Tues. May–Oct., Mon. and Tues. Nov.–Apr.) serves such entrées as Chinese five-spice duck breast and filet mignon. You can enjoy your breakfast in the dining room, in the garden, or on the front porch with a view of Main Street. There's a two-night minimum on weekends, three on holidays. *✉ 9 S. Main St., 18938 ☎ 215/862–1231 ⎙ 215/862–6939 🌐 www.themansioninn.com 3 rooms, 4 suites Restaurant, cable TV, in-room DVDs, Internet; no kids under 14, no smoking ▭ AE, MC, V BP.*

$$ **Logan Inn.** Established in 1727 as an extension of the Ferry Tavern, this inn once accommodated passengers riding the ferry to Lambertville. George Washington is said to have stayed here at least five times—and one can only imagine what he would think of the crowds of shoppers who stroll past the inn, smack dab in the busiest part of town. Rooms have original and reproduction Colonial and Victorian furnishings and canopy beds; some have river views. The friendly restaurant ($$–$$$$) has three menus: lunch (11–4), dinner (4–closing), and a popular all-day tavern menu, with such favorites as nachos, buffalo wings, salads, and burgers. The Magnolia Terrace is a seasonal outdoor bar. *✉ 10 W. Ferry St., 18938 ☎ 215/862–2300 ⎙ 215/862–3931 🌐 www.loganinn.com 16 rooms Restaurant, cable TV, bar ▭ AE, D, DC, MC, V Closed Jan.–mid-Feb. CP.*

$–$$ **Hotel du Village.** Flower-filled grounds surrounding this old stone boarding school create the feeling of an English manor house. The guest rooms have country-style furniture. You can enjoy dinner in the French restaurant ($$$; closed Mon. and Tues.), either in a Tudor-style dining room or on the sunny porch. Chef Omar Arbani prepares beef fillet with béarnaise sauce, sweetbreads with mushrooms in Madeira sauce, and fillet of sole in curried butter. Desserts are extravagant. *✉ 2535 N. River Rd., 18938 ☎ 215/862–9911 ⎙ 215/862–9788 🌐 www.hotelduvillage.com 19 rooms Restaurant, 2 tennis courts, pool, no-smoking rooms; no room TVs ▭ AE, DC, MC, V CP.*

★ **$–$$$** **Wedgwood Inn.** The accommodations at this B&B include two 1870 Victorians (including a blue "painted lady" with a gabled roof, porch, and a porte cochere) and a Federal-style 1840 stone manor house. Just steps from Main Street, the inn has 2 acres of parklike grounds with colorful gardens. Every room has some Wedgwood china in it, and many have two-person whirlpool tubs, wood-burning stoves, fireplaces, and private porches. A Continental breakfast (dietary restrictions accommodated) is served in the breakfast room, on the porch or in the gazebo, or in your room. At night, sip the hosts' homemade almond liqueur. For a fee you can have tennis and pool privileges at a nearby club. *✉ 111 W. Bridge St., 18938 ☎ 215/862–2570 ⎙ 215/862–3937 🌐 www.wedgwoodinn.com 14 rooms, 5 suites Some kitchenettes, Wi-Fi, concierge, free parking, some pets allowed; no TV in some rooms, no smoking ▭ AE, MC, V CP.*

Nightlife & the Arts

The **Bucks County Playhouse** (✉ 70 S. Main St. ☎ 215/862–2041 🌐 www.buckscountyplayhouse.com), housed in a historic mill, stages Broadway musical revivals. Shows have included *Phantom of the Opera* and *Godspell.* The season runs from March to December.

There are crowds every night at **The Raven** (✉ 385 W. Bridge St. ☎ 215/862–2081 🌐 www.theravenresort.com), the town's oldest gay bar. Sunday afternoons, when men and women enjoy the sunny terrace, are most popular.

Sports & the Outdoors

New Hope Cyclery (✉ 404 York Rd. ☎ 215/862–6888) rents mountain bikes for $32 a day. The staff can direct you to scenic bike routes.

North of New Hope, **West End Farm** (✉ River Rd. ☎ 215/862–5883) offers one-hour escorted rides on horseback along the Delaware Canal for $40 per person; call to make a reservation.

Shopping

New Hope's streets are lined with shops selling a touristy mix of upscale and lowdown. Very nice arts and crafts and handmade accessories, antiques, and jewelry are juxtaposed with campy vintage items and kinky adult paraphernalia. In what other town this size would you find an entire store devoted to spicy foods, including "hot" chocolate?

ANTIQUES **Hobensack & Keller** (✉ 57 W. Bridge St. ☎ 215/862–2406) stocks antique and reproduction garden statues, cast-iron furniture, fencing, and Oriental rugs. **Katy Kane** (✉ 34 W. Ferry St. ☎ 215/862–5873) is the place for vintage and designer clothing, accessories, and fine linens. The shop is open by appointment only.

ART Many artists live in Bucks County, and numerous galleries showcase paintings and sculpture. The New Hope Information Center can tell you about other galleries. The **Golden Door Gallery** (✉ 52 S. Main St. ☎ 215/862–5529) displays works by Bucks County painters, sculptors, and printmakers, as well as by artists from other parts of the country.

BOOKS The crowded shelves at **Farley's Bookshop** (✉ 44 S. Main St. ☎ 215/862–2452 🌐 www.farleysbookshop.com) hold plenty of choices, including books about the area.

CRAFTS A branch of the Lambertville store of the same name, **A Mano Gallery** (✉ 128 S. Main St. ☎ 215/862–5122) stocks jewelry, clay, wood, glass, and other decorative items. You'll find art glass and jewelry at **Topeo** (✉ 35 N. Main St. ☎ 215/862–2750). There are contemporary crafts in a mixture of media at **Topeo South** (✉ 15 N. Main St. ☎ 215/862–4949).

Lambertville

❻ *Across the Delaware River from New Hope.*

If you're interested in New Hope's refrain but prefer it in a lower key, head directly across the Delaware River. You'll find more charm and even better antiques in this New Jersey village. You can't swing a cabriole leg without hitting an antiques shop, as there are some 30 dealers in the tiny town, as well as a delightfully chic assemblage of boutiques, art galleries, and fine restaurants. One of Lambertville's chief pleasures doesn't involve commerce at all: the towpath along the Delaware Canal is a bucolic retreat for strolling, running, or biking. Heading south takes you to the popular Washington Crossing State Park; the less busy northern route leads past other appealing river hamlets.

Where to Stay & Eat

$$–$$$$ Fodor'sChoice ★ ✕ **Hamilton's Grill Room.** This casually elegant eatery has earned a fine reputation for its changing menu of simply prepared Mediterranean-inspired meat and fish dishes. As the name suggests, an open grill—the centerpiece of the main dining room—figures in the kitchen's preparations. Starters might include shad roe with capers, butter, and lemon, or chilled asparagus and calamari *escabèche* (marinated and served cold). Entrées often include grilled breast and leg of duck with dates and almonds or grilled tuna with avocado chutney. The terrace has been enclosed for year-round dining; in winter it's a glass-walled garden room, while in summer the doors fold up to catch the breeze. ✉ *8 Coryell St.* ☎ *609/397–4343* ▭ *AE, D, DC, MC, V* *BYOB* ⊙ *No lunch.*

$$–$$$ ✕ **DeAnna's.** Known for its homemade ravioli and pasta dishes (Gorgonzola cream sauce is a specialty), DeAnna's also has plenty of fish and meat dishes. The cozy space, which feels like a 1940s supper club, has three dining areas: one with banquettes and colorful pillows, another with couches, and a third, downstairs, with long farm tables (perfect for larger parties). In summer there is covered outdoor dining. A Venetian glass chandelier hangs above the wood bar faced in iridescent black glass tiles. ✉ *54 N. Franklin St.* ☎ *609/397–8957* ▭ *MC, V* ⊙ *Closed Mon. No lunch.*

★ **$$–$$$** ✕ **Manon.** The mural of Van Gogh's *Starry Night* on the ceiling transports you to a whimsical corner of Provence at this French bistro that's both farmhouse cozy and white-linen refined. Start with the warm goat cheese salad or country pâté, and follow it up with the bouillabaisse or rack of lamb with thyme. ✉ *19 N. Union St.* ☎ *609/397–2596* ▭ *No credit cards* *BYOB* ⊙ *Closed Mon. and Tues. No lunch.*

$ ✕ **Full Moon.** This funky eatery, decorated with mirrors and neon, surveys a wide range of cuisines—from Asian to Cajun to Mediterranean. Breakfast specialties include omelets and egg dishes, some served with the signature hollandaise sauce. Lunch options include a cheesesteak with top-round beef, chicken-and-walnut salad, and Portobello mushrooms topped with cheese and sautéed with onions and peppers in pesto olive oil. Dinner is served only on the full moon, and the menu changes each month. You might have to choose between filet mignon topped with Gorgonzola, and pork tenderloin with rhubarb chutney. ✉ *23 Bridge St.* ☎ *609/397–1096* ▭ *No credit cards* ⊙ *Closed Tues.*

$ ✕ **Siam.** You don't come here for fancy decor or polished service; both are as plain and straightforward as they come. You come for the delicious Thai food. You could easily make a meal of the tasty appetizers: pork satay, panfried wontons, rich chicken-and-coconut soup, and vermicelli salad with shrimp and ground pork. But it would be a shame not to save room for the curries and the coconut-milk ice cream. ✉ *61 N. Main St.* ☎ *609/397–8128* ▭ *No credit cards* *BYOB* ⊙ *Closed Mon. No lunch Tues.*

★ **$–$$$** ✕ **Inn at Lambertville Station.** Each guest room at this small hotel overlooks the Delaware River. All are decorated with antiques and reproduction furnishings in styles ranging from Parisian to New Orleanian to Asian; suites have sitting areas and gas fireplaces. The inn's restaurant ($$–$$$) and bar are housed in an 1867 stone building designed by Thomas Ustick Walter, architect of the dome on the U.S. Capitol, as the headquarters of the Belvidere-Delaware Railroad. The contemporary American menu changes twice a year but often includes filet mignon or pan-roasted Atlantic salmon with a lemon-dill aioli. A casual pub serves sandwiches and snacks. Continental breakfast is served in your room. ✉ *Bridge St. and the Delaware, 08530* ☎ *609/397–4400 or 800/524–1091* 📠 *609/397–4262* 🌐 *www.lambertvillestation.com* *37 rooms, 8 suites* *Restaurant, cable TV, Internet, bar, meeting rooms; no smoking* 💳 *AE, MC, V* 🍽 *CP.*

★ $$$–$$$$ **Lambertville House.** This former stagecoach stop—dating to 1812—overlooks the compact downtown. The handsome stone building is steps away from the antiques shops of North Union Street and about a block from the bridge to New Hope. Rooms, all with whirlpool tubs and most with gas fireplaces, are furnished with period reproductions. On the 1st floor is Left Bank Libations, a cozy spot for cocktails with an inviting outdoor porch that's open seasonally. Privileges at a local fitness center are included. ✉ *32 Bridge St., 08530* ☎ *609/397–0200 or 888/867–8859* 📠 *609/397–0511* 🌐 *www.lambertvillehouse.com* *20 rooms, 6 suites* *Cable TV, Internet, bar, no-smoking rooms* 💳 *AE, D, MC, V* 🍽 *CP.*

Shopping

Antiques shops, furniture stores, and galleries line Union Street, heading north from Bridge Street, and the intersecting cross streets. This is where the serious antiques collectors—as well as those seeking contemporary crafts and furniture—shop.

A Mano Gallery (✉ 42 N. Union St. ☎ 609/397–0063) stocks jewelry, glass, kaleidoscopes, and wearable art, as well as contemporary furniture. **Broadmoor Antiques** (✉ 6 N. Union St. ☎ 609/397–8802) packs in 10 rooms of paintings, antiques, and decorative items. **Greene and Greene Gallery** (✉ 32 Bridge St. ☎ 609/397–7774) refers to contemporary furniture designer Jeffrey Greene and his wife. The store carries Greene's lovely hardwood furniture as well as fine jewelry, glass, ceramics, textiles, and other art for the home. The **Orchard Hill Collection** (✉ 22 N. Union St. ☎ 609/397–1188) has an array of Dutch-Colonial antiques and handcrafted furniture.

need a break?

Tired from too much antiquing? Stop by **Lambertville Trading Company** (✉ 43 Bridge St. ☎ 609/397–2232) for some homemade goodies (the lemon bars are highly recommended) and a cappuccino. You can browse through the assortment of coffees and teas or hop on a stool to mull over your next shopping stop.

You can discover art deco treasures, toy trains, porcelain, and memorabilia from the '60s and '70s in the 60 antiques shops at the **Golden Nugget Antique Flea Market** (✉ 1850 River Rd. ☎ 609/397–0811 🌐 www.gnmarket.com), open Wednesdays and weekends 6–4. Sunday is the biggest day, with more than 400 outdoor vendors competing for your business.

Lahaska

7 *3½ mi west of Lambertville.*

Shopping packs in the crowds here, primarily because of the boutiques at Peddler's Village. If bargains are your goal, you can also find outlet stores here. Along U.S. 202 between New Hope and Lahaska you'll see many antiques shops.

Where to Stay & Eat

$$$–$$$$ ✕ **Waterlilies.** Don't let the diner exterior fool you. Inside, red tablecloths and a cheery atmosphere set the scene for good sandwiches and salads at lunch and Italian fare at dinner. Take a break from shopping to dig into a Cobb salad, Greek chicken wrap, or Maryland crab cake sandwich. At night fortify yourself with everything from veal to fresh seafood. Soup, salad, and sides are included. ✉ *U.S. 202 and Rte. 263* ☎ *215/794–8588* ▭ *MC, V* *BYOB* ⊗ *No dinner Mon.*

$$$–$$$$ **Fodor'sChoice ★** **Barley Sheaf Farm.** Sometimes a disaster—like the 2004 fire that destroyed part of this estate—becomes an opportunity to create something special. Once the home of playwright George S. Kaufman, the heavily damaged Manor House, whose original section dates back to 1740, has been totally restored, including the mansard roof and exposed stone walls. Its large suites (named for Kaufman works) have gas fireplaces and whirlpool tubs. While the Manor House features European and American antiques, the Guest Cottage has an Arts and Crafts aesthetic. The 19th-century barn has original exposed beams and ladders. Whether art nouveau, Empire, or Asian, the antiques are exceptional. The ornate Chinese wedding bed in the barn's Deep Tangled Wildwood Suite is a favorite. In addition to in-room spa services and homemade breakfasts in the dining room, there is also piano or guitar music on Fridays. ✉ *U.S. 202, Holicong 18928* ☎ *215/794–5104* *215/794–5332* ⊕ *www.barleysheaf.com* *16 suites* *Some kitchens, cable TV, Internet, pool, 2 ponds, massage, meeting rooms, some pets allowed; no smoking* ▭ *AE, D, DC, MC, V* *BP.*

$$–$$$$ **Golden Plough Inn.** Nestled within Peddler's Village, the main building of this inn has 22 spacious guest rooms, many with four-poster beds, rich fabrics, and cozy window seats that evoke 19th-century Bucks County. All rooms come with a complimentary split of champagne, and some have a fireplace or whirlpool bath. The remainder of the guest rooms are scattered about the village—in an 18th-century farmhouse, a historic carriage house, and in Merchant's Row. There's a complimentary Continental breakfast or a credit toward breakfast on the à la carte menu at the Spotted Hog. ✉ *Peddler's Village, U.S. 202 and Street Rd., 18931* ☎ *215/794–4004* *215/794–4008* ⊕ *www.goldenploughinn.com* *70 rooms* *Restaurant, refrigerators, cable TV, Internet, no-smoking rooms* ▭ *AE, D, DC, MC, V* *CP.*

★ $–$$ **Ash Mill Farm.** Past a pasture of grazing and bleating sheep, a handsome taupe manor house dating to 1790 is now a country B&B. Indefatigable innkeeper David Topel and Beau, his golden retriever, provide a warm welcome. Ornate moldings and four-poster beds satisfy those who love vintage, while flat-screen TVs and wireless Internet access attract those who can't leave modern life behind. Fun details include window sashes transformed into mirrors. In addition to the main house, you can stay in the charming Shepherd's Cottage, with light-wood paneling, a potbellied stove, kitchenette, whirlpool tub, and a glass door that the sheep press their noses to. David's buffet breakfasts—with healthy and decadent options, such as challah French toast with grilled maple mango—can be enjoyed outdoors on the deck or in the breakfast room. ✉ *5358 York Rd. Holicong 18928* ☎ *215/794–5373* 🖷 *215/794–2308* 🌐 *www.ashmillfarm.com* *4 rooms, 2 suites* *Some kitchenettes, cable TV, Wi-Fi; no kids under 12, no smoking* 💳 *AE, MC, V* *BP.*

Shopping

Peddler's Village (✉ U.S. 202 and Rte. 263 ☎ 215/794–4000 🌐 www.peddlersvillage.com) began in the early 1960s, when the late Earl Jamison bought a 6-acre chicken farm, moved local 18th-century houses to the site, and opened a Carmel, California–inspired collection of specialty shops and restaurants. The 75 shops in the now 42-acre village peddle books, toys, leather goods, jewelry, candles, and other items. The Grand Carousel, a restored 1922 merry-go-round, still works. Crowd-drawing seasonal events include May's Strawberry Festival and September's Scarecrow Festival.

Penn's Purchase Factory Outlet Stores (✉ 5881 York Rd., at U.S. 202 ☎ 215/794–0300) include more than 40 shops selling name-brand merchandise at discount prices. You'll find Brooks Brothers, Coach, Easy Spirit, Geoffrey Beene, Izod, Nine West, Orvis, and Nautica. All 15 buildings in this complex have been designed in an Early American country style that harmonizes with the look of Peddler's Village, across the road.

Near Peddler's Village, **Rice's Market** (✉ 6326 Greenhill Rd., Solebury ☎ 215/297–5993) is an open-air market with bargains on new and used items, including clothing, toys, produce, meats, and baked goods. There are some antiques and collectibles, too. It's open Tuesday (year-round) and Saturday (March–December) 7–1:30.

Buckingham

8 *2 mi west of Lahaska, 12 mi north of Langhorne.*

This village, which dates to the Colonial era, remains primarily rural and is the site of many large farms.

Bucks County's first winery, **Buckingham Valley Vineyards,** is a small family-owned operation that produces estate-bottled varietals. Walk past the outdoor sculpture and into the rustic tasting room, where you should sample wines from left to right (dry to sweet). You can stroll through the vineyards and pop downstairs to the cellar to see barrels and a champagne-riddling machine, which gently turns and tilts over a period of weeks. Bring a picnic and buy a bottle to accompany it.

✉ *1521 Rte. 413, 2 mi south of U.S. 202* ☎ *215/794–7188* 🌐 *www.pawine.com* 🎫 *Free* ⏲ *Tues.–Sat. 11–6, Sun. noon–5.*

Where to Stay

$$ **Mill Creek Farm.** Like most old Bucks County farmhouses (the oldest room dates to 1730), this one has been expanded over the years. Today it's a relaxed B&B far enough from U.S. 202 to be a real country retreat. Curl up by the Mercer-tile fireplace in the library, pay a visit to the thoroughbreds who gallop nearby, or gaze at the creek and pond from the glass-walled dining room. The guest rooms are named for presidents. The George Washington Suite has a stone-wall master bedroom and a second, whimsically painted bedroom with a children's play area. ✉ *2348 Quarry Rd., 18912* ☎ *215/794–3121* 📠 *215/794–7898* 🌐 *www.millcreekfarmbb.com* *4 rooms, 1 suite* *Tennis court, pool, fishing; no room phones, no TV in some rooms, no smoking* 💳 *AE, MC, V* 🍽 *BP.*

Shopping

At **Brown Brothers,** three or four auctioneers simultaneously conduct auctions in various categories—jewelry, silver, linens, tools, books, frames, furniture, and box lots. ✉ *Rte. 413, south of Rte. 263* ☎ *215/794–7630* ⏲ *June–Aug., Thurs. 3–9:30; Sept.–May, Sat. 8–3.*

Doylestown

9 *4 mi west of Buckingham.*

The county seat, this completely charming small town showcases Early American architecture. You'll find Federal-style brick buildings on Lawyers' Row and gracious Queen Anne, Second Empire, and Italianate homes scattered about the nearby streets. The historic district, nearly 1,200 buildings, is listed on the National Register of Historic Places. Here you'll find the locally owned shops and restaurants (Starbucks notwithstanding) that are fast disappearing elsewhere in the county.

Doylestown's most unusual buildings are those created by the eccentric Henry Chapman Mercer. An expert in prehistoric archaeology, a homespun architect, and a writer of Gothic tales, Mercer is best remembered for three brilliantly theatrical structures, including the Mercer Museum, on what is known as Mercer Mile. All are constructed with reinforced concrete, using a technique perfected by Mercer in the early part of the 20th century.

You almost expect to see a dragon puffing smoke outside **Fonthill,** Henry Chapman Mercer's storybook home. Don't be at all surprised if you see one inside. The Harvard-educated millionaire began building the house in 1908, modeling it after a 13th-century castle. Outside, it bristles with turrets and balconies. Inside, the multilevel structure is truly mazelike. The concrete castle is built from the inside out—without using blueprints—resulting in a jumble of differently shaped rooms (44 in all) and stairways (following close behind with 32). Gothic doorways, dead-end passages, and inglenooks add to the fairy-tale effect. Ancient tiles

CloseUp

AMONG FRIENDS

*"W*HEN WILL THE MEETING START?" *you might wonder as you sit in silence on one of the many wooden benches facing each other in a Quaker meetinghouse. It already has. Unprogrammed Quaker meetings (the type practiced in Bucks County) are unlike most other church services. There is no minister to deliver a sermon or lead the congregation in prayer. Instead Quakers believe that all people "have that of God within them" and therefore do not require a go-between. So Quakers, also called the Religious Society of Friends, sit in silent worship and speak when they are moved to speak. The silence speaks volumes.*

Prominent area Quakers in history include William Penn, founder of Pennsylvania, and Edward Hicks, famous for painting The Peaceable Kingdom. *Though Quakerism has changed since their time, the key "testimonies," or general tenets, remain those of simplicity, integrity, equality, community, stewardship, and peace. It's not surprising then that most Quaker meetinghouses are simple structures with little ornamentation. Local meetings you might consider attending include Buckingham (5684 York Rd., Lahaska), Doylestown (95 E. Oakland Ave.), Falls (Meetinghouse Sq., near New Falls and Tyburn Rds.), Newtown (219 Court St.), Solebury (Sugan Rd., 2 mi north of U.S. 202), Wrightstown (Rte. 413), and Yardley (65 N. Main St.). Worship—at 10 or 11 on Sunday—provides an hour of thoughtful and spiritual quiet before you rush off to resume your hectic day. "So how will I know when the meeting is over?" you might also wonder. It ends with the shaking of hands, appropriate for a gathering of Friends. For more information, go to (www.quakersbucks.org.)*

---

that Mercer found around the world as well as Arts and Crafts tiles from his own kilns (depicting scenes from the *Bible* to *Bluebeard*) seem to cover every surface—floors, walls, columns, and ceilings. To see this amazing incrustation, however, you must take a tour (reservations suggested). These begin every hour. ✉ *E. Court St. and Swamp Rd. (Rte. 313)* ☎ *215/348–9461* 🌐 *www.fonthillmuseum.org* 🎫 *$9, $12 includes Mercer Museum* 🕑 *Mon.–Sat. 10–5, Sun. noon–5.*

The **Moravian Pottery and Tile Works,** on the grounds of the Fonthill estate, still produces Arts and Crafts–style tiles from Mercer's designs. These tiles adorn such well-known structures as Grauman's Chinese Theater in Hollywood as well as many of the homes and sidewalks of Doylestown. The late author and Bucks County resident James Michener described them as follows: "Using scenes from the Bible, mythology, and history, Henry Chapman Mercer produced wonderfully archaic tiles about 12 or 14 inches square in powerful earth colors that glowed with intensity and unforgettable imagery." You can take a self-guided tour past artisans at work in the 1912 factory, which resembles a Spanish mission. ✉ *130 Swamp Rd. (Rte. 313)* ☎ *215/345–6722* 🌐 *www.buckscounty.org/departments/tileworks* 🎫 *$3.50* 🕑 *Daily 10–4:45.*

In the center of town, the **Mercer Museum,** opened in 1916, displays Mercer's collection of tools, including more than 50,000 objects from before the steam age. An archaeologist, Mercer worried that the rapid advance of industrialization would wipe out evidence of pre-industrial America. Consequently, from 1895 to 1915 he scoured the back roads of eastern Pennsylvania, buying folk art, tools, and articles of everyday life to display in another of his concrete castles. In what amounts to a six-story attic, log sleds, cheese presses, fire engines, boats, and bean hullers are suspended from walls and ceilings and crammed into rooms organized by trade or purpose. Interactive activities and a special audio guide channel keep children amused. ✉ *84 S. Pine St.* ☎ *215/345–0210* 🌐 *www.mercermuseum.org* 🎟 *$8, $12 includes Fonthill* ⏲ *Mon. and Wed.–Sat. 10–5, Tues. 10–9, Sun. noon–5.*

Named for the late best-selling novelist and Doylestown native, the **James A. Michener Art Museum,** across the street from the Mercer Museum, has a permanent collection and changing exhibitions that focus on 19th- and 20th-century American art, especially those by Bucks County artists. It's known for its collection of early-20th-century Pennsylvania impressionists, representing such artists as Edward Redfield and Daniel Garber. The museum occupies the buildings and grounds of the former Bucks County jail, which dates from 1884. A 23-foot-high fieldstone wall surrounds seven galleries, an outdoor sculpture garden and a Gothic-style warden's house. There's also a re-creation of Michener's Doylestown study. A branch is in New Hope. ✉ *138 S. Pine St.* ☎ *215/340–9800* 🌐 *www.michenermuseum.org* 🎟 *$6.50* ⏲ *Mid-Apr.–mid-Oct., Tues., Thurs., and Fri. 10–4:30, Wed. 10–9, Sat. 10–5, Sun. noon–5; mid-Oct.–mid-Apr., Tues.–Fri. 10–4:30, Sat. 10–5, Sun. noon–5.*

need a break?

If you're early enough, you can get a yummy croissant or melt-in-your-mouth sticky bun from **La Maison Cheese** (✉ 51 W. State St. ☎ 215/348–7543) to fortify you for your day of sightseeing.

Driving up to the **National Shrine of Our Lady of Czestochowa,** you can't help but realize that you're not in Kansas anymore. This enormous Polish spiritual center has drawn millions of pilgrims, including Pope John Paul II, since its opening in 1966. The complex includes a modern church with huge stained-glass panels depicting the history of Christianity in Poland and the United States. The gift shop and bookstore sell religious gifts, many imported from Poland, and the cafeteria serves hot Polish and American food on Sunday. ✉ *Ferry Rd., off Rte. 313* ☎ *215/345–0600* 🌐 *www.czestochowa.us* 🎟 *Free* ⏲ *Daily 9–4:30.*

Where to Stay & Eat

$$–$$$$ ✕ **Domani Star Cucina Italiana.** The atmosphere is lively and a bit noisy in the good-size dining room, where you can look out the big picture window at the street or stroll over to inspect the open kitchen. This Italian favorite is one of Doylestown's few BYOB eateries. Try ordering the *cellantani con salsiccia casalinga, scarola, e mozzarella affumicato.* It's quite a mouthful, but then so is the dish itself: cellantani pasta with homemade fennel sausage, sautéed escarole, and smoked mozzarella topped with a spicy plum tomato–cream sauce. Other options include crab cakes with Sicilian caper sauce and filet of beef with a Gorgonzola–pine nut crust. ✉ *57 W. State St.* ☎ *215/230–9100* 💳 *AE, D, MC, V* *BYOB* ⊙ *No lunch Sun.*

$$–$$$ ✕ **Siam Cuisine at the Black Walnut Cafe.** Soft music fills the violet-hued dining rooms of this 1846 Federal-style town house, and lights sparkle in the trees in the rear garden. There are even a few tables out front if you'd like to engage in Doylestown's favorite pastime—people-watching. Wherever you eat, the French-Thai fusion cuisine is top-notch. Start with a Thai sampler and move on to sautéed veal champignon, Siamese duck, or pad thai. Finish off your dinner with such desserts as lemon meringue tart or chocolate mousse. ✉ *80 W. State St.* ☎ *215/348–0708* 💳 *AE, D, MC, V* ⊙ *Closed Mon.*

★ ¢ ✕ **Lilly's.** From the whisk-shaped door handles to the TV- and movie-themed menu, Lilly's is full of fun. This busy downtown lunch spot serves fresh salads, wraps, paninis, soups, and pastas, which you can eat in the small, lively dining room or take home. Try the Chicken Run (tarragon-chicken salad, snow pea sprouts, and tomatoes on seven-grain bread) or the Miami Vice (barbecue pork layered with ham, cheese, and red onions and stuffed in a pita). Check the blackboard for the Daily Dagwood specials. A light breakfast of Danish, muffins, bagels, and fresh fruit is also served. ✉ *1 W. Court St.* ☎ *215/230–7883* 💳 *AE, MC, V* ⊙ *Closed Sun. No dinner.*

$$–$$$ **1814 House Inn.** You can walk to museums, shops, and restaurants from this B&B in the heart of Doylestown. Known originally as the Hargrave House, it was completely renovated in 2002. Rooms are outfitted with 19th-century antiques, including several four-poster beds, electric fireplaces or Franklin stoves, and Mercer tiles. Five rooms have whirlpool tubs. A full country breakfast is served in the dining room on weekends (Continental on weekdays), or you can avail yourself of the goodies left in the common room throughout the day, where you can also use a computer. Afternoon tea is available by request. ✉ *50 S. Main St., 18901* ☎ *215/340–1814 or 800/508–1814* 📠 *215/340–2234* 🌐 *www.1814houseinn.com* *7 rooms* *Cable TV, in-room data ports, kitchenettes* 💳 *AE, MC, V* *CP, BP.*

$$ **Doylestown Inn.** Guests have been coming to this Victorian hotel in the middle of town since 1902. Dark woods and traditional furnishings set the tone in the guest rooms, which are on the 3rd floor, above two levels of office and retail space. Some of the rooms have whirlpool tubs and fireplaces. Rates include a certificate good for a Continental breakfast at Starbucks. ✉ *18 W. State St., at Main St., 18901* ☎ *215/345–6610* 📠 *215/348–9940* 🌐 *www.doylestowninn.com* *11 rooms* *Cable TV, in-room data ports, minibars* 💳 *AE, MC, V* *CP.*

Nightlife & the Arts

One of those independent throwbacks of which Doylestown residents are so proud, the community-owned **County Theater** (✉ 20 E. State St. ☎ 215/345–6789 🌐 www.countytheater.org) is an art deco movie house that screens foreign and independent films.

Shopping

Doylestown is filled with the kind of specialty shops that are just plain fun to browse through. They carry housewares and women's wear, gifts and antiques, and whatever you need for your favorite hobby (there are several knitting shops, for example). A shelf of staff choices is the first thing you come to at the laid-back **Doylestown Bookshop** (✉ 16 S. Main St. ☎ 215/230–7610). Grab a drink from the fridge and settle in.

Perkasie

6 mi north of Doylestown.

Writer Pearl S. Buck, best known for her novel *The Good Earth,* lived outside this small town, and her country house has been designated a National Historic Landmark. Two of the area's covered bridges are nearby, as well.

The **Pearl S. Buck House** is filled with the writer's collection of Asian and American antiques and personal belongings. Green Hills Farm is the country house where she wrote nearly 100 novels, children's books, and works of nonfiction while raising seven adopted children and caring for many others. The house still bears the imprint of the girl who grew up in China and became the first American woman to win both the Nobel and Pulitzer prizes. Pearl S. Buck International, which supports displaced children in Asia, has offices on the 68-acre property. ✉ *520 Dublin Rd., off Rte. 313* ☎ *215/249–0100 or 800/220–2825* 🌐 *www.pearl-s-buck.org* 🎟 *$6* 🕙 *Tours Mar.–Dec., Tues.–Sat. 11, 1, and 2, Sun. 1 and 2.*

Sports & the Outdoors

Haycock Riding Stables (✉ 1035 Old Bethlehem Rd., off Rte. 313 ☎ 215/257–6271) escorts riders on one- and two-hour trips through lovely Nockamixon State Park. It's closed Monday, except on holiday weekends; reservations are suggested.

Carversville

⓫ *4 mi northeast of Lahaska.*

One pleasure of traveling in Bucks County is driving on lovely back roads and discovering tiny old mill villages such as Carversville. If you're traveling east from Lahaska, make a left turn onto Aquetong Road and into one of the most beautiful areas of the state.

At the **Carversville General Store** (✉ Carversville and Aquetong Rds. ☎ 215/297–5353), locals gather for gossip and take-out coffee and pick up gourmet picnic supplies and other groceries.

Where to Eat

★ $$$–$$$$ ✕ **Carversville Inn.** Its out-of-the-way location has made this circa-1813 inn one of the area's best-kept secrets. Chef Will Mathias's regional American cuisine with a Southern flair is a local favorite. The menu changes seasonally, but you can always count on flavorful dishes such as shrimp étouffée or roast rack of lamb with a pine-nut crust. ✉ *Carversville and*

Aquetong Rds. ☎ 215/297–0900 ▭ AE, D, MC, V ⊗ Closed Mon. No lunch Tues.

Lumberville

⓬ *3 mi northeast of Carversville.*

In tiny Lumberville you can picnic along the Delaware Canal or on Bull's Island, accessible by the footbridge across the Delaware River. The 1803 Lumberville Store, touted as the country's oldest continually operating general store, is the focus of village life—the place to mail letters, buy groceries, and rent a bicycle. Across the street stands the Black Bass Hotel, a famous Colonial-era inn that was once the country retreat of President Grover Cleveland. To get here from Carversville, take Fleecy Dale or Old Carversville roads (ignore the ROAD CLOSED sign—it's been there for years). Both of these backcountry roads lead to River Road and Lumberville.

Where to Stay & Eat

¢–$$ **Black Bass Hotel.** This inn has been a favorite stopover along the Delaware River since 1760. Although it sits snug within a region that witnessed many events of the American Revolution, don't look for any GEORGE WASHINGTON SLEPT HERE plaques: the owners were loyalists to the British Crown, and the walls here are still adorned with British royal memorabilia. A truly wayside inn, the Black Bass also has an excellent restaurant ($$$–$$$$) serving dishes like lobster bouillabaisse and cumin-rubbed pork chops. A deck overlooking the river (enclosed in winter) is perfect for dinner. ✉ *3774 River Rd., 18933* ☎ *215/297–5770* 📠 *215/297–0262* 🌐 *www.blackbasshotel.com* *9 rooms, 2 with bath* *Restaurant; no room TVs, no kids under 13, no smoking* ▭ *AE, D, DC, MC, V* 🍽 *CP.*

Sports & the Outdoors

The **Lumberville Store** (✉ River Rd. ☎ 215/297–5388) rents mountain bikes for $25 a day. The staff can direct you to the best bike routes.

Point Pleasant

⓭ *2 mi north of Lumberville.*

This town's location on the Delaware River makes it a focus for recreational activities. It's a lovely area to explore, and two of the county's covered bridges are a few miles northwest of town. Two fine parks, Tohickon Valley County Park (Point Pleasant) and Ralph Stover State Park (Pipersville), are joined along Tohickon Creek near town.

More than 100,000 people a year—from toddlers to grandparents—negotiate the Delaware in inner tubes, rafts, canoes, and kayaks from **Bucks County River Country** (✉ 2 Walters La. ☎ 215/297–5000 🌐 www.rivercountry.net). But even when the river is a mass of yellow and green tubes, it's still a relaxing trip. The cost is $14 to $19 per person for tubing, $21 to $34 per person for rafts, canoes, and kayaks. From May to October, a bus transports you upriver to begin two- to four-hour floats back to the starting point. No food, cans, or bottles are permitted.

Wear sneakers or sandals you don't mind getting wet, and be sure to slather on lots of sunscreen; life jackets are available at no charge. Reservations are required.

need a break?

If you're floating down the river, what can you do when you get hungry? Stop for a bite along the way, of course. The **River Hot Dog Man** sells chicken sandwiches, hamburgers, and, of course, hot dogs at prices that are nearly as inflated as your tube. You can't beat the location: on an island about halfway down the longer float.

Between the villages of Point Pleasant and Erwinna run some of the most verdant stretches of the **Delaware Canal towpath,** parallel to River Road. This is the section of Bucks County that is reminiscent of the Cotswolds of England, with bridge-keeper lodges and corkscrew bends in the road.

Erwinna

14 *7 mi north of Point Pleasant.*

The bucolic river town of Erwinna is a fine place to unwind. There are three covered bridges nearby, and you can visit a park and a local winery. Nearby Tinicum was once home to writers Dorothy Parker and S. J. Perelman.

One of the county's most popular parks, 126-acre **Tinicum Park** (✉ River Rd. ☎ 215/757–0571) has areas set aside for hiking, picnicking, and fishing. On weekend afternoons from May through September (or by appointment), you can tour the park's **Erwin-Stover House** (☎ 215/489–5133), an 1800 Federal house with 1840 and 1860 additions.

Sand Castle Winery opens its doors for tastings and tours of its vineyard and underground wine cellar. The 20-minute tour doesn't require reservations. ✉ *755 River Rd.* ☎ *610/294–9181 or 800/722–9463* 🌐 *www.sandcastlewinery.com* *$5* ⏲ *Weekdays 9–6, Sat. 10–6, Sun. 11–6.*

Where to Stay & Eat

★ $$–$$$ **EverMay on-the-Delaware.** Dating to the 1700s but enlarged and remodeled in the 19th and 20th centuries, this cream-color country inn sits on 25 acres between the river and the canal and is known as much for its restaurant ($$$$) as for its lodging. Chef Andrew Little creates an impressive prix-fixe seven-course dinner—offered at one seating on weekends only—that includes a glass of champagne. His regional American menu leans heavily on fresh produce from nearby farmers. Rooms are upstairs in the main house (request one with a river view), carriage house, cottage, and barn and are appointed with Victorian furnishings. ✉ *889 River Rd., 18920* ☎ *610/294–9100* 📠 *610/294–8249* 🌐 *www.evermay.com* *18 rooms* *Restaurant, Internet; no kids, no smoking* *AE, D, MC, V* *CP.*

★ $–$$$ **Golden Pheasant Inn.** One of the prettiest places along the Delaware Canal, this 1857 Bucks County landmark has been restored as a rustic yet elegant French auberge by Michel and Barbara Faure, a husband-and-wife team of chef and hostess. Dining is beneath potted plants and the stars in the solarium restaurant ($$$–$$$$), or in the tavern room, with its working fireplace and pierced-tin chandeliers. A former chef at Paris's Ritz Hotel, Michel deliciously melds the culinary traditions of the new and old worlds. The menu changes seasonally, but might include roasted pheasant in a white wine sauce or shrimp with a spicy tomato creole sauce. Dinner is served Wednesday through Sunday, and brunch is a Sunday ritual. Upstairs, the guest rooms have four-poster beds and river or canal views; these are often booked months in advance. Note that some rooms face River Road, at times a heavily trafficked thoroughfare. ✉ *River Rd., 18920* ☎ *610/294–9595 or 800/830–4474* 📠 *610/294–9882* 🌐 *www.goldenpheasant.com* *5 rooms, 1 suite* *Restaurant, cable TV, Internet* 💳 *AE, D, DC, MC, V* 🍽 *CP.*

Upper Black Eddy

⓯ *6 mi north of Erwinna.*

This is another Bucks County river town that's a fine place in which to relax or explore the countryside. You can drive across the river here to Milford and explore the Jersey side of the Delaware. A few miles south of Milford are the antiques shops and restaurants of pretty Frenchtown. After visiting Frenchtown you can recross to Uhlerstown and drive back north to Upper Black Eddy.

Where to Stay

$$–$$$ **Bridgeton House on the Delaware.** Wide screened porches and a terrace provide close-up views of the Delaware River and the bridge to Milford, New Jersey. This 1836 brick inn is decorated in the Arts and Crafts style; guest rooms have folksy murals on the walls and ceilings. A two-course country breakfast is served, as are afternoon tea and sherry. Request a river view, as those facing the Delaware have French doors leading to private screened porches. In the modern penthouse, the marble fireplace and huge windows are delightful. The boathouse, with a whirlpool tub, patio, fireplace, and kitchenette, can accommodate a family of four. ✉ *1525 River Rd., 18972* ☎📠 *610/982–5856* 🌐 *www.bridgetonhouse.com* *8 rooms, 3 suites, 1 cottage* *In-room data ports, some kitchenettes; no TV in some rooms, no smoking* 💳 *AE, MC, V* 🍽 *BP.*

Kintnersville

⓰ *5 mi northwest of Upper Black Eddy.*

Near the pleasures of the river and the towpath, the hamlet of Kintnersville is also a few minutes from 5,000-acre Nockamixon State Park, a popular spot for boating, swimming, biking, and hiking. You can explore the scenic back roads and farm country of northern Bucks County, too.

Where to Stay

$–$$ **Bucksville House Bed & Breakfast.** This country-style inn was a stagecoach stop for more than a century, and later served a different mission as a speakeasy during Prohibition. The original 1795 building has fireplaces in all of the guest rooms; plenty of antique quilts, baskets, and country-style furniture add warmth. On the inn's 4½ acres are a large pond and an herb and perennial garden. In summer the full breakfast—dishes might include fluffy three-cheese omelets or fresh fruit parfaits—is served on a modern octagonal deck; at other times you eat in an enclosed gazebo. ✉ *4501 Durham Rd., 18930* ☎📠 *610/847–8948 or 888/617–6300* 🌐 *www.bucksvillehouse.com* *5 rooms* *Library; no room TVs, no smoking* 💳 *AE, D, MC, V* 🍽 *BP.*

BUCKS COUNTY A TO Z

To research prices, get advice from other travelers, and book travel arrangements, visit www.fodors.com.

BUS TRAVEL

Greyhound Lines has two buses a day between Doylestown and Philadelphia. The trip takes 80 to 90 minutes and costs $9.50 each way.

Greyhound ☎ 800/231–2222 🌐 www.greyhound.com.

CAR TRAVEL

From Philadelphia the most direct route to Bucks County is I–95 north, which takes you near sights in the southern part of the county. From the last exit before you cross into New Jersey, you can turn left (north) on Taylorsville Road and then right (east) on Woodside Road to head directly to Route 32, which runs along the Delaware River past Washington Crossing Historic Park. If your destination is New Hope or farther north, stay on Taylorsville Road until it merges with River Road to avoid the perennially closed bridge north of Washington Crossing. New Hope is about 40 mi northeast of Philadelphia.

EMERGENCIES

Doylestown Hospital ✉ 595 W. State St., Doylestown ☎ 215/345–2200.

LODGING

B&BS Bucks County Bed & Breakfast Association of Pennsylvania represents nearly 50 inns within Bucks County and Hunterdon County, New Jersey.

Reservation Service **Bucks County Bed & Breakfast Association of Pennsylvania** Box 154, New Hope 18938 ☎ 215/862–2570 🌐 www.visitbucks.com.

TOURS

Bucks County Carriages shows off the area on 20-minute horse-drawn carriage tours. Horses are "parked" at the Logan Inn in New Hope, near the bakery in Peddler's Village, and at the Lambertville Station in Lambertville, New Jersey. There are daytime and evening rides, depending on the season and departure location. A ride to a catered picnic and customized tours are available by reservation.

Marlene Miller of Executive Events has customized group tours and tour groups for individual travelers in 28-passenger minivans. Some trip themes include covered bridges, historic mansions, arts, wineries, antiques, and shopping.

Wings of Gold pilots 30-, 60-, and 90-minute hot-air-balloon flights over central Bucks County. Flights leave from Richboro or Lahaska and are scheduled within two hours of sunrise or sunset, when the winds are usually calm. The cost is $95 to $225 per person.

Bucks County Carriages ☎ 215/862-3582 ⊕ www.buckscountycarriages.com. **Ghost Tours of New Hope** ☎ 215/343-5564. **Marlene Miller of Executive Events** ☎ 215/766-2211. **Wings of Gold** ☎ 215/244-9323 ⊕ www.wingsofgold.biz.

TRAIN TRAVEL

The Southeastern Pennsylvania Transportation Authority provides frequent service from Philadelphia's Market Street East, Suburban, and 30th Street stations to Doylestown on the R5 line. The trip takes up to 85 minutes, depending on the number of local stops.

SEPTA ☎ 215/580-7800 ⊕ www.septa.org.

TRANSPORTATION AROUND BUCKS COUNTY

Bucks County is a large area—40 mi long and up to 20 mi wide—and is almost impossible to tour without a car. Main roads are River Road (Route 32), U.S. 202, and Route 611. One great pleasure of a visit here can be exploring country back roads.

VISITOR INFORMATION

The Bucks County Conference & Visitors Bureau provides a wealth of information, including a useful visitors guide. The Central Bucks Chamber of Commerce has brochures with walking tours and other information. The New Hope Information Center covers many nearby towns in addition to New Hope.

Bucks County Conference & Visitors Bureau ✉ 3207 Street Rd., Bensalem 19020 ☎ 800/836-2825 ⊕ www.experiencebuckscounty.com. **Central Bucks Chamber of Commerce** ✉ 252 W. Swamp Rd., Doylestown 18901 ☎ 215/348-3913 ⊕ www.centralbuckschamber.com. **New Hope Information Center** ✉ 1 W. Mechanic St., at Main St., New Hope 18938 ☎ 215/862-5880 ⊕ www.newhopepa.com.

Pennsylvania Dutch Country

With Hershey & Gettysburg

10

WORD OF MOUTH

"Strasburg Railroad is a fun trip through Amish Country. There is lots of shopping along Rt. 30 with the Rockvale Outlet Center—it's huge! I would also suggest that you drive on some of the roads off Rt. 30 just to see all the wonderful farms in the area."

—beth48

"I would recommend picking up a [personal] guide at the Mennonite center to drive around with you. My guide took us around the backroads and answered all of my curious questions. We stopped at the house of an Amish woman who sold her quilts out of her barn, and we also visited an ice cream and candle making business being run by Amish women."

—julie21486

www.fodors.com/forums

By Laura Knowles Callanan

NEATLY PAINTED FARMHOUSES dot the countryside of Lancaster County, nearly 65 mi west of Philadelphia. Whitewashed fences outline pastures, and the landscape looks like a patchwork quilt of squares and rectangles. On the back roads, the Amish travel in horse-drawn buggies and lead a lifestyle that has been carried on for generations.

Here, the plain and fancy live side by side. You can glimpse what rural life was like 100 years ago because whole communities of the "Plain" people—as members of the Old Order Amish are called—shun telephones, electricity, and the entire world of American gadgetry. Clinging to a centuries-old way of life, the Amish, one of the most conservative of the Pennsylvania Dutch sects, eschew the amenities of modern civilization, using kerosene or gas lamps instead of electric lighting, and horse-drawn buggies instead of automobiles. Ironically, in turning their backs on the modern world, the Amish have attracted its attention.

Today the county's main roads are lined with souvenir shops and sometimes crowded with busloads of tourists. The area's proximity to Philadelphia and Harrisburg has brought development as non-Amish farmers sell land. In fact, the National Trust for Historic Preservation has put Lancaster County on its list of the nation's most endangered historic places because of rapid suburbanization. But beyond the commercialism and development, general stores, one-room schoolhouses, country lanes, and tidy farms remain. You'll find instructive places to learn about the Amish way of life, pretzel factories to tour, quilts to buy, and a host of railroad museums to explore.

Exploring Pennsylvania Dutch Country

The city of Lancaster is at the heart of Pennsylvania Dutch Country, quite literally in its center. East of the city, you'll find towns such as Intercourse and Bird-in-Hand, with markets, outlet shops, and sights that interpret Amish life. Also nearby is Strasburg, with its railroad museums. Less than half an hour north of Lancaster, the historic towns of Ephrata and Lititz are near farmers' markets and antiques malls. The quiet western part of Lancaster County has the Susquehanna River towns of Columbia and Marietta, as well as country towns to the north. If you're on an extended tour of south-central Pennsylvania, you can also explore Gettysburg and Hershey, which are both west of the county.

The Amish are not the only reason to explore Lancaster County. Lancaster, which the English named after Lancashire, is an intriguing place. This appealingly residential city of row houses is one of the nation's oldest inland cities, dating from 1710. Historic sites in the area include Wheatland, the home of U.S. President James Buchanan. Around Lancaster you can visit the Landis Valley Museum, devoted to rural life before 1900. The Ephrata Cloister provides a look at a religious communal society of the 1700s. And Main Street in Lititz, founded in 1756, is an architectural treat.

Western Lancaster County, which includes the towns of Marietta, Mount Joy, and Columbia, is a quieter part of the county, where you can bi-

Most people come to Lancaster County to get a glimpse of the Amish and their lifestyle. The territory covered is not that large, and you can see many area sights in a week. If you have only a couple of days, you'll probably want to concentrate on key Amish towns and Lancaster.

Numbers in the text correspond to numbers in the margin and on the Lancaster County map.

If you have **2 days**

Begin your tour of Amish Country in **Intercourse** 2 and visit People's Place, a cultural interpretation center with good introductory films and an exhibit for children. If you'd rather see the area by Amish buggy, follow Route 340 west to **Bird-in-Hand** 3 and take a tour with Aaron & Jessica's Buggy Rides. Also in this area are such attractions as the Amish Farm and House and the Amish Experience. Farmers' markets and shops easily fill the day before you head to **Lancaster** 1 for the night. On your second day, explore this historic city. The Lancaster Cultural History Museum shows the work of Lancaster County artists and craftspeople, past and present. The Historic Lancaster Walking Tour is a 90-minute stroll through the heart of town. On Tuesday, Friday, or Saturday, be sure to visit the Central Market, with its open-air stalls brimming with produce and baked goods. Antiques lovers may want to see Historic Rock Ford Plantation.

If you have **4 days**

Follow the 2-day itinerary above; spend another night in Lancaster and on your third day, continue to explore the **Lancaster** 1 area. While in the city, visit Wheatland and the Hans Herr House. Take an hour or two to explore the country roads east of the city. Drive the side roads between Routes 23 and 340 to see Amish farms (the ones with windmills and green blinds) along the way. Then head up the Oregon Pike (Route 272) to visit the Landis Valley Museum, an outdoor museum of Pennsylvania German rural life and folk culture before 1900, and drive on to **Ephrata** 5 or **Lititz** 7, either of which is good for an overnight. On Day 4, you can visit the Ephrata Cloister, tour a pretzel or chocolate museum in Lititz, or, depending on the day of the week, spend the day shopping for antiques in **Adamstown** 6. Another choice for your fourth day is to spend time in **Strasburg** 4, which has the don't-miss Strasburg Rail Road and the Amish Village.

If you have **7 days**

Follow the four-day itinerary for the beginning of your trip. On Day 5, head west to the sleepy towns of Marietta, Columbia, and Mount Joy; any of these is fine for your overnight. The river town of **Columbia** 8 has the excellent National Watch and Clock Museum, as well as Wright's Ferry Mansion, the former residence of English Quaker Susanna Wright. The restored town of **Marietta** 9 is perfect for strolling and browsing. You can tour a historic brewery in **Mount Joy** 11 or take the wine-tasting tour at the **Nissley Vineyards and Winery Estate** 10, near Bainbridge. You can devote days 6 and 7 to **Hershey** 13 or to touring the Civil War battlefields and museums of **Gettysburg** 14.

cycle down winding lanes, sample local wines and authentic Mennonite cooking, and explore uncrowded villages. Its history is rooted in the Colonial period. The residents are of Scottish and German descent, and architecture varies from log cabins to Victorian homes.

If you've brought your children as far as Lancaster, you may want to continue northwest to Hershey, the "Chocolate Town" founded in 1903 by Milton S. Hershey. Here the number-one attraction is Hersheypark, a theme park with kiddie and thrill rides, theaters, and live shows. Or you may wish to journey southwest to the Civil War battlefields and museums of Gettysburg, also within driving distance.

About the Restaurants

Like the German cuisine that influenced it, Pennsylvania Dutch cooking is hearty and uses ingredients from local farms. Though their numbers are dwindling, there are still a few traditional Pennsylvania Dutch restaurants where you can dine family style. Expect fried chicken, ham, and roast beef, often accompanied by dried corn, buttered noodles, mashed potatoes, pepper cabbage, and "chowchow" (pickle relish). There are always traditional "sweets and sours," vegetable dishes made with a vinegar-and-sugar dressing. This is the way the Amish, who hate to throw things out, preserve leftover vegetables.

Be sure to indulge your sweet tooth with shoofly pie (made with molasses and brown sugar), *snitz* (dried apple) pie, and other kinds of pies, even for breakfast. Bake shops proudly point out that this region invented the hole in the doughnut by cutting out the center of *fastnacht* (a deep-fried potato pastry); in fact, the English word "dunk" comes from the Pennsylvania Dutch *dunke.*

Lancaster County has numerous reasonably priced family restaurants, along with a number of eateries offering more exotic fare. The cuisine is changing and expanding to include many flavors beyond traditional Amish. Unless otherwise noted, liquor is served.

About the Hotels

Lancaster County lodgings are much like the people themselves—plain or fancy. You can rough it in one of the many campgrounds in the area, stay at a historic inn, or indulge yourself at a luxurious resort. A good selection of moderately priced motels caters to families. Although hotels welcome guests year-round, rates are highest in summer. Some inns and bed-and-breakfasts have minimum stays in high season.

Many working Amish and non-Amish farms throughout Lancaster County welcome guests to stay for a few days to observe and even participate in farm life. Operated as bed-and-breakfast establishments with a twist, the farms invite you to help milk the cows and feed the chickens, and afterward share a hearty breakfast with the farmer and his family or help with other farm chores. Reservations must be made weeks in advance, as most farms are heavily booked in summer. The Pennsylvania Dutch Convention & Visitors Bureau has a listing of all area B&Bs and farms that welcome guests.

History & Culture

A visit to Lancaster County and the surrounding area captures a lot of history in a relatively small space. In towns such as Bird-in-Hand and Intercourse, you can see the Amish living their traditional lifestyle. Museums and activities help interpret complex social and religious history; a drive along country roads off the beaten path also gives you a feeling for this way of life. The city of Lancaster has Revolutionary War sites and President James Buchanan's home, Wheatland. Even if you're not a history buff, a trip to Gettysburg, site of the pivotal 1863 Civil War battle, can be a moving experience.

Shopping

Shoppers in Lancaster County can find everything from farmers' markets to hundreds of outlet stores. The county's main arteries, U.S. 30 and Route 340, are lined with gift shops and outlets. Some outlets are factory stores, with top-quality goods at good discounts.

On Sunday antiques hunters frequent the huge antiques malls along Route 272 between Adamstown and Denver. As many as 5,000 dealers may turn up on Extravaganza Days, held in late spring, summer, and early fall. You can spend hours browsing among old books and prints and looking at Victorian clothing, pewter, silver, pottery, and lots of furniture. Or you can stop in a store along a country road to shop for the crafts and handmade quilts for which the area is famous. Galleries, boutiques, roadside stands, and farmers' markets abound, with a temptingly wide variety of merchandise.

WHAT IT COSTS

	$$$$	$$$	$$	$	¢
RESTAURANTS	over $26	$20–$26	$14–$20	$8–$14	under $8
HOTELS	over $240	$190–$240	$140–$190	$90–$140	under $90

Restaurant prices are for one main course at dinner. Hotel prices are for two people in a standard double room in high season.

Timing

Lancaster County can be hectic, especially on summer weekends and in autumn when the fall foliage attracts crowds. Farmers' markets and family-style restaurants overflow with people. The trick is to visit the top sights and then get off the beaten path. If possible, plan your trip for early spring, September, or Christmas season, when the area is less crowded. You should note that although many restaurants, shops, and farmers' markets close Sunday, commercial attractions remain open.

AROUND LANCASTER

The city of Lancaster has plenty to see and makes a good base for exploring the surrounding countryside. East of the city, between Routes

340 and 23 in towns with names such as Intercourse, Blue Ball, Paradise, and Bird-in-Hand, lives most of Lancaster County's Amish community. Strasburg, to the southeast, has sights for train buffs. No more than 12 mi north of Lancaster, Ephrata and Lititz are lovely historic towns.

When you are visiting among the Amish, remember to respect their values. They believe that photographs and videos with recognizable reproductions of them violate the biblical commandment against making graven images. Out of respect, you should refrain from photographing the Amish.

Lancaster

❶ *75 mi west of Philadelphia.*

Near the heart of Pennsylvania Dutch Country, Lancaster is a colorful small city that combines Colonial and Pennsylvania Dutch influences. During the French and Indian War and the American Revolution, its craftsmen turned out fine guns, building the city's reputation as the arsenal of the colonies. On September 27, 1777, Lancaster became the nation's capital for a day, as Congress fled the British in Philadelphia. Today markets and museums preserve the area's history. East of town on U.S. 30 are some of the area's more commercial attractions, such as miniature golf and fast-food eateries.

Fodor's Choice ★ A must-see in Lancaster City is the Romanesque **Central Market,** constructed in 1889. The market began as open-air stalls in 1742. Here local people shop for fresh fruits and vegetables, meats (try the Lebanon bologna), fresh flowers, and baked goods such as sticky buns and shoofly pie. Central Market has the distinction of being the oldest continuously operating farmers' market in the country. ✉ *Penn Sq.* ☎ *717/291–4723* ⊙ *Tues. and Fri. 6–4, Sat. 6–2.*

The **Demuth Foundation** includes the restored 18th-century home, studio, and garden of Charles Demuth (1883–1935), one of America's first modernist artists. A watercolorist, Demuth found inspiration in the geometric shapes of machines and modern technology, as well as the flowers in his mother's garden. Several of his works are on display. The gallery also features a changing exhibit of regional and national artists. The complex includes the oldest operating tobacco shop in the country, which dates back to 1770. ✉ *120 E. King St.* ☎ *717/299–9940* 🌐 *www.demuth.org* 🎫 *Donation requested* ⊙ *Feb.–Dec., Tues.–Sat. 10–4, Sun. 1–4.*

The Old City Hall, reborn as the **Lancaster Cultural History Museum,** documents the Colonial history of the region and the culture of the Pennsylvania German settlers. The museum showcases the timeless work of Lancaster County artisans and craftspeople—clocks, furniture, homemade toys, rifles, and *Fraktur* (documents in a style of calligraphy with folk art decorations). ✉ *King and Queen Sts. on Penn Sq.* ☎ *717/299–6440* 🌐 *www.lancasterheritage.com* 🎫 *$6, $10 includes admission to the Lancaster Quilt & Textile Museum* ⊙ *Tues.–Sat. 10–5, Sun. noon–5.*

Not far from Central Market, the **Lancaster Quilt & Textile Museum** has a breathtaking display of Amish quilts and other textiles. The quilts were

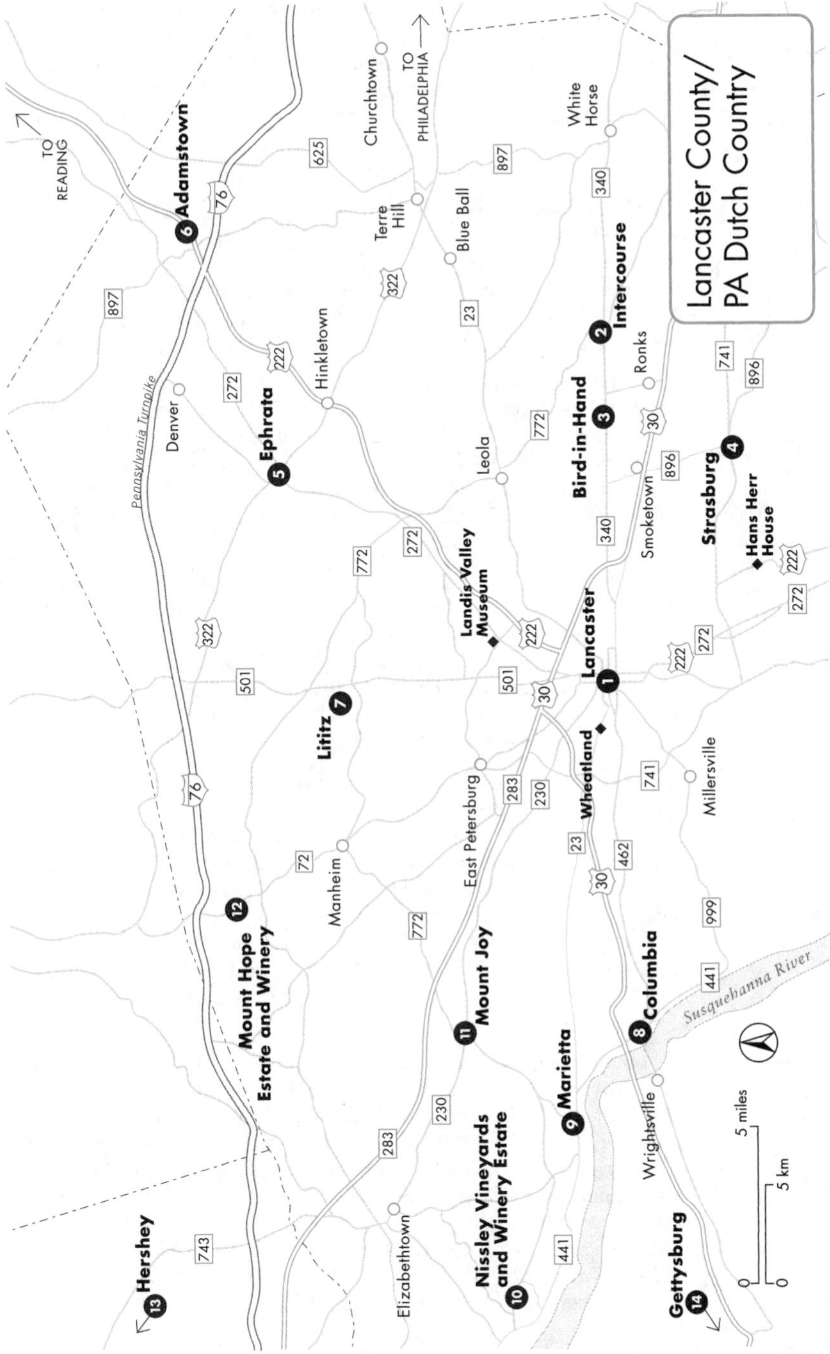
Lancaster County/
PA Dutch Country
1 Lancaster
2 Intercourse
3 Bird-in-Hand
4 Strasburg
5 Ephrata
6 Adamstown
7 Lititz
8 Columbia
9 Marietta
10 Nissley Vineyards and Winery Estate
11 Mount Joy
12 Mount Hope Estate and Winery
13 Hershey
14 Gettysburg
Hans Herr House
Landis Valley Museum
Wheatland
TO READING
TO PHILADELPHIA
Pennsylvania Turnpike
Susquehanna River
Churchtown
Terre Hill
Blue Ball
White Horse
Hinkletown
Denver
Leola
Ronks
Smoketown
Millersville
East Petersburg
Manheim
Elizabethtown
Wrightsville
76
222
322
30
283
897
625
340
23
272
772
741
896
501
230
462
72
999
441
743
5 miles
5 km
0
0

collected in the 1970s by the Esprit Company, where they were displayed in its San Francisco headquarters. Now the quilts have come home to their roots, dramatically displayed with their rich colors and bold designs. This is the place to see authentic Amish quilts, as well as changing exhibits of other crafts. ✉ *37 Market St.* ☎ *717/299–6440* 🌐 *www.lancasterheritage.com* 🎫 *$6, $10 includes admission to the Lancaster Cultural History Museum* ⏲ *Tues.–Sat. 10–5, Sun. noon–5.*

The **Historic Lancaster Walking Tour** is a 90-minute stroll through the heart of this old city by costumed guides who impart anecdotes about notable points of interest. There are also themed tours. Tours of the six-square-block area depart from the downtown visitors center. ✉ *S. Queen and Vine Sts.* ☎ *717/392–1776* 🎫 *$7* ⏲ *Apr.–Oct., Tues., Fri., and Sat. at 10 and 1, Sun., Mon., Wed., and Thurs. at 1; Nov.–Mar., by reservation.*

The **Historic Rock Ford Plantation** is the restored home of General Edward Hand, Revolutionary War commander, George Washington's confidant, and member of the Continental Congress. Eighteenth-century antiques and folk art are displayed in the 1794 Georgian-style mansion. There are changing exhibits in the Kauffman Barn. ✉ *881 Rock Ford Rd.* ☎ *717/392–7223* 🌐 *www.rockfordplantation.org* 🎫 *$5* ⏲ *Apr.–Oct., Tues.–Fri. 10–4 and Sun. noon–4.*

Now owned by Hersheypark, the 44-acre **Dutch Wonderland** features rides and activities. Designed by and for kids, this amusement park is especially suited for families with younger children. Most rides, such as the roller-coaster, merry-go-round, and giant slide, are quite tame. ✉ *2249 U.S. 30, east of Lancaster* ☎ *717/291–1888* 🌐 *www.dutchwonderland.com* 🎫 *$29* ⏲ *Memorial Day–Labor Day, daily 10–6; Labor Day–Oct. and Easter–Memorial Day, weekends 10–6.*

★ The **Hans Herr House,** the oldest in Lancaster County, is considered the best example of medieval-style German architecture in North America. The subject of several paintings by Andrew Wyeth, it was the Colonial home of the Herr family, to whom the Wyeths were related. Today the house is owned by the Lancaster Mennonite Historical Society, which educates the public about the Mennonite religion. The 45-minute tour covers the grounds and the 1719 sandstone house, a former Mennonite meeting place. It's 5 mi south of Lancaster off U.S. 222. ✉ *1849 Hans Herr Dr.* ☎ *717/464–4438* 🌐 *www.hansherr.org* 🎫 *$5* ⏲ *Apr.–Nov., Mon.–Sat. 9–4.*

Fodor's Choice ★ The **Landis Valley Museum** is an open-air museum of Pennsylvania German rural life and folk culture before 1900. Started by brothers Henry and George Landis, the farm and village are now operated by the Pennsylvania Historical and Museum Commission. You can visit more than 15 historical buildings, from a farmstead to a country store, with costumed guides providing interesting bits of history. There are demonstrations of skills such as spinning and weaving, pottery making, and tinsmithing. Many of the crafts are for sale in the Weathervane Shop. ✉ *2451 Kissel Hill Rd., off Oregon Pike (Rte. 272)* ☎ *717/569–0401* 🌐 *www.landisvalleymuseum.org* 🎫 *$9* ⏲ *Mar.–Dec., Mon.–Sat. 9–5, Sun. noon–5.*

★ **Wheatland** was the home of the only U.S. president from Pennsylvania, James Buchanan, who served from 1857 to 1861. The restored 1828 Federal-style mansion and outbuildings display the 15th president's furniture just as it was during his lifetime. A one-hour tour includes a profile of the only bachelor to occupy the White House. There are holiday candlelight tours with costumed guides. It's off of Route 23, 1½ mi west of Lancaster. ✉ *1120 Marietta Ave.* ☎ *717/392–8721* 🌐 *www.wheatland.org* 🎫 *$7* ⏲ *Apr.–mid-Dec., daily 10–4.*

Where to Stay & Eat

$$$–$$$$ ✕ **Carr's Restaurant.** Owner Tim Carr and chef Michael White have created a refreshingly simple and appealing restaurant with the look of a French café. Fresh meats, fowl, vegetables, and fruits are featured. A signature dish is the organic grilled chicken with potato salad and green beans in mustard vinaigrette. There is also a carry-out food store and a stall at nearby Central Market. ✉ *Market and Grant Sts., across from Central Market* ☎ *717/299–7090* 💳 *AE, D, DC, MC, V* ⏲ *Closed Mon.*

$$$–$$$$ Fodor's Choice ★ ✕ **Gibraltar.** A Mediterranean flair makes this seafood restaurant especially appealing. The decor is dramatic, with sunny yellows accented by cobalt blue. The freshly baked bread is served with olive oil, not butter. The menu changes weekly, with selections that might include a hearty fisherman's chowder, cumin-dusted halibut with lobster risotto, and potato gnocchi with mushroom ragout. The trendy Aqua Bar is a popular weekend spot with an extensive wine selection. ✉ *931 Harrisburg Pike* ☎ *717/397–2790* 💳 *AE, MC, V* ⏲ *No lunch.*

$$$–$$$$ Fodor's Choice ★ ✕ **The Log Cabin.** It's no wonder that generations have made this their special-occasion place for timeless fare such as filet mignon au poivre. The steaks as well as lamb chops, veal, and poultry are prepared on a charcoal grill in this 1928 expanded log cabin set on a wooded hillside. The atmosphere in the 10 candlelighted dining rooms is elegant, and there's an impressive collection of 18th- and 19th-century American paintings. The restaurant is about 6 mi northeast of Lancaster. ✉ *11 Lehoy Forest Dr., off Rte. 272, Leola* ☎ *717/626–1181* 💳 *AE, MC, V* ⏲ *No lunch.*

$$–$$$ Fodor's Choice ★ ✕ **Lily's on James.** This is the newest location for Lily's, the creation of chef Steve Brown. Known for its "American fare with flair," Lily's on James has the same menu as its sibling in Ephrata, including the popular (and pretty) raspberry chicken with Brie and almonds, and horseradish-crusted Atlantic salmon. You can also dine on lighter fare, such as the Cobb salad. ✉ *300 W. James St.* ☎ *717/509–1069* 💳 *AE, D, DC, MC, V.*

$$–$$$ ✕ **Mazzi Designed Dining.** Chef Ralph Mazzocchi prepares a blend of Mediterranean, Asian, and American fare in a lush setting with golden stucco walls, heavy oak furnishings, and lots of greenery. Among the many favorites are Chilean sea bass, American-style paella, and Thai chicken with coconut milk and green curry. The eatery is 7 mi northeast of Lancaster. ✉ *46 Deborah Dr., off Rte. 23, Leola* ☎ *717/656–8983* 💳 *AE, D, DC, MC, V.*

$$–$$$ ✕ **The Meritage.** Meritage is hidden away in Place Marie, a quiet shopping mall in Lancaster. Owners David and Linda Eshleman are highly experienced as chef and manager, respectively. The setting is warm and intimate, with a stone-and-brick wall in the dining area. In warm weather, the enclosed outdoor dining area is a delight. Selections include hazelnut sea scallops, Atlantic salmon with pearl pasta, and horseradish-crusted rack of lamb. The wine list is extensive. ✉ *51 N. Market St.* ☎ *717/396–1189* ▭ *AE, D, DC, MC, V* ⊗ *Closed Sun. No lunch Mon.*

$ ✕ **Lancaster Dispensing Co.** Relaxed, fun, and casual, this eatery is next to Central Market. Fajitas, salads, sandwiches, and pita pizzas are served until midnight in a stylish, boisterous, Victorian-style pub. The selection of imported beers is extensive. There's live music on weekends. ✉ *33–35 N. Market St.* ☎ *717/299–4602* ▭ *AE, D, MC, V.*

¢–$ ✕ **The Pressroom.** The menus look like newspapers at this casual bistro in an old warehouse. The classic mahogany bar adds to the atmosphere. The open kitchen has an exposed baking hearth. Some dishes, such as the Blondie breaded flounder, are named for characters from the funny pages. There is a nice selection of crab cakes, burgers, salads, and pasta dishes. In summer the brick patio is a pleasant outdoor dining spot. ✉ *26–28 W. King St.* ☎ *717/399–5400* ▭ *AE, MC, V.*

$–$$ **Best Western Eden Resort Inn.** Attractive grounds and spacious rooms with Colonial-style furnishings make your stay here pleasant. The inn has an indoor pool and whirlpool under a retractable roof—quite a hit with the kids. The chef at Arthur's is noted for delicious seafood and pasta dishes; more casual food is served at Garfield's. If you're spending a few days in the area, consider one of the extended-stay suites. ✉ *222 Eden Rd., U.S. 30 and Rte. 272, 17601* ☎ *717/569–6444 or 800/528–1234* 🖷 *717/569–4208* 🌐 *www.edenresort.com* *276 rooms, 42 suites* *2 restaurants, room service, in-room data ports, in-room safes, refrigerators, tennis court, 2 pools, gym, sauna, lounge* ▭ *AE, D, DC, MC, V* *CP.*

★ $–$$ **King's Cottage.** An elegant 1913 Spanish-style mansion on the National Register of Historic Places has been transformed into this B&B. The blend of architectural elements includes an art deco fireplace and stained-glass windows. Several rooms have whirlpools and fireplaces, including the 1st-floor bedroom chamber. An outdoor hot tub accented by a soothing goldfish pond and patio are pleasant in warmer weather. The price includes full breakfast and afternoon tea. ✉ *1049 E. King St., 17602* ☎ *717/397–1017 or 800/747–8717* 🖷 *717/397–3447* 🌐 *www.kingscottagebb.com* *7 rooms, 1 cottage* *In-room hot tubs* ▭ *D, MC, V* *BP.*

$–$$ **Lancaster Host Resort and Conference Center.** This sprawling family resort is in the heart of the busy Pennsylvania Dutch tourist area and features cherrywood furnishings. You can jog or rent a bike and ride around the beautifully landscaped golf course and grounds. ✉ *2300 Lincoln Hwy. E (U.S. 30), 17602* ☎ *717/299–5500 or 800/233–0121* 🌐 *www.lancasterhost.com* *330 rooms, 8 suites* *2 restaurants, room service, in-room data ports, driving range, 18-hole golf course, miniature golf, putting green, 2 tennis courts, 2 pools, bicycles, basketball, piano bar, convention center, meeting rooms* ▭ *AE, DC, MC, V.*

$ **Lancaster Hilton Garden Inn.** An elegant, contemporary hotel popular with business travelers, the Garden Inn has oversize rooms, many with cathedral ceilings and large writing desks. There's free coffee in the rooms. The hotel is in a corporate center on the edge of town. ✉ *101 Granite Run Dr., Rtes. 72 and 283, 17601* ☎ *717/560–0880 or 877/782–9444* 🖷 *717/560–5400* 🌐 *www.hiltongardeninn.com* *156 rooms* *Restaurant, room service, Internet, indoor pool, gym, hot tub, laundry facilities, laundry service, business services, meeting room* 💳 *AE, D, DC, MC, V.*

$ **Willow Valley Family Resort and Conference Center.** Smorgasbord meals, large rooms, a duck pond, and indoor pools make this large, stylish resort a great family place. Rooms are spread out over three buildings; those in the Atrium Building surround a striking skylighted lobby. The extensive Sunday brunch in the Palm Court is a favored feast. Since the resort is Mennonite-owned, liquor is not permitted on the premises. ✉ *2416 Willow St. Pike, 17602* ☎ *717/464–2711 or 800/444–1714* 🖷 *717/464–4784* 🌐 *www.willowvalley.com* *342 rooms, 50 suites* *2 restaurants, 9-hole golf course, 2 tennis courts, 3 pools, gym, hot tub, sauna, steam room, basketball, recreation room, playground, business services, meeting rooms* 💳 *AE, D, DC, MC, V.*

Nightlife & the Arts

The 1,600-seat **American Music Theatre** (✉ 2425 Lincoln Hwy. E ☎ 717/397–7700 or 800/648–4102 🌐 www.americanmusictheatre.com) presents full-scale original musical productions and an annual Christmas show. There are late-morning, afternoon, and evening shows. Each season there are 40–50 celebrity concerts with performers such as Roberta Flack, Johnny Mathis, the Beach Boys, and Peter, Paul, and Mary.

The draws at the 400-seat **Dutch Apple Dinner Theater** (✉ 510 Centerville Rd., at U.S. 30 ☎ 717/898–1900 🌐 www.dutchapple.com) are the candlelight buffet and Broadway musicals, such as *Cats, Miss Saigon,* and *Oklahoma!* Call for reservations.

A National Historic Landmark, the 1853 **Fulton Opera House** (✉ 12 N. Prince St. ☎ 717/397–7425 🌐 www.fultontheatre.org) has been sumptuously renovated. It is home to the Fulton Theater Company, the Actors Company of Pennsylvania, the Lancaster Symphony Orchestra, and the Lancaster Opera. Recent shows have included *Crazy for You* and *Carousel.*

Shopping

CRAFTS Although craftspeople in the Lancaster County area produce fine quilts and needlework, much of the best work is sold to galleries around the country and never shows up in local shops. Still, there are some good places you can check.

The **Olde Mill House Shoppes** (✉ 105 Strasburg Pike ☎ 717/299–0678), one of the area's oldest country stores, stocks a fine selection of pottery, folk art, and country-style furniture. Among the few places that carry fine local crafts is the **Weathervane Shop** (✉ 2451 Kissel Hill Rd. ☎ 717/569–9312) at the Landis Valley Museum. Many of the items are made on the premises, and they include everything from braided rugs to cane chairs.

OUTLETS U.S. 30 is lined with outlet malls. With more than 120 stores, from Bass to Nike, **Rockvale Square Outlets** (✉ U.S. 30 and Rte. 896 ☎ 717/293–9595) is the largest outlet center in Lancaster. The **Tanger Outlet Center** (✉ 311 Outlet Dr., U.S. 30 E ☎ 717/392–7260 🌐 www.tangeroutlet.com) is a collection of 60 upscale outlets, including Banana Republic, Ralph Lauren, and J. Crew.

Intercourse

❷ *10 mi east of Lancaster.*

The town's odd name came from the Colonial term for intersection. At the intersection of Routes 340 and 772, this town is a center of Amish life. Between Intercourse and up the road to Bird-in-Hand, the Amish way of life can be explored by observing their farms, crafts, quilts, and various educational experiences.

The **People's Place** is a "people-to-people interpretation center," providing an excellent introduction to the Amish, Mennonite, and Hutterite communities. There's a gallery showcasing the paintings of local communities by P. Buckley Moss and an extensive bookshop with cookbooks and other titles. Across the street you'll find the People's Place Quilt Museum and the Olde Country Store, with handcrafted furniture, quilts, folk art, and other items. ✉ *3513 Old Philadelphia Pike (Rte. 340)* ☎ *717/768–7171 or 800/390–8436* 🌐 *www.thepeoplesplace.com* *Free* ⏲ *Memorial Day–Labor Day, Mon.–Sat. 9:30–8; Labor Day–Memorial Day, Mon.–Sat. 9:30–5.*

Where to Stay & Eat

$–$$ ✕ **Stoltzfus Farm Restaurant.** Homemade Pennsylvania Dutch foods are served family style in this small country farmhouse. Many of the ingredients are grown on the farm. Most dishes, such as the ham loaf with vinegar and brown sugar, are so tasty that you'll likely want the recipes—and the owners happily supply them. The price is $15.50 for adults. ✉ *Rte. 772 E, ½ mi east of Rte. 340* ☎ *717/768–8156* 💳 *AE, D, MC, V* ⏲ *Closed Sun. and Dec.–Mar.*

¢–$ ✕ **Kling House.** This family home has been converted into a pleasant, casual restaurant serving innovative breakfast and lunch selections. Favorites include the sticky bun bread pudding for breakfast and the cranberry chicken salad sandwich for lunch. The complimentary appetizer of crackers with cream cheese and red-pepper jam is a treat, as are the homemade soups and desserts, such as luscious shoofly pie and extra fluffy coconut cream pie. A children's menu is available. It's open for breakfast and lunch throughout the year, but open for dinner only Thursday to Saturday evenings from April to November. ✉ *Kitchen Kettle Village, Rtes. 340 and 772* ☎ *717/768–8261* 💳 *D, MC, V* ⏲ *Closed Sun.*

¢ ⛺ **Spring Gulch Resort Campground.** Glorious farmland and forest are the setting for the pleasantly shaded campsites ($31.50–$49.50) and a limited number of rental cottages ($65–$130). A full schedule of weekend activities includes country dances and chicken barbecues. Campsites range from bare-bones tent sites to fully equipped RV sites with electric, water, sewer, and cable hook-ups. ✉ *Rte. 897 between Rtes.*

340 and 322, New Holland 17557 ☎ 717/354–3100 or 800/255–5744 🌐 www.springgulch.com 500 sites, 4 cottages Miniature golf, tennis court, fitness center, 2 pools, lake, fishing, volleyball, recreation room.

Shopping

Amishland Prints (✉ 3504 Old Philadelphia Pike ☎ 717/768–7273) sells prints depicting the Amish in rural daily life as well as landscapes by well known artist and folklorist Xtian Newswanger. Other local artists like Freiman Stoltzfus, Susie Riehl, and Liz Hess also show their work here.

Fodor'sChoice ★ The 39 shops of **Kitchen Kettle Village** (✉ Rte. 340 ☎ 717/768–8261 or 800/732–3538) showcase local crafts ranging from leather goods to music boxes. There's also an abundance of relishes, jams, and jellies that you can sample before you buy. Kling House serves local dishes, and stands sell ice cream, fudge, and other goodies. The shops are closed on Sunday.

The **Old Road Furniture Company** (✉ 3457 Old Philadelphia Pike ☎ 717/768–0478 or 800/760–7171) has lovely furniture handcrafted by Amish and Mennonite craftspeople. You'll find harvest and farm tables, chairs, chests, cupboards, storage cabinets, and desks. The company specializes in custom orders. The store is closed on Sunday.

Bird-in-Hand

3 *3 mi west of Intercourse.*

This village, like many others, took its name from the sign hanging on an early tavern. Today it's a center for the Pennsylvania Dutch farming community.

At Plain & Fancy Farm, the **Amish Experience** is a multimedia theatrical presentation about the history of the Amish, using multiple screens, three-dimensional sets, and special effects. In *Jacob's Choice,* the teenage main character struggles between traditional ways and the temptations of the modern world. A $28.95 package includes the show, the Amish Country Homestead, and Amish Country Tours, a bus tour of the farmlands. *✉ 3121 Old Philadelphia Pike (Rte. 340), between Bird-in-Hand and Intercourse ☎ 717/768–8400 🌐 www.amishexperience.com $7.95, $11.95 includes Amish Country Homestead ⏲ Apr.–June, Mon.–Sat. 8:30–5, Sun. 10–5; July–Oct., Mon.–Sat. 8:30–8, Sun. 10:30–5; Nov.–Mar., daily 10–5; shows on the hr.*

The **Amish Country Homestead,** a re-creation of a nine-room Old Order Amish house, is the fictional home of the characters in the Amish Experience film *Jacob's Choice.* On a guided tour of nine furnished rooms, you can learn about the culture and clothing of the Amish and how they live without electricity. The house is part of Plain & Fancy Farm. *✉ 3121 Old Philadelphia Pike (Rte. 340), between Bird-in-Hand and Intercourse ☎ 717/768–3600 $7.95, $11.95 includes the Amish Experience ⏲ July–Oct., Mon.–Sat. 9:45–6:45; Apr.–June and Nov., Mon.–Sat. 9:45–4:15; Dec.–Mar., weekends 9:45–4:15.*

Aaron & Jessica's Buggy Rides offers four tours of the Amish countryside, each about 3½ mi and a half hour long, taking passengers through a covered bridge in an authentic Amish carriage. The rides depart from Plain & Fancy Farm. ✉ *3121 Old Philadelphia Pike (Rte. 340), between Bird-in-Hand and Intercourse* ☎ *717/768–8828* 🌐 *www.amishbuggyrides.com* 🎫 *$10* 🕑 *Mon.–Sat. 8 AM–dusk.*

On **Abe's Buggy Rides,** is a 2-mi spin down country roads in an Amish buggy with a real Amish driver, who provides a friendly chat about the customs of the Pennsylvania Dutch and the sights along the way. ✉ *2596 Old Philadelphia Pike (Rte. 340)* ☎ *717/392–1794* 🎫 *$10* 🕑 *Mon.–Sat. 9 AM–dusk.*

The **Amish Farm and House** has 40-minute tours through a 10-room circa-1805 house furnished in the Old Order Amish style. A map guides you to a waterwheel, lime kiln, and even a traditional covered bridge. One of the older attractions in the area, it dates back to 1955. ✉ *2395 Lincoln Hwy. E, Smoketown* ☎ *717/394–6185* 🌐 *www.amishfarmandhouse.com* 🎫 *$6.95* 🕑 *Apr.–May and Sept.–Oct., daily 8:30–5; June–Aug., daily 8:30–6; Nov.–Mar., daily 8:30–4.*

The **Folk Craft Center** includes a museum, shops, and a bed-and-breakfast, housed in 18th- and 19th-century buildings. The museum presents an authentic overview of the lifestyles and culture of the Pennsylvania Germans, with displays of pottery, glassware, toys, and household implements. An antique loom is on exhibit in the main building. Woodworking and print-shop demonstrations show early techniques. In spring and summer the ornamental and herb gardens come alive with color. Amish quilts and pillows, hooked rugs, punched tinware, and other crafts are for sale in the shops. The B&B, in an 1851 farmhouse, has three rooms filled with handmade furnishings and crafts. ✉ *441 Mt. Sidney Rd., ½ mi west of Bird-in-Hand, Witmer* ☎ *717/397–3609* 🌐 *www.folkcraftcenter.com* 🎫 *Donation requested* 🕑 *Apr.–Nov., Mon.–Sat. 10–5; Dec., Feb., and Mar., Sat. 10–5.*

Where to Stay & Eat

$$ ✕ **Good 'N Plenty.** If you don't mind sharing the table with a dozen or so others, you'll be treated to a family-style meal of hearty regional fare like baked country ham, crispy fried chicken, chowchow, mashed potatoes, and traditional sweets and sours. More than 650 can be served at a time in this bustling family-style restaurant, set within a remodeled Amish farmhouse. The all-you-can-eat meal is $17. ✉ *Rte. 896, ½ mi north of U.S. 30* ☎ *717/394–7111* 💳 *MC, V* 🕑 *Closed Sun. and Jan.*

$$ ✕ **Plain & Fancy Farm.** You'll get heaping helpings of stick-to-your-ribs Pennsylvania Dutch food at this family-style restaurant. The rustic, county feeling is accented by the pine paneling in the dining room. Selections include fried chicken, roast beef, and chicken potpie. Also on the grounds are specialty shops selling everything from quilts to baked goods, and attractions like the Amish Experience. ✉ *3121 Old Philadelphia Pike (Rte. 340), between Bird-in-Hand and Intercourse* ☎ *717/768–4400* 💳 *AE, MC, V.*

¢–$ ✕ **Amish Barn.** Pennsylvania Dutch cuisine—generous helpings of meat, potatoes, and vegetables, plus breads and pies—is served in this family-style eatery. You can also choose from an à la carte menu. Apple dumplings and shoofly pie are specialties. Breakfast is available, too. No liquor is served. ✉ *3029 Old Philadelphia Pike (Rte. 340)* ☎ *717/768–8886* ▭ *AE, D, MC, V.*

★ ¢–$ ✕ **Bird-in-Hand Family Restaurant.** This family-owned diner has a good reputation for hearty Pennsylvania Dutch home cooking. The big attraction is the huge weekday lunch buffet with selections that often include chicken potpie, fried chicken, pork and sauerkraut, and oyster pie. No liquor is served. ✉ *2760 Old Philadelphia Pike (Rte. 340)* ☎ *717/768–8266* ▭ *MC, V* ⊗ *Closed Sun.*

★ ¢–$ ✕ **Miller's Smorgasbord.** The spread here is lavish, with a good selection of Pennsylvania Dutch foods at the daily smorgasbord from noon to 7 PM. The Sunday breakfast buffet features omelets, pancakes, eggs cooked to order, fresh fruits, pastries, bacon, sausage, potatoes, and much more. ✉ *2811 Lincoln Hwy. E, U.S. 30, Ronks* ☎ *717/687–6621* ▭ *AE, D, MC, V.*

$ **Bird-in-Hand Family Inn.** The rooms are simple, clean, and comfortable, and the staff is friendly at this family-run motel. The property offers a host of recreational opportunities. ✉ *2740 Old Philadelphia Pike (Rte. 340), 17505* ☎ *717/768–8271 or 800/537–2535* 🖷 *717/768–1768* 🌐 *www.bird-in-hand.com/familyinn* *125 rooms, 4 suites* *Restaurant, refrigerators, miniature golf, tennis court, 2 heated indoor pools, 1 outdoor pool, lake, gym, hot tub, bicycles, basketball, playground* ▭ *AE, D, DC, MC, V.*

¢–$ **Bird-in-Hand Village Inn and Suites.** Decorated with floral wall coverings and handmade quilts, this three-story country-style inn's old-fashioned flavor is beautifully preserved. Built in 1734 to serve travelers along the Old Philadelphia Pike, the inn now offers such modern comforts as cable TV and whirlpool tubs. Continental breakfast, an evening snack, and a two-hour tour of the area are included in the price. Guests have pool and tennis privileges at the nearby Bird-in-Hand Family Inn. ✉ *2695 Old Philadelphia Pike (Rte. 340), 17505* ☎ *717/293–8369 or 800/914–2473* 🌐 *www.bird-in-hand.com/villageinn* *15 rooms, 9 suites* *Some in-room hot tubs, cable TV, fireplaces* ▭ *AE, D, MC, V* *CP.*

¢ **Historic Mill Bridge Village and Camp Resort.** This campground is adjacent to a restored 18th-century village that was home to Herr's Grist Mill. Campers get free admission to the village, which has a farm, grist mill, and one of the longest covered bridges in the area. There's a general store, café, and snack bar on the premises. ✉ *S. Ronks Rd., ½ mi south of U.S. 30, Ronks 17579* ☎ *717/687–8181 or 800/645–2744* 🌐 *www.millbridge.com* *101 sites, 2 resort cabins* *Snack bar, fishing, swimming pool.*

Shopping

Bird-in-Hand Farmers Market (✉ 2710 Old Philadelphia Pike ☎ 717/393–9674) consists of produce stands, gift shops, and a snack counter. It's open weekends all year, as well as Thursdays July to October and Wednesdays April to June and November.

Strasburg

❹ *5 mi south of Bird-in-Hand.*

Although settled by French Huguenots, the village of Strasburg is today a community of Pennsylvania Dutch. It is best known as the railroad center of eastern Pennsylvania; railroad buffs can easily spend a day here. You can also visit the Amish Village, which has buildings typical of the area.

The **Amish Village** offers guided tours through an authentically furnished Amish house. Afterward you can wander around the village, which includes a barn, one-room schoolhouse, a blacksmith shop, village store, and an operating smokehouse built by Amish craftsmen. From December to February, only the house is open. ✉ *Rte. 896 between U.S. 30 and Rte. 741* ☎ *717/687–8511* 🎟 *$6.75* 🕓 *Mar.–June and Sept.–Nov., daily 9–5; June–Aug., daily 9–6.*

What started as a family hobby in 1945 with a single train chugging around the Groff family Christmas tree is now the **Choo-Choo Barn, Traintown, USA.** This 1,700-square-foot display of Lancaster County in miniature has 20 trains, mainly in O-gauge, with 150 animated scenes, including an authentic Amish barn raising, a huge three-ring circus with animals and acrobats, and a blazing house fire with fire engines rushing to the disaster. Periodically, the overhead lights dim and the scene turns to night, with streetlights and locomotive headlights glowing in the darkness. ✉ *Rte. 741 E., near Fairview Rd.* ☎ *717/687–7911* 🌐 *www.choochoobarn.com* 🎟 *$5.50* 🕓 *Apr.–Dec., daily 10–5.*

The **National Toy Train Museum,** the showplace of the Train Collectors Association, displays antique and modern toy trains. The museum has five huge operating layouts, with toy trains from the 1800s to the present, plus nostalgic films and hundreds of locomotives and cars in display cases. ✉ *Paradise La., north of Rte. 741* ☎ *717/687–8976* 🌐 *www.traincollectors.org* 🎟 *$3* 🕓 *May–Oct. and Christmas wk, daily 10–5; Apr. and Nov.–mid-Dec., weekends 10–5.*

★ The **Railroad Museum of Pennsylvania and the Railway Education Center,** across the road from the Strasburg Rail Road, holds 75 pieces of train history, including 13 colossal engines built between 1888 and 1930; 12 railroad cars, including a Pullman sleeper; and memorabilia documenting the history of Pennsylvania railroading. More than 50 of the pieces of equipment are kept indoors in the Rolling Stock Hall. ✉ *300 Paradise La., off Route 741* ☎ *717/687–8628* 🌐 *www.rrmuseumpa.org* 🎟 *$7* 🕓 *May–Oct., Mon.–Sat. 9–5, Sun. noon–5; Nov.–Apr., Tues.–Sat. 9–5, Sun. noon–5.*

The **Strasburg Rail Road** makes a scenic 45-minute round-trip excursion through Amish farm country from Strasburg to Paradise on a rolling antique chartered in 1832 to carry milk, mail, and coal. Called America's oldest short line, the Strasburg run has wooden coaches pulled by an iron steam locomotive. You can lunch in the dining car or buy a box lunch in the restaurant at the station and have a picnic at Groff's Grove along the line. Visit the Reading Car No. 10, a restored business car that carried the top brass of the Philadelphia and Reading Railroad back in the early 1900s. Trains usually depart hourly. Dinner trains, which board at 6:30, run April to November. ✉ *Rte. 741, ½ mi east of Strasburg* ☎ *717/687–7522* 🌐 *www.strasburgrailroad.com* 🎟 *$9.75–$15.50* ⏲ *Mid-Feb.–mid-Apr. and Nov.–mid-Dec., weekends noon–2; mid-Apr.–Oct., weekdays 11–4, weekends 11–5.*

Where to Stay & Eat

$$$–$$$$ ✕ **Iron Horse Inn.** Owners Richard and Denise Waller (of the nearby Limestone Inn) continue the tradition of this rustic candlelight pub with a menu that features steaks, seafood, salads, and home-style desserts like warm apple pie. The bar features a number of microbrews. Housed in the original 1780s Hotel Strasburg, the restaurant and pub are open throughout the year. ✉ *135 E. Main St.* ☎ *717/687–6362* 💳 *AE, D, DC, MC, V.*

¢–$$ ✕🏨 **Netherlands Inn.** This is a real Dutch inn, not to be confused with Pennsylvania Dutch. In springtime bright orange tulips line the brick walkways. The owners, originally from Holland, have added light natural woods and subdued colors. The Bistro restaurant ($$–$$$) features innovative cuisine like maple–butternut squash bisque and cod with a cashew crust, as well as treats created by the pastry chef. The luxurious Spa Orange provides massages, foot and nail treatments, body wraps, and aromatherapy with 21 different scents. ✉ *Historic Dr., off Rte. 896, 17579* ☎ *717/687–7691 or 800/872–0201* 📠 *717/687–6098* 🌐 *www.netherlandsinn.com* 🛏 *102 rooms, 9 suites* 🏊 *2 restaurants, pool, gym, hot tub, massage, spa, bicycles* 💳 *AE, D, DC, MC, V.*

$ 🏨 **Hershey Farm Restaurant and Motor Inn.** This motel just south of Bird-in-Hand overlooks flower and vegetable gardens, a picture-perfect pond, and a farm. Simply furnished rooms are available in three buildings: Country Meadows, Carriage House, and Farm House. The restaurant serves a complimentary breakfast smorgasbord and reasonably priced buffet and à la carte meals featuring homegrown produce. Walking trails lace the grounds. ✉ *Rte. 896, Ronks 17572* ☎ *717/687–8635 or 800/827–8635* 📠 *717/687–8638* 🌐 *www.hersheyfarm.com/motorinn.htm* 🛏 *57 rooms, 2 suites* 🏊 *Restaurant, cable TV, pool, playground, no-smoking rooms* 💳 *AE, D, MC, V* 🍽 *BP.*

$ 🏨 **Limestone Inn Bed and Breakfast.** Richard and Denise Waller are the gracious hosts at this 1786 Georgian-style home, listed on the National Register of Historic Places. The formal living room, library, and sitting room with a fireplace are nice places to relax, as is the fishpond in the small garden. The guestrooms feature Amish quilts and four-poster beds; each has a private bath, and some have old-fashioned claw-foot tubs. The hearty breakfast might include cinnamon-raisin French toast, eggs with country sausage, or creamed chipped beef with parmesan cheese. The B&B is in the center of the village, within walking distance of many attractions. ✉ *33 E. Main St., 17579* ☎ *717/687–8392 or 800/278–8392* 📠 *717/687–8366* 🌐 *www.thelimestoneinn.com* 🛏 *6 rooms* 🏊 *Dining room, library* 💳 *AE, D, MC, V* 🍽 *BP.*

¢–$ 🏨 **Strasburg Village Inn.** This circa-1788 house in the heart of town has rooms elegantly appointed in the Williamsburg style. Most have a canopy or four-poster bed; three have whirlpool baths. A sitting room is on the 2nd floor; an old-fashioned porch overlooks Main Street. A made-to-order breakfast is served each morning. ✉ *1 W. Main St., 17579* ☎ *717/687–0900 or 800/541–1055* 🌐 *www.strasburg.com* *5 rooms, 5 suites* *Some in-room hot tubs, cable TV* *AE, D, MC, V* *BP.*

¢ **Mill Stream Country Inn and Restaurant.** This freshly renovated motel overlooking a pretty stream has long been a popular choice. Guests have exercise privileges at the Willow Valley Family Resort in Lancaster. Breakfast is available in the restaurant. Alcohol is not served. ✉ *Rte. 896, 17576* ☎ *717/299–0931* *717/295–9326* 🌐 *www.willowvalley.com/millstrhome.htm* *52 rooms, 2 suites* *Restaurant, cable TV, pool, no-smoking rooms* *AE, D, MC, V* *BP.*

Ephrata

5 *22 mi north of Strasburg, 12 mi northeast of Lancaster.*

This is a classic American town, with old-fashioned streets, a variety of shops selling locally made crafts, and an entertaining farmers' market. Except for the Ephrata Cloister, there's little to remind you of the town's austere beginning as a religious commune.

★ The **Ephrata Cloister** preserves the remains of a religious communal society founded in 1728 by German immigrant Conrad Beissel. The monastic society of brothers and sisters lived an austere life of work, study, and prayer. They ate one meal a day of grains, fruits, and vegetables and encouraged celibacy. They even slept on wooden benches with wooden "pillows." Known for its a cappella singing and publishing, the society lived and worked in a cluster of striking buildings with steep-roofed medieval-style architecture. The last sister died in 1813. Guides lead 45-minute tours of three restored buildings, after which you can browse through the stable, print shop, and crafts shop. There's also on-site archaeological research. ✉ *Rtes. 272 and 322* ☎ *717/733–6600* 🌐 *www.ephratacloister.org* *$7* *Mon.–Sat. 9–5, Sun. noon–5.*

Fodor'sChoice ★ Friday is bustling at the **Green Dragon Farmers Market and Auction,** one of the state's largest farmers' markets, occupying 30 acres. The 400 indoor and outdoor stands run by Amish and Mennonite farmers sell meats, cheeses, fruits, vegetables, baked goods, flowers, and crafts. It's a traditional agricultural market with a country-carnival atmosphere. There's also a flea market and an evening auction of small animals. ✉ *955 N. State St., off Rte. 272* ☎ *717/738–1117* 🌐 *www.greendragonmarket.com* *Fri. 9–9.*

Where to Stay & Eat

$$–$$$ Fodor'sChoice ★ ✕ **Lily's on Main.** The food is artistically presented in a stylish art deco setting; tables are draped with crisp white linens and topped with a single lily. Favorite dishes include raspberry chicken with Brie and almonds, horseradish-crusted Atlantic salmon, and grilled meat loaf with roasted onion gravy. You can also dine on lighter fare, such as the salad with pears and blue cheese. The gorgeous view overlooking town is another plus. There is also a second location at the corner of Mulberry and James streets in downtown Lancaster. ✉ *124 E. Main St., in the Brossman Business Complex* ☎ *717/738–2711* 💳 *AE, D, DC, MC, V.*

★ ¢–$ ✕ **Nav Jiwan Tea Room.** This delightful café in Ten Thousand Villages takes you to destinations far and near. On any given week the menu may feature foods from India, Mexico, Laos, Haiti, Ethiopia, Nepal, the Philippines, Tanzania, Indonesia, or Thailand. The bountiful Friday evening buffet offers a sampling of foods from the featured country. The lunch entrées are prepared and served in an authentic style. ✉ *240 N. Reading Rd.* ☎ *717/721–8400* 💳 *D, MC, V* ⊙ *Closed Sun. No dinner Mon.–Thurs.*

$–$$ ✕ **The Inns at Doneckers.** Three properties dating from the 1770s to the 1920s have been tastefully furnished with French country antiques and decorated by hand stenciling. Rooms are light and airy; suites have fireplaces and whirlpool baths. At the inn's Restaurant at Doneckers ($$$–$$$$; closed Wed. and Sun.), classic and country French cuisine is served downstairs amid Colonial antiques and upstairs in a country-garden setting. Among the menu selections are mushroom cappuccino (a tasty soup) and crab galette (delicious crab cakes). The service is attentive and the wine cellar extensive. ✉ *318–333 N. State St., 17522* ☎ *717/738–9502 or 800/377–2206* 🌐 *www.doneckers.com* *35 rooms, 10 suites, 2 lofts* *Restaurant, some in-room hot tubs, shops* 💳 *AE, D, DC, MC, V* *CP.*

$–$$ **Smithton Inn.** This B&B, a stagecoach inn built in 1763, has been authentically restored and filled with hand-tooled furniture that is true to the period. Some rooms have fireplaces and canopy beds; the 3rd-floor suite has a skylight, cathedral ceiling, and Franklin stove. Pleasant luxuries are oversize pillows, feather beds, and bouquets of flowers. A huge dahlia garden is the outdoor centerpiece, accented by a lily pond and fountain. Full breakfast is included. ✉ *900 W. Main St., at Academy Dr., 17522* ☎ *717/733–6094 or 877/755–4590* 🌐 *www.historicsmithtoninn.com* *7 rooms, 1 suite* *Some in-room hot tubs, refrigerators* 💳 *AE, MC, V* *BP.*

Fodor's Choice ★

Shopping

CRAFTS **Ten Thousand Villages** (✉ Rte. 272, north of Ephrata Cloister ☎ 717/721–8400 🌐 www.tenthousandvillages.com) lets you shop with a social conscience. Run by the Mennonite Central Committee, it is designed to benefit artisans in low-income countries. The vast store stocks more than 3,000 items—including jewelry, needlework, baskets, toys, rugs, and clothing—from more than 30 countries. The Oriental Rug Room has hand-knotted Persians, Bokharas, Kilims, Dhurries, and Afghani tribal rugs crafted by fairly paid adult labor. Sales in January and July offer excellent bargains. Sample a different country's cuisine each week in the Nav Jiwan Tea Room.

Adamstown

❻ *21 mi northeast of Lancaster on Rte. 222 and Rte. 272.*

Known as "Antiques Capital USA," Adamstown has dozens of shops, galleries, and markets selling goods from bygone eras. The bigger markets, such as Renninger's Antique Market and Stoudt's Black Angus Antiques Mall, have aisles and aisles of collectibles, including furniture, toys, jewelry, crystal, china, glassware, linens, and coins. For outdoor antiquing, there's nothing like Shupp's Grove, with acres of shady woods filled with an array of antiques and collectibles. There are many other smaller markets and galleries.

Where to Stay & Eat

$$–$$$$ ✕ **Stoudt's Black Angus.** Prime rib from certified Angus beef is the specialty of this Victorian-style restaurant, adjacent to the Black Angus Antiques Mall. Innovative dishes like grilled lime-and-peppercorn sea bass and beef with portobello mushrooms are complemented by German dishes such as Wiener schnitzel. Stoudt's beer, brewed right next door, is on tap. On weekends from August to October, a Bavarian-style festival with bands and a pig roast takes over Brewery Hall. Stop at Eddie's Breads for old-fashioned favorites like walnut-raisin bread. ✉ *Reading Rd. (Rte. 272)* ☎ *717/484–4385* ▭ *AE, DC, MC, V* ⊗ *No lunch Mon.–Thurs.*

★ $–$$ **Inns at Adamstown.** These two elegant Victorian inns are less than a half block from each other. Both the Adamstown Inn and the Amethyst Inn have spacious rooms with private baths, handmade quilts, fresh flowers, and lace curtains. A number of the rooms have whirlpools, fireplaces, and European-style steam showers. Set high on a hill, the Amethyst Inn is a true Painted Lady, with an exterior clad in deep eggplant, forest green, amethyst, and gold. There's even an old English sheepdog to greet you. A hearty Continental breakfast is served each morning in the Adamstown Inn's dining room. ✉ *62 W. Main St., 17522* ☎ *717/484–0800 or 800/594–4808* 🌐 *www.adamstown.com* *10 rooms* *Dining room, some in-room hot tubs; no kids under 12, no smoking* ▭ *AE, MC, V.*

Shopping

The huge **Renninger's Antique and Collector's Market** (✉ Rte. 272, ½ mi north of Pennsylvania Tpke. Exit 21 ☎ 717/336–2177) draws thousands of collectors and dealers on Sunday from 7:30 to 5. Nearly 400 indoor stalls, open year-round, overflow with every conceivable type of antique; on good-weather days, the outdoor flea market adds to the selection. There are food stands, too.

★ **Shupp's Grove** (✉ Off Rte. 897, south of Adamstown ☎ 717/484–4115 🌐 www.shuppsgrove.com), the oldest of the Adamstown antiques markets, has acres of dealers in a tree-shaded grove. Tables are piled with antiques, art, and collectibles. The market is open weekends from April through October, 7–5. Extravaganzas offer fascinating displays of antiques and collectibles.

At **Stoudt's Black Angus Antiques Mall** (✉ Rte. 272 ☎ 717/484–4385) more than 500 dealers display old books and prints, estate jewelry, linens, china and glassware, coins, and plenty of furniture, inside and outside. There's also a restaurant. The mall is open Sunday, 7:30–5.

Lititz

❼ *10 mi southwest of Ephrata.*

Lititz was founded in 1756 by Moravians who settled in Pennsylvania and created their own private community. Lititz's historic character re-

THE PENNSYLVANIA DUTCH

__THE COUNTRY'S LARGEST__ and oldest settlement of Plain people—more than 85,000 people in more than 41 Amish, Mennonite, and Brethren sects—makes Lancaster County their home. Collectively, the sects are known as the Pennsylvania Dutch. Despite their name, they aren't Dutch at all, but descendants of German and Swiss immigrants who came to the Lancaster area to escape religious persecution. Because of a misunderstanding of the word Deutsch, *meaning "German," they became known as the "Dutch."*

The Mennonite movement, named after its leader, Dutch Catholic priest Menno Simons, began in Switzerland in the early 16th century, the time of the Reformation. This radical religious group advocated nonviolence, separation of church and state, adult baptism, and individual freedom in choosing a religion. In 1710 eight families led by Mennonite bishop Hans Herr accepted William Penn's invitation to settle in Lancaster County. In 1693 Swiss Mennonite bishop Jacob Amman, whose stricter interpretation of church tenets had attracted a following, broke off from the movement and formed his own group, the Amish. Like the Mennonites, the Amish came to live in Lancaster County.

Lancaster County has the second-largest Amish community in the country, with an estimated 22,000 Old Order Amish. That the number of Amish has doubled in the past two decades suggests that theirs is still a viable lifestyle. The eight Amish, 24 Mennonite, and nine Brethren groups differ in their interpretations of the Bible, their use of technology, the value they place on education, their use of English, and their degrees of interaction with outsiders. Brethren and Mennonite groups use modern conveniences more than Old Order Mennonites and Amish sects do, particularly the Old Order Amish, who shun technology.

The Amish religion and way of life stress separation from the world, caring for others of the faith, and self-sufficiency. The Amish, who reject compulsory school attendance and military registration, do not accept social-security benefits or purchase life or property insurance. Old Order Amish send their children to one-room schoolhouses with eight grades to a room. They avoid public schools to prevent the exposure of their children to the influence of "outsiders." Though Amish students study many of the traditional subjects, they learn less about science and technology. The Supreme Court has ruled that Amish children need not attend school beyond the eighth grade, after which students learn agriculture, building trades, and domestic skills at home.

Lancaster County's Amish can be recognized by their clothing, which is similar to that worn by their ancestors. Dress and grooming symbolize each person's role in Amish society. Men must begin to grow a beard upon marriage, and they wear several different styles of hats to distinguish their age, status, and their religious district. Amish women wear full-length dresses, capes, and aprons. Those who are baptized wear white organdy caps and don't cut their hair.

The Amish do change and update some rules themselves. Some have telephones for emergency use only; many will accept a ride in an automobile or take public transportation. The Amish live a rich life of discipline and caring. They seek to be at peace with themselves, their neighbors, their surroundings, and their God.

mains, with tree-shaded streets lined with 18th-century houses and shops selling antiques, crafts, clothing, and gifts. This is a great town for walking; be sure to see the beautiful Moravian church, which dates back to 1787 and served as a hospital to treat the wounded during the Revolutionary War.

At the **Julius Sturgis Pretzel House,** the oldest pretzel bakery in the United States, the dough is knotted by hand and baked in brick ovens the same way Julius Sturgis did it in 1861. At the end of the 20-minute guided tour, you can try your hand at the almost extinct art of pretzel twisting. *219 E. Main St. 717/626–4354 $2 Mon.–Sat. 9–5.*

The first thing you notice in Lititz is the smell of chocolate emanating from the **Wilbur Chocolate Company.** Their Candy Americana Museum and Factory Candy Outlet is a small museum of candy-related memorabilia with a large retail store filled with brand name chocolates made with Wilbur Chocolate and signature Wilbur Buds. *48 N. Broad St. 717/626–3249 Free Mon.–Sat. 10–5.*

Where to Stay & Eat

★ ¢–$ **General Sutter Inn.** Built in 1764, this is the oldest continuously run inn in Pennsylvania. It was named after the man who founded Sacramento in 1839, only to lose his home during the frenzy of the gold rush. He retired in Lititz while seeking to be reimbursed by Washington. The inn is on the main square of Lititz, within easy walking distance of the historic district. The 1764 Restaurant ($$–$$$$) offers fine dining with an artistic flourish; favorite selections include crab cakes, veal tenderloins with mushrooms, and Pennsylvania trout. In warm weather, the brick patio is a favorite dining spot. *14 E. Main St., corner of Rtes. 501 and 772, 17543 717/626–2115 717/626–0992 www.generalsutterinn.com 12 rooms, 3 suites Restaurants, café, bar, no-smoking rooms AE, D, MC, V.*

★ $–$$ **Swiss Woods.** Innkeepers Werner and Debrah Mosimann designed this chalet while they were still living in Switzerland. They planted it on 30 acres, creating an open and airy, European-style B&B with light pine furnishings, contemporary country decor, and goose-down comforters. Nestled on the edge of the woods overlooking Speedwell Forge Lake, the chalet is surrounded by extensive flower gardens. Each room has its own patio or balcony. *500 Blantz Rd., 17543 717/627–3358 or 800/594–8018 717/627–3483 www.swisswoods.com 6 rooms, 1 suite Boating, fishing, hiking AE, D, MC, V BP.*

WESTERN LANCASTER COUNTY

You can avoid the crowds and commercialism of parts of eastern Lancaster County by staying in the peaceful towns along or near the Susquehanna River, including Columbia, Marietta, and Mount Joy. There's plenty of scenery and Colonial history to explore, and you can sample good Mennonite food here.

Columbia

8 *10 mi west of Lancaster.*

They're quiet towns now, but Columbia and other river communities were bustling in the days when boats were one of the easiest methods of transporting goods. Eighteenth-century Quaker missionary John Wright worked in this area, and two of his sons set up a ferry that became an important destination for settlers moving west. Today there are several museums and the tranquil countryside to explore.

★ The **National Watch and Clock Museum** exhibits more than 12,000 timepieces and time-related items, including early sundials and water clocks; a 19th-century Tiffany globe clock; a German Black Forest organ clock with 94 pipes; moon-phase wristwatches; and the showstopper, the Engle Clock, an 1878 timepiece intended to resemble the famous astronomical cathedral clock of Strasbourg, France. You can also see what a century-old clock shop and a modern watch factory look like. ✉ *514 Poplar St.* ☎ *717/684–8261* 🌐 *www.nawcc.org* 🎫 *$7* ⏲ *Tues.–Sat. 10–5.*

Built in 1869, the **Market House and Dungeon** is one of the oldest farmers' market sites in the state. The basement really was a dungeon; you can still see the ground-level windows through which prisoners were shoved down a chute into the darkness. ✉ *308 Locust St., off Rte. 441* ☎ *717/684–5249* 🌐 *www.parivertowns.com.*

Wright's Ferry Mansion was the residence of English Quaker Susanna Wright, a silkworm breeder whose family helped open the area west of the Susquehanna. The 1738 stone house showcases period furniture in the William & Mary and Queen Anne styles and a great collection of English needlework, ceramics, and glass, all predating 1750. ✉ *38 S. 2nd St.* ☎ *717/684–4325* 🎫 *$5* ⏲ *May–Oct., Tues., Wed., and Sat. 10–3.*

Where to Stay & Eat

$–$$$ ✕ **Prudhomme's Lost Cajun Kitchen.** Owned by David and Sharon Prudhomme, relatives of the famous Paul Prudhomme of New Orleans, this Cajun-style restaurant attracts visitors from as far away as Philadelphia and Baltimore. You can dine on authentic Louisiana fare, such as crawfish étouffée, blackened catfish, gumbo, jambalaya, and fried alligator. The dishes are prepared as hot as you like, or more mild mannered with reduced spices. ✉ *Rte. 462 and Cherry St.* ☎ *717/684–1706* 💳 *AE, D, MC, V* ⏲ *No dinner Sun.; no lunch Mon.*

¢–$ 🏨 **The Columbian.** This Victorian mansion in the heart of the village has a tiered staircase that leads to rooms filled with antiques. Several rooms have fireplaces. The rate includes a country breakfast with such favorites as baked peach pancakes or cheese and egg casserole seasoned with herbs from the garden. ✉ *360 Chestnut St., 17512* ☎ *717/684–5869 or 800/422–5869* 🌐 *www.columbianinn.com* 🛏 *4 rooms, 1 suite* 👍 *Playground; no smoking* 💳 *MC, V* 🍴 *BP.*

Marietta

9 *8 mi northwest of Columbia.*

Almost half of the buildings in Marietta are listed on the National Register of Historic Places; the architecture ranges from rustic log cabins to elegant Federal and Victorian homes. This restored river town, now seeing new life as an artists' community, is perfect for a stroll past the well-preserved facades of art galleries and antiques shops.

10 At the 52-acre **Nissley Vineyards and Winery Estate,** you can review the grape-growing process on a self-guided tour. This scenic winery, which produces award-winning vintages, has tastings and a shop with bottles for sale. You can picnic on the grounds. In summer there's a concert series with jazz, big band, and folk music. The winery is northwest of Marietta near Bainbridge. ✉ *140 Vintage Dr., 1½ mi off Rte. 441* ☎ *717/426–3514* 🌐 *www.nissleywine.com* 🎟 *Free* ⏲ *Mon.–Sat. 10–5, Sun. 1–4.*

Where to Stay

$ **Olde Fogie Farm Bed and Breakfast.** Even grown-ups get to act like kids, thanks to the warmth and humor of owners Tom and Biz Fogie. On this fun-filled farm you can milk the goats and bottle-feed the calves. The accommodations have names like the Hayloft Suite and the Pig Pen Room. The old frame home has an Amish cookstove; the property has a creek, a playhouse, and a stable for pony rides. The swimming pool has waterfalls and a sitting area. A hearty breakfast is included if you stay in one of the rooms; guests in the apartments are given ingredients to make their own. ✉ *106 Stackstown Rd., 17547* ☎ *717/426–3992 or 877/653–3644* 🌐 *www.oldefogiefarm.com* *2 rooms, 2 apartments* *Pond, hot tub* *MC, V* *BP.*

Shopping

George's Woodcrafts (✉ 9 Reichs Church Rd. ☎ 717/426–1004 or 800/799–1685) sells handcrafted furniture for every room in the house in walnut, oak, maple, and cherry. You can watch items being made and then place an order. The store is closed Sunday.

Mount Joy

11 *5 mi northeast of Marietta.*

A historic brewery and some good restaurants are the highlights of this little town. Dating from before the Civil War, **Bube's Brewery** is the only brewery in the United States that has remained intact since the mid-19th century. A guided tour takes you 43 feet below the street into the brewery's vaults and passages, which were built in a cave; these passages also served as part of the Underground Railroad. There are also ghost tours for $2. ✉ *102 N. Market St.* ☎ *717/653–2056* 🌐 *www.bubesbrewery.com* 🎟 *Free* ⏲ *Tours Memorial Day–Labor Day, daily 10–5.*

Where to Stay & Eat

$$–$$$ ✕ **Groff's Farm.** People are so taken with this restaurant's hearty Mennonite fare that owner Betty Groff has published a cookbook. Candlelight, fresh flowers, and country-style fabrics contribute to the homey

ambience at this 1756 farmhouse. House specialties include chicken Stoltzfus (creamy chicken with pastry squares), farm relishes, and cracker pudding. Dinner begins with seven sweets and sours. Dinner is à la carte or family-style, but served at your own table. ✉ *650 Pinkerton Rd.* ☎ *717/653–2048* ▭ *AE, D, DC, MC, V* ⊙ *Closed Sun. and Mon.*

$–$$$ ✕ **Bube's Brewery.** Three different restaurants are found on the grounds of this old brewery. The Bottling Works, in the original bottling plant, serves steaks, burgers, and subs at lunch and dinner. A shady terrace lets you dine outdoors in the summer. Alois presents prix-fixe six-course dinners featuring entrées such as duck breast with cantaloupe salsa. "Martini czar" Andrew Gerofsky works his magic at the bar. The dinner-only Catacombs serves traditional steak and seafood dishes in the brewery's cellars. Dinners with a medieval, pirate, or Roman theme take place every Sunday night. Reservations are required for Alois and the Catacombs. ✉ *102 N. Market St.* ☎ *717/653–2056* ▭ *AE, D, MC, V.*

$ **Rocky Acre Farm.** The ideal family getaway, this 200-year-old stone farmhouse was once a stop on the Underground Railroad. This is a dairy farm with calves to feed and cows to milk. Children love the abundance of kittens, roosters, and sheep, as well as the fishing and boating in the creek. There are also free pony, barrel train, and tractor rides. ✉ *1020 Pinkerton Rd., 17552* ☎ *717/653–4449* ⊕ *www.rockyacre.com* *8 rooms, 2 efficiency units* *Boating, fishing* ▭ *No credit cards* *BP.*

Manheim

7 mi northeast of Mount Joy.

Baron Henry William Stiegel founded the small town of Manheim and manufactured Stiegel glassware here in the 18th century. Today a major draw is a winery and fairgrounds a few miles north of town.

12 The **Mount Hope Estate and Winery** is an elegant 19th-century mansion surrounded by a vineyard. The mansion and its gardens are on the National Register of Historic Places. Originally built in 1800 in Federal style, the house was renovated in 1895 with Victorian flourishes and enlarged to its current 32 rooms. Turrets, hand-painted 18-foot ceilings, Egyptian marble fireplaces, gold-leaf wallpaper, and crystal chandeliers are just some of the decorative elements. The winery bottles about 30 vintages; complimentary tastings are held in the wine shop. Call ahead for tours of the house. ✉ *Rte. 72, 5 mi north of Manheim* ☎ *717/665–7021* ⊙ *Mon.–Sat. 10–5, Sun. 11–5.*

The seasonal **Pennsylvania Renaissance Faire,** on the grounds of the Mount Hope Estate and Winery, transforms the winery into an extensive 16th-century English village ruled by Her Majesty Queen Elizabeth I. The lively action includes street performers, human chess matches, jousting and fencing tournaments, knighthood ceremonies, street performances, craft demonstrations, battling pirates, jesters, medieval food, and Shakespearean plays performed on outdoor stages. ✉ *Rte. 72, 5 mi north of Manheim* ☎ *717/665–7021* ⊕ *www.parenfaire.com* *$23.95* ⊙ *Mid-Aug.–mid-Oct., weekends 10–6:30.*

Where to Stay & Eat

$–$$ ✕ **The Cat's Meow.** In a restored 1869 railroad hotel, this eatery has the atmosphere of a speakeasy from the Roaring Twenties. Newspapers from the era and gangster portraits add to the period flavor. Entrées include broiled crab cakes, stuffed salmon, and excellent tenderloin tips with mushrooms. ✉ *215 S. Charlotte St.* ☎ *717/664–3370* ▭ *AE, D, MC, V.*

¢ **Jonde Lane Farm.** This homey B&B is run by the Nissleys, a Mennonite family. Breakfast is served every day but Sunday at this 20-acre working farm, where you can savor country life, surrounded by ponies, chickens, goats, sheep, and cats. The four guest rooms include one designed for families that can sleep six. There's also a fishing pond. ✉ *1103 Auction Rd., 17545* ☎ *717/665–4231* *4 rooms, 2 with private bath* *Fishing* ▭ *MC, V* *Closed Thanksgiving–Easter* *BP.*

HERSHEY & GETTYSBURG

It's easy to combine a trip to Lancaster County with two popular sights not more than an hour's drive from Lancaster. Hershey, to the northwest, has an amusement park and some chocolate-theme attractions. Gettysburg, to the southwest, is the county seat of Adams County and the site of Gettysburg National Military Park and museums that examine the significance of the Civil War battle.

Hershey

13 *30 mi northwest of Lancaster.*

Hershey is Chocolate Town, a community built around a chocolate factory and now home to a huge amusement park, the Hershey Museum, and other diversions for children and adults. Founded in 1903 by confectioner Milton S. Hershey, a Mennonite descendant, it celebrates chocolate without guilt, from streetlights shaped like foil-wrapped candies to avenues named Chocolate and Cocoa. Hershey is also known as a fine golf center.

At **Hersheypark** you can enjoy thrilling rides and socialize with 6-foot-tall Hershey Bars and Reese's Peanut Butter Cups. Touted as "the Sweetest Place on Earth," the park has more than 100 landscaped acres, with 60 rides, five theaters, and ZooAmerica, an 11-acre wildlife park with more than 200 animals. Begun in 1907, Hersheypark is prized as one of America's cleanest and greenest theme parks. Among its historical rides are the Comet, a 1946-vintage wooden roller coaster, and a carousel built in 1919 that has 66 hand-carved wooden horses. For thrill seekers, some of the newer rides include the exciting Lightning Racer double-track wooden racing coaster, the Great Bear steel inverted coaster, and the Roller Soaker—half roller coaster, half water ride. There are also big name concerts and sporting events at Hersheypark Stadium, the Pavilion, and the Giant Center. ✉ *Hersheypark Dr., Rte. 743 and U.S. 422* ☎ *717/534–3090* *www.hersheypa.com* *$39.95* *Memorial Day–Labor Day, daily 10–10 (some earlier closings); May and Sept., weekends only, call for hrs.*

At **Hershey's Chocolate World,** a 10-minute automated ride takes you through the steps of producing chocolate, from picking the cocoa beans to making candy bars in Hershey's kitchens. This is the town's official visitor center, so you can get information while tasting your favorite Hershey confections and buying gifts in a spacious conservatory filled with tropical plants. *Park Blvd.* *717/534–4900* *www.hersheypa.com* *Free* *Spring and fall, daily 9–5; summer, daily 9–8.*

★ The **Hershey Museum** preserves the story of Milton S. Hershey, who founded the town bearing his name and just about everything in it. The main exhibition, *Built on Chocolate,* showcases Hershey memorabilia, including chocolate-bar wrappers and cocoa tins that show their evolution through the years, and black-and-white photos of the town from the '30s, '40s, and '50s contrasted with color photos of the same sites today. There are also exhibits that document the daily lives of Pennsylvania Germans and a display of Native American art and artifacts from Hershey's personal collection. A children's area provides a hands-on experience. *170 W. Hersheypark Dr.* *717/534–3439* *www.hersheypa.com* *$7* *Daily 10–5.*

Hershey Gardens began with a single 3½-acre plot of 7,000 rosebushes and has grown to include 10 theme gardens on 23 landscaped acres, along with 1,200 varieties of roses and 22,000 tulips. The gardens come to life in spring as thousands of bulbs burst into bloom. Flowering displays last until fall, when late roses open. Kid-theme areas include a butterfly house and a children's garden. *Hotel Rd. near Hotel Hershey* *717/534–3492* *www.hersheygardens.org* *$7* *Apr.–Sept., daily 9–6, Oct., daily 9–5.*

off the beaten path

INDIAN ECHO CAVERNS – One of the largest caves in the northeastern United States has a 45-minute guided walking tour of its underground wonderland. The temperature is always around 52°F, so bring a sweater; strollers are not allowed. The children can enjoy panning for gold at Gem Mill Junction. There's the Expressions gift shop with gemstones and souvenirs, and a picnic area. The caverns are about 3 mi west of Hershey. *Off U.S. 322, Hummelstown* *717/566–8131* *$10* *Memorial Day–Labor Day, daily 9–6; Labor Day–Memorial Day, daily 10–4.*

Where to Stay & Eat

$$$–$$$$ **Brian Kent's Restaurant.** Chef Brian Matlick blends the freshest ingredients in new ways for stellar dining in a beautiful setting. Among the chef's unusual creations are pecan-crusted chicken with roasted garlic potatoes and seared tuna with bok choy. *934 E. Chocolate Ave.* *717/533–3529* *www.briankents.com* *AE, D, DC, MC, V* *Closed Sun. and Mon. No lunch.*

¢–$ **Hershey Pantry.** The decor is warm and homey in this family-friendly restaurant that serves generous portions of simple food made with fresh ingredients. The menu includes sandwiches, salads, and homemade desserts; the hearty breakfasts are notable. *801 E. Chocolate Ave.* *717/533–7505* *No credit cards* *Closed Sun.*

$$$$ **Fodor'sChoice** ★ **Hotel Hershey.** The grande dame of Hershey, this gracious Mediterranean villa–style hotel is a sophisticated resort with plenty of options for recreation, starting with the golf course that wraps around the hotel. Inspired by the fine European hotels Milton S. Hershey encountered in his travels, elegant touches abound, from the mosaic-tile lobby to rooms with maple armoires, paintings by local artists, and tile baths. The Spa at the Hotel Hershey has body treatments that include chocolate bean polish, cocoa butter scrub, chocolate fondue wrap, and a whipped cocoa bath. Outdoor activities include carriage rides, a ropes course, and nature trails. ✉ *Hotel Rd.* ☎ *717/533–2171 or 800/533–3131* 🌐 *www.hersheypa.com* *234 rooms, 20 suites* *3 restaurants, coffee shop, room service, cable TV, 9-hole and 18-hole golf courses, 3 tennis courts, 2 pools (1 indoor), gym, sauna, spa, bicycles, basketball, lounge, babysitting, laundry service, concierge, business services, meeting rooms* 💳 *AE, D, DC, MC, V.*

$$–$$$ **Hershey Lodge & Convention Center.** This bustling expansive modern resort caters to both families and business travelers. There are four restaurants, including the upscale Fireside Steakhouse. The hotel hosts groups of up to 1,300 in its Chocolate Ballroom, and it can be hectic during conventions. Ask for a room in the Guest Tower. ✉ *W. Chocolate Ave. and University Dr., 17033* ☎ *717/533–3311 or 800/533–3131* 🌐 *www.800hershey.com* *665 rooms, 28 suites* *3 restaurants, coffee shop, room service, cable TV, miniature golf, 2 tennis courts, 3 pools (1 indoor), gym, basketball, 2 lounges, recreation room, babysitting, laundry service, concierge, convention center* 💳 *AE, D, DC, MC, V.*

Sports & the Outdoors

The **Country Club of Hershey** (✉ 1000 E. Derry Rd. ☎ 717/533–2464) maintains two private 18-hole courses, which are available to guests of the Hotel Hershey. Greens fees are from $60 to $90. **Spring Creek Golf** (✉ 450 E. Chocolate Ave. ☎ 717/533–2847), a 9-hole course, was originally built by Milton Hershey for youngsters to hone their strokes. Greens fees are around $11.

Shopping

Crossroads Antiques Mall (✉ Intersection Rtes. 322 and 743 ☎ 717/520–1600) has more than 90 dealers and an assortment of antiques and collectibles. It's housed in Hershey's largest circular barn. The mall is open Thursday to Monday, 10–5:30.

Ziegler's in the Country (✉ Rte. 743 ☎ 717/533–1662) is on a restored 1850s homestead, with several buildings from that era. An air-conditioned barn has space for 92 dealers and an herb and body products shop (open on weekends). Hours are Thursday to Monday, 9–5.

Gettysburg

14 *53 mi west of Lancaster on U.S. 30.*

"The world will little note, nor long remember, what we say here, but it can never forget what they did here." These words from Abraham Lincoln's famous address were delivered in Gettysburg to mark the dedication of its national cemetery in November 1863. Four months earlier, from July 1 to 3, 51,000 Americans were killed, wounded, or counted as missing in the bloodiest battle of the Civil War. The events that took place in Gettysburg during those few days marked the turning point in the war. Although the struggle raged on for almost two more years, the Confederate forces never recovered from their losses.

At the national military park and at 20 museums in Gettysburg, you can recapture the power of those momentous days. You can see battlefields such as Little Round Top, Big Round Top, and Devil's Den. A $95-million project is underway for a stately visitor center, museum, outdoor amphitheater, and battlefield restoration at Gettysburg National Military Park. The museum will enable the park to preserve and display its extensive collection of Civil War artifacts, while the battlefield will be restored to its 1863 appearance.

The **Cyclorama Center** contains the 360-foot circular Gettysburg Cyclorama, a painting that depicts Pickett's Charge at Gettysburg. It's one of the last surviving cycloramas, displayed since 1884. There's also a 20-minute film on the battle. ✉ *97 Taneytown Rd., near visitor center* ☎ *717/334–1124* 🌐 *www.nps.gov/gett* 🎟 *$3* 🕒 *Showings daily, every 30 min, 9–4:30.*

★ The **Eisenhower National Historic Site** was the country estate residence of President Dwight D. Eisenhower, who bought it in 1950. He and his wife used it as a weekend retreat and a meeting place for world leaders. From 1961 until his death in 1969, it was the Eisenhowers' full-time residence. The brick-and-stone farmhouse is preserved in 1950s style. The farm adjoins the battlefield and is administered by the Park Service, which sells daily ticketed tours only on a first-come, first-served basis at the Gettysburg National Military Park Visitor Center. ✉ *Off Millerstown Rd.* ☎ *717/338–9114* 🌐 *www.nps.gov/eise* 🎟 *$5.50* 🕒 *Apr.–Oct., daily 9–5; Nov.–Mar., Wed.–Sun. 9–5.*

General Lee's headquarters. General Robert E. Lee established his personal headquarters in this old stone house, which dates from the 1700s. On July 1, 1863, Lee made plans for the Battle of Gettysburg in this house. The home now holds a collection of Civil War artifacts and has a museum store. ✉ *Rte. 30 W, 8 blocks west of Lincoln Sq.* ☎ *717/334–3141* 🎟 *$2* 🕒 *Mar.–Nov., daily 9–9.*

The **Gettysburg Tour Center** is the departure point for two-hour narrated tours of the battlefield. Open-air double-decker buses depart every 15–45 minutes. ✉ *778 Baltimore St.* ☎ *717/334–6296* 🎟 *$16.95* 🕒 *Jan.–June and Sept.–Dec., daily 9–5; July and Aug., daily 9–9.*

★ There are few landmarks as touching as the **Gettysburg National Military Park,** where General Robert E. Lee and his Confederate troops encountered the Union forces of General George Meade. There are more than 1,300 markers and monuments honoring the casualties of the battle in the 6,000 acre park. More than 30 mi of marked roads lead through the park, highlighting key battle sites. In the first week of July, Civil War reenactors dress in period uniforms and costumes to commemorate the three-day battle. ✉ *97 Taneytown Rd.* ☎ *717/334–1124* 🌐 *www.nps.gov/gett* 🎟 *Free* 🕒 *Park roads 6 AM–10 PM.*

The **Gettysburg National Military Park Visitor Center** distributes a free map with an 18-mi driving tour through the battlefield, as well as an orientation program, Civil War exhibits, and schedules of ranger-conducted programs. The Park Service also provides free walking-tour maps. Private, licensed guides may also be hired at the center. To best understand the battle, begin by viewing the **Electric Map,** which uses colored lights to illustrate the three-day battle. The $3 presentation begins every 45 minutes. ✉ *97 Taneytown Rd.* ☎ *717/334–1124* 🎫 *Free* ⏲ *Daily 8–5, later summer hrs.*

The **Gettysburg National Cemetery,** dedicated by President Abraham Lincoln in his Gettysburg Address on November 19, 1863, is now the final resting place of more than 7,000 servicemen and their dependents. ✉ *Off Baltimore Pike, across from visitor center* 🎫 *Free* ⏲ *Daily dawn–dusk.*

The **Hall of Presidents and First Ladies** meticulously reproduces in wax the likenesses of the nation's chief executives from George Washington to George W. Bush, as well as their wives dressed in their inaugural gowns. The museum also contains a room displaying paintings by President Dwight D. Eisenhower. ✉ *789 Baltimore St.* ☎ *717/334–5717* 🎫 *$6.95* ⏲ *June–Aug., daily 9–9; Mar.–May and Sept.–Nov., daily 9–5.*

The **Lincoln Room Museum** in the Willis House is where Abraham Lincoln stayed and completed his Gettysburg Address on November 18, 1863. Through a tape featuring a re-creation of Lincoln speaking his thoughts, doubts, and dreams on that day, you can learn the story behind his words and understand what motivated them. ✉ *12 Lincoln Sq.* ☎ *717/334–8188* 🌐 *www.gettysburg.com* 🎫 *$3.50* ⏲ *Summer, daily 9–7:30; reduced hrs off-season.*

The **Lincoln Train Museum** reenacts the president's journey from Washington to Gettysburg in November 1863. A 12-minute ride simulates the sights and sounds, and features actors portraying the reporters and officials on the train. You can also see the 1890 caboose, model train display, and military rail collection. ✉ *425 Steinwehr Ave.* ☎ *717/334–5678* 🎫 *$6.95* ⏲ *May and June, daily 9–9; July and Aug., daily 9 AM–10 PM; Sept. and Nov., daily 9–5.*

The **National Civil War Wax Museum** presents the story of the Civil War era and the Battle of Gettysburg through more than 200 life-size figures in 30 scenes, including a reenactment of the Battle of Gettysburg and an animated Abraham Lincoln delivering his Gettysburg Address. ✉ *297 Steinwehr Ave.* ☎ *717/334–6245* 🎫 *$5.50* ⏲ *Daily 9–5, with extended seasonal hrs.*

The **Schriver House** was the home of George and Henrietta Schriver and their two children, and shows what civilian life was like during the war. After George joined the Union troops and his family fled to safety, the home was taken over by Confederate sharpshooters, two of whom were killed in its garret during the battle. The restored home is a recipient of the Pennsylvania State Historic Preservation Award. ✉ *309 Baltimore St.* ☎ *717/337–2800* 🌐 *www.shriverhouse.com* 🎫 *$5.75* ⏲ *Mon.–Sat. 10–5, Sun. noon–5.*

Soldier's National Museum was the headquarters for Union General Oliver O. Howard during the Battle of Gettysburg, later becoming the Soldiers National Orphanage. It now has 60 displays of more than 5,000 Civil War items. ✉ *777 Baltimore St.* ☎ *717/334–4890* 🎫 *$6.95* ⏲ *June–Aug., daily 9–9; Mar.–May and Sept.–Nov., daily 9–5.*

Where to Stay & Eat

$–$$$ ✕ **Blue Parrot Bistro.** This bustling bar and restaurant is within walking distance of many attractions. The Blue Parrot serves an eclectic selection of creatively prepared dishes, including salads, soups, and sandwiches. Innovative entrées include chicken souvlaki salad. ✉ *35 Chambersburg St.* ☎ *717/337–3739* 💳 *MC, V* ⏲ *Closed Mon.*

★ $–$$ ✕🏨 **Historic Farnsworth House Restaurant & Inn.** Civil War–era dishes such as game pie, peanut soup, pumpkin fritters, and spoon bread are the specialty at this historic dining room ($$–$$$). The 1810 building has more than 100 bullet holes from the battle. The tranquil outdoor garden has sculptures and fountains. Each guest room is lushly and individually decorated with lace canopy beds, period sewing machines, Victrolas, and antique clothing. The inn conducts ghost tours of Gettysburg for $6 that begin with dramatizations and stories in the basement's Mourning Theater. There's an art and book gallery, as well as a Civil War memorabilia shop. ✉ *401 Baltimore St.* ☎ *717/334–8838* 🌐 *www.farnsworthhousedining.com* 🛏 *11 rooms* 👍 *Restaurant* 💳 *AE, D, MC, V* 🍽 *BP.*

¢–$ ✕🏨 **Historic 1776 Dobbin House Tavern and Gettystown Inn.** Overlooking the spot where Lincoln gave his Gettysburg Address, this inn has period furnishings and four-poster beds. There are also guest rooms in two adjacent buildings. The Dobbin House Tavern ($$–$$$) was built in 1776, making it the oldest building in town. American and Colonial fare such as barbecued ribs and salmagundi (salad containing greens, vegetables, and cooked meats) are served in the tavern's six rooms with fireplaces and antiques. You can dine in wing chairs in the parlor, take your meal in the spinning room, or have dinner in your room. There is also the more casual Springhouse Tavern, with sandwiches and other light fare. ✉ *89 Steinwehr Ave., 17325* ☎ *717/334–2100* 🌐 *www.dobbinhouse.com* 🛏 *4 rooms, 4 suites* 👍 *2 restaurants, shop, business services* 💳 *AE, MC, V* 🍽 *BP.*

$–$$ 🏨 **Baladerry Inn.** During the Battle of Gettysburg, this 1812 home on the edge of the battlefield served as a field hospital. Today it serves breakfast to the guests who overnight here, in the main house or in the carriage house. The carefully restored rooms are filled with antiques; many have fireplaces. Those on the ground floor of the carriage house have their own patios. ✉ *40 Hospital Rd., 17325* ☎ *717/337–1342* 🌐 *www.baladerryinn.com* 🛏 *9 rooms* 👍 *Tennis court; no kids under 12* 💳 *AE, D, MC, V* 🍽 *BP.*

$–$$ 🏨 **Historic Best Western Gettysburg Hotel 1797.** Built before the Civil War, this hotel is in the heart of the downtown historic district. Prominent guests have included Carl Sandburg, Henry Ford, and General Ulysses S. Grant. During the Cold War, the hotel served as President Eisenhower's national operations center while he was recuperating at his nearby home. Rooms are furnished in traditional style, and suites have fireplaces and whirlpool baths. There's a cannonball from the battle that's still embedded in the brick wall across the street. ✉ *1 Lincoln Sq., 17325* ☎ *717/337–2000 or 800/528–1234* 🖷 *717/337–2075* 🌐 *www.gettysburg-hotel.com* *67 rooms, 27 suites* *Restaurant, room service, in-room data ports, microwaves, refrigerators, pool, bar, business services, no-smoking rooms* 💳 *AE, D, DC, MC, V.*

$ **James Gettys Hotel.** It flourished in the 1920s, and is now an affordably priced, attractively furnished suites-only hotel. Each suite has a sitting room with a kitchenette including a refrigerator, microwave oven, and small dining table. A Continental breakfast is brought to each room. At the neighboring Thistlefields Tea Room, you can relax with full English afternoon tea. ✉ *27 Chambersburg St., 17325* ☎ *717/337–1334 or 888/900–5275* 🖷 *717/334–2103* 🌐 *www.jamesgettyshotel.com* *11 suites* *Kitchenettes, microwaves, refrigerators, laundry service* 💳 *AE, D, MC, V* *CP.*

¢ **Artillery Ridge Campground.** You can pitch a tent or park an RV a mile south of the Gettysburg National Military Park Visitor Center. Horse owners can even bring their steeds. Families may enjoy the fishing pond. ✉ *610 Taneytown Rd., 17325* ☎ *717/334–1288* *45 tent sites, 105 camper or RV sites* *Pool, fishing, bicycles, horseback riding* 💳 *D, MC.*

Shopping

Gallon Historical Art (✉ 9 Steinwehr Ave. ☎ 717/334–8666) exhibits original paintings and prints of Gettysburg battle scenes by Dale Gallon, the town's artist-in-residence.

The Horse Soldier (✉ 777 Baltimore St. ☎ 717/334–0347) carries one of the country's largest collections of military antiques—everything from bullets to discharge papers. Its Soldier Genealogical Research Service can help you find your ancestors' war records prior to 1910. The store is closed Wednesday.

PENNSYLVANIA DUTCH COUNTRY A TO Z

To research prices, get advice from other travelers, and book travel arrangements, visit www.fodors.com.

BUS TRAVEL

Greyhound Lines has several daily runs between Philadelphia and Lancaster's R&S Bus Terminal. The ride takes about 2½ hours. For transportation to Hershey, you can take Greyhound to the Harrisburg station, which is 15 minutes away from Hershey—most resorts have a shuttle service.

Greyhound Lines ✉ 22 W. Clay St. ☎ 800/231–2222 🌐 www.greyhound.com.

CAR TRAVEL

From Philadelphia, take the Schuylkill Expressway (I–76) west to the Pennsylvania Turnpike. Lancaster County sights are accessible from Exits 20, 21, and 22. Another option is to follow U.S. 30 west from Philadelphia, but be prepared for a lot of traffic. It's about 65 mi to the Pennsylvania Dutch Country.

EMERGENCIES

Lancaster County has four emergency rooms: Community Hospital of Lancaster, Lancaster General Hospital, Lancaster Regional Medical Center, and Ephrata Community Hospital. For nonemergency referrals, contact the Lancaster City & County Medical Society.

Ambulance, fire, and police ☎ 911.

Hospitals **Heart of Lancaster Hospital** ✉ 1500 Highlands Dr., Lititz ☎ 717/625-5000. **Community Hospital of Lancaster** ✉ 1100 E. Orange St. ☎ 717/239-4000. **Lancaster General Hospital** ✉ 555 N. Duke St. ☎ 717/290-5511. **Lancaster Regional Medical Center** ✉ 250 College Ave. ☎ 717/291-8211. **Ephrata Community Hospital** ✉ 169 Martin Ave., Ephrata ☎ 717/738-6420. **Lancaster City & County Medical Society** ☎ 717/393-9588.

Pharmacies **CVS Pharmacy** ✉ 1643½ Lincoln Hwy., Lancaster ☎ 717/394-5121. **Weis Pharmacy** ✉ 1603 Lincoln Hwy. E, Lancaster ☎ 717/394-9826.

LODGING

B&BS Lancaster County Bed-and-Breakfast Inns Association is a group of 16 B&Bs in the area.

Reservation Services **Lancaster County Bed-and-Breakfast Inns Association** ✉ 2835 Willow St. Pike, Willow Street 17548 ☎ 717/464-5588 or 800/848-2994 ⊕ www.padutchinn.com.

TOURS

At Plain & Fancy Farm, Amish Country Tours has large bus or minivan excursions. Most popular is the two-hour Amish farmlands trip, with a visit to a farmhouse, a wine tasting, and shopping for crafts; tours to Hershey are available on Tuesdays. Brunswick Tours has private guides who accompany you in your car. The company also has a self-guided audio tour with 28 stops that begins at the Pennsylvania Dutch Convention & Visitors Bureau and takes three to four hours. The Mennonite Information Center has local Mennonite guides who join you in your car. These knowledgeable escorts lead you to country roads, produce stands, and Amish crafts shops and also acquaint you with their religion.

Glick Aviation, at Smoketown Airport, offers 18-minute flights in a four-seater plane (pilot plus three) that gives you a splendid aerial view of rolling farmlands.

Fees & Schedules **Amish Country Tours** ✉ 2596 Old Philadelphia Pike ☎ 717/768-3600 or 800/441-3505 ⊕ www.amishexperience.com. **Brunswick Tours** ✉ National Wax Museum, U.S. 30 E, Lancaster ☎ 717/397-7541 or 800/979-8687 ⊕ www.brunswicktours.com. **Glick Aviation** ✉ 311 Airport Dr., off Rte. 340, Smoketown ☎ 717/394-6476 ⊕ www.airvav.com/q08/glick. **Mennonite Information Center** ✉ 2209 Millstream Rd., Lancaster ☎ 717/299-0954 ⊕ www.mennoniteinfoctr.com.

TRAIN TRAVEL

Amtrak has regular service from Philadelphia's 30th Street Station to the Lancaster Amtrak station. The trip takes 80 minutes.

Amtrak ✉ 53 McGovern Ave. ☎ 215/824-1600 or 800/872-7245 ⊕ www.amtrak.com.

TRANSPORTATION AROUND LANCASTER COUNTY

A car is the easiest way to explore the many sights in the area; it also lets you get off the main roads and into the countryside. Lancaster County's main arteries are U.S. 30 (also known as the Lincoln Highway) and Route 340 (also called Old Philadelphia Pike). Some pleasant back roads can be found between Routes 23 and 340. Vintage Road is a country road running north over U.S. 30 and then along Route 772 west to Intercourse. You get a look at some of the farms in the area and also see Amish schoolhouses, stores, and the Amish themselves. Remember that you must slow down for horse-drawn buggies when you're driving on country roads.

VISITOR INFORMATION

The Pennsylvania Dutch Convention & Visitors Bureau is the welcome center for Pennsylvania Dutch Country, with a wide selection of brochures, maps, and other materials, as well as direct connections to hotels. There's also a multi-image presentation, "Lancaster County: People, Places & Passions," that serves as a good introduction to the area. It's open Monday–Saturday 8:30–5 and Sunday 9–5 in summer. The Mennonite Information Center serves mainly to "interpret the faith and practice of the Mennonites and Amish to all who inquire." It has information on local inns and Mennonite guest homes as well as a 20-minute video about the Amish and Mennonite people. It's open Monday through Saturday 8–5. The Susquehanna Heritage Tourist Information Center has information about visiting the Susquehanna River town of Columbia. The Gettysburg Convention and Visitors Bureau, in the former Western Maryland Railroad Passenger Depot, has free brochures and maps of area attractions. Be sure to pick up a self-guided walking-tour map of the town's historic district, centered on Baltimore Street. You'll find a number of museums along the route, as well as markers that point out homes and sites significant to the history of the town and to the battle.

Pennsylvania Dutch Convention & Visitors Bureau ✉ 501 Greenfield Rd., Lancaster 17601 ☎ 717/299-8901 or 800/735-2629 🌐 www.padutchcountry.com. **Mennonite Information Center** ✉ 2209 Millstream Rd., Lancaster 17602 ☎ 717/299-0954 or 800/858-8320 🌐 www.mennoniteinfoctr.com. **Susquehanna Valley Chamber of Commerce and Visitor Center** ✉ 445 Linden St., Box 510, Columbia 17512 ☎ 717/684-5249 🌐 www.parivertowns.com. The **Gettysburg Convention and Visitors Bureau** ✉ 35 Carlisle St. ☎ 717/334-6274 🌐 www.gettysburg.com.

UNDERSTANDING PHILADELPHIA & THE PENNSYLVANIA DUTCH COUNTRY

HALLOWED GROUND: A WALK AT GETTYSBURG

Prologue

In his address at the dedication of the cemetery for Union soldiers killed in the battle of Gettysburg, President Abraham Lincoln acknowledged that "in a larger sense, we can not dedicate—we can not consecrate—we can not hallow this ground. The brave men, living and dead, who struggled here, have consecrated it, far above our power to add or detract."

More than any other place in the United States, this battlefield is indeed hallowed ground. Perhaps no word in the American language has greater historical resonance than Gettysburg. For some people Lexington and Concord, or Bunker Hill, or Yorktown, or Omaha Beach would be close rivals. But more Americans visit Gettysburg each year than any of these other battlefields—perhaps than all of them combined.

And Gettysburg resonates far beyond these shores. At least sixty thousand foreigners are among the nearly two million annual visitors to the battlefield. In 1851 the British historian Sir Edward Creasy wrote a famous book titled *Fifteen Decisive Battles of the World.* The last of the fifteen was Waterloo, fought in 1815. After the American Civil War, Creasy published a new edition with a sixteenth decisive battle—Gettysburg.

During the bicentennial commemorations of the American Revolution in 1976, a delegation of historians from the Soviet Union visited the United States as a goodwill gesture, to take part in these events. A colleague of mine on the history faculty at Princeton University was one of their hosts. When they arrived, he asked them which historic sites they wanted to visit first—perhaps Independence Hall in Philadelphia, or maybe Williamsburg and Yorktown in Virginia, or Lexington and Concord in Massachusetts. But their answer was none of these. They wanted to go first to Gettysburg.

Why Gettysburg? asked my astonished colleague. It had nothing to do with the American Revolution. To the contrary, replied the Russians; it had everything to do with the Revolution. In Lincoln's words, it ensured that the nation founded in 1776 would not "perish from the earth." These Soviet historians may have been more familiar with Lincoln's Gettysburg Address than was my colleague. They knew that the famous opening words of that address—"Four score and seven years ago"—referred to the founding of the United States in 1776, and that Gettysburg was the battlefield on which thousands gave the last full measure of devotion that the nation might live. These Russians also wanted to see Gettysburg first because they compared it to their battle of Stalingrad in World War II—it was the costliest battle in America's own Great Patriotic War that turned the tide toward ultimate victory.

In 1896 the United States Supreme Court handed down a decision that has stood for more than a century as a landmark in the struggle for historic preservation of hallowed ground. Not surprisingly, that decision grew out of events surrounding the recent creation of Gettysburg National Military Park. The Gettysburg Electric Railway Company had built a trolley line over the southern part of the battlefield to carry tourists to Devil's Den and the Round Tops. The park wanted to buy the land and restore it to its 1863 appearance, which of course would mean removal of the trolley line. The company refused to sell. The government began proceedings to seize the land under the power of eminent domain. The case went to the Supreme Court, where the government argued that "the ground whereon great conflicts have taken place, especially those where great interests or principles were at stake, becomes at once of so much public interest that its preservation is essentially a matter of public concern." Nowhere were such great principles at stake more than at Gettysburg, which embodied "the national idea and the principle of the indissolubility of the Union."

The Court agreed. The justices ruled unanimously that Gettysburg was vested with such importance for the fate of the United States that the government had the right to "take possession of the field of battle, in the name and for the benefit of all the citizens of the country. Such a use seems. so closely connected with the welfare of the republic itself as to be within the powers granted Congress by the Constitution for the purpose of protecting and preserving the whole country."

* * *

THE BATTLE OF GETTYSBURG WAS AN *event* without equal in its connection "with the welfare of the republic itself," as the Court put it. But what is Gettysburg as a place? It is a battlefield of about ten square miles (five miles from north to south and two miles from east to west, not counting East Cavalry Field) surrounding a county-seat town of about eight thousand people today, 2,400 at the time of the battle in 1863. It is located seventy-five miles north of Washington, 115 miles west of Philadelphia, and only eight miles north of the Mason-Dixon Line, which forms the border between Pennsylvania and Maryland. From the town of Gettysburg a dozen historic (and modern) roads radiate to every point of the compass—a major reason why a great battle was fought there, for the road network enabled the armies to concentrate there quickly after the opening clashes.

Although it is the home of Gettysburg College and of a Lutheran theological seminary, the main business of Gettysburg today is tourism. Most of those nearly two million visitors to the battlefield spend money in town. Many tourist services flourish, from restaurants and motels to shops selling every kind of trinket and relic, from "ghost tours" and a wax museum to bookstores and picture galleries. Some of these businesses are cheek by jowl with the National Military Park, which includes more than four thousand acres on which most of the fighting took place during those first three days of July 1863.

No tourists came to Gettysburg before that time. It was then a market town for a large and prosperous agricultural hinterland. The area was a famous fruit-growing region; no fewer than thirty-eight orchards existed on what became the battlefield. All of them are gone today except part of the famous Peach Orchard where the Confederates broke Dan Sickles's line on July 2, plus two ornamental fruit orchards on Cemetery Hill and at the site of the Bliss farm, across which some of the Pickett-Pettigrew attackers marched on July 3. The Park Service has long-term plans to plant replica orchards where they existed in 1863—but don't hold your breath waiting for it to happen.

I have lost count of the number of times I have been to Gettysburg. I have toured the battlefield by car, by bus, on a bicycle, and on foot. Over the past twenty years I have taken Princeton students, alumni, friends, and miscellaneous groups on at least two dozen tours of the battlefield. I have made so many visits to the college and town, as well as the battlefield, that Gettysburg has become almost a second home. I honestly believe that if I were blindfolded and winched down from a helicopter to any spot on the battlefield on a moonlit night, I could remove the blindfold and identify my surroundings within minutes.

I would not have known where I was on many parts of the battlefield in 1863, however. Not only did all those orchards exist then, but there are also some six hundred acres of woods today that were cleared then, and about 150 acres of cleared land today that were wooded in 1863. Another six hundred acres of woods that existed in the same places then as now were woodlots in 1863, where farmers harvested dead trees and some live ones for fuel and fencing. They also allowed livestock to graze in some of these woodlots, which kept them free from undergrowth. Many of the woodlots were therefore open and parklike in 1863, enabling troops to move through and fight in them where saplings and undergrowth today would make such activities impossible.

The Park Service plans to remove 150 acres of woods that did not exist in 1863, to reforest fifty acres (plus the orchards) where woods did exist in 1863, and to cull some trees from the six hundred acres of woodlots. When they have done so, it will be easier to see and understand the lines of sight, approach, and combat that existed in 1863 (though the culled woodlots will soon grow up in brush and saplings again in the absence of grazing livestock, for which the Park Service has no plans). Until (and even after) this cutting and culling happens, however, the first thing a tour guide must tell listeners is to imagine a cleared field or a parklike woodlot where there are thick woods today, or imagine an orchard or a grove where there are none today. Such a feat of imagination is not always easy.

What brought those 165,000 soldiers—75,000 Confederate, 90,000 Union—to Gettysburg during the first three days of July 1863? Why did they lock themselves in such a deathgrip across these once bucolic fields until 11,000 of them were killed and mortally wounded, another 29,000 were wounded and survived, and about 10,000 were "missing"—mostly captured. By way of comparison, those 50,000 casualties at Gettysburg—27,000 Confederate, 23,000 Union—were almost ten times the number of American casualties on D-Day, June 6, 1944. (Because of incomplete records, the number of Confederate casualties at Gettysburg is an estimate. Such estimates range from 23,000 to 28,000.) What was accomplished by all of this carnage? Join me for a walk on this hallowed ground, where we will try to answer these questions.

Day Two: July 2, 1863

. . . We can easily find our way to the Twentieth Maine monument, about 250 yards southwest of the Little Round Top parking area. When I first visited Gettysburg in the 1960s, scarcely any tourist knew about the Twentieth Maine, and few ever saw its monument, which is tucked away from the others that are back on the west face of Little Round Top. After *The Killer Angels* was published in 1974 and won the Pulitzer Prize, the Park Service put up a sign pointing to the regiment's monument and position. After Ken Burns's video documentary *The Civil War* in 1990, which prominently featured Chamberlain, and the movie *Gettysburg* in 1993, two interpretive markers, more directional signs, a paved walkway, and an auxiliary parking lot just below the monument materialized. Now this site is the most heavily visited in the Park.

Joshua Lawrence Chamberlain became an iconic figure in the 1990s. More people on the tours I have led want to see where he fought than anything else. Powerful emotions have gripped some of them as they stared at the simple stone and bronze monument and their imaginations drifted back to those desperate moments about 7:00 P.M. on that July 2. I remember one such occasion in particular. In April 1987 I took a group of Princeton students on a tour of the battlefield, as I have done many times. This year one of those students had written her senior thesis on Chamberlain, but had never before actually been to Gettysburg. As we came to the place where the Twentieth Maine fought, she could no longer hold back the tears.

Nor could the rest of us. Although I have experienced other powerful emotions while walking Civil War battlefields, none has ever matched that April day in 1987. The world has little noted what I said there, but it can never forget what they did there.

Several of Chamberlain's ancestors had fought in the American Revolution. His father had wanted young Lawrence (as his family called him) to pursue a military career. But his mother wanted him to become a clergyman. She seemed to have gotten her way; Lawrence graduated Phi Beta Kappa from Bowdoin and earned a B.D. from Bangor Theological Seminary. In 1855 he accepted a professorship at Bowdoin, succeeding Calvin Stowe, whose wife, Harriet Beecher Stowe, had written *Uncle Tom's Cabin* while Chamberlain was a student there. Chamberlain knew Mrs. Stowe, and like thousands of others he was moved by her novel to work for the abolition of slavery.

In 1862 he got his chance. Although thirty-three years old and the father of three children, he considered it his duty to fight for Union and freedom. To dissuade him, Bowdoin offered him a two-year sabbatical to study in Europe. Instead, Chamberlain went to the state capital and accepted a commission in the newly organized Twentieth Maine. He was probably the only officer in either army who could read seven foreign languages—these seven, at least: Greek, Latin, Arabic, Hebrew, Syriac, French, and German.

As the shadows lengthened toward evening on July 2, Chamberlain found himself responsible for preventing the enemy from rolling up the Union left. His orders from [Brigadier General Strong] Vincent were to 'hold that ground at all hazards." Chamberlain soon found out what that meant. For more than an hour, repeated assaults on Vincent's brigade (eventually reinforced by another brigade) surged back and forth, constantly increasing the pressure on the left flank held by the Twentieth Maine. Chamberlain and his senior captain, Ellis Spear (one of Chamberlain's former students at Bowdoin), extended and bent back their line in an attempt to prevent this disaster. Meanwhile, off to Chamberlain's right, on the west face of Little Round Top, the battle raged fiercely as Alabama and Texas regiments advanced from boulder to boulder up the hill. Vincent was mortally wounded, a colonel and the general commanding the reinforcing brigade were killed, and the commander of an artillery battery that had struggled into position was also killed.

* * *

CHAMBERLAIN SEEMED LIKELY TO MEET THE SAME FATE. He had already been slightly wounded twice. With a third of his four hundred men down and the rest of them nearly out of ammunition, with the enemy apparently forming for yet another assault, the Twentieth Maine seemed finished. As Chamberlain later wrote, at this crisis "my thought was running deep. Five minutes more of such a defensive, and the last roll-call would sound for us. Desperate as the chances were, there was nothing for it but to take the offensive. I stepped to the colors. The men turned toward me. One word was enough,—'BAYONET!' It caught like fire, and swept along the ranks." With a wild yell, the survivors of this two-hour firefight, led by their multilingual fighting professor, lurched downhill in a bayonet charge against the shocked Alabamians. The Twentieth drove them across the front of the next Union regiments in line, the Eighty-third Pennsylvania and the Forty-fourth New York, and together these three regiments captured more than two hundred of them (Chamberlain claimed almost four hundred).

The hero-worship of Chamberlain has prompted a minor backlash among some historians and park rangers who have grown tired of exaggerated questions and claims by visitors who want to see where Chamberlain performed these exploits. The revisionists claim that the men of the

Twentieth spontaneously charged, or that Ellis Spear deserves the credit for the bayonet assault (though no one denies that it was Chamberlain who gave the order to fix bayonets). They quote the report of Colonel William C. Oates, commander of the Fifteenth Alabama (who, like Chamberlain, later became governor of his state), that he was in fact preparing to withdraw when the Twentieth Maine came screaming down the hill, and that the withdrawal was a retreat, not a rout. Oates doth protest too much. But there is no doubt that the Alabamians were exhausted and dehydrated after seemingly endless uphill fighting following a twenty-five-mile march to the battlefield.

It seems clear, however, that Chamberlain deserved the Congressional Medal of Honor he won for the defense of Little Round Top. He went on to become one of the war's most extraordinary soldiers. He rose to brigade command and, on June 18, 1864, was shot through the pelvis while leading his brigade in an assault at Petersburg. Such wounds were almost always fatal; Ulysses S. Grant promoted the supposedly dying colonel to brigadier general on the field–one of only two such occasions in the war. Chamberlain beat the odds and recovered to lead his brigade in the final campaign to Appomattox. At the battle of Quaker Road on March 29, 1865, he took another bullet, this one just below the heart, where it would have killed him had it not been deflected around his ribs by a leather case of field orders in his breast pocket. Chamberlain suffered two cracked ribs and a bruised arm, but continued to lead his brigade in several more fights during the next eleven days until the surrender at Appomattox. So impressed was Grant with his fighting professor that he selected Chamberlain to take charge of the Army of Northern Virginia's formal surrender at Appomattox.

In 1886, Chamberlain and other veterans of the Twentieth Maine returned to Gettysburg to dedicate their monument on Little Round Top. As we stand at the same spot, listen to Chamberlain's words on that occasion: "In great deeds, something abides. On great fields something stays. Forms change and pass; bodies disappear, but spirits linger, to consecrate the ground for the vision-place of souls. And reverent men and women from afar, and generations that know us not and that we know not of, heart-drawn to see where and by whom great things were suffered and done for them." Little wonder that my students could not hold back the tears when I read these words to them here in 1987.

CHRONOLOGY

Colonial

1643 The Swedes, under Governor Johan Printz, establish their New Sweden colony at Tinicum Island, making it the first permanent settlement in Pennsylvania.

1655 The Dutch, spurred on by New Amsterdam Director General Peter Stuyvesant, take over New Sweden.

1674 The Treaty of Westminster ends hostilities between the Dutch and the English and turns Dutch colonies, including Pennsylvania, over to the English.

1681 William Penn petitions King Charles II to grant him land in the New World for a Quaker colony as repayment for a debt owed to his late father. The huge parcel of land, known as Pennsilvania or Penn's Woods, makes William the largest landholder in the British Empire—after the king.

1682 William Penn establishes the city of Philadelphia—Greek for "City of Brotherly Love."

1701 Penn grants Pennsylvania residents the Charter of Privileges, establishing broadminded provisions for religious freedom and a structure for government that became a model for the U.S. Constitution.

1728 Pioneering botanist John Bartram plants America's first botanical garden on the banks of the Schuylkill River.

1731 The Philadelphia Library, the first public institution of its kind in America, was founded by Benjamin Franklin, Thomas Hopkinson, Thomas Cadwalader, and others.

1751 To commemorate the 50th anniversary of the Charter of Privileges and to "Proclaim Liberty thro' all the Land," the Liberty Bell is commissioned from a foundry in England.

1754 The Philadelphia Stock Exchange (PHLX) opens, making it the first stock exchange in America. Transactions take place at City Tavern.

Revolutionary

1774 The First Continental Congress meets in Carpenters' Hall in Philadelphia to address a declaration of rights and grievances to King George III.

1775 At a meeting of the Second Continental Congress, George Washington is appointed commander-in-chief of the Continental Army.

1776 The Continental Congress, meeting in the Assembly Room at the State House, adopts the Declaration of Independence. The Liberty Bell rings to signal the first public reading of that document. Washington crosses the Delaware River from Bucks County to Trenton to defeat the Hessians on Christmas night.

1777 The American Revolution rages in Philadelphia and its surrounding areas. The British, under General Howe, defeat Washington's army at the Battle of Brandywine. Howe then marches on Philadelphia and takes the city without opposition. Washington tries to drive the British out of Germantown, but his army is thwarted at the Battle of Germantown. The British put Fort Mifflin under siege. The Continental Army begins its winter encampment at Valley Forge. The Continental Congress flees to York and adopts the Articles of Confederation of the new United States of America.

1778 The British withdraw from Philadelphia. Washington's troops march out of Valley Forge to intercept the British at Monmouth.

1780 Pennsylvania becomes the first state to abolish slavery.

1787 The Constitutional Convention, representing 12 states, meets in the Pennsylvania State House in Philadelphia and signs the U.S. Constitution, sending it to the states to ratify.

1792 The Bank of North America adopts dollars and cents instead of shillings and pence, and the nation's first mint opens in Philadelphia.

1793 Washington's inauguration for his second term is held in Congress Hall. The city's yellow fever epidemic causes George and Martha Washington to move to Germantown and take up residence in Deshler-Morris House.

19th Century

1800 The nation's capital is moved from Philadelphia to Washington, D.C.

1805 The Pennsylvania Academy of the Fine Arts, an art school and museum and the nation's first art institution, is founded in Philadelphia, where painters such as Gilbert Stuart, Benjamin West, and the Peale family have already made the city famous.

1809 The Walnut Street Theatre opens. Today it's the oldest English-language theater in continuous use in the United States.

1812 The Academy of Natural Sciences is founded, making it now the oldest science research institution in the Western Hemisphere.

1823 The Pennsylvania Railroad begins construction on the state's first railroad, linking Philadelphia and Lancaster and giving birth to the Main Line.

1829 The Eastern State Penitentiary, at the time the most expensive building in America, is built. It becomes a model of penal design around the world.

1857 Napoleon Le Brun and Gustav Runge design the lavish Academy of Music. Today it is oldest surviving European-style grand opera house in the United States.

1874 The Zoological Society of Philadelphia opens the nation's first zoo in a 42-acre Victorian garden set in a corner of Fairmount Park.

1890 Cyrus H. K. Curtis launches the Curtis Publishing Company, which includes the *Ladies Home Journal* and the *Saturday Evening Post*. The latter had circulation of over 1 million copies a week by 1909.

20th Century

1900 After 30 years of construction, City Hall, topped by a 37-foot bronze statue of William Penn, is completed. It remained the tallest building in the city for 87 years.

1901 On New Year's Day, the city celebrates with the first official Mummers Parade, although clubs had been parading unofficially since 1876.

1905 Confectioner William Hershey opens the world's largest chocolate manufacturing plant and builds the town of Hershey around it.

1926 The Benjamin Franklin Bridge is built to span the Delaware River between Philadelphia and New Jersey; it's the longest suspension bridge in the world at the time.

1932 Culinary history is made when Pat Olivieri, the legendary "King of Steaks," invents the cheese steak. His South Philadelphia concession is still in operation to this day.

1946 The first fully electronic computer, ENIAC (an acronym for Electronic Numerical Integrator and Computer), is invented by Physics Professor John Mauchly and Teaching Assistant John Presper Eckert at the University of Pennsylvania.

1987 The 61-story Liberty Place office and retail complex opens in Center City, breaking the 100-year-old agreement limiting buildings in Center City to the height of the William Penn statue atop City Hall.

BOOKS & MOVIES

Books

Fiction. "Writing fiction set in Philadelphia is tough," says novelist Steve Lopez. "There is nothing you can make up that is any more unbelievable than what actually happens here." Nonetheless, Lopez succeeded with *Third and Indiana,* a hard-edged story set in Philadelphia's "badlands"; *The Sunday Macaroni Club;* and *Land of Giants. God's Pocket,* by Pete Dexter; *South Street,* by David Bradley; and *Payback,* by Philip Harper, also capture the grittier side of the City of Brotherly Love. John Edgar Wideman's *Philadelphia Fire* won the PEN/Faulkner award for 1991. His latest book, *Two Cities,* is set in Philadelphia and Pittsburgh. Lisa Scottoline writes highly entertaining legal thrillers about an all-female law firm in Philadelphia.

Michael Shaara's Pulitzer prize–winning *The Killer Angels* is a gripping account of the battle at Gettysburg.

History & Background. *Philadelphia: A 300-Year History,* with essays edited by Russell F. Weigley, is the best overall text. Ron Avery condenses those three centuries into the compact, easy-to-read *A Concise History of Philadelphia.* Catherine Drinker Bowen's *Miracle at Philadelphia* tells the story of the Constitution. In *Philly Firsts,* Janice L. Booker explores the unique ideas, products, and inventions that the city's natives have dreamed up—from Girl Scout cookies to the tranquilizing chair.

For biographies of seven Philadelphians, read *Philadelphia: Patricians and Philistines, 1900 to 1950,* by John Lukacs. *Puritan Boston and Quaker Philadelphia,* by the late E. Digby Baltzell, is a scholarly work that compares the two cities. *Christopher Morley's Philadelphia* is edited by Ken Kalfus. Robert Lawson's *Ben and Me,* a classic children's story, gives a mouse's view of Ben Franklin's life.

Buzz Bissinger's *A Prayer for the City* assesses the struggles and achievements of Mayor Ed Rendell during the 1990s. *South Philadelphia,* by *Philadelphia Inquirer* reporter Murray Dubin, is both a memoir and an oral history that describes a well-known neighborhood. Harry D. Boonin's illustrated *The Jewish Quarter of Philadelphia: A History and Guide 1881–1930* traces the story of the area around South Street.

The Foundation for Architecture's *Philadelphia Architecture: A Guide to the City* contains maps, photos, biographies of noted Philadelphia architects, and descriptions of almost 400 sites. *Historic Houses of Philadelphia,* by Roger W. Moss, includes stunning color photos and historical notes about 50 of the area's museum homes. Francis Morrone's 1999 *Architectural Guidebook to Philadelphia* is illustrated with photographs.

Movies

The Philadelphia Story (1940), starring Cary Grant, Katharine Hepburn, and Jimmy Stewart, is a comedy of manners about the search for love in high society. *Rocky,* with Sylvester Stallone (1976), and its four sequels describe the adventures of an underdog Philadelphia boxer. Director John Landis's *Trading Places* (1982) stars Eddie Murphy and Dan Akroyd—the opening credits pan across the city. In *Witness* (1985), Philadelphia police detective Harrison Ford lives undercover with the Amish.

Philadelphia (1993) stars Tom Hanks as a lawyer who is dismissed from his job because he is battling AIDS. The four-hour movie *Gettysburg* (1993), based on Michael Shaara's novel *The Killer Angels,* captures the intensity of the Civil War battle. Terry Gilliam's *12 Monkeys* (1995), starring Brad Pitt and Bruce Willis, is a dizzying tale set in both normal 1996

Philly and an eerily empty post-apocalyptic version of the city. Philadelphia filmmaker M. Night Shyamalan shot two movies in his hometown—*The Sixth Sense* (1999) and *Unbreakable* (2000). His third effort, *Signs* (2002), has aliens visiting a farm in Bucks County.

Philly doubled for 1870s New York in *Age of Innocence* (1993). The corner of 3rd and Arch streets in Old City, along with its closely surrounding blocks, was transformed into a mid-1880s Cincinnati shopping district, complete with horse-drawn carriages, for *Beloved* (1998).

INDEX

J

K

L

M

N

NOTES

NOTES

NOTES

NOTES